International Environmental Governance

International Environmental Law

VOLUME 10

The titles published in this series are listed at *brill.com/iel*

International Environmental Governance

Towards UNEPO

By

Bharat H. Desai

TUTA SUB AEGIDE PALLAS · 1683 ·

BRILL
NIJHOFF

LEIDEN | BOSTON

This publication has been typeset in the multilingual "Brill" typeface. With over 5,100 characters covering Latin, IPA, Greek, and Cyrillic, this typeface is especially suitable for use in the humanities.
For more information, please see www.brill.com/brill-typeface.

ISSN 1873-6599
ISBN 978-90-04-21454-5 (hardback)
ISBN 978-90-04-21455-2 (e-book)

This book is printed on acid-free paper.

FSC www.fsc.org MIX Paper from responsible sources FSC® C109576

Printed by Printforce, the Netherlands

For all those who believe in the truism that:
The Earth has enough for everyone's need but not for anyone's greed

Contents

Foreword IX
Nicholas Robinson
Preface XII

PART 1
The Debate

1 Governing the Environment: An Introduction 3
2 Designing the International Environmental Institutions 20
3 International Environmental Institutions: An Overview 46

PART 2
Efforts at Revitalization

4 The Quest for a UN Specialized Agency for the Environment 81
5 UNEP: A Global Environment Authority? 97
6 Mapping the Future of International Environmental Governance 148
7 Revitalizing International Environmental Institutions 168

PART 3
Sectoral Law Making

8 Multilateral Environmental Agreements 221

PART 4
The Future

9 Conclusions 265

PART 5

Appendices

I UN GA Resolution 67/290, 9 July 2013 277

II UN GA Resolution 67/251, 13 March 2013 285

III UNEP GC as First Universal Session, Decision 27/2, 22 February 2013 289

IV UN GA Resolution 67/213, 21 December 2012 290

V UNEP GC Twelfth Special Session, Decision SS XII/3, 20-22 February 2012 294

VI The Nairobi-Helsinki Outcome, 23 November 2010 296

VII UN GA Mandated 'Informal Consultation' Co-Chair Report, 10 February 2009 301

VIII UN Secretary-General's High-Level Panel Report, 9 November 2006 (Excerpts) 309

IX The Cartagena Intergovernmental Group of Ministers Report, 6 February 2002 315

X The Intergovernmental Group of Ministers on IEG, First Meeting, 18 April 2001 335

XI The Malmö Ministerial Declaration, 31 May 2000 349

XII UN GA Resolution 53/242, 10 August 1999 355

XIII The Secretary-General's Report on Environment & Human Settlements, 6 October 1998 359

XIV The Nairobi Declaration, 7 February 1997 398

Index 401

Foreword

Bharat H. Desai's insightful proposals and informative analysis comes at a critical moment for the international debates on environmental governance. Once the United Nations General Assembly resolves on the content of its new Sustainability Goals, nations will have a common set of objectives by which to harmonize their national programs toward global environmental security. All social and economic development depends on the natural environment. The "Airpocoplyse" in Chinese cities besieged by extreme air pollution, the social turmoil accompanying the desiccation of soils and expanding deserts of northern Africa, the pollution of drinking water across many region, and displacement of people from the rising sea levels on all marine coast lines: These are but a few of the challenges the UN Sustainability Goals must contend with.

As Dr. Desai makes clear, the 1972 UN General Assembly's model of a small UN Environment Programme has been insufficient to help nations stem the accumulating degradation of the environment across the globe. Nations had warning of this in the 1972 UN Stockholm Conference on the Human Environment, and in the 1992 UN "Earth Summit" (The UN Conference on Environment and development) in Rio de Janeiro. "The Future We Want" in 2012, at the UN "Rio+20" conference, reaffirmed the prior recommendations for action to avert further environmental degradation. Dr. Desai parses and leads us through the on-going inter-governmental dialogue toward finding a consensus on new frameworks of cooperative environmental governance.

The question remains, however, how should international environmental governance be accomplished? : International Environmental Law provides the framework through which governments seek to arrest environmental degradation and build patterns of "sustainable" development. As humans currently add 2 billion more inhabitants to the Earth, the natural systems of the planet experience irreversible changes. Some laws rapidly cope with change, as is the case of the Vienna Convention for the Protection of the Stratospheric Ozone Layer, while others boast but limited success, as mounting biodiversity losses attest world-wide or is evidenced by the gridlock of the multilateral negotiations for addressing climate change (most famously the Copenhagen meetings of State Parties to the UN Framework Convention on Climate Change in December of 2009). Why does one treaty work well and another perform poorly? How are international laws enforced and implemented nationally and locally? How do nations set environmental benchmarks or empirically quantifiable goals? What can be done to enhance the effectiveness of International Environmental Laws? This book examines such questions.

"The Earth is one but the world is not." This declaration, which sums up the challenges addressed through International Environmental Law, appears in the 1987 report of the United Nations World Commission on Environment and Development, *Our Common Future* (also known as the "Brundtland Commission" report), published by Oxford University Press, 1987, available in paperback and also available at www.un-documents.net/wced-ocf.htm. *Our Common Future* launched the UN General Assembly decisions to convene the 1992 Earth Summit and its endorsement of "sustainable development" in Agenda 21, and spurred negotiation of several multilateral environmental agreements (MEAs). The MEAs comprise a latticework of treaties that set international norms and procedures to protect the environment. While International Environmental Law is grounded in "public international law," the law governing nation states, it is equally based upon national (termed "municipal" by international lawyers) environmental laws of each country and political subdivision. Whether as a set of treaties or national laws, environmental law is the product of what society learns from the environmental sciences, or experiences in the unprecedented environmental disruptions now emerging recurrently in all Earth's regions. "*Airpocolypse*" is the term in use today for the acute air pollution in Chinese cities; this is both a local and a national and an international issue. How does law address this problem, at each level?

The practitioner of International Environmental Law (whether a scholar, a lawyer or a scientist or an NGO leader or government official or corporate executive) functions in a multi-disciplinary world, one in which familiarity with the basics of the environmental sciences is essential to understanding and applying the law. Determining how each nation's distinctive legal system responds to environmental problems is discerned through the study of "Comparative Environmental Law in Global Legal Systems" [F&ES 828b, taught by Prof. Nicholas Robinson and Prof. Lye Lin Heng, of the National University of Singapore, as an intensive daily seminar, February 5–18, 2014]. How different countries implement agreed international environmental law norms depends significantly on their legal traditions, whether the Common Law, Civil Law, Socialist Law, Islamic Law or other theocratic legal traditions, or Customary Law. These legal traditions are touched upon in the study of International Environmental Law, in order to illustrate the varied ways nations implement the same international obligations. These could also richly contribute in implementing new UN "Sustainability Goals, but a framework is needed to enable them to each contribute, equitably and openly, to the common cause. http://digitalcommons.pace.edu/perl/vol29/iss2/. At the national level, significant reforms are emerging to better enforce environmental protection laws. For example, some 500 environmental courts now exist in more than 50 nations [see the Symposium on "*Environmental Courts and Tribunals: Improving Access to Justice and Protection of the Environment Around the World*" (*Pace Environmental law Review* (*PELR*), Winter, 2012); available at http://digitalcommons.pace.edu/perl/vol29/iss2/].

Yet, the rapid emergence of International Environmental Law since 1972 has not stemmed the accumulation of radical impacts on the planet Earth. Scientific evidence suggests that Earth has left the Holocene and entered a new geological epoch, the *Anthropocene* (see Will Steffen, Paul J. Crutzen, and John R. McNeill, "Are Humans Now Overwhelming the Great Forces of Nature?" *Ambio*, vol. 36, no. 8, 2007; available at http://allenpress.com/pdf/ambi-38-08-06_614.621.pdf). As the above-mentioned course examines contemporary International Environmental Law, students are asked to consider whether laws conceived in the mind-set of the Holocene remain adequate for the *Anthropocene*. What progressive developments will be required to enhance the efficacy of International Environmental Laws? The answers to these questions lie in the realms of international cooperation. Nations need a framework within which to foster cooperation around shared environmental norms. It is not enough to have treaties; there must be capacity building and coordination in the implementation of the treaties. Ecosystems are linked globally, but nations divide up the world into sovereign States along arbitrary lines, too weakly united by public international law. Just as UNEP fostered the enactment of environmental statutes in many nations, so now a UN presence is needed to foster cooperation in implementation of these laws.

International Environmental Governance is at cross-roads. If it continues as it is now, it will fail the "peoples of the United Nations." If nations provide steps toward establishing a progressive framework for environmental collaboration, through the good offices of the United Nations, a new road can be taken. The adoption of the UN Sustainability Goals needs to be accompanied by new institutional frameworks. The two must go together. Dr. Desai's timely analysis in this book can assist diplomats and scholars, citizens and civil servants alike in finding the new roads forward. This study brings a clarion voice to rally anew the international cooperation needed to ensure that the peoples of the Earth may share in the fruits of the Earth, to realize their fundamental human rights, and to equitably act as stewards of the planet. How nations respond to the proposals in this book will help determine whether the International Environmental Laws conceived in the mind-set of the Holocene can remain adequate for the Anthropocene. Dr. Desai offers progressive ideas and proposals that will be required to enhance the efficacy of International Environmental Laws in the coming years.

Nicholas A. Robinson
University Professor for the Environment, Pace University, New York and Former Chair of the IUCN World Commission on Environmental Law

Preface

This work culminates research engagement concerning the process of 'institutionalization' in the field of International Environmental Law that commenced in 1997. It coincided with adoption of the Nairobi Declaration by the UNEP Governing Council (on 7 February 1997). In the wake of this process, a modest effort has been made to understand innovative law-making and institution-building processes at work. Cumulatively, they underscore the organic linkage between law and institutions, art and craft of institution building, atmospherics and posturing witnessed at intergovernmental meetings as well as fascinating pattern at work on institutionalized intergovernmental environmental cooperation. In turn, it has set in motion a gigantic enterprise on 'governance' of the environment as a best humanly possible effort for preserving the fabric of life and, in turn, our own survival on this small endangered planet.

The book includes some of the chapters drawn from the author's work published in the area of international environmental governance (IEG) in various journals of international repute during the period of 2000–2013. This specifically applies to chapter 3 in Part I on *The Debate* and chapters 4 to 7 in Part II on *Efforts at Revitalization*. This scholarly journey on IEG received a boost with my stay as the Alexander von Humbolt Fellow at Institute of International Law at University of Bonn during 1998-99. During the period, an invited lecture at Environment & International Law Unit of the Legal Department of the World Bank (Washington DC) on 15 January 1999 resulted in first outlining of the proposals for United Nations Environment Protection Organization (UNEPO) as well as mandate for a 'new trust' to revive the UN Trusteeship Council. It was followed by another special invited presentation on 9 March 1999 at Max-Planck Institute for Public International Law (Heidelberg). These lectures resulted in publication of two articles: "International Environmental Institutions: An Overview" in Rudolf Dolzer et.al ed., *Protecting Our Environment*, St. Augustine: KAS, 2000 as well as "Revitalizing International Environmental Institutions: The UN Task Force Report and Beyond" in the *Indian Journal of International Law* (vol. 40, no. 3, 2000). It essentially comprised launch of the process of revitalization of United Nations Environment Programme (UNEP) through 1997 Nairobi Declaration, 1998 report of the UN Task Force on Environment and Human Settlements, the UN Secretary-General's suggestion concerning a new 'trust' for the environment and the UN general Assembly resolution 53/242 of 10 August 1999. It continued with the publication of "Mapping the Future of International Environmental Governance" in the *Yearbook of International Environmental Law* (vol. 13, 2002) that covered significant developments in the launch of Global Ministerial Environment Forum

(GMEF) and Environment Management Group (EMG). The abiding interest as well as other noteworthy developments in the field resulted in an invitation by the United Nations University's Institute for Environment & Human Security (Bonn) for the *Bonn Open Lecture* on 26 October 2005. It was published as "UNEP: A Global Environment Authority?" in *Environmental Policy & Law* (vol. 36, no. 3–4, 2006). The stock-taking and assessment of developments in the field, prior to the Rio+20 Summit (20–22 June 2012), took the shape of an invited article on "The Quest for a UN Specialized Agency for the Environment" in special issue of *The Round Table: The Commonwealth Journal of International Affairs* (vol. 101, no. 2, 2012). Thus, in effect, these four contributions of 2000, 2002, 2006 and 2012, though separate; still represent the process of continuation that covered scholarly assessment of progressive developments relevant at the time. Each of them were designed as composite stand alone articles and hence cover some repetition and overlapping that was essential to provide complete picture on the theme as at the time for readers of each of the international journals/yearbook that published them.

Thus, in order to preserve the integrity and originality of the abovementioned five articles as well as to reflect gradual progression in intergovernmental deliberations on the subject, it has been decided to publish these articles in their original form – except some figures and tables as indicated at appropriate places – since they comprise scholarly analyses and historical record of the period. Due permissions have been procured from all the publishers of the said publications. The author expresses deep sense of gratitude to the respective editors and publishers for the permission to use them in this volume. They seek to provide an authentic glimpse of those prevailing times when the intergovernmental deliberations sought to grapple with impasse over the negotiations on IEG. As a corollary, the work also includes select primary documents that provide reference value for intergovernmental processes that became milestones for the IEG. Effort was made to find the rarely available original instruments and include them year-wise (latest being the first) as they provide progressive account of the marathon IEG process during 1997 to 2013 period.

The abovementioned concerted processes reflected efforts to break the gridlock by finding innovative tailor-made solutions that suited best at the time; for instance, clustering of issue based MEAs (chemicals), coming up of a new international environmental institution (CSD), Environment Management Group (EMG), Global Ministerial Environment Forum (GMEF), replacement of CSD with new High Level Political Forum (HLPF) as well as closer of GMEF, and conversion of the 58 member UNEP Governing Council into the universal-membership UN Environment Assembly (UNEA) in which all 193 State Members will participate. The idea of this book, in essence, is to provide an analytical scholarly account both as a privy to the process as well as a ring-side view on the momentous IEG juggernaut during the said 1997–2013 period, consolidate the work done as well as place these seminal publications, along with other chapters, together in a single volume so as to provide an authoritative and analytical reference tool for teaching, research as well as a guide for future IEG negotiations.

The author would like to express gratitude to the Alexander von Humboldt Stiftung whose generous award as well as warm hospitality of my academic host, Rudolf Dolzer (Institute of International Law, University of Bonn) facilitated the initial basis and genesis of this work (during 1998–99) possible. Subsequent brief spells of research work at Bonn and Geneva based MEA secretariats as well as Max-Planck Institute of Public International Law (Heidelberg) proved rewarding for this scholarly work. I am thankful to all these institutions.

I would also like to thank other international institutions as well as personalities whose works as well as, where possible, discussions provided food for thought in the arduous task that I was privileged to be engaged in and have thoroughly enjoyed. It included graphic story-telling by the MEA insiders; expression of frustration by the incumbent UNEP executive directors for the roadblocks; fatigue and disappointment by the ambassadors who coordinated the IEG consultations with sovereign states and civil society groups; encouraging words and valuable help by some scholars as well as rare dose of sarcastic comments such as "you seem to be the only UNEP supporter left out in the field", notwithstanding the fact that the author had never visited UNEP headquarters (Nairobi)! It happened, as a sheer coincidence, subsequently only in May 2010 as a part of ICIMOD delegation for the CBD meeting held at the UN compound in Nairobi.

I express deep sense of gratitude to Nick Robinson whose generous foreword graces this book. It was Nick who provided me the prestigious perch of Pace University School of Law (New York) to deliver the *Fourth Gilbert and Sarah Kerlin Lecture* (27 October 2003) on "The Future of International Environmental Governance: Johannesburg and Beyond".

I express sincere thanks to Balraj K Sidhu whose tireless and sincere assistance made this book possible in the midst of consistent pressure of academic and other parallel works concerning initiatives that I undertook to build and coordinate three futuristic inter-disciplinary and *Inter-University Consortiums* (themes: cryosphere, atmospheric aerosols and geo-spatial information systems). Thanks are also due to Tomme R Young for suggestions on outline of the book. Marie M Sheldon deserves gratitude for immense patience and gentle reminders to ensure that the work is brought out at the earliest notwithstanding several unforeseen obstacles that littered the path.

Over the seventeen long years, this work has been driven purely by passion, hard work, determination and genuine scholarly quest for a workable blueprint of IEG. It is nothing short of a miracle that a scholar could give effect to such a work single-handedly without any kind of project funding support, amidst enormous academic engagement, a host of unforeseen difficulties, with only very few scholarly voices of support and in spite of 'location' disadvantage for being based far away from decision-making centers of the world. It could be attributed to an invisible energy flow from a different Realm. One can only hope that this modest effort will contribute in the emergence of an IEG architecture that could include an efficient and effective blueprint for governance of MEAs, final up gradation of UNEP into a UN specialized agency – to be called UNEPO to preserve an organic link with UNEP – as a logical step of 'creeping' institutionalization in the near future and mandate for a 'new trust' to revive the UN Trusteeship Council to supervise simmering challenges of the global environment and the commons on the *Only One Earth* that, so far, we have.

Bharat H Desai

PART 1

The Debate

CHAPTER 1

Governing the Environment

An Introduction

There have been intense intergovernmental deliberations in recent years on issues concerning 'governance'[1] in the field of environment. It, basically, reflects a process and encompasses role of the institutions that provide platforms for international cooperation to address a variety of global environmental problems. As such the act of 'governance' is an inclusive process comprising different tools, techniques and regulatory instruments to attain results desired by the sovereign states. There are mainly two trends that are under scanner in the matter: setting up of regime-specific institutions that cater to sectoral regulatory frameworks (popularly known as multilateral environmental agreements); and institutions that are set up as a 'follow up' to global environmental conferences or assigned with a specific intergovernmental environmental task. These processes, cumulatively, reflect the process of 'institutionalization' in the field of environment. Interestingly, most of these institutions are creatures of legal tools and reflect consensual process at work. Once in the saddle, these institutions play crucial role in the law-making process too. In view of the growing environmental challenges as well as demands of the prevailing time, there has been proliferation and, in turn, clogging of institutions that cater to institutionalized international environmental cooperation.

The debate is quite challenging one. It has now come to be widely popularized under the rubric of *international environmental governance* (IEG) especially since the Governing Council of United Nations Environment Program (UNEP) decided to 'revitalize' the entity in 1997.[2] After a series of intergovernmental ministerial confabulations as well as yearly consideration at UNEP Governing Council meetings, the matter received a sudden boost in January 2006 when the then President of the UN General Assembly (currently UN Deputy Secretary-General from 1 July 2012), Jan Elliason, sought to follow up

1 The dictionary meaning of 'governance' (from Collins English Dictionary – Complete & Unabridged 10th Edition, 2009) is as follows: "the action, manner, or system of governing"; see http://dictionary.reference.com/browse/governance?s=t.

2 Since 1997 Nairobi Declaration on the Role and Mandate of the United Nations Environment Program (UNEP); Decision 19/1 adopted at the 19th Session (27 January to 7 February 1997) of the UNEP Governing Council (Nairobi); available at http://www.unep.org/Documents.multilingual/Default.asp?DocumentID=96&ArticleID=1458&l=en.

 | DOI 10.1163/9789004214552_002

the 2005 World Summit Outcome. He launched *Informal Consultative Process on the Institutional Framework for the United Nations (UN) Environmental Activities* led by Permanent Representatives of Mexico and Switzerland to the UN.

The UN Secretary-General also announced establishment of a *High level Panel on UN System-wide Coherence in the Area of Development, Humanitarian Assistance and the Environment.*[3] The said High-level Panel emphatically recommended (on 9 November 2006) that:

> UNEP should be upgraded and have real authority as the environmental policy pillar of the UN system, backed by normative and analytical capacity and with broad responsibility to review progress towards improving the global environment.[4]

The issue of UNEP's 'up-gradation', however, still remains a subject of deliberations at intergovernmental level as well as among the scholars and the civil society groups. There appears to be good amount of divergent views in this matter.

Sui Generis *Treaty-Making*

There is also a web of over five hundred environment related multilateral agreements and institutions aimed at responding to environmental problems ranging from wetlands of international importance and migratory species of wild animals to ozone layer depletion and climate change to persistent organic pollutants and mercury. The manner in which these sector-specific environmental institutions have been established, to a large extent, been *ad hoc*, diffused, and somewhat chaotic. It is mostly because the creation of institutions for environmental governance has run parallel with random

3 The then UN Secretary-General Kofi Annan established the High-Level Panel co-chaired by Prime Ministers of Norway, Pakistan and Mozambique on 15 February 2006 as a follow-up to the 2005 *World Summit Outcome.* For the communication of the Secretary-General and composition of the 13 member panel (with UNDP and IFAD as ex-officio members) co-chaired by Pakistan, Mozambique and Norway see http://www.un.org/ga/president/60/summitfollowup/060215sg.pdf.

4 United Nations, *Delivering as One: Report of the Secretary-General's High-Level Panel on UN System-wide Coherence in the Areas of Development, Humanitarian Assistance and the Environment*, 9 November 2006, New York, pp. 1–42 at 6; available at http://www.un.org/events/panel/resources/pdfs/HLP-SWC-FinalReport.pdf.

emergence of environmental issues onto national and international political agendas.[5]

Since the early 1970s a large number of MEAs in the area of ocean, atmosphere, nature, wastes and fisheries have been concluded with institutional arrangements that set up a conference or a meeting of the parties (COP/MOP) with decision-making powers, a secretariat, and specialist subsidiary bodies.[6] These institutions are considered 'autonomous' as they are, generally, not considered as traditional inter-governmental organizations (IGOs). They remain distinct both from the state parties to a particular agreement and from the existing IGOs. Moreover, they have their own in-built law-making competence as well as compliance mechanisms.[7] These treaty organs comprise the COP/MOP, a secretariat and specialized subsidiary bodies. They have emerged as a new breed of multilateral environmental institutions. These international environmental institutions (IEIs) are fulfilling a range of interrelated functions including: awareness raising and agenda setting; collecting, processing and disseminating information; laying down international standards and regulations; capacity building; providing financial and technical assistance; avoiding and settling disputes.[8]

It is fair to say that IEIs do seek to fulfill their functions within the limits of their own given mandates to protect the environment. However, existing multilateral institutions and structures are inadequate to meet the simmering global environmental challenges being faced by the international society. Chapter 38 of Agenda 21 calls for restructuring and revitalization of the UN system to implement Agenda 21 and other outcomes of UNCED.[9] Many suggestions and proposals have been made for that purpose including for

---

5 United Nations University, *International Environmental Governance: The Question of Reform: Key Issues and Proposals Preliminary Report* (UNU/IAS, March 2002).

6 For detailed discussion about these institutional arrangements see, generally, Bharat H. Desai, *Multilateral Environmental Agreements: Legal Status of the Secretariats* (New York, NY: Cambridge University Press, 2010); R.R. Churchill and Geir Ulfstein, "Autonomous Institutional Arrangements in Multilateral Environmental Agreements: A Little-Noticed Phenomenon in International Law", *American Journal of International Law*, Vol. 94, 2000, pp. 623–659; V. Röben, "Institutional Developments under Modern International Environmental Agreements", *Max Plank Yearbook Of United Nations Law*, Vol. 4, 2000, pp. 363–443.

7 Churchill and Ulfstein, ibid, at 623.

8 Jack Werksman, Ed., *Greening International Institutions* (London: Earthscan, 1996), at pp. xiii–xvii.

9 See Bharat H. Desai, "Revitalizing International Environmental Institutions: The UN Task Force Report and Beyond," *Indian Journal of International Law*, Vol. 40, 2000, pp. 455–504, at pp. 471–504.

establishment of new institutions and structures to address environmental issues in a more holistic way.

In the past more than a decade, there has been growing international concern over proliferation of legal and institutional arrangements aimed at addressing specific environmental problems. This concern relates not only to establish a functional framework for coordinated international action but also for maximizing the limited resources available for environment protection.[10]

This lack of coherence in the international environmental governance system can also be attributed to the complexities of environmental issues involved and the sui *generis* nature of multilateral environmental treaty-making processes. As such international environmental governance – as a process – could be realized through establishment of inter-linkages of multilateral institutions that require structural changes in existing institutions and/or the creation of new institutions.

Catalyst Institution

UNEP was established by the UN General Assembly in 1972 to meet the "urgent need for a permanent institutional arrangement within the United Nations System for the protection and improvement of the environment".[11] UNEP is the designated authority of the United Nations system in environmental issues at the global and regional level. Its mandate is to coordinate the development of environmental policy consensus by keeping the global environment under review and bringing emerging issues to the attention of governments and the international community for action.[12]

United Nations Environment Programme (UNEP) was established as a follow-up to the first UN Conference on Human Environment (UNCHE). In the post-Stockholm era, UNEP has emerged as the centre-piece of the UN's efforts to protect the global environment. At the institutional level, UNEP has simply

10 United Nations," Report of the Secretary-General on Environment and Human Settlements", *UNGA/A/RES/53/242*, 105th plenary meeting, 28 July 1999, p. 28.

11 See, for more details, Bharat H. Desai, "Mapping the Future of International Environmental Governance," *Yearbook of International Environmental Law*, vol. 13, 2002, pp. 43–61.

12 The mandate and objectives of UNEP emanate from United Nations General Assembly resolution 2997 (XXVII) of 15 December 1972 and subsequent amendments adopted at UNCED in 1992, the Nairobi Declaration on the Role and Mandate of UNEP, adopted at the Nineteenth Session of the UNEP Governing Council, and the Malmö Ministerial Declaration of 31 May, 2000.

been a *programme*, a subsidiary organ of the UN General Assembly. Though, *prima facie*, UNEP does not possess the legal status of an independent international organization, it does not appear to have deprived it of some measure of international legal personality since it is required to fulfill specific tasks on the international plane (such as entering into headquarters agreement with the host country). In the preparatory stage, there was considerable caution as well as even possible envy and turf guarding by existing UN specialized agencies that played role in environmental matters. For example, it was UNESCO that played crucial role for crystallization of two global conventions: 1971 convention on wetlands of international importance (Ramsar) as well as 1972 world heritage convention. It seems convergence of several factors at the time played role in stonewalling creation of a new UN specialized agency for the environment.

The institutional structure thrown up by UNCHE was the result of a need within the UN system to have a specialized entity to promote international cooperation in the field of the environment. UNEP was designed to perform a vital role in the entire process. This new quasi-autonomous entity of Environment Secretariat within the UN, headed by the Executive Director, was carved out to serve as a *focal point for environmental action and coordination within the United Nations system.*

Since it was decided to be a *programme* within the UN, the enabling General Assembly resolution described it merely as "institutional and financial arrangements for international environmental cooperation". Its 58-member Governing Council was given a mandate that includes promotion of "*international cooperation in the field of the environment*" and to provide *"general policy guidance for the direction and coordination of environmental programmes within the United Nations system"*.

The Stockholm mandate required UNEP to act as a main fulcrum, both in terms of coordinating activities and programmes within the UN system as well as in terms of triggering international environmental cooperation. As a UN programme, in terms of hierarchy, it is responsible and reports to the General Assembly through the Economic and Social Council. UNEP appears to have achieved considerable success in galvanizing international environmental concerns. However, it was left to be just one of the UN programmes, having been denied even the status of a '*specialized agency*' (as per Article 57 and 63 of the UN Charter) for 'environmental' purposes on the specious ground that such an agency for the environment would result in duplication of activities and would compound already serious problems of coordination. It was also argued that it made no sense to remove these activities from existing specialized agencies and place them in a new agency. It seems there was an undercurrent within the UN system pushed by some of the specialized agencies that were not in favor of a new agency designed for protection of the environment.

The Conscience Keeper

UNEP have attained considerable success in galvanizing action on international environmental concerns, and laying down the threshold of environmental behavior globally.[13] UNEP initiated the preparation of the 1992 Convention on Biological Diversity (CBD). UNEP and WMO co-sponsored the Intergovernmental Panel on Climate Change (IPCC) or the negotiation of a climate regime culminating in the adoption of the United Nations Framework Convention on Climate Change (UNFCCC) in 1992. UNEP also provided substantive support and expertise for the conclusion of the 1994 Convention to Combat Desertification in Those Countries Experiencing Serious Drought and/or Desertification, Particularly in Africa (the Desertification Convention). It initiated the regional seas programme for eighteen regions with fourteen conventions and thirteen Action Plans, as well as their thirty-three protocols. UNEP plays a significant role for administering five MEA secretariats of the 1973 Convention on International Trade in Endangered Species of Wild Fauna and Flora (CITES), the 1979 Bonn Convention on the Conservation of Migratory Species of Wild Animals (CMS), the 1985 Vienna Convention and the 1987 Montreal Protocol, the 1989 Basel Convention and CBD.

It has been felt that UNEP's ability to set the global environmental agenda has come to be severely constrained by its organizational structure and unpredictable funding. Such inherent weakness could be a product of half-hearted political support to this international environmental institution. In spite of this, however, it seems no mean achievement that UNEP could contribute significantly in terms of development of both hard law and soft law. In fact, UNEP has been regarded, in the words of the UN Secretary-General, as the *environmental conscience* of the United Nations.

The gradual inroads made by other agencies of the UN system in environmental matters, as a peripheral concern within their own functional jurisdiction, also appear to have contributed to the dilution of UNEP's authority. It seems, in the euphoria of the 1992 Rio Earth Summit, UNEP was not paid any prominent attention and it was relegated to the background. In a way it contributed in 'dwarfing' of UNEP as it became just a cog in the machine

---

13 See, Desai (2000), n.9, at p. 462.

rather than an effective environmental conscience-keeper of the UN. Moreover, the gradual institutional clogging in the environmental field, emergence of other high-profile actors and multiplicity of environmental institutions has also had a negative effect on UNEP's role.

Quest for Revitalization

UNEP's Governing Council responded to declining resources and eroding authority by seeking to reassert the programme's pre-eminence in the field of environment. With adoption of the 1997 *Nairobi Declaration* by the Governing Council, serious efforts were launched to 'revitalize' UNEP. The Nairobi Declaration was followed by inauguration of the *Töpfer Task Force* by the UN Secretary-General in early 1998. The Task Force's report (June 1998) was duly examined by the General Assembly, which, in turn, gave direction for a series of institutional steps both within the UN Secretariat as well as at the intergovernmental level. It brought into being two forums, namely the Environmental Management Group (EMG), for inter-agency environmental coordination within the UN system, and the Global Ministerial Environment Forum (GMEF), for high-level policy dialogue at the intergovernmental level. The UN General Assembly has provided an overarching political guidance to the entire process, coupled with crucial policy direction.

It was recognized early on in the discussion on international environmental governance (IEG) reform that any major change in UNEP's situation, would require high-level ministerial intervention. Thus, launching of the GMEF represented a bold political initiative to revive the sagging fortunes of UNEP. It was also an attempt to regain policy coherence in the field of environment. In the post-Johannesburg Summit (2002) period, States were facing a litmus test of their sincerity to grapple effectively with the problems afflicting IEG. UNEP has been focus of the IEG process though the process is not 'UNEP-centric'. It was predicted that cumulative effect of the main policy options that emerged from the process – including universal membership and a secure funding base – would be decisive for the future of UNEP. It was expected that universal membership, as compared to mere participation, would bring about more legitimacy as well as authority to work of the Governing Council as well as contribute to widening of the funding base. It is noteworthy that there is a remarkable recent trend of "greening" of the existing UN organs. It has also been felt that the creation of new subsidiary organs within the UN system such as CSD (now closed) and High Level Political Forum (HLPF) on Sustainable Development on the one hand and development of environmental treaty organs on the other hand, have contributed in dilution of UNEP's mandate and authority.[14]

UNEP has been criticized for its insufficient clout because it has been unable to fulfill its original mandate as a 'catalyst' to promote international co-operation in the UN system due to growing complexities of environmental problems. A diagnosis of its health has shown several responsible factors that include size of its secretariat, insufficient budget, location of its headquarters, lower voice of its Executive Director in the UN Secretary-General's cabinet, lower status of environmental matters in the over-crowded schedule of the Second Committee of the UN General Assembly, and duplication of its functions with the other UN organs.[15]

Issue of 'Up-Gradation'

In institutional terms, a UNEP with Governing Council (now redesignated as the UN Environment Assembly) of 'universal membership' could formally emerge as a global environmental forum that acts as a global environmental authority as well as reflects the wishes and expectations of all the members of the United Nations. This reform, coupled with adequate, stable and predictable funding, could provide, in due course, a basis for elevating UNEP to the level of a UN *specialized agency* that has been variously designated as United Nations Environment Protection Organization (UNEPO),[16] UN Environment

14 See detailed discussion, see Bharat H. Desai, "Revitalizing International Environmental Institutions: The UN Task Force Report and Beyond," *Indian Journal of International Law*, Vol. 40, 2000, pp. 468–471; Bharat H. Desai, "The Quest for a UN Specialized Agency for the Environment", *The Round Table: The Commonwealth Journal of International Affairs*, vol. 101, no. 2, 2012, pp. 167–179; available at: http://dx.doi.org/10.1080/00358533.2012.661528; J. Werksman, Ed., Greening International Institutions (London: Earthscan, 1996).

15 Paul C. Szasz, *Restructuring the International Organizational Framework*, in: E.B. Weiss, Ed., Environmental Change and International Law (Tokyo: UNU, 1992) pp. 340–351.

16 For details of 1999 UNEPO proposal see Desai, n.14. Bharat H. Desai, "The Quest for a UN Specialized Agency for the Environment", *The Round Table: The Commonwealth Journal of International Affairs*, vol. 101, no. 2, 2012, pp. 167–179; available at: http://dx.doi.org/10.1080/00358533.2012.661528. Also see, Bharat H Desai, "Whither International Environmental Governance? Research Journey From The World Bank to Rio+20"; available at: http://www.jnu.ac.in/SIS/MakingSISVisible/Presentations/Whither%20International%20Environmental%20Governance.pdf.

Organization (UNEO)[17] and World Environment Organization (WEO).[18] There is already a strong undercurrent that favors such an 'up-gradation' of UNEP as shown by a series of recent deliberations at the meetings of the UNEP Governing Council/Global Ministerial Environment Forum meetings held especially during the period of 2000 to 2013.

The advantages and disadvantages of having a specialized agency for environment protection will need to be considered in terms of the possibility of improvement over the existing situation. The core issue in the matter remains the question of elevating existing UNEP's status or carving out a *de novo* global environmental organization. The history of institution building shows that it is difficult and cumbersome to create a new organization. Moreover, it would be a fallacy to presume that a brand new entity such as a world environment organization (WEO) would be more effective than UNEP. It is also important not to lose sight of the argument that UNEP is still the closest we have come to a WEO. It worked as such during the first two decades of its existence. Still, to impart credibility and authority to this beleaguered entity, several elements could be considered necessary for emergence of UNEP as a *specialized agency*. If the 'form' and 'perceptions' are key factors in determining authority of an international environmental institution, especially in view of multiplicity of actors, UNEP would qualify for that through the trappings of a UN 'specialized agency'. This development (as and when it materializes in due course) would take UNEP closer to being what may be called the United Nations Environment Protection Organization (UNEPO).

Any such exercise will need to remain within the UN system for credibility and wider acceptability among States. The process, content and range of institutional restructuring within the UN system for this purpose will depend upon the political will of the sovereign states, which may consist of mergers of some existing UN departments and programmes in the new specialized agency with UNEP at its core. Elevating UNEP to the level of a *specialized agency* also appears to be a pragmatic course of action compared to creating a *de novo*

---

17 Maria Ivanova, "Assessing UNEP as Anchor Institution for the Global Environment: Lessons for the UNEO Debate", Working Paper No. 05/01, New Haven, 24 May 2005; available online at http://www.yale.edu/gegproject/uneo-wp.pdf; Andreas Rechkemmer (Ed.), *Uneo – Towards an International Environment Organization: Approaches to a Sustainable Reform of Global Environmental Governance* (Nomos Publishers, 2005); Bharat H. Desai, "The Quest for a UN Specialized Agency for the Environment", *The Round Table: The Commonwealth Journal of International Affairs*, vol. 101, no. 2, 2012, pp. 167–179; available at: http://dx.doi.org/10.1080/00358533.2012.661528.

18 Ole Kristian Fauchald, *International Environmental Governance: A Legal Analysis of Selected Options* (Lysaker: Fridtjof Nansen Institute, 2010), p. 11.

organization with a new bureaucracy, which may jettison UNEP. Such an approach, favored by some due to deep disdain for its location in Nairobi (being the only important UN institution located in a developing country), will amount to throwing way baby with the bath water, and hence prove counter-productive. As such, the future direction in this respect will be dictated more by the political will of States, how far they wish to go in the process, how best they want to translate their international environmental commitments into action, and how much they are willing to allow transparency in the functioning of different international institutional structures in order to address the global environmental challenge.

The Restructuring

As today's architects of reform seek to improve the complex system of global environmental governance, they face the task of rethinking existing structure of IEG for concerted efforts at the international level to address the global environment concerns. While the scope and scale of environmental concerns have changed and actors in the environmental field have proliferated, the crux of the debate remains the same—how does the international system implement an effective environmental policy and law that take into account the concerns of developed and developing countries. In this regard, the contemporary process of consultations among governments is actively searching for innovative ways to reform the governance architecture for the environment.

Two reform initiatives for the IEG architecture are currently under way at the United Nations: 1) the implementation phase of the recommendations of the High-Level Panel on UN System-Wide Coherence and 2) the informal consultations on international environmental governance held under the auspices of the UN General Assembly. These policy debates seek to outline an optimal institutional form and function for the global environmental governance system.

UNGA Informal Consultations

The UN General Assembly President mandated Informal Consultation Process (Co-chaired by UN Permanent Representatives of Mexico and Switzerland) sought to carry out extensive consultation with UN member states as well as other institutions and experts. This enabled them to come out with 14 June 2007 Options Papers on key issues under consideration. The said paper in fact sought to analyze weaknesses of the existing system and suggested seven 'building blocks' for strengthened international environmental governance system. The co-chairs also proposed that by the end of the sixty-second session of the UN General Assembly, terms of reference could be decided for formal negotiations on 'transformation' of the IEG system.

In this context, the author was invited by the Informal Consultation Co-Chairs to present his views on 26 November 2007 in New York City on the proposal for UNEP's up-gradation into a UN 'specialized agency (UNEPO) as well as a wide-range of issues coming within the rubric of international environmental governance.[19] The presentation looked at several 'building blocks' to address the crisis of international environmental governance. It comprised future of central environmental institutional structure (UNEP), synergies and inert-linkages among multilateral environmental agreements as well as need for an environmental 'supervisory' organ at the UN headquarters – such as the possible revival of the UN Trusteeship Council.[20] Apart from this, a detailed presentation was made on the 1999 proposal of this writer on 'up-gradation' of UNEP into a UN specialized agency which could be called UN Environment Protection Organization (UNEPO). It underscored the necessity of carving out an institutional structure for environmental governance, the present position of UNEP, misconceptions about role of UNEP, 'dwarfing' of UNEP, difficulties in coordination in work of the UN's environmental related institutional structures, ambiguities in using the terms "revitalizing UNEP", declining voluntary financial contribution to UNEP by member states in the post-1992 Rio Earth Summit period etc. In view of series of problems and decline in political confidence of the sovereign states in UNEP, this proposal for UNEPO has sought to 'upgrade' UNEP into a 'specialized agency' of the UN system.

19 On the proposal for a 'specialised agency' and detailed blueprint of the structure for such an agency to be called United Nations Environment Protection Organisation (UNEPO), see lecture seminar by Bharat H. Desai, "Revitalising International Environmental Institutions: The UN Task Force Report and Beyond" at Environment and International Law Unit of the World Bank, Washington D.C., on 15 January 1999.

20 For a detailed proposal on the revival of the Trusteeship Council and, as a corollary, relevant amendments to Articles 87 and 88 of the UN Charter required for the purpose, see Bharat H. Desai, "Revitalizing International Environmental Institutions: The UN Task Force Report and Beyond," *Indian Journal of International Law*, Vol. 40, 2000, pp. 455–504 at 485–486 and 498–503.

Proposal for UNEPO

The UNEPO proposal has suggested detailed structure with a plenary body (General Conference/ Council), subsidiary organs such as Science & Technology Council, Environmental Policy & Law Council, Environmental Emergencies Relief Council and a Bureau as well as a Secretariat headed by the Director-General. It has also drawn mandate of the proposed entity as well as its relationship with the United Nations through special 'relationship agreement'. For practical considerations and aversion of the UN Member States, UNEPO could be established through 'up-gradation' of the existing UNEP and not as a *de novo* new entity. An intergovernmental treaty could form a basis for such transformation. Its location will need to be in developing country and Nairobi could continue as the headquarters. Its funding contribution can follow the UN scale of assessment or even current pattern of 'voluntary indicative scale of assessment'.

There appears to be an urgent need for strengthening the UN's environmental institutional framework and augmenting coordination so as to avoid duplication and wastage of resources. UNEP – being UN's environmental conscience – has the best credentials to spearhead the process. Given the political will and emergence of consensus among key sovereign actors, there appears to be strong justification – growing support of more than 50 states – for UNEP's up gradation into a UN specialized agency. The exact structure of such exercise could be drawn from experiences and existing models of 'specialized agencies' within the UN system. It, however, seems that the proposed structure will need to be *sui generic* 'specialized agency' for the environment in view of nature and uniqueness of this functional area. The contours of such an entity could emerge on the basis of 'expectations' (content) of the sovereign states from institutionalized international environmental cooperation. Such 'expectations', duly supported by necessary wherewithal, could throw up an appropriate 'form' for the said entity.

In this context the Global Ministerial Environmental Forum/Tenth Special Session of UNEP Governing Council at Monaco (20–22 February 2008) provided an indication as regards strengthening IEG as rooted in the Cartagena Package of 15 February 2002 and "need for and modalities of a possible resolution by the UN General Assembly". It was also expected that the input for the proposed GA resolution will be provided by the UN General Assembly President mandated Informal Consultation Co-Chairs that could "set the format for future talks". It seems, however, that in spite of best efforts, many of the key states were wary of such a move. As such the Co-Chairs had to abandon their effort and seek further political guidance. In the aftermath of this disappointment resulting from the said Informal Consultation Process, baton was passed back to the UNEP GC, which adopted decision 25/4 (20 February 2009)[21] and decision SS. XI/1 (26 February 2010)[22] to establish a regionally representative Consultative Group of Ministers or High-level Representatives. It met in Nairobi (7–9 July 2010) and in Espoo (21–23 November 2010). The suggestions on the table included: enhancing UNEP; establishing a UN specialized agency; and enhancing institutional reforms and streamlining existing structures. The outcome of the process was expected to feed into the work of the 26th UNEP GC, 65th UN General Assembly session and the Prep-Com for the UN Conference on Sustainable Development (UNCSD; Rio+20). The 11th Special Session of the GC/GMEF also reiterated the general consensus as regards role of UNEP in the architecture of IEG as:

> We remain committed to strengthening the role of the United Nations Environment Programme as the leading global environmental authority that sets the global environmental agenda, that promotes the coherent implementation of the environmental dimension of sustainable development within the United Nations system, and that serves as an authoritative advocate for the global environment, as set out in the Nairobi Declaration of 1997.[23]

The 26th session of the UNEP Governing Council/Global Ministerial Environment Forum (GC-26/GMEF) took place (during 21–24 February 2011) with 1000 participants from 140 countries. The GC-26/GMEF concluded its work by adopting 17 decisions on issues relating to, *inter alia*, chemicals and waste management; the world environment situation; IEG; an intergovernmental science-policy platform on biodiversity and ecosystem services (IPBES); South-South cooperation; and strengthening international cooperation for environmental crisis response.[24] On the issue of IEG, it reiterated stance as decided in the *Nairobi-Helsinki Outcome* that it should form the basis of any

21 See, http://www.unep.org/gc/gc25/proceedings-docs.asp.

22 See, http://www.unep.org/gc/GCSS-XI/proceeding_docs.asp.

23 See the Nusa Dua Declaration adopted by Ministers of Environment and Heads of Delegations at the eleventh special session of the UNEP (United Nations Environment Programme) Governing Council/Global Ministerial Environment Forum,held in Bali, Indonesia in February 2010; available at http://www.unep.org/gc/gcss-xi/downloads/nusa_dua_declaration.pdf.

24 See, Proceedings of the Governing Council/Global Ministerial Environment Forum at its twenty-sixth session, UNEP/GC.26/19, Nairobi, 21–24 February, 2011; available at, http://www.unep.org/gc/gc26/docs/Proceedings/K1170817_E-GC26-19_Proceedings.pdf.

discussion in the Preparatory Committee for the UNCSD.[25] UNEP celebrated its 40th anniversary at the 12th Special Session of its GC/GMEF (during 20 to 22 February 2012).[26] The session extended an opportunity, both to take stock of the past 40 years and to prepare for a meaningful and decisive outcome at the Rio+20 Summit. As a corollary, the UN General Assembly resolution 67/213 (see Appendices, p.284), taking note of the UNEP GC report, provided an inkling of things to come (see Appendices, p.294). The Assembly resolved to:

> (a) Strengthen and upgrade the United Nations Environment Programme in the manner set out in subparagraphs (a) to (h) of paragraph 88 of the outcome document, entitled "The future we want"...(b)Establish universal membership in the Governing Council of the United Nations Environment Programme, and mandates it, as from its first universal session to be held in Nairobi in February 2013...[27]

Thus, it seems, the long winding and arduous process of positioning UNEP to be the "principal United Nations body in the field of environment" as well as "leading global environmental authority that sets the environmental agenda" (1997 Nairobi Declaration) has now come full circle. The advent of *universal membership* of the UNEP GC is a watershed development in the incremental process of up-gradation of UNEP. It has provided virtual trappings of an international organization to UNEP without formally declaring it to be so. Thus UNEP has been taken closer to being a *proto-specialized agency* under the UN system that underscores its *sui generis* legal status.

The UNEP GC did host its 27th Session in its new incarnation of a UN environment program with *universal membership* i.e. all the 193 member states of the United Nations automatically become member of the UNEP Governing Council as compared to its earlier status with limited 58 members elected by the General Assembly. Thus the new structure now obviates the need for any formal role of the General Assembly to elect members of its plenary body – to

25 Ibid, Decision 26/1: International environmental governance, 24 February, 2011, at pp. 11–12.

26 For more details see, http://www.unep.org/gc/gcss-xii/.

27 See the Report of the Governing Council of the United Nations Environment Programme on its twelfth special session and on the implementation of section IV.C, entitled "Environmental pillar in the context of sustainable development", of the outcome document of the United Nations Conference on Sustainable Development, General Assembly resolution 67/213 of 21 December 2012, para 4 (a) and (b); available at: http://www.unep.org/gc/gc27/Docs/GA-RES-67-213-UNEP.pdf.

be now known as the UN Environment Assembly. It is significant snap of the umbilical cord with the UN General Assembly of which UNEP still technically remains a subsidiary organ. At the first universal session, the Governing Council adopted its rules of procedure and decided to hold one regular session every two year.[28] More significantly, and indicative of the future things to come, the GC also recommended that the General Assembly formally endorse this specially tailored attire of universal membership and provide it commensurate nomenclature (see Appendices, p. 293):

> *Recommends* to the General Assembly that the Governing Council of the United Nations Environment Programme, an intergovernmental body established pursuant to article 22 of the United Nations Charter, be renamed as the United Nations Environment Assembly of the United Nations Environment Programme;[29]

This remarkable change has *de facto* sought to elevate the status of plenary body of UNEP – called the UN Environment Assembly – akin to the plenary organ of any other sixteen specialized agency of the United Nations. Since the plenary body itself has been upgraded both with universal membership and given the nomenclature of the *Assembly*, the artificial and temporary construct of the GMEF outlived its utility. Hence it was decided to jettison GMEF after a life span of 12 years (having started with the Malmo Ministerial Declaration of 2000). It is also major milestone for the UNEP GC to be re-designated as the UN Environment Assembly. The decisions of the outgoing Governing Council needed to be given a formal political endorsement by the UN General Assembly. As a corollary, the UN General Assembly has resolved (see Appendices, p.289):

1. *Takes note* of Governing Council decision 27/2 of 22 February 2013, by which the Governing Council invited the General Assembly to adopt a

---

28 See Rule 1 of Decision 27/1 on New Rules of Procedure (1 to 72) adopted at the Twenty-seventh session of the Governing Council/ Global Ministerial Environment Forum on 22 February 2013; UN Doc. UNEP/GC.27/17 of 12 March 2013; available at: http://www.unep.org/GC/GC27/Docs/Proceedings/K1350945.pdf.

29 See Para 1 of Decision 27/2 on Implementation of paragraph 88 of the Outcome Document of the United Nations Conference on Sustainable Development, ibid. Also see UN Doc. A/CONF.216/L.1 of 19 June 2012; Report of the UN Conference on Sustainable Development; available at http://www.uncsd2012.org/content/documents/814UNCSD%20REPRT%20final%20revs.pdf, p. 17. The UN General Assembly, vide resolutivon 66/288 of 27 July 2012, duly endorsed the UNCSD Outcome Document annexed thereto; available at: http://www.un.org/en/ga/search/view_doc.asp?symbol=%20A/RES/66/288.

resolution to change its designation to the United Nations Environment Assembly of the United Nations Environment Programme, it being understood that this change of designation in no way changes, nor will change, the present mandate, aims and purposes of the United Nations Environment Programme or the role and functions of its governing body;

2. *Decides* to change the designation of the Governing Council of the United Nations Environment Programme to the United Nations Environment Assembly of the United Nations Environment Programme.[30]

This placed the stamp of approval of the General Assembly on the re-designing of the existing architecture of environmental governance.

Conclusion

Over the years, the churning on governance of the environment has assumed various meanings and shapes as well as witnessed sprouting of different forums. Interestingly, the global conferencing technique – that at the outset brought UNEP into being – still remains pivotal *mantra* (*raison de etre*) of all the four major inter-governmental milestones in the field – UNCHE (1972), UNCED (1992), WSSD (2002) and UNCSD (2012). In spite of all the cacophony, atmospheric and posturing, these global conferences have generated vital awareness, steam and drive to push for formulations and institutional structures as deemed best at a given time. It also underscores the truism that – alike humans that form them – the institutions of governance play a subtle law-making role and are also not infallible. It is interesting to see how 'perform or perish' motto works in actual practice as an underpinning of institutionalized intergovernmental environmental cooperation. Moreover, institutions also face envy and need to guard their turf, they become victim of circumstances and also run into the proverbial 'glass ceiling'. It is this quest for breaking the ceiling – not allowing UNEP to become a UN specialized agency – that has become a crucial chapter in the search for just, equitable, democratic and transparent architecture of international environmental governance.

The reluctance of many of the sovereign states is borne out of perceived fears and fuelled by envy from other institutional actors in the field. Thus, even

30 See the General Assembly resolution 67/251 on Change of the designation of the Governing Council of the United Nations Environment Programme, 13 March 2013; UN Doc. A/RES/67/251, 25 July 2013; available at: http://www.un.org/ga/search/view_doc.asp?symbol=A/RES/67/251.

as different pieces of the jigsaw are now gradually falling into place, UNEP's emergence as a 'specialized agency' seems to be written on the wall – just like nomenclature 'to be born a nation' characterized plight of Namibia for decades. Thus it seems to be no longer a question 'why' but 'when' and 'how'. The question of a 'new trust' for the UN Trusteeship Council that still forms part of the UN Charter and lies dormant, can also be addressed as a part of the larger issue of UN reform as and when conducive climate and sagacity come to the fore. It will vindicate the time tested truism that both law and institutions must change with changing circumstances as well as needs of the society at a given time. One hopes that 'doing' rather than 'talking' becomes the mantra in the governance of the environment during this crucial century for survival of life on this endangered planet.

CHAPTER 2

Designing the International Environmental Institutions

Introduction

In our global quest for interdependence as well as coexistence and cooperation, there has been momentous growth in the corpus of international institutions in the past one century. A closer scrutiny of the institution building quest of sovereign states reveals a remarkable effort to attain balance between the idealistic notions of international cooperation and the practical constraints emanating from assertions of sovereignty as well as national interests of the states. It has kept pace with changing needs of the international community to regulate its affairs, especially through means of institutionalized forms of cooperation.

The proliferation of these human institutions has not been an easy one. It had several twists and turns as well as ran into problems from time to time since they cannot often be seen to be crossing the invisible demarcation line as regards vital national interests of the sovereign states. As such these institutions and the efforts at institution building, become products of complex processes[1] as per prevailing circumstances at the time. In order to understand the process at work through intergovernmental efforts, one needs to examine the issues such as sovereignty, membership, legal personality, internal law, coordination, contribution of respective states as well as the decision making process that play a decisive role in the evolution of the institutions. Since the establishment of the United Nations, international institutions have provided useful forums for international cooperation on a variety of issues. The growth of functional international organizations (specialized agencies), functional commissions and regional commissions as well other programs within the UN system provide living testimony to the craving for *institutionalization* of international cooperation.

We notice the web of institutionalization has been slowly but steadily spreading in the last four decades in the field of international environmental

1 For more details on international institution building process see, Bharat H Desai, *Institutionalizing International Environmental Law* (Ardsley, New York: Transnational Publishers, 2004), pp. 17–62.

 | DOI 10.1163/9789004214552_003

law. Interestingly, the international law-making process in the environmental field is generally molded by international institutions, which act as catalysts, stimulators and sometimes even active participants in the process notwithstanding the fact that the final call is taken by the sovereign states. As a corollary, the environmental law-making process underlines a remarkable symbiosis between development of law as well as institution in the field. The growing corpus of multilateral environmental agreements (MEAs)[2] has significantly contributed to the proliferation of international institutions. They cater to regulatory requirements under the relevant MEAs. As compared to these regime specific institutions, several specialized environmental institutions (IEIs) like the United Nations Environment Program (UNEP),[3] the Global Environment Facility (GEF)[4] and the Commission on Sustainable Development (CSD)[5] – now replaced by the High-Level Political Forum on Sustainable Development (HLPF)[6] – have come on the international scene.

The advent of MEAs and other IEIs (especially over a period of past four decades) show persistent growth in institutional actors – and clogging of the space – in the environmental field. There does not seem to be any coherent long-term strategy at work for the purpose under a single or unified institutional umbrella. It has, in turn, contributed in making the IEI scenario much more complex. Moreover, it does pose a significant challenge in addressing issues of institutional coordination, inter-linkages as well as synergy.

---

2 For a detailed examination of the phenomenon of MEAs, see Bharat H. Desai, *Multilateral Environmental Agreements: Legal Status of the Secretariats* (New York: Cambridge University Press, 2010).

3 See the UN General Assembly resolution 2997 (XXVII) on *Institutional and financial arrangements for international environmental co-operation*, 15 December 1972; available at http://www.un.org/en/ga/search/view_doc.asp?symbol=A/RES/2997%28XXVII%29&Lang=E&Area=RESOLUTION.

4 The Global Environment Facility was launched as a pilot project just prior to the 1992 Rio Earth Summit. However, due to issues concerning democratic structure and transparency, it led to its restructuring in 1994. See *Instrument for the Establishment of the Restructured Global Environment Facility*; available at http://www.thegef.org/gef/sites/thegef.org/files/publication/GEF_Instrument3.pdf. Also see http://www.thegef.org/gef/.

5 See the General Assembly resolution 47/191 on Institutional arrangements to follow up the United Nations Conference on Environment and Development adopted at 47th Session on 22 December 1992; available at http://www.un.org/documents/ga/res/47/ares47-191.htm.

6 See the General Assembly resolution 67/290 on *Forum and organizational aspects of the high-level political forum on sustainable development* adopted at 67th Session on 9 July 2013; available at http://www.un.org/en/ga/search/view_doc.asp?symbol=A/RES/67/290.

As a plenary organ of the United Nations, the General Assembly has provided crucial guidance to the whole process even as the technique of 'global conferencing' has become popular and come to stay.[7] In the environmental arena, the General Assembly has acted as 'conductor of a grand orchestra' that provides political direction to States, notwithstanding the inbuilt Charter limitation that it can only make *recommendations* through its resolutions.[8] The Assembly has adopted, often without a vote, resolutions comprising constituent instruments of specialized environmental institutions such as UNEP and the CSD. In this context, an analytical study on the designing of IEIs with a focus on the CSD and its recent replacement by HLPF is a good example of changing character of designing trend-at-work. The establishment of the CSD was seen as one of the main outcomes of 1992 UNCED especially since it was agreed that the follow-up activities would be vital for sustainable development. However, there has been consistent concern as regards ability of the CSD to fulfill its mandate for follow up on the Rio sustainable development agenda. Even within the UN parlance, it was widely felt for some time that the CSD was a 'talk shop' as well as a waste of time and resources. This disenchantment of the member states and stakeholders with respect to working of the CSD finally led to end of the road for it after twenty year long journey. It started with the Rio Summit (1992) and ended with the Rio+20 Summit (2012). It seems the CSD provided a good perch to sovereign states to 'talk' about sustainable development as the agenda came to be seen in full glare during 2002 Johannesburg Summit. By the time of the Rio+20 Summit, it outlived its symbolic utility even as a 'talk shop' to those who had sought to bring the CSD into being even at the cost of undermining authority of the UN's 'environmental conscience' – UNEP.

7 See, generally, Peter M Haas, "UN Conferences and Constructivist Governance of the Environment", *Global Governance*, Vol. 8, 2002, pp. 73–91.

8 There has been a great debate concerning the nature and legal effect of the resolutions of the UN General Assembly. It has been observed that the records of the United Nations Conference on International Organization (UNCIO) at San Francisco do not provide an authoritative interpretation of what exactly was envisaged by the use of the word 'recommendations' in Articles 10 to 14 of the Charter; see F. Blaine Sloan, 'The Binding Force of a 'Recommendation' of the General Assembly of the United Nations', *British Yearbook of International Law* (BYIL), vol. 25, 1948, pp. 7, 10. Also see Rosalyn Higgins, 'The Development of International Law by the Political Organs of the United Nations', *ASIL Proceedings*, vol. 59, 1965, p. 117; *Preface* by Wolfgang Friedmann in Obed Y. Asamoah, *The Legal Significance of the Declarations of the General Assembly of the United Nations* (The Hague: Martinus Nijhoff, 1966), p. v; Stephen M. Schwebel, 'The Effect of Resolutions of the UN General Assembly on Customary International Law', ASIL *Proceedings*, vol. 73, 1979, p. 301.

The UN Conference on Sustainable Development (UNCSD) in its outcome document – *The Future We Want*[9] – spelled out creation of a new institution called as the *High-Level Political Forum(HLPF) on Sustainable Development.*[10] In carving out a new institutional structure the states derive lessons from past experiences of international institution-making. The HLPF is expected to start its work from where the CSD has left it. In this context, one could seek to make sense of original brief of the CSD, what went wrong with the CSD in fulfilling the Rio mandate and discuss institutional design of the new entity – HLPF. As a successor to the CSD, would HLPF be able to stand up to the challenge, learn lessons from the CSD experience and throw its political weight behind the sustainable development agenda at all levels (including the UN) are some of the pertinent issues that need to be probed. HLPF has just had the first inaugural session (it followed the last CSD session on 20 September 2013)[11] on 24 September 2013. Still, in the formative years of this new forum, it is likely to face some teething troubles. The significance attached by sovereign states to this new political forum will underscore its legitimacy and provide it with necessary impetus to carry forward the sustainable development agenda.

Multiplicity of Institutions

It is rather revealing that in the past four decades (since 1972 Stockholm Conference), most of the developing countries have witnessed massive environmental deterioration in the wake of sudden industrialization, explosive urbanization and population explosion. In fact, the capacity of a number of developing countries to manage their environment – so as to secure the well-being of their people – is also coming under severe stress, following rapid population growth, its uneven distribution and inadequate socio-economic

9 See the UN General Assembly resolution 66/288 [A/66/288], adopted at the 66th Session on 11 September 2012, pp. 1–53; available at http://www.un.org/en/ga/search/view_doc.asp?symbol=%20A/RES/66/288.

10 The High-level Political Forum came to be established vide the General Assembly resolution 67/290 of 9 July 2013; see UN Doc.A/RES/67/290 of 23 August 2013; available at http://www.un.org/ga/search/view_doc.asp?symbol=A/68/588&Lang=E.

11 The First Meeting of the High Level Political Forum was held on 24 September 2013 at the Trusteeship Council Chamber in New York; see UN Doc.A/68/588 of 13 November 2013; available at: http://www.un.org/ga/search/view_doc.asp?symbol=A/68/588&Lang=E. Also see *Earth Negotiations Bulletin*, vol. 33, no. 1, 27 September 2013; available at http://www.iisd.ca/hlpf/hlpf1/.

development.[12] They have provided enough room for most of the environmental disasters resulting from human quest for development.[13] Consequently, inter-governmental environment cooperation at the global level was considerably intensified. In order to meet simmering global environmental challenges, all the states, both industrialized and developing ones, need to cooperate with each other as closely as possible.[14] However, the four decade long efforts to develop a sound environmental and developmental partnership between the North and the South have been hampered seriously by a number of disparities. Therefore, bridging the North – South divide appears to be a prerequisite for any successful global environmental cooperation. Most of the people in the developing world are acutely aware that there are "two worlds, two planets, two humanities". As Mahbub ul Haq had prophesized:

> (O)ur two worlds, while they touch and meet, they rarely communicate. And it is that process of real communication, real dialogue, that we have to encourage today in case we have to equip ourselves to deal with the problems of this world.[15]

In this context, the UN General Assembly took cognizance of the report of the World Commission on Environment and Development (WCED).[16] As a follow up to it, the Assembly subsequently decided to convene[17] a United Nations Conference on Environment and Development (UNCED) in Brazil, to coincide with the World Environment Day on 5 June 1992. The enabling resolution of the General Assembly set up a Preparatory Committee (PrepCom) to address an ambitious agenda. One of the important mandates given to the UNCED was:

---

12 Bharat H Desai, "Destroying the global environment", *International Perspectives,* November/December 1986, pp. 27–29. Also see, Bharat Desai, "Threats to World Ecosystem: A Role for Social Scientists", *Social Science & Medicine,* vol. 35(4), 1992, pp. 589–596.

13 See, generally, Barbara Ward, "Only One Earth", *The UNESCO Courier,* January 1973, pp. 8–10; available at, http://unesdoc.unesco.org/images/0007/000748/074879eo.pdf (visited on 7 December 2013).

14 See, Bharat H Desai, "Environment and Development: Making Sense of Predicament of the Developing Countries", *World Focus,* May 2013, pp. 1–8 at 3. Also see, Bharat H. Desai, "Managing Ecological Upheavals: A Third World Perspective", *Social Science & Medicine,* vol. 30 (10), 1990, pp. 1065–1072 and Bharat H. Desai, "Threats to the World Eco-system: A Role for Social Scientists", *Social Science & Medicine,* vol. 35 (4), 1992, pp. 589–596.

15 See, Desai (2013), *Ibid* at p. 4.

16 See General Assembly resolution 42/187 on 11 December 1987: UN Doc. A/42/427. annex.

17 The General Assembly resolution 44/228 of 22 December 1989: see, UN GAOR Supp. 49, p. 151: UN Doc. A/44/49. 1989 (UNCED resolution).

> To promote the further development of international environmental law, taking into account the declaration of the United Nations Conference on the Human Environment, as well as the special needs and concerns of the developing countries, and to examine in this context the feasibility of elaborating general rights and obligations of States, as appropriate, in the field of the environment, and taking into account relevant existing international legal instruments.[18]

The General Assembly again emulated the example of UNEP in carving out institutional arrangement following the 1992 Rio Earth Summit. One of the basic objectives of the UNCED was to "promote the development or strengthening of appropriate institutions" apart from specifying responsibilities of the UN system as a follow-up to its recommendations. Following the biggest ever coming together of Heads of State/Governments on an environment and development platform, the UNCED adopted a draft resolution on institutional arrangement. Essentially, it relied upon the chapter on international institutional arrangements[19] in Agenda 21 and endorsed recommendation for the establishment of a high level Commission on Sustainable Development (CSD). The UNCED draft resolution IV[20] (for adoption by the Assembly) as well as the Secretary-General's report[21] recommended that the ECOSOC set up the proposed CSD as one of its functional commissions in accordance with Article 68 of the Charter. It was explicitly proposed to ensure an effective follow-up to the Conference, enhance international cooperation and rationalize the intergovernmental decision-making capacity for the integration of environment and development issues.

The Assembly took note of the UNCED report[22] and quickly adopted[23] the proposed draft resolution. This gave mandate to the ECOSOC to proceed to

---

18 The UNCED resolution, Part I, para 15(d).

19 See Chapter 38 of Agenda 21 in Nicholas A. Robinson (ed.) *Agenda 21: Earth's Action Plan* (New York: Oceana. 1993), pp. 604–619.

20 Report of the United Nations Conference on Environment and Development, Rio de Janerio, 3–14 June 1992, Doc. A/CONF.151/26, vols. I, II and Corr. I and III.

21 See UN Doc. A/47/598 & Add.1.

22 The General Assembly resolution 47/190 took note of the Report of the United Nations Conference on Environment and Development on 22 December 1992. It also decided to include in the provisional agenda of 48th session and subsequent sessions an item entitled "Implementation of decisions and recommendations of the United Nations Conference on Environment and Development", *Yearbook of the United Nations*, vol. 46, 1992, p. 675.

23 Adopted by the General Assembly as resolution 47/191 of 22 December 1992.

establish a new institutional structure as one of its functional commissions. Finally, the ECOSOC, acting under the authority of the Assembly resolution, proceeded to establish the CSD. Thus, unlike in the case of the setting up of UNEP, this time Assembly did not prefer to establish new institutional structure for the UNCED follow-up under its own aegis. Instead, it requested the ECOSOC to establish the CSD and take it under its wings as one of the functional commissions. As such, the CSD became a subsidiary organ of the ECOSOC. The primary authority and mandate, however, for the CSD flows from the General Assembly resolution. The subtle difference in the nuanced approach in institution designing is quite apparent. The resultant institutional entity, established by the ECOSOC, carried a special mandate. Though it was narrower, its political profile was expected to be higher. Thus it is interesting to find that through the authority of a General Assembly resolution, two institutional structures came to be created within the UN system in 1972 (UNEP) and 1992 (CSD). Both of these became subsidiary organs of different UN organs (UNGA and ECOSOC), within the meaning of Article 7(2) of the Charter though with different nomenclature (one is a program and the other was a functional commission). In both the cases, it is the Assembly resolution that served as a basic instrument, forsaking the need for any international legal agreement for the purpose.

The creation of this new UN environmental institution was viewed as indirectly contributing to the dilution in UNEP's authority as regards institutionalized international environmental cooperation.[24] In that sense UNCED's negative implication, for UNEP as well as in the setting up of the CSD, also came to be viewed as ineffective for the global environmental agenda:

> In hindsight, Rio indirectly contributed to UNEP's weakness while adding the CSD that failed to raise the profile of the international environmental agenda. The implications of this institutional weakness have become increasingly apparent while the state of much of the environment has kept on deteriorating. The proliferation of environmental secretariats for individual conventions, located in different parts of the world, has highlighted the lack of a forceful central institution. Fragmentation and lack of coordination grew, rather than the integrated approach, which has rightly become the hallmark of the modern environmental paradigm.[25]

---

24 Bharat H Desai, "UNEP: A Global Environmental Authority?", *Environmental Policy and Law*, 2006, Vol. 36 (3/4), pp. 137–157, at 142. Also see, Bharat H. Desai, 'UNEP: Coming out of Coma', *Down To Earth*, 9(20), 2001, p. 49.

25 Rudolf Dolzer, 'Time for Change', *Our Planet* (UNEP), vol. 9, no. 1, 1997, p. 19.

By 1998, as a part of an overall effort to reform the UN system, the UN Secretary-General established a UN Task Force on Environment and Human Settlements, which was headed by UNEP's then Executive Director, Klaus Töpfer.[26] The Töpfer task force identified 'proliferation'[27] of environmental institutions that changed the UN's environmental structure as well as led to the creation of institutional structures parallel to UNEP and the CSD.[28] In the view of the Töpfer task force, this proliferation gave rise to "substantial overlaps, unrecognized linkages and gaps".[29] The task force expressed the concern that:

> These flaws are basic and pervasive. They prevent the UN system from using its scarce resources to best advantage in addressing problems that

26 In early 1998, the UN secretary-general set up a high-level twenty-one-member United Nations Task Force on Environment and Human Settlements. It comprised ministers, government advisors, and members of the civil society as well as representatives from the UN Secretariat. It was headed by Klaus Töpfer, who was the executive director of UNEP. The task force presented its report to the secretary – general on 15 June 1998. See *UN Task Force on Environment and Human Settlements, Report to the Secretary-General,* 15 June 1998 [on file with the author]. Also see UN, *Report of the Secretary-General 'Environment and Human Settlements,'* 6 October 1998, UN Doc. A/53/463, Annex, at 11–28; and UN, *Report of the Secretary-General on Environment and Human Settlements, Presented to the UNGA at Its Fifty-Third Session,* 20th Session, 6 January 1999, Doc.UNEP/GC.20/INF/13; available at: http://www.un.org/en/ga/search/view_doc.asp?symbol=A/RES/53/242&Lang=E.

27 There has been proliferation of environmental institutions in the post-UNCED period, including the Commission on Sustainable Development [hereinafter CSD], the Inter-Agency Committee on Sustainable Development, and the Global Environment Facility. Similarly, considerable 'greening' of other development-oriented international institutions can be seen within the UN system, such as World Health Organization, the World Meteorological Organization, the Food and Agriculture Organization, the United Nations Educational, Scientific and Cultural Organization [hereinafter UNESCO] as well as the UN's regional economic commissions (the Economic Commission for Africa, the Economic Commission for Europe, the Economic Commission for Latin America and the Caribbean, the Economic and Social Commission for Asia and the Pacific, and the Economic and Social Commission for Western Asia).

28 Bharat H Desai, "Revitalizing international environmental institutions: The UN Task Force and Beyond", *Indian Journal of International Law,* Vol. 40, pp. 455–504 at 471.

29 See UN Task Force on Environment and Human Settlements, *Report to the Secretary-General,* 15 June 1998 (on file with the author), pp. 29–30 (hereinafter the *Task Force Report*). Also see UN, *Report of the Secretary-General 'Environment and human settlements',* Doc.A/53/463, Annex, pp. 11–28, 6 October 1998 at 85; available at: http://www.un.org/documents/ga/docs/53/plenary/a53-463.htm; UNGA Res.53/242 of 28 July 1999; available at: http://www.un.org/en/ga/search/view_doc.asp?symbol=A/RES/53/242&Lang=E.

> are crucial to the human future; harm the credibility and weight of the United Nations in the environmental arena; and damage the UN's working relationship with its partners in and outside of Government.[30]

A variety of reasons can be found for this multiplicity of institutions, including the growth in *ad hoc,* piecemeal and sectoral environmental law-making, which was represented by the MEAs; periodic efforts at 'global conferencing'[31] on the environment and sustainable development, represented by the Rio and Johannesburg summits; as well as the creation of more permanent structures with mandates that overlap with UNEP's existing or potential mandate, such as the Global Environment Facility (GEF) and the Commission on Sustainable Development (CSD). In the environmental arena, as noted earlier, the UN General Assembly has provided crucial political guidance to States, acted as a catalyst for the law-making process, and adopted resolutions comprising constituent instruments for some of the specialized environmental institutions including UNEP and the CSD. The role that is being played by these institutions has often resulted in overlapping of jurisdictions, working at cross-purposes, turf wars and precious resources being wasted.[32] Cumulatively, they have not helped in efficiently and effectively realizing the goal of institutionalized international environmental cooperation. At the same time, the multiplicity of institutions has also made the task of coordination very difficult. In fact, lack of coordination has emerged as one of the major challenges of international environmental governance. Recent academic studies have concluded that the current system of international environmental governance is "not only too complicated, but it is also steadily getting worse".[33]

It is in this context that the coming up of the new institutional structure of HLPF – as a replacement of twenty-year-old CSD – does pose an interesting scenario amidst wide skepticism on the creation of multiple IEIs. Nevertheless, the birth of HLPF with its special mandate could essentially be a product of the "com-

30 Ibid.

31 For details of a series of UN convened global conferences, see United Nations, *The World Conferences: Developing Priorities for the 21st Century* (New York: UN, 1997).

32 Bharat H Desai, "Strengthening International Environmental Governance: Some Reflections", in Smitu Kothari, Imtiaz Ahmed, Helmut Reifeld (ed.), *The Value of Nature: Ecological Politics in India*, Konrad Adenauer Stiftung, Rainbow Publishers, 2000, pp. 221–242.

33 See United Nations University, *International Sustainable Development Governance: the Question of Reform: Key Issues and Proposals*, Final Report 10 (Tokyo: UNU/IAS, 2002), pp. 4–48.

pelling force of circumstances"[34] or "evident need"[35] arising from institutionalized international environmental cooperation. The shape of such an international institution generally reflects the balance of power and realities of international life.

Working of the CSD

As mentioned in the preceding section, the CSD was designed as a high level environmental institution especially to ensure implementation of Agenda 21. The General Assembly was called upon to specify the organizational modalities for the setting up of the the CSD. Therefore, the Assembly adopted resolution[36] to this effect, detailing an institutional structure for the new body. The primary functions[37] of the CSD revolved around the Rio mandate and specifically it was expected to oversee implementation of Agenda 21.

---

34 J L Brierly, *The Law of Nations: An Introduction to the International Law of Peace*, 4th edition (Oxford: Clarendon Press) 1949, p. 94.

35 See, D W Bowett, *The Law of International Institutions*, 4th edition (London: Stevens & Sons) 1982, p. 1.

36 The General Assembly resolution 47/191 was adopted without vote on 22 December 1992; see, for full text of the resolution, Yearbook of the United Nations, Vol. 46, 1992, pp. 676–680. Also see, A.E. Boyle et. al (eds.), *Basic Documents on International Law and the Environment* (Oxford: Clarendon, 1995), pp. 658–665.

37 The General Assembly resolution 47/191, as an instrument constituting CSD, provides for the following functions:

(a) To monitor progress in the implementation of Agenda 21 and activities related to the integration of environmental and developmental goals throughout the United Nations system through analysis and evaluation of reports from all relevant organs, organizations, programmes and institutions of the United Nations system dealing with various issues of environment and development, including those related to finance;

(b) To consider information provided by Governments, for example, in the form of periodic communications or national reports regarding the activities they undertake to implement Agenda 21, the problems they face, such as problems related to financial resources and technology transfer, and other environment and development issues they find relevant;

(c) To review the progress in the implementation of the commitments set forth in Agenda 21, including those related to the provision of financial resources and transfer of technology;

(d) To review and monitor regularly progress towards the United Nations target of 0.7 per cent of the gross national product of developed countries for official development assistance; this review process should systematically combine the monitoring of the implementation of Agenda 21 with the review of financial resources available;

It was firmly placed within the UN system as a functional commission[38] of ECOSOC. As such, the task of the CSD was to assist, advice, make recommendations and provide reports to the ECOSOC concerning the mandate assigned to it. In a sense the CSD remained primarily a monitoring body for the Rio mandate. It was also regarded as "facilitator with the potential to harness public support to influence course of governments and institutional programmes".[39] Interestingly, the CSD's mandate gave a hint as regards issue

(e) To review on a regular basis the adequacy of funding and mechanisms, including efforts to reach the objectives agreed in chapter 33 of Agenda 21, including targets where applicable;

(f) To receive and analyse relevant input from competent non-governmental organizations, including the scientific and the private sector, in the context of the overall implementation of Agenda 21;

(g) To enhance the dialogue, within the framework of the United Nations, with non-governmental organizations and the independent sector, as well as other entities outside the United Nations system;

(h) To consider, where appropriate, information regarding the progress made in the implementation of environmental conventions, which could be made available by the relevant conferences of parties;

(i) To provide appropriate recommendations to the General Assembly, through the Economic and Social Council, on the basis of an integrated consideration of the reports and issues related to the implementation of Agenda 21;

(j) To consider, at an appropriate time, the results of the review to be conducted expeditiously by the Secretary-General of all recommendations of the Conference for capacity-building programmes, information networks, task forces and other mechanisms to support the integration of environment and development at regional and subregional levels; see n. 35, *ibid.*

38 The ECOSOC has been empowered to set up "commissions in economic and social fields and for the promotion of human rights and such other commissions as be required for the performance of its functions". The ECOSOC draws its power for the purpose from Article 68 of the Charter. However, there is also a general power to set up "subsidiary organs" is available under Article 7(2) of the Charter, apart from the power to "adopt its own rules of procedure" under Article 72(1). ECOSOC has used this power to set up commissions and subsidiary organs for a variety of purposes in the economic and social fields. It has set up nine functional commissions concerning Social Development, Crime Prevention and Criminal Justice, Narcotic Drugs, Science and Technology for Development, Sustainable Development, Status of Women, Population and development, Statistical Commission and United Nations Forum on Forests. As well as five regional commissions for Africa (ECA), Europe (ECE), Latin America and the Caribbean (ECLAC), Asia and the Pacific (ESCAP) and Western Asia (ESCWA); see, United Nations, *Basic Facts about United Nations* (New York: UN, 2004), p. 139.

39 Razali Ismail, "Agenda 21 and the UN Commission on Sustainable Development", Massachusetts Institute of Technology, Global Accords for Sustainable Development: Symposium Report (Cambridge, MA: MIT, 1997), p. 30.

of 'turf' and potential place of UNEP within the UN hierarchy. For instance, it stated that:

> To monitor progress in the implementation of Agenda 21 and activities related to the integration of environmental and developmental goals throughout the United Nations system through *analysis and evaluation of reports from all relevant organs, organisations, programmes and institutions of the United Nations system* dealing with various issues of environment and development, including those related to finance (emphasis added).[40]

Thus, it required reporting from UNEP to the CSD. It presented an interesting legal situation wherein a subsidiary organ of the General Assembly was required to report to another subsidiary organ created by the ECOSOC. It may not be a coincidence that international institutional arrangements under Agenda 21 first dealt with the mandate and structure of the CSD, followed by recognizing the need for an "enhanced and strengthened role for UNEP and its Governing Council".[41] It seemed to ominously signify that during the Rio process and its aftermath, the UN member states had less confidence in UNEP than in the high-profile CSD.

The CSD comprised 53 members elected by the ECOSOC for a period of three years. It also had a small Bureau[42] consisting of a chairperson, three vice-chairpersons and a rapporteur to be elected from each of the regional groups as well as a High-level Advisory Board of eminent persons having recognized expertise in the field. Apart from the CSD member states, other members of the UN and its specialized agencies as well as accredited entities could participate in the work of the CSD as observers. It also provided for involvement of a host of other intergovernmental organizations as well as international institutions to assist and advise the Commission in the performance of its functions. Significantly, in consonance with the role earmarked by Agenda 21, the CSD could also provide for effective participation of non-governmental organizations and other major groups[43] in the deliberations.

---

40 The General Assembly resolution 47/191, para 3 (a); see *Yearbook of the United* Nations, vol. 46, 1992, p. 676. Also see Agenda 21, Chapter 38, para 13 (a).

41 *Ibid*, para 11 to 13 and para 21 to 23. Also see, Bharat H Desai, "UNEP: A Global Environmental Authority?", *Environmental Policy and Law*, 2006, Vol. 36 (3/4), pp. 137–157.

42 See the General Assembly resolution 47/191, n. 40, para 11.

43 Agenda 21 has earmarked roles for various major groups consisting of women, children and youth, indigenous people and their communities, non-governmental organizations, local authorities, workers and trade unions, business and industry, scientific and technological community as well as farmers; see Agenda 21, n. 166, Chapters 24 to 32.

In view of marathon job of implementation of Agenda 21, the CSD sought to carry out the task by examining thematic clusters in its yearly work. Initial tasking for the purpose was done in its organizational session in 1993 which provided the framework as well as guided the process of the program of work.[44] The nineteenth special session of the General Assembly (1997) reviewed the work and prepared the CSD's multi-year programme of work for 1998–2002[45] period. It recognized that while much still had to be done, the Commission "has catalyzed new action and commitments and had contributed to the new deliberations on sustainable development".[46] However, the General Assembly

44 The first Session of the CSD took place in New York from 14–25 June 1993, Report of the session could be accessed at: http://www.un.org/ga/search/view_doc.asp?symbol=E/CN.17/1993/3/Add.1&Lang=E.

45 The CSD programme of work covers sectoral themes on strategic approaches to freshwater management (1998), oceans and seas (1999), integrated planning and management of land resources (2000) and atmosphere/energy (2001). The cross-sectoral themes would cover transfer of technology/capacity building/education/science/awareness raising (1998), consumption and production patterns (1999), financial resources/trade and investment/economic growth (2000) and information for decision-making and participation as well as international cooperation for an enabling environment (2001).

46 The recommendations of the Nineteenth Special Session of the General Assembly regarding working methods of the CSD provided as follows:

a. Greater involvement of ministers and high-level national policy makers responsible for specific economic and social sectors, together with ministers and policy makers responsible for environment and development with the high-level segment that needs to be more interactive and should concentrate on priority issues;
b. Continue to provide a forum for the exchange of national experience and best practices including through voluntary national communications or reports and to consider more effective modalities for the further implementation of commitments in Agenda 21 with appropriate emphasis on means of implementation;
c. Take into account regional developments and provide a forum for exchange of regional experiences and initiatives for sustainable development including through modalities for possible national reviews of regional implementation of the countries who voluntarily agree to do so;
d. Establish closer interaction with international financial, development and trade institutions;
e. Strengthen its interaction with major groups, including through better use of focused dialogue sessions and round tables;
f. Organize its multiyear work programme in the most effective and productive way.
g. The inter-sessional ad hoc working groups should help to focus the Commission's sessions by identifying key elements to be discussed and important problems to be addressed within specific items of the Commission's programme of work.

did underscore the need for improvement in working methods of the CSD in the implementation of its mandate.[47]

At the CSD-11 [48] an agreement was reached on its future program and organization of work for a 15 year period from 2004–05 to 2016–17.[49] The program envisaged seven two-year cycles with a review year and a policy year. It was decided that the review year would discuss the themes while the policy year would adopt policy decisions. It is to be noted that the Commission was able to complete only four cycles before it has been replaced by the High-Level Political Forum on Sustainable Development.[50] Though the multi-year program was introduced with an aim to make the agenda more predictable and ensure better preparation for all stakeholders. However, this step appears to not have gone well with the member states as it sought to make working of the CSD quite rigid and did not allow it to address critical contemporary challenges as well as new or emerging issues. In fact the technique of multi-year program has not helped the Commission much in raising its profile as a specialized

---

See the General Assembly 19th Special Session, 23 to 28 June, 1997, Supplement no. 2, resolution A/S-19/33; available at: http://www.un.org/en/ga/search/view_doc.asp?symbol=A/S-19/33&Lang=E.

47 See the UN Secretary-General' focused report prepared (in pursuance of the General Assembly resolution 67/203) on *Lessons learned from the Commission on Sustainable Development: Report of the Secretary General;* Doc.A/67/757 of 26 February 2013, at pp. 5–6; available at: http://www.un.org/ga/search/view_doc.asp?symbol=A/67/757&Lang=E.

48 The 11th Session of the CSD took place in New York during 28 April to 9 May 2003. An estimated 40 ministers, senior representatives of the governments, heads of the UN agencies and other international organizations as well as more than 900 representatives of non-governmental organizations and other stakeholders took part in this session of CSD; see, http://www.un.org/ga/search/view_doc.asp?symbol=E/CN.17/2003/6&Lang=E.

49 At its eleventh session the CSD decided that its multi-year programme of work beyond 2003 would be organized on the basis of seven two-year cycles, with each cycle focusing on selected thematic clusters of issues. It included water, sanitation and human settlement (2004–05), energy for sustainable development, industrial development, air pollution/atmosphere and climate change (2006–07), agriculture, rural development, land, drought, desertification and Africa (2008–09), transport, chemicals, waste management, mining, a ten year framework of programmes on sustainable consumption and production patterns (2010–11), forests, biotechnology, biodiversity, tourism and mountains (2012–13), oceans and seas, marine resources, small island developing states, disaster management and vulnerability (2014–15), overall appraisal of implementation of Agenda 21, the programme of further implementation of Agenda 21 and the Johannesburg Plan of Implementation (2016–17), *ibid.*

50 See, the General Assembly resolution 67/290 of 9 July 2013 on the format and organizational aspects of the high-level political forum on sustainable development; available at: http://www.un.org/ga/search/view_doc.asp?symbol=A/67/L.72&Lang=E.

body on sustainable development. On the contrary, it was pulled up for being an environmental body, ignoring the other key dimensions of sustainable development, that is, social and economic aspects! The cluttering of too many issues that do not seem to be in sync with each other often prevented in-depth discussions. In fact a discord on one of the issues jeopardized negotiation on the others. As a result, often the outcome was disappointing since no consensus could be arrived at and pending issues remained stranded. Hence, undertaking the whole process of preparation, discussion and negotiation in the sessions of the CSD proved to be a non-starter and added little value to its profile.

The CSD's task was, generally, based upon national reports to be submitted by the states. In fact, reporting as a tool was required to provide input for the annual sessions of the CSD. However, the task of reporting was 'voluntary' for all the entities including states, such as multilateral financial institutions, convention secretariats, international organizations and non-governmental organizations. The CSD's experience with national reports could be rated as mixed and varied.[51] Most of the states have been submitting reports as a *voluntary exchange of information* rather than any obligation *per se*. Even after twenty years of its existence, the CSD was not able to come out with any guidelines for reporting. Thus it made the whole exercise futile as no uniform level was fixed to review progress as regards implementation. The Commission did juggle in ensuring implementation at the national level by spurring innovative methods like developing national sustainable development strategies (NSDS) as well as sustainable development indicators (SDI). However, it was unable to undertake any systematic monitoring and review of such measures thereby never getting to know how far these measures were effective in supporting implementation of any of the consensual issues on sustainable development. Therefore, lack of effective review mechanism on country progress reports and commitments as well as no data on compliance with its own decisions did decisively hamper functioning of the CSD. As a result, the Commission started to lose its luster and effectiveness as regards implementation of sustainable development agenda as well as its decision-making processes and outcomes.

51 The number of national reports received by CSD during the initial years was: 152 (1992), 53 (1994), 59 (1995), 41 (1996) and 97 (1997). The largest number of national reports came in the wake of organization of UNCED and there were no reports in 1993 as it was CSD's organizing year. It is quite revealing as to how seriously countries have been taking the reporting task to annual CSD meetings; for details see, Farhana Yamin, "The CSD Reporting Process: A Quite Step Forward for Sustainable Development", *Yearbook of International Co-operation on Environment and Development*, 1998–99, pp. 51–61 at 58.

One of the major activities followed up by the CSD was the issue of forests. Due to lack of consensus at UNCED, the so called 'forestry principles'[52] ended up having a peculiar status. In order to build upon this, the CSD initially launched an intergovernmental panel on forests (1995–97), which was followed up by an intergovernmental forum on forests (1997–99). Since the states were unable to reach any consensus on the critical issues concerning forests, it was decided to establish yet another forum to carry forward debate on the issue. The CSD-8 handed over the matter of establishment of the UN Forum on Forests (UNFF)[53] to ECOSOC. In October 2000, UNFF came to be established, for a five year period, as a subsidiary organ of ECOSOC. Still, consensus remained elusive as regards having a legal instrument on forests due to sharply divergent views of the states.[54] In addition to this, it also recommended to the General Assembly to establish the UN Informal Consultative Process on Oceans to review developments in ocean affairs.[55] The recommendation of the second session of the CSD also led to processes to establish the Rotterdam Convention on Prior Informed Consent[56] (PIC)

52 See Non-legally Binding Authoritative Statement of Principles for a Global Consensus on the Management, Conservation and Sustainable Development of all Types of Forests, *Environmental Policy and Law*, vol. 22, issue 4, 1992, pp. 269–271.

53 The United Nations Forum on Forests (UNFF) came to be established as a subsidiary organ of the Economic and Social Council of the UN by resolution 2000/35 of 18 October 2000. It has 'universal' membership. Therefore all states members of the UN and states members of the specialized agencies can fully participate in the Forum with voting rights. For the first time the issue of forests has been put in charge of proper institutional mechanism (instead of an ad hoc one) and as a subsidiary organ of one of the principal UN organs. Its objective is to promote the implementation of internationally agreed actions on forests at the national, regional and global levels. See, UNFF website at http://www.un.org/esa/forests/.

54 For a detailed discussion on the international forests protection negotiations and the debate surrounding it, see Bharat H Desai, "Forests, International Protection", R. Wolfrum (ed), *Max Planck Encyclopedia of Public International Law* (OUP: Oxford 2008–2011), May 2011; see http://www.mpepil.com/.

55 The seventh session of CSD in 1999 made recommendation in its report on Oceans and Seas; available at, http://www.un.org/ga/search/view_doc.asp?symbol=E/CN.17/1999/4&Lang=E.

56 The Convention on the Prior Informed Consent Procedure for Certain Hazardous Chemicals and Pesticides in International Trade was adopted at Rotterdam on 10 September 1998. It seeks to curtail the $1.5 trillion trade in hazardous pesticides and chemicals; see UNEP, *Annual Report 1998* (Nairobi: UNEP, 1998), p. 7 and 21. For text of the Rotterdam PIC Convention see UNEP/FAO/PIC/CONF.5 of 17 September 1998. Also see, http://www.pic.int/TheConvention/Overview/TextoftheConvention/tabid/1048/language/en-US/Default.aspx.

and the Stockholm Convention on Persistent Organic Pollutants[57] (POPs). The Commission has also been the only forum reviewing the implementation of outcomes of global conferences on Small Island developing states (SIDS).[58] Apart from this, the CSD has served as an important platform for the Major Groups to develop their relationships with the United Nations and among themselves. It particularly ensured the involvement of the Major Groups in the CSD process by providing them due space to intervene during discussions.[59] CSD literally took their participation in the discussions 'from the corridors' to the high table. This considerably enhanced the outlook of the CSD showing great potential as a platform for dialogue and exchange of best practices between stakeholders of all types, including those organizations and implementers that have a substantial political, intellectual and operational presence in the field. However, the impact of multi-stakeholder dialogues on the actual decision making process as well as their engagement in the implementation of sustainable development remains a moot question.

To mark the thirtieth anniversary of the Stockholm Conference and to organize the ten-year review of progress achieved in implementation of the outcome of the 1992 UNCED, the CSD was put in charge of preparatory work of the World Summit on Sustainable Development (WSSD). The mandate[60]

57 The Conference of Plenipotentiaries on the Stockholm Convention on Persistent Organic Pollutants was held during 22–23 May 2001 in Stockholm (Sweden). The POPs Convention was formally adopted on 22 May 2001. It was to remain open for 'signature' at the United Nations Headquarters until 22 May 2002. As on 03 December 2013, the Convention was signed by states 152 and ratified by 179 states; for text of convention see, http://chm.pops.int/TheConvention/Overview/TextoftheConvention/tabid/2232/Default.aspx.

58 For more details see, the sixth session of CSD held in 1998; documents available at, http://sustainabledevelopment.un.org/index.php?menu=1182.

59 Felix Dodds, R Gsrdiner, et al., "Post-Johannesburg: The Future of the Commission on Sustainable Development", Stakeholder Forum Paper, No. 9, November 2002; available at, http://www.earthsummit2002.org/es/issues/Governance/csdfuture-2.pdf.

60 While adopting the resolution at its 55th Session, the General Assembly expressed deep concern that, "despite the many successful and continuing efforts of the international community since the Stockholm Conference and the fact that some progress has been achieved, the environment and the natural resource base that support life on earth continue to deteriorate at an alarming rate". The Assembly also emphatically stated that, "Agenda 21 and the Rio Declaration on Environment and Development should not be renegotiated and that the review should identify measures for the further implementation of Agenda 21 and the other outcomes of the United Nations Conference on Environment and Development, including sources of funding"; see the General Assembly resolution A/RES/55/199 of 20 December 2000, paras 2, 16 and 17; available at, http://www.un.org/en/ga/search/view_doc.asp?symbol=A/RES/55/199&Lang=E.

for the purpose was given by the UN General Assembly so that the CSD, as a preparatory committee,[61] could undertake the comprehensive review and assessment of progress achieved in implementation of Agenda 21 (1992) and the *Program for the Further Implementation of Agenda 21* (1997). In this capacity, as a PrepCom for the Johannesburg Summit, the CSD organized four meetings during a period of one year where the central thrust was laid on the implementation of the commitments that states had already made rather than undertaking any new commitments. Therefore, a detailed Johannesburg Plan of Implementation[62] (JPOI) was worked out. It brought out a political declaration that provided stocktaking of the history of three decades (from Stockholm to Rio de Janerio to Johannesburg) of efforts for environment protection. The JPOI also underscored the need to undertake institutional reforms whereby the Commission was required to place more emphasis on actions that enabled implementation at all levels, including promoting and facilitating partnerships involving Governments, international organizations, major groups and relevant stakeholders for the implementation of Agenda 21. It was also recommended that:

> (T)the Commission should focus on the cross-sectoral aspects of specific sectoral issues and provide a forum for the better integration of policies, including through interaction among ministers dealing with the various dimensions and sectors of sustainable development through the high-level segments; focus on actions related to the implementation of Agenda 21, limiting negotiations in the sessions of the Commission to every two years; and limit the number of themes addressed at each session.[63]

---

61 Report of the Commission on Sustainable Development acting as a Preparatory Committee for the World Summit on Sustainable Development, Organizational Session (30 April – 2 May 2001), General Assembly Official Records, 56th Session, Supplement no. 19 (A/56/19), 20 June 2001.

62 The Plan of Implementation of the World Summit on Sustainable Development adopted at the 17th plenary meeting, 4 September 2002; see United Nations, Report of the World Summit on Sustainable Development, Johannesburg (South Africa), 26 August – 4 September 2002, A/CONF.199/20 (New York: UN, 2002) pp. 1–173 at 8 to 72; available at, http://www.un.org/esa/sustdev/documents/WSSD_POI_PD/English/WSSD_PlanImpl.pdf.

63 Lessons learned from the Commission on Sustainable Development: Report of the Secretary General, General Assembly resolution, A/67/757, at pp. 6–7; available at, http://www.un.org/ga/search/view_doc.asp?symbol=A/67/757&Lang=E.

In addition, the JPOI stated in its recommendations the need to give greater attention to the scientific contributions to sustainable development. Ironically, the forum met with criticism that its policy decisions have not been sufficiently based on scientific findings, even though, science and technology was engaged as one of the nine major groups.[64]

It seems that during the twenty-year work journey of the CSD, the states did come to rely upon it as a crucial dialogue forum on issues concerning sustainable development. During its entire life-span, the CSD did become important platform in raising awareness about the sustainable development and contributed to 'pushing the envelope' in the areas of forests, chemicals, energy and oceans. CSD's annual deliberations in New York and their contribution for injecting the sustainability agenda in the policy-making processes within national jurisdictions did not seem very promising. Moreover, along with UNFF, it represented fragmentation of the environmental and sustainable agenda. It appears to have contributed in further marginalization as well as causing deleterious effect on UNEP's authority to set the global environmental agenda.[65] Cumulative effect of the above mentioned factors was enough to create disenchantment among the states and other stakeholders to think about utility and even closer of the CSD. This did come about when the member states finally decided on 21 December 2012[66] that the CSD would have its last session immediately prior to the convening of the first meeting of the HLPF on sustainable development in order to ensure a smooth institutional transition. The CSD-20, which was designated as the last session of the Commission, took place on Friday 20 September 2013.[67] It effectively brought the curtain down on a UN entity whose continuation probably no one was any longer willing to support. It is a graphic story of an international institution that almost died unsung and there was none to even shed a tear for it.

64 Ibid at p. 13.

65 Bharat H Desai, "The Quest for a United Nations Specialized Agency for the Environment", *The Roundtable: The Commonwealth Journal of International Affairs,* vol. 101(2), 2012, pp. 167–179. Also see Bharat H. Desai, "UNEP: A Global Environmental Authority?", vol. 36, no. 3–4, 2006, pp. 137–157.

66 See, the General Assembly resolution 67/203 of 21 December 2012, Implementation of Agenda 21, the programme for the further implementation of Agenda21 and the outcomes of World Summit on Sustainable Development and of the United Nations Conference on Sustainable Development, available at, http://www.un.org/ga/search/view_doc.asp?symbol=A/RES/67/203&Lang=E.

67 See, the Report on Conclusion of the work of the Commission on Sustainable Development; available at, http://www.un.org/ga/search/view_doc.asp?symbol=E/2013/L.38&Lang=E.

Advent of the High-Level Political Forum

The goal for reform of the institutional architecture for sustainable development is a continuous process that begun, though naively, at Stockholm (1972) and took concrete shape over the years especially at Rio (1992), Johannesburg (2002) and became more emphatic in the recently held Rio+20 summit (2012). In the run-up to Rio+20, discussions on the sustainable development framework veered around the issue if the CSD could be transformed into a Sustainable Development Council (SDC) or whether to abolish it altogether.[68] However, the governments eventually decided to close down the Commission and replace it with a High-Level Political Forum (HLPF), a hybrid body that will operate under the auspices of both the Economic and Social Council (ECOSOC) and the General Assembly. The establishment of the High-level Political Forum on Sustainable Development was called for by the UN Conference on Sustainable Development[69] (UNCSD or Rio+20) in June 2012 in its outcome document, *The Future We Want.*[70] It categorically stated that:

> We decide to establish a universal intergovernmental high-level political forum, building on the strengths, experiences, resources and inclusive participation modalities of the Commission on Sustainable Development, and subsequently replacing the Commission. The high-level political forum shall follow up on the implementation of sustainable development and should avoid overlap with existing structures, bodies and entities in a cost-effective manner.[71]

68 Maria Ivanova, "Reforming the Institutional Framework for Sustainable Development", Outreach, September 2013; available at, http://www.stakeholderforum.org/sf/outreach/index.php/component/content/article/177-68-ga/1415-reforming-the-institutional-framework-for-sustainable-development.

69 The United Nations Conference on Sustainable Development – or Rio+20 – took place in Rio de Janeiro, Brazil on 20–22 June 2012. The General Assembly vide resolution 64/236 of 24 December 2009 decided to organize the United Nations Conference on Sustainable Development at the highest possible level in 2012, as well as its resolution 66/197 of 22 December 2011. See, Report of the United Nations Conference on Sustainable Development, A/CONF.216/16, 20–22 June 2012; available at, http://www.uncsd2012.org/content/documents/814UNCSD%20REPORT%20final%20revs.pdf.

70 The outcome document of the United Nations Conference on Sustainable Development is entitled "The future we want". The General Assembly adopted it vide resolution A/RES/66/288, 27 July 2012; available at, http://www.un.org/ga/search/view_doc.asp?symbol=A/RES/66/288&Lang=E.

71 *Ibid,* paragraph 84.

In fact, the President of the 67th session of the General Assembly called on the ambassadors from Brazil and Italy to conduct informal consultations on the format and organizational modalities of HLPF.[72] These consultations began in January 2013 and concluded with the adoption of resolution 67/290 on 9 July 2013 (see Appendices, p.277).[73] The HLPF has an intergovernmental character and its mandate includes providing:

> (P)olitical leadership, guidance and recommendations for sustainable development, follow up and review progress in the implementation of sustainable development commitments, enhance the integration of the three dimensions of sustainable development in a holistic and cross-sectoral manner at all levels and have a focused, dynamic and action-oriented agenda, ensuring the appropriate consideration of new and emerging sustainable development challenges.[74]

Though the new body will replace the CSD yet it draws upon the strengths, experiences, resources and inclusive participation modalities of the CSD.[75] It means the starting point of HLPF would be from where the CSD has left its work. Nevertheless, it has been especially created to address the shortcomings of the current system. The HLPF is based on the premise to operate at the highest political level and, therefore, it will be convened at the level of Heads of State and Government every four years under the aegis of the UN General Assembly. Its participation would be universal, as opposed to the 53 member CSD. In intervening years, the HLPF will be convened for eight days under the auspices of ECOSOC and include a three day ministerial segment.

Thus, it seems, HLPF also does not have any independent legal status (alike the CSD). On the contrary, it has two masters – UNGA and ECOSOC – that will control its agenda. This hybrid organizational structure throws up several issues that need to be addressed. There are concerns about the new arrangement as it could become obstacle in giving coherent and focused treatment to the agenda for sustainable development. A universal model of high-level

---

72 See Letter of 18 December 2012 from the President of the General Assembly to Permanent Representatives of Brazil and Italy; available at: http://www.un.org/en/ga/president/67/letters/pdf/rio_20_18_dec_2012.pdf.

73 The General Assembly adopted resolution 67/290 on 9 July 2013 on the format and organizational aspects of the high-level political forum on sustainable development; available at, http://www.un.org/ga/search/view_doc.asp?symbol=A/67/L.72&Lang=E.

74 *Ibid*, para 2.

75 *Ibid*, Preamble, para 3.

decision making has the advantage of widespread legitimacy, but has a limited capacity for deliberation and it diffuses peer pressure. The limited frequency of high-level meetings raises the challenge of addressing new and current issues as well as having a dynamic agenda. As such, the HLPF will need to balance its mandate to "provide political leadership" and "agenda setting" that could provide an independent high-level voice for sustainable development with its close organizational and political relationship to ECOSOC and the UNGA.[76]

The HLPF has been specifically created to integrate "in a holistic and cross-sectoral manner at all levels" the "three dimensions" of sustainable development – economic, social and environmental. The scope of the sustainable development agenda is quite broad and the field has grown manifold since the first UN Conference on Human Environment (Stockholm, 1972). At the same time, the agenda of sustainable development forms the mandate of many other UN agencies, regional organizations, the World Bank and the WTO, as well as a wide variety of partnerships and relatively autonomous non-state or hybrid governance systems. In a situation such as this, it is a challenging task for HLPF to provide leadership and galvanize the agenda for sustainable development at all levels of the UN and beyond.

Another remarkable facet of the new institutional incarnation is the inclusion of "other relevant stakeholders" in the HLPF mandate.[77] It implies stakeholders other than those mentioned in Agenda 21 could now participate in the meetings of HLPF. The more inclusive language in the HLPF's mandate highlights the challenge of ensuring inclusive and fair access as well as the need to engage and attract the widest possible range of relevant stakeholders. It could impart HLPF with much needed legitimacy and provide effective leadership in the field. Furthermore, bringing more transparency and clarity, the constitutive General Assembly resolution emphatically lays down that the Major Groups and other stakeholders will be allowed to (i) attend all official meetings of the forum; (ii) have access to all official information and documents; (iii) intervene in official meetings; (iv) submit documents and present written and oral contributions; (v) make recommendations; and (vi) organize side events and round tables.[78]

---

76 See Steven Bernstein, "The Role and the Place of the High-Level Political Forum in Strengthening the Global Institutional Framework for Sustainable Development", September 2013; available at, http://sustainabledevelopment.un.org/content/documents/2331Bernstein%20study%20on%20HLPF.pdf.

77 The General Assembly resolution 67/290 on 9 July 2013 on the Format and Organizational Aspects of the High-level Political Forum on Sustainable Development, para 16; available at, http://www.un.org/ga/search/view_doc.asp?symbol=A/67/L.72&Lang=E.

78 Ibid, paragraph 15.

The new forum appears to be sensitive to the needs and concerns of the developing countries. It envisages providing adequate space and time for the discussion on sustainable development challenges faced by the developing countries. In order to facilitate participation of the least developed countries, the travel expenses would be borne under the regular budget of United Nations.[79] Meanwhile, the UNCSD outcome document *The Future We Want* has mobilized more than 700 voluntary commitments with an estimated valuation in excess of US$500 billion. These commitments have now grown to more than 1,400 with a value greater than US$600 billion – or nearly 1 percent of global annual GDP.[80] The figures do indicate that in the future the cost burden on the developing countries and least developed countries for implementing sustainable development agenda would become enormous. In this regard, the HLPF's role would become crucial in the implementation of its assigned mandate in these countries by providing vital impetus on financing for sustainable development.

The Road Ahead

In the era of institutional proliferation, the advent of HLPF is a logical corollary to legal and policy frameworks in addressing sustainable development goals having a global character. The carving out of a new HLPF squarely reflects the demands of the time as well as balancing of the interests of the sovereign states. The process of institution designing has witnessed qualitative and quantitative changes over a period of years which reflects constant efforts to find solutions to various challenges of the time. The precise nature of the role to be played by HLPF will depend upon the mandate of its constituent instrument, the exigencies of situation and the expectation of sovereign States from it. HLPF may be regarded as *locus classicus* for institutionalized sustainable development cooperation. The birth of HLPF at the UNCSD (Rio+20), as a part of UN system, followed the realization that "the need for an improved and more effective institutional framework for sustainable development". It is designed to perform a vital role in the entire process. As UNGA President John Ashe succinctly put it in his closing remarks at the HLPF inaugural meeting:

---

79 Ibid, paragraph 25.

80 Report on Fulfilling the Rio+20 Promises: Reviewing Progress since the UN Conference on Sustainable Development; Stakeholder Forum and Natural Resources Defense Council, September 2013; available at, http://www.stakeholderforum.org/fileadmin/files/rio-20-report.pdf.

> The decision of Rio+20 to establish a high-level political forum is a powerful step in mainstreaming sustainable development in the post-2015 agenda. The Forum will be a home for the international community to address and coordinate the entirety of sustainable development issues. As guardian of sustainability, it can provide a platform for leaders to reflect on today's priorities, not in isolation but holistically.[81]

The inaugural meeting of the HLPF (24 September 2013), under the auspices of the UNGA, presented an opportunity to open a new chapter in sustainable development governance.[82] With the participation of presidents, prime ministers and vice presidents, it did become a 'high-level' meeting.[83] It also appeared as a change from the CSD in the sense that environment ministers were not the only ones in the room. Speakers included ministers of foreign affairs, development cooperation, multilateral affairs, irrigation and water resources management, social development, and trade, leading to more of a balance between the three dimensions of sustainable development. The presence of the President of the World Bank Group and the Managing Director of the IMF provided some kind of gravitas, and demonstrated the importance that the financial institutions will lend to the process. The session was divided into several segments that featured the three themes: "From vision to action," "Global partnerships for development to create jobs and improve sustainable lifestyles," and "Mapping the way forward for eradicating poverty and achieving sustainable development". The Heads of State and Government, Ministers and other leaders articulated a number of concrete proposals on the role of the HLPF that (i) it should include stakeholders; (ii) it should emphasize accountability; (iii) it should review the post-2015 development agenda and the implementation of the Sustainable Development Goals (SDG); and (iv) it should examine issues from scientific and local perspectives. In view of this, the new forum could be said to reflect a new chapter in the story of sustainable development governance.

The HLPF's increased political weight, compared to the CSD, is especially relevant to the extent to which it could present a unified and independent voice for sustainable development. In particular, a clear division of labor

81 Earth Negotiations Bulletin (ENB), "*Summary of the First Meeting of the High Level Political Forum on Sustainable Development* (24 September 2013)", Vol. 33, no. 1, 27 September 2013, p. 9; available at, http://www.iisd.ca/hlpf/hlpf1/.

82 The President of General Assembly convened the inaugural meeting of HLPF, summary of the first meeting; available at, http://www.un.org/ga/search/view_doc.asp?symbol=A/68/588&Lang=E.

83 See ENB, n. 81, p. 9; available at, http://www.iisd.ca/hlpf/hlpf1/.

between the environment and sustainable development institutions will be important to avoid perpetuating the dynamic that led to the institutional reform in the first place. Without clear roles and responsibilities, there is a danger of overlap, duplication, and turf wars among the new HLPF, the reformed ECOSOC, the UNEP with universal membership, and other UN institutions and the multilateral environmental agreements.

At the same time, with rights come obligations and contain an implicit challenge for the stakeholders – they need to deliver as well as the governments ought to do. In a novel experiment, the stakeholders have been given a critical mandate by the HLPF document – to help develop and implement sustainable development policies. In addition, the document encourages stakeholders to be responsible for the development of modalities for engagement, asking them to establish and maintain effective coordination mechanisms for participation in this *sui generis* forum.

Conclusion

The growth of international environmental institutions is indeed remarkable in the annals of institutionalized intergovernmental cooperation. These institutional structures reflect the need for interdependence in the arena of global protection of the environment. One can witness innovations in the process of art and craft of institution building which are designed to cater to the nature and location of the environmental problems as well as expectation of the sovereign states. Most of the institutions also appear to be mirror images of the experiences of the states within their domestic sphere. As such they are expected to adjust to the changing circumstances and priorities of the states. The entry of HLPF on the radar screen of sustainable development agenda is largely seen as a welcome and timely step. It is also expected to fill the void left by its predecessor the CSD. There are genuine expectations from it to spearhead and get the goal of sustainable development internalized at all the levels. However, the way forward for the HLPF may not be very easy as the legacy and experience of the CSD underscores. It has been entrusted with a challenging responsibility. Only time could provide answers to doubts raised by some that the penchant at UN conferences to create new institutional structures every time leads to more talk shops, work overlap, additional burden on already fund starved UN, turf wars and institutional clogging.

In view of complex challenges that are expected to confront us in the foreseeable future, the HLPF shall have to tread the difficult path with caution, pragmatism and effectiveness to ensure implementation of global sustainable development agenda as well as our long term well being. Meanwhile, in the midst of the present debate on international environmental governance within the UN system, states would need to streamline priorities, provide adequate wherewithal and define expectations from the institutions. Any exercise for creation of a new institution will need to be guided by the ground realities and must be based on consensus among the sovereign states through a democratic and transparent manner. It remains to be seen as to how the HLPF measures up to the simmering global challenge of sustainable development. It also presents an opportunity to ensure that environment and development equilibrium does not deter or cause stagnation in the path of development, as most of the developing countries perceive it in the interests of their teeming millions of citizens. Only time will tell if the HLPF is able to stand up to the challenge of simmering global *problematique* entrusted to it.

CHAPTER 3

International Environmental Institutions

An Overview

Introduction

The increasing interdependence among states has laid solid foundations for international environmental cooperation. Though state sovereignty and territorial integrity still form the fulcrum around which international relations are conducted, yet there is a remarkable openness about inter-state interactions. In fact, with the surrender of old colonial possessions and assertion of the principle of self-determination by nations and peoples, a host of new state entities have appeared on the international horizon. This has necessitated international law to adapt to the needs and aspirations of these "new" entities. As such, the horizontal as well as vertical expansion of international law has brought about a transformation in its role as protecting the interests, to some extent, of the small and weak states as compared to its earlier role as a handmaiden for furthering only the interests of powerful states. An effort has been made to provide an overview of the international environmental institutions (IEIs), in their varied origins, forms and mandates. It does not, however, seek to provide an in-depth review of performance of these IEIs.

Institutional Proliferation

The proliferation in the number of states, more than three and half times the United Nations (UN) members in 1945 has put its own pressure in terms of addressing problems of the burgeoning humanity. The economic and social field is one of the most hard pressed. The international institutional forms have provided useful forums for international cooperation on a wide range of issues. The growth of functional international organizations (specialized agencies), functional commissions, and regional commissions as well as other programs, as a part of the UN system, provide living testimony to the craving for institutional forms of international cooperation. Some writers have

* Published as a chapter in Rudolf Dolzer and Josef Thesing (ed.), *Protecting our Environment: German Perspectives on a Global Challenge* (Sankt Augustin: Konrad-Adenauer-Stiftung, 2000), pp. 231–265.

 | DOI 10.1163/9789004214552_004

viewed such adaptation, especially by some of the specialized agencies, as a survival instinct:

> (N)number of UN agencies charged with aiding economic development felt threatened by the impact of the new interest in environment protection...(which led to) reorganize their programs in order to protect their budgets and preserve the integrity of their mandate.[1]

The gradual so-called *greening* of multilateral financial institutions such as the World Bank also reflects an effort to thwart criticisms concerning their lending operations having deleterious effect on environment as well as to keep pace with the changing agenda of international environmental cooperation. There are also scores of other intergovernmental and non-governmental organizations, outside the UN system, which fulfill the growing need for this purpose. The increasing concerns among states for some of the world *problematique*[2] have contributed in no less measure to the proliferation of international institutions. The "organizational explosion"[3] has even been compared with the much talked about population explosion. The argument has been put forward that some of these *problematique* pose a challenge of "global governance."[4] There are, however, differences in views regarding the need for any such "governance," especially by the UN, and the means to attain it.[5]

---

1 See Ernst B. Haas, Mary Pat Williams and Don Babi, *Scientists and World Order* (Berkeley: University of California Press, 1977), p. 182.

2 The *problematique* which have come to be considered as global, as compared to international, include a wide array of issues such as rapidly shrinking natural resource base, degradation of the environment, population explosion, traffic in narcotics, terrorism transboundary movements of hazardous substances and wastes, pervasive poverty and lack of development etc.

3 See, generally, James N. Rosenau, "Organizational Proliferation in a Changing World" in Commission on Global Governance (CGG), *Issues in Global Governance* (London: Kluwer International, 1995), pp. 371–403.

4 For instance see, generally, Peter H. Sand, *Lessons Learned in Global Environmental Governance* (Washington D.C.: World Resources Institute, 1990), pp. 1–60, *Peter M. Haas and Ernst B. Haas*, "Learning to Learn: Some Thoughts on Improving International Governance of the Global *Problematique*" in CGG, *Issues in Global Governance* (London: Kluwer International, 1995), pp. 295–332; Rahmatullah Khan, "The Thickening Web of International Law," ibid., pp. 249–262; *Peter M. Haas*, "Global Environmental Governance," ibid., pp. 333–369.

5 The idea of using the UN as an instrument for the purpose has been disfavored by many, especially in view of the inherent weaknesses of the system and the pitfalls; see, e.g., Khan, n. 4, p. 255 and 260.

The growing institutionalization is inextricably linked to the increase in the number of states on the international scene. The participation of a large number of states in international environmental negotiations underscores their desire to be part of the process. The role of small states, island states and large number of least developed as well as developing states has injected the law-making as well as institution-building processes with a much needed legitimacy. In many of the cases, these states are reluctant participants in a process which, they perceive, is of remote concern to them and issues impinge upon their much cherished sovereignty. This is reflected in the concerns expressed by a large number of states in the international environmental negotiations for multilateral environmental agreements (MEAs) as well as at various global fora. They have, in turn, brought the issues of *ethics* and *equity* in sharp focus between the northern industrialized countries and the southern developing countries. As a result, attention has been focused on the international environmental institutions, to make their functioning democratic, transparent and reflective of the needs and aspirations of the disadvantaged countries.

IEIs as Legal Creatures

All the IEIs invariably have a basis in their constituent instruments. The constituent instruments may be in the form of a multilateral environmental agreement, constitution of an international organization, a special international instrument or a resolution adopted by a plenary organ of an international organization (IO), such as the UN General Assembly. In each of such cases, what matters is *content* and not the *form* of the instrument as well as *intention* of the states. As the international treaty practice reveals, states would like to go for an institution as well as provide a legal basis to it, in a form which is convenient to them. As soon as the institutional form takes shape, it will come to acquire necessary legal personality, which will be essential for carrying out its mandate. The legal capacity of concerned institutions is circumscribed by their constituent instruments, form in which they are clothed, functions assigned as well as intention of the states. One of the main attributes of legal personality includes capacity to enter into international agreements with other entities and states. The governing bodies of the IEIs have the final authority in the matter. If the constituent instrument is silent on the issue, intention of the parties will need to be deciphered.

One may even argue that the IEIs based upon resolutions of the General Assembly (GA) – United Nations Environment Programme (UNEP) and Commission on Sustainable Development (CSD) – also have considerable operational room. The functioning of UNEP is a classical example in this context. The basis of its mandate from a GA resolution did not put constraints upon it to act as a fulcrum of inter-governmental action in environmental matters. The fact that the GA resolutions, as constituent instrument of IEI, are generally adopted in such cases *without vote* is significant. It may well be considered as reflective of consent of states in the matter. It can be regarded as a mere coincidence of bringing an IEI into existence through a resolution of plenary organ of an international organization. The inherent logic in this *modus vivendi* may be attributed to convenience of states. The constituent instrument of an IEI based upon a resolution of an organ of international organization, will apparently appear to be less cumbersome, as compared to negotiating and bringing into effect a separate international agreement for the purpose. The GA resolution, serving as a constituent instrument, in such cases can be regarded as *no less* significant than an international agreement which establishes an IEI.

The IEIs which come into being as legal creatures do generally have well defined mandates. However, the actual functioning of the institutions has to take cognizance of the realities of international life and the exigencies of the situation. All international institutions have to face this challenging task to keep pace with requirements of the states, which are the final arbiters of their destiny. Significantly, almost all institutions often rely upon their implied powers, which are not explicitly found in the basic instrument but regarded as essential to carry out the tasks assigned to them. IEIs are no exception. UNEP's constituent instrument does not mention its role in international environmental law-making, which, it seems, has come to be regarded as its "cornerstone."[6] The exercise of such *implied* powers imparts latitude as well as facilitates in actual governance. The attitude of states, especially in the Governing Council of UNEP, can act as a barometer for endorsement of exercise of such implied powers. In this sense, as creatures of legal regimes, IEIs evolve as dictated by the interests of the states.

Institutional Forms

The emergence of international environmental institutions as a specialized set of structures has been, in a sense, a logical corollary to the growth of

6 Elizabeth Dowedeswell, "Implementation: Enhancing the Effectiveness of International Environmental Law" in Scandinavian Seminar College, *Implementing Environmental Conventions: Papers from the Second High-level Nordic Policy Seminar* Copenhagen (Denmark), 28 October 1994, p. 39.

international environmental law. In fact, the organic linkage between "substantive law and institutions" in this rapidly growing field has been regarded as very close as compared to any other field of international law.[7] It takes varied forms and, generally, an international instrument either in the form of a convention or a resolution of an international organization, provides a basis for it. The need for an institutional form arises especially in order to supervise implementation of the relevant conventions, provide a forum for law-making and to ensure adaptability of the convention to changing needs.

In fact, it is common knowledge that MEAs enshrine some institutional form to give effect to the defined objective of the agreement. The institutional structures differ and are specifically designed to cater to the requirements of a given environmental issue sought to be addressed. In this context, Said Mahmoudi has observed:

> The role, scope and competence, and legal status of international environmental institutions have varied depending upon the types of environmental problems they deal with, the geographical location of the problems, the nature of the problems and most importantly, the priorities of the states concerned.[8]

In carving out a new institutional structure, the states derive lessons from the past, experiences of other international institutions and sometimes even domestic environmental institutions. The resultant product, however, reflects the demands of the time as well as balancing of the states' interests. The functions of IEIs are primarily determined by their constituent instruments. Most IEIs are permanent structures which cater to the goals designed by states for them.

It has been often taken for granted that a MEA needs to be equipped with necessary institution. Thus, generally speaking, IEIs provide the basis for institutionalized international environmental cooperation and serve as the tools to translate goals of MEAs into action. As such, institutionalized environmental cooperation appears in various shapes, shades as well as forums including entities such as intergovernmental commissions, intergovernmental panels or negotiating committees, conference of parties and intergovernmental organizations, multilateral development banks and specialized international

7 See the remarks by the Chair Said Mahmoudi in the Panel Discussion on "Environment: New Institutional Challenges," American Society of International Law (90th Annual Meeting), *Proceedings*, vol. 90, 1996, p. 488.

8 Ibid.

environmental institutions. They operate both within the United Nations system and outside it.

The international law-making process, especially in the field of environment, is generally molded by international institutions which act as catalysts, stimulators and sometimes even active participants in the process. Some of the prominent intergovernmental and non-governmental organizations such as IUCN and WWF have also made important contributions in the emergence of soft law instruments as well as international agreements. Interestingly, the environmental law-making process inevitably throws up some institutional forms too. It underlines a remarkable symbiosis between growth of law as well as institutions in this field. The growth in MEAs has significantly contributed to the proliferation of institutions specific to the area. They cater to the needs of the specific regulatory requirements under the relevant MEA. As compared to these regime-specific institutions, several specialized environmental institutions like the United Nations Environment Programme (UNEP), the Commission on Sustainable Development (CSD), the Global Environment Facility (GEF) etc. have come on the international scene. The growth of MEAs and IEIs, especially over the past three decades or so, shows persistent fragmentation of environmental institutional space as compared to any coherent strategy under a single or unified institutional umbrella. This has, in turn, also contributed in making the environmental institutional scenario much more complex, apart from posing a significant challenge of institutional coordination.

Types of IEIs

An examination of the role performed by varied international institutional forms in the field of environment protection and natural resources conservation can include broad categories of functional international organizations, specialized environmental institutions, regime-specific institutions as well as role of the multilateral development banks. Interestingly, most of the environmental institutional space is carved out in and around the UN system. Each of these institutional form derives mandate from its respective constituent instrument, carve out role at its own initiative or due to pressure of its constituency, try to grapple with an environmental issue as per its own understanding and may or may not coordinate action with others. As a result, there appears to be significant institutional fragmentation as well as *clogging* in the field, apart from the problems of duplication, overlapping of jurisdiction, bureaucratization and, often, confusion. It also leads to high-profile role for some due to political weight given by the states, whereas some others' authority have seen decline. The issue of coordination of work of varied IEIs is becoming complex and currently poses a challenge.

Role of Functional Organizations

Much before the advent of the specialized international environmental institutions, the task of addressing environmental issues was quite low key. In fact, prior to the 1972 Stockholm Conference, global environmental issues had not even surfaced. Apart from the specialized environmental institutions and convention-based institutional forms, some of the international organizations (IOs) have also played an important role for protection of the environment. Such organizations derive their mandate from respective constitutions. All of these IOs are now *specialized agencies* of the UN. These *specialized agencies*, as intergovernmental organizations (IGOs), have played limited roles, within their respective functional area, for protection of the environment. These include some of the earliest IOs like International Labour Organization (ILO), Food and Agricultural Organization (FAO), United Nations Educational, Social and Cultural Organization (UNESCO), World Health Organization (WHO) and World Meteorological Organization (WMO). In a bid to strengthen the international institutional arrangements following the 1992 UNCED, Agenda 21 called for the overall guidance to be provided by the General Assembly.[9] It mainly underscored institutional arrangements within the UN system and duly supported by multilateral financial institutions. Also prominent global non-governmental organizations (NGOs) like World Conservation Union (IUCN) as well as World Wide Fund for Nature (WWF) are exclusively mandated to work for the protection of environment and conservation of natural resources.

The task of dealing with some of the environmental problems was sought to be performed by functional international organizations, which came to be conferred with the status of *specialized agencies*[10] under the UN Charter.

---

9 Nicholas A. Robinson (Ed.), *Agenda 21: Earth's Action Plan* (New York: Oceana 1993), Chapter 38, par. 1 and 2, p. 604.

10 The United Nations Charter describes various specialized international institutions as *specialized agencies* under Art. 57. They are established under an international agreement and wide international responsibilities in areas such as economic, social, cultural, educational, health, and related fields. In 1945 when the Charter was drafted, environmental issues had not yet become global concern, and hence, no specific mention of "environmental" in the areas mentioned. However, they can be covered under the general category

Some of these agencies had enabling powers under their original constitutions for environmental matters or came to incorporate them by subsequent amendments. A notable aspect in exercise of constituent powers by the specialized agencies is that their ambit has been circumscribed by respective functional areas. In spite of this, they did lay down, to some extent, both legal and institutional frameworks for regulation of issues such as health and safety of workers, quality of soil and forests, marine pollution, protection of world cultural and heritage sites, environment and health, global monitoring of weather, safety and precaution in cases of nuclear accidents etc.

As early as 1919, the ILO came to be set up along with the League of Nations. The mandate of ILO was international regulation of "humane"[11] working conditions of the labour, which includes "sickness, disease and injury arising out of his employment."[12] This provided a broad menu for the ILO to act upon through its regulatory conventions. Some of these conventions have a direct bearing on the environmental aspects, including health and safety of workers, such as working environment (1977), safety and health (1988) as well as environment and cultures of the indigenous peoples (1989)[13] and chemicals in workplace (1990). Similarly, the constitution of UNESCO aimed at contributing to peace and security by promoting collaboration among nations through

"and related fields" under Art. 57. It is the Economic and Social Council (ECOSOC) of the UN which has been conferred with the power – subject to the General Assembly's approval under Art. 63 – to bring these agencies into relationship with the UN. A *relationship agreement* entered into between the ECOSOC and the concerned agency takes shape following negotiations. After the *relationship agreement* is approved by the UN General Assembly as well as the General Assembly/Conference of the concerned agency, a Protocol is generally signed between the UN Secretary-General and the Director-General of the agency to bring the *relationship agreement* into force.

11 See Report of the Commission on International Labour Legislation of the Peace Conference, appointed by the Versailles Peace Conference on 31 January 1919; reproduced in *International Conciliation*, vol. II, May-December 1919, Preamble to the *Draft Convention Creating a Permanent Organization for the Promotion of the International Regulation of Labour Conditions*, p. 863.

12 Preamble to the Constitution of the International Labour Organization; Amended Text vide Instrument of Amendment adopted by the 29th Session of the International Labour Conference, Montreal, 9 October 1946; see UNTS, vol. 15, 1948, p. 40.

13 The ILO Convention (No. 169) Concerning Indigenous and Tribal Peoples in Independent Countries specifically sought to ensure special measures for "safeguarding the persons, institutions, property, labour, cultures and environment of the peoples concerned" (Art. 4); see 28 *International Legal Materials* (I.L.M.) 1382, 1385 (1989).

education, science and culture.[14] However, in view of the growing concerns for environmental issues immediately preceding the Stockholm Conference, UNESCO initiated an ambitious Man and the Biosphere (MAB) programme which succeeded in carving our biosphere reserves across the world. Moreover, two landmark international conventions on wetlands[15] as well as cultural and natural heritage[16] have been framed under the auspices of UNESCO. Under the MAB it proposed to study the relationship between humans and their environment. In the case of the FAO of the United Nations, forestry and fisheries hold important positions in its portfolio of work alongside food, nutrition, rural development and agriculture.

The role played by these various functional international organizations is noteworthy; however, they were not strictly speaking international environmental institutions *per se*. As such, their primary concern was to address matters falling within their respective functional jurisdiction, with environment protection either a coincidence or a peripheral concern. In an exceptional case such as the FAO, its constitution can be regarded to have originally provided for an explicit mandate for recommending national and international action for the "conservation of natural resources."[17] In fact, the term "agriculture" in FAO's parlance includes fisheries, marine products, forestry, and primary forest product.[18] FAO's initiatives concerning plant genetic resources (1983),[19]

---

14 In the immediate aftermath of the Second World War, the collective concern for destructive human tendencies was given effect to in the Preamble of the UNESCO Constitution as "since wars begin in the minds of men, it is in the minds of men that the defenses of peace must be constructed" and hence the goals of UNESCO were placed in the wider context of human enlightenment; for Constitution of the UNESCO see UNTS, vol. 4, 1947, pp. 276–301.

15 See Ramsar Convention on Wetlands of International Importance Especially as Waterfowl Habitat, Ramsar, 2 February 1971. It entered into force on 21 December 1975; see *UNTS*, vol. 996, p. 245. Also see 22 I.L.M. 698 (1982).

16 Convention for the Protection of the World Cultural and Natural Heritage, Paris, 16 November 1972. It entered into force on 15 July 1977; see 11 I.L.M. 1358 (1972).

17 Constitution of the Food and Agriculture Organization, Art. I Par.1 (c); see *Yearbook of the United Nations*, 1946–1947, p. 694.

18 FAO Constitution, Article XVI.

19 FAO initiated *International Undertaking on Plant Genetic Resources* was adopted in Rome on 23 November 1983. It entered into force on 1 January 1984. Till February 1997, 113 countries had adhered to it. Its objectives are to ensure that plant genetic resources are conserved and are made as widely available as possible for plant breeding as well as conservation and use of PGR for economic and/or social interest etc. The Undertaking is overseen by the FAO Commission on Genetic Resources for Food and Agriculture; see for

the forestry sector concerning the Tropical Forestry Action Plan (1985) and sustainable forest management[20] are noteworthy.

Most of the other functional organizations have also from time to time trodden on a path of environment protection, closer to their own area of work. For instance, the International Atomic Energy Agency (IAEA) is mandated for development and practical application of atomic energy for peaceful uses. It has been authorized to lay down, in collaboration with the UN system, "standards of safety for protection of health and minimization of danger to life and property."[21] In the aftermath of the Chernobyl nuclear power plant accident, it proceeded to swiftly adopt two conventions on Early Notification of a Nuclear Accident (1986) and Assistance in the Case of a Nuclear Accident or Radiological Emergency (1986).[22] Moreover, it has recently adopted a "code of practice"[23] concerning international transboundary movement of radioactive

---

details Yearbook of International Cooperation on Environment and Development, 1998–1999, pp. 162–164.

20 See generally, FAO, The Road From Rio: Moving Forward in forestry (Rome: FAO, 1994); FAO, Harmonization of Criteria and Indicators for Sustainable Forest Management, FAO/ITTO Consultation, Rome, 13–16 February 1995: Also see Rome Statement on Forestry, Ministerial Meeting on forestry, Rome, 16–17 March 1995, which was adopted unanimously by Ministers from 54 countries as well as senior government officials from other 70 countries.

21 See Art. III (A) (6), Statute of the International Atomic Energy Agency, New York (UNHQ), 26 October 1956; *UNTS*, vol. 276, 1957. p. 6.

22 Both these convention were drafted by a group of governmental experts, following a decision of the Board of Governors of the IAEA during a meeting at Vienna, 21 July-15 August 1986. They were adopted by the IAEA General Conference in September 1986 and both conventions opened for signature on 26 September 1986. The Early Notification convention came into force on 27 October 1986 and the Assistance convention came into force on 26 February 1987; see for the texts 25 I.L.M. 1370, 1377 (1986).

23 The General Conference of IAEA requested [in Resolution GC (XXXII)/RES/490] the Director-General "to establish a representative technical working group of experts with the objective of elaborating an internationally agreed code of practice for international transactions involving nuclear wastes." The Technical Group established by the DG drafted a Code of Practice on the issue, which was designed to serve as guidelines in ensuring the safety of international transboundary movements of radioactive waste. Under the Code, which is advisory in nature, every state is required to ensure safe management and disposal of such radioactive wastes within its jurisdiction or control and "protection of human health and the environment." It also underscores internationally accepted norms of "prior notification and consent" of sending, receiving and transit states for any transboundary movement of radioactive wastes; see IAEA General Conference Resolution [GC(XXXIV)/939] of 21 September 1990 adopting the Code of Practice as well as for the text of the Code see 30 I.L.M. 556, 564 (1991).

waste. In the case of the International Maritime Organization (IMO), it has adopted a series of conventions for regulation of oil pollution[24] resulting from ships and various offshore activities, affecting the marine environment.

In this context, one may surmise that influence of the historic Stockholm Conference was decisive in adjusting gears to keep in tune with changing needs of the time. This logical trend, especially in the post-Stockholm period, may be regarded as responsible for institutional fragmentation in the environmental field. Thus several functional institutions playing their roles in respective jurisdictions can be said to have affected the reach as well as authority of a specialized international environmental institution such as UNEP.

Specialized Environmental Institutions

The *ad hoc* role played by some of the UN affiliated functional international organizations resulted from the fact that environment protection was at best their peripheral concern. The need for a specialized environmental institutional structure, as a part of the UN system was widely debated during the 1972 (UNCHE). It led to the birth of United Nations Environment Programme (UNEP), as a fulcrum of UN's activities in the environmental field.

(a) *UNEP*

In the post-Stockholm era, the UNEP has generally been the centerpiece of the UN's efforts for the protection of the global environment. At the institutional level, UNEP has been just a programme,[25] a subsidiary organ of the UN General Assembly. Though its legal status is not of an independent international organization, this does not appear to have deprived this UN body of "international legal personality since it is required to fulfill certain tasks on the international

24 For instance, International Convention on Oil Pollution Preparedness, Response and Cooperation (1990); 30 I.L.M. 733, 735 (1991).

25 It was established by virtue of the General Assembly's Resolution 2997 (XXVII) of 15 December 1972, which set out the institutional and financial arrangements for launching of the UNEP. Its establishment was again reaffirmed by the General Assembly Resolution 32/112 of 16 December 1976. The UNEP comprises of the institutional machinery of the Governing Council (comprising now 58 members) of the United Nations Environment Programme, the Environment Secretariat headed by the Executive Director of the Programme, the Environment Fund and the Environment Coordination Board.

plane,"[26] in consonance with the Advisory Opinion of the International Court of Justice in the *Reparations*[27] case. In the preparatory stage, there was considerable caution as regards creation of a new set of international institutions. In fact, the UN Secretary-General's Report to the Preparatory Committee underscored this:

> a) Any organizational arrangement should be based first on agreement about what needs to be done. Until this is reached, no firm decision can be made on the ways and means to be adopted.
> b) All functions that can best be performed by existing organizations should be assigned to those organizations, both international and national, most capable of carrying them out effectively. *No unnecessary new machinery should be created.*
> h) *The United Nations should be the principal centre for international environment cooperation.*
> i) The organization of environmental activities within the United Nations should be so designed as to strengthen and reinforce the entire United Nations system (emphasis added).[28]

Therefore, the institutional structure thrown up by the UNCHE was the result of a clear felt need within the UN system to have an exclusive entity to cater to the requirement of providing a platform for international environmental cooperation. UNEP was in fact designed to perform a vital catalytic role in the entire process. This new quasi-autonomous entity of Environment Secretariat within the UN, headed by the Executive Director, was carved out to serve as a *focal point for environmental action and coordination within the United Nations*

26 Patricia W. Birnie and Alan E. Boyle, *International Law and the Environment* (Oxford: Clarendon Press, 1992), p. 35.

27 In this landmark Opinion, the International Court of Justice (ICJ), with reference to the legal competence of the United Nations, observed: "In the opinion of the Court. The Organization was intended to exercise and enjoy, and is in fact exercising and enjoying, functions and rights which can only be explained on the basis of the possession of a large measure of international personality and the capacity to operate upon an international plane. It is at present the supreme type of international organization, and it could not carry out the intentions of its founders if it was devoid of international personality. It must be acknowledged that its Members, by entrusting certain functions to it, with the attendant duties and responsibilities, have clothed it with the competence required to enable those functions to be effectively discharged"; see ICJ Reports (1949), p. 179.

28 See Report of the Secretary-General to the Third Session of the Preparatory Committee, U.N.Doc. A/CONF.48/PC.11, 30 July 1971, p. 222.

system.[29] Since it was decided to be merely a programme within the UN, the enabling General Assembly Resolution did not even carry the name of the new entity as its title, which was described as "Institutional and financial arrangements for international environmental cooperation." Its 58 member Governing Council[30] has been given the mandate which includes the following primary functions:

a) To promote international cooperation in the field of the environment and to recommend, as appropriate, policies to this end;
b) To provide general policy guidance for the direction and coordination of environmental programmes within the United Nations system;[31]

Therefore, the Stockholm mandate required UNEP to act as a *catalyst*, both in terms of coordinating activities and programmes within the UN system as well as in terms of triggering international environmental cooperation rather than "initiating or mandating environmental programmes on its own account."[32] Since it is one of UN's own programmes, it is responsible to and reports to the General Assembly through the Economic and Social Council.[33]

The UN system has had, even prior to the setting up of the UNEP, several specialized and related agencies which were dealing with environment related functions as a part of their own functional areas. These included agencies such as Food and Agriculture Organization (FAO), United Nations Educational, Scientific and Cultural Organization (UNESCO), World Bank (IBRD), World

---

29 See Report of the UNCHE, Note 1, Ch. III, part II. Also see the General Assembly Resolution A/RES/2997 (XXVII) of 15 December 1972, part II, p. 3 in United Nations General Assembly Official Records, 26th Session, Supp. No. 30, p. 43.

30 The 58 members of the UNEP Governing Council are to be elected by the UN General Assembly, for a period of three years on the following basis: (a) Sixteen seats for African States; (b) Thirteen seats for Asian States; (c) Six seats for Eastern European States; (d) Ten seats for Latin American States; (e) Thirteen seats for Western European and other States; see UNGA Res. 2997 I, Part I, par. 1.

31 Ibid., Part I, par. 2 (a) and (b).

32 Birnie and Boyle, n. 26, p. 42.

33 The enabling resolution requires that "the Governing Council" shall report annually to the General Assembly through the Economic and Social Council, which will transmit to the Assembly such comments on the report as it may deem necessary, particularly with regard to questions of coordination and to the relationship of environmental policies and programmes within the United Nations system to overall economic and social policies and priorities; see UNGA Res. 2997, Part I, par. 3.

Health Organization (WHO), World Meteorological Organization (WMO), International Maritime Organization (IMO) and International Atomic Energy Agency (IAEA). In spite of this, the fact that a specialized environmental programme was created, underscored the need for a hub or focal point within the UN system. In fact it has been regarded, in the words of the UN Secretary General, as the "environmental conscience of the United Nations."[34] It was in a way reflection of the consensus that:

> (T)he key international environmental institutions should be intergovernmental in character. Governments are not prepared to surrender authority to a supranational agency that could bind them to act against their will. Governments may, however, be willing to delegate authority to international entities to act in carefully prescribed areas under norms and policies already agreed upon...the central machinery for environmental cooperation should be within the framework of the United Nations...as the central world institution for global cooperation.

Keeping in view these goals, UNEP seems to have attained considerable success in galvanizing international environmental concerns. In turn, it propelled intergovernmental efforts to lay down the threshold limits of environmental behaviour. One of the important achievements of UNEP has been the Regional Seas Programme,[35] which facilitated crystallization of more than thirty environmental agreements as well as regional Action Plans. It has also effectively translated its catalyst role into action through an ambitious Montevideo Programme[36] I (1981) and II (1993). As a result, it has contributed through evolution of several international environmental agreements, development of *soft law* through principles, standards and guidelines as well as contributed in the development of environmental law and policy at the national level. Some of the important MEAs in which UNEP has contributed in various degrees include the 1979 Convention on Migratory Species of Wild Animals

34 Kofi A. Annan, "An Indispensable Contribution," *Our Planet*, vol. 9, no. 1, 1997, p. 4.

35 The Oceans and Coastal Areas Programme Activity Centre (OCA/PAC) of the UNEP is responsible for this Programme. In fact the UNEP provides secretariat facilities to several of the Regional Seas Conventions.

36 See Report of the Ad Hoc Meeting of Senior Government Officials Experts in Environmental Law, UNEP/GC 10/5/Add.2, Annex, Ch. 11 (1981) and UNEP, Programme for the Development and Periodic Review of Environmental Law for the 1990s (Nairobi, June 1993), pp. 1–17. Also see Yearbook of the United Nations, vol. 36, 1982, p. 1030 and Yearbook of the United Nations, vol. 47, 1993, pp. 820–821.

(Bonn Convention),[37] the 1985 Vienna Convention and 1987 Montreal Protocol for the Protection of the Ozone Layer,[38] and the 1989 Basel Convention on the Control of Transboundary Movement of Hazardous Wastes and their Disposal.[39] During the preparatory process for the 1992 United Nations Conference on Environment and Development (UNCED), it played an important role in the framing of the Convention on Biological Diversity (CBD).[40] UNEP even provides secretariat services for five international environmental conventions (CITES, CMS, Ozone, Basel and CBD).[41]

It is also no mean achievement that UNEP could contribute significantly to the development of both hard law and soft law during a quarter century of its existence. The gradual inroads made by other agencies of the UN system in environmental matters, as a part of their own functional jurisdiction, contributed to the dilution of UNEP's authority. It was at the initiative of UNEP that the Brundtland Commission[42] came to be established and, in turn, at whose recommendation the 1992 United Nations Conference on Environment and Development (UNCED) was convened by the General Assembly.[43] However the "expert 'watchdog'"[44] and "environmental conscience" of the UN

37 Convention on the Conservation of Migratory Species of Wild Animals (Bonn), 1979. It came into force on 1 November 1983; see 19 I.L.M. 15 (1980).

38 Convention for the Protection of the Ozone Layer (Vienna), 1985. It came into force on 22 September 1988. The Protocol on Substances that Deplete the Ozone Layer (Montreal), 1987. It came into force on 1 January 1989; see 26 I.L.M. 1529, 1550 (1987). The UNEP headquarters in Nairobi houses the Secretariat of the Ozone Regime.

39 Convention on the Control of Transboundary Movement of Hazardous Wastes and Their Disposal (Basel), 1989. It came into force on 24 May 1992; see 28 I.L.M. 657 (1989).

40 Convention on Biological Diversity (Rio de Janeiro), 1992. It came into force on 29 December 1993; see 31 I.L.M. 822 (1992).

41 In doing so the concerned Conference of Parties (COP) of the Convention seeks to take advantage of the established administrative structure of UNEP. Whenever UNEP (which is also a subsidiary organ of the UN General Assembly), as an international environmental institution, undertakes to carry out the function of the Convention Secretariat it will be subject to the authority of the COP as far as those specific functions of the Convention are concerned. For an exposition on this relationship see UN Doc. UNEP/DEP/Coord.4/3/COR.1, 4 January 1996.

42 The World Commission on Environment and Development (*WCED*), headed by the former Norwegian Prime Minister was established pursuant to the UNEP Governing Council decision UNEP/GC.11/3 on 23 May 1983. The WCED report Our Common Future (published by Oxford Uni. Press, Oxford, 1987) was endorsed by the UN General Assembly Resolution A/RES/42/187 on 11 December 1987.

43 See the UN General Assembly Resolution 43/196 (1988).

44 Kofi A. Annan, "An Indispensable Contribution," *Our Planet*, vol. 9, No. 1, 1997, p. 4.

was not even assigned with the "preparation of the follow-up conference to Stockholm." In the euphoria of the Earth Summit, UNEP did not find any prominent attention.

(b) *CSD*

The Commission on Sustainable Development (CSD) is a major institutional product of the United Nations Conference on Environment and Development (UNCED). Unlike UNEP, which emerged after the 1972 UNCHE, CSD was designed as an environmental institution at a high level, especially to ensure implementation of Agenda 21. In fact Agenda 21 explicitly envisaged the establishment of CSD. In a chapter on "international institutional arrangement," CSD was to be the only major institutional addition to the UN system to ensure:

> (E)ffective follow-up of the Conference, as well as to enhance international cooperation and rationalize the intergovernmental decision-making capacity for the integration of environment and development issues and to examine the progress in the implementation of Agenda 21 at the national, regional and international levels, a high-level Commission on Sustainable Development should be established.[45]

The General Assembly was called upon to specify the organizational modalities for the setting up of CSD. However, this came about not through the drafting of a special constituent or an international agreement. Instead, the Assembly adopted a resolution[46] to this effect, detailing the institutional structure of the new body. Alike UNEP, the Assembly resolution serves as a constituent instrument for CSD too.

The primary functions[47] of CSD revolve around the Rio mandate and specifically implementation of Agenda 21. It has been firmly placed within the UN

---

45 Agenda 21, Chapter 38, para 11; see *Nicholas A. Robinson* (Ed.), Agenda 21: Earth's Action Plan (New York: Oceana, 1993), p. 607.

46 The General Assembly Resolution 47/191 was adopted, *without vote*, on 22 December 1992; see, for full text of the resolution, Yearbook of the United Nations (YUN), vol. 46, 1992, pp. 676–480.

47 The Assembly Resolution 47/191, as an instrument constituting CSD, provides the following functions:
(a) To monitor progress in the implementation of agenda 21 and activities related to the integration of environmental and developmental goals throughout the United Nations system through analysis and evaluation of reports from all relevant organs, organizations, programmes and institutions of the United Nations system dealing with various issues of environment and development, including those related to finance; (b) To consider infor

system, as a *functional commission*[48] of the Economic and Social Council. As such, the task of the CSD is to assist, advice and make recommendations and reports to the ECOSOC concerning the mandate assigned to it. It has been often dubbed as a "talk shop," though at a high level. In a sense, CSD remains

---

mation provided by Governments, including, for example, in the form of periodic communications or national reports regarding the activities they undertake to implement Agenda 21, the problems they face, such as problems related to financial resources and technology transfer, and other environment and development issues they find relevant; (c) To review the progress in the implementation of the commitments contained in Agenda 21, including those related to the provision of financial resources and transfer of technology; (d) To review and monitor regularly progress towards the United Nations target of 0.7 per cent of the gross national product of developed countries for official development assistance. This review process should systematically combine the monitoring of the implementation of Agenda 21 with the review of financial resources available; (e) To review on a regular basis the adequacy of funding and mechanisms, including efforts to reach agreed objectives of chapter 33 of Agenda 21, including targets where applicable; (f) To receive and analyse relevant input from competent non-governmental organizations, including the scientific and the private sector, in the context of the overall implementation of Agenda 21; (g) To enhance the dialogue, within the framework of the United Nations, with non-governmental organizations and the independent sector, as well as other entities outside the United Nations system; (h) To consider, where appropriate, information regarding the progress made in the implementation of environmental conventions, which could be made available by the relevant Conference of Parties; (j) To provide appropriate recommendations to the General Assembly, through the Economic and Social Council, on the basis of an integrated consideration of the reports and issues related to the implementation of Agenda 21; (k) To consider, at an appropriate time, the results of the review to be conducted expeditiously by the Secretary-General of all recommendations of the Conference for capacity building programmes, information networks, task forces and other mechanisms to support the integration of environment and development at regional and subregional levels.

48 The ECOSOC has been empowered to set up "commissions in economic and social fields and for the promotion of human rights, and such other commissions as may be required for the performance of its functions." The ECOSOC draws its power for the purpose from Article 68 of the Charter. However, there is also a general power to set up "subsidiary organs" is available under Art. 7(2) of the Charter, apart from the power to "adopt its own rules of procedure" under Art. 72(1). ECOSOC has used this power to set up commissions and subsidiary organs for a wide variety of purposes in the economic and social fields. It has set up 8 functional commissions concerning Social Development, Human Rights, Narcotic Drugs, Science and Technology for Development, Sustainable Development, Status of Women, Population and Development and Statistical Commission as well as 5 regional commissions for Africa (ECA), Europe (ECE), Latin America and the Caribbean (ECLAC), Asia and the Pacific (ESCAP) and Western Asia (ESCWA); see *United Nations*, Basic Facts About the United Nations (New York: UN, 1998), pp. 21–22.

primarily a monitoring body for the Rio mandate. It has also been regarded as "facilitator with the potential to harness public support to influence course adjustments of governments and institutional programmes."[49] The CSD comprises 53 members, elected by the ECOSOC for a period of three years. It also has a small Bureau[50] consisting of a chairperson, three vice-chairpersons and a rapporteur to be elected from each of the regional groups as well as a High-level Advisory Board of eminent persons having recognized expertise in the field. Apart from CSD member states, other member states of the UN and its specialized agencies, observer entities can participate in the work of CSD as observer. It also provides for involvement of a host of other intergovernmental organizations as well as international institutions to assist and advise the Commission in the performance of its functions. Significantly, in consonance with the role earmarked by Agenda 21, CSD can also provide for effective participation of non-governmental organizations and other major groups[51] in the deliberations.

The CSD, in view of the marathon job of reviewing and monitoring the progress in the implementation of Agenda 21, is to carry out the task by examining *thematic clusters* in its yearly work. The initial task for the purpose was done in its organizational session in 1993, which provided the framework as well as guided the process of programme of work. In fact, Agenda 21 itself grouped various chapters into nine[52] broad clusters. The nineteenth special session of the General Assembly reviewed this work and prepared CSD's multi-year

49 Razali Ismail, "Agenda 21 and the UN Commission on Sustainable Development," Massachusetts Institute of Technology, Global Accords for Sustainable Development: Symposium Report (Cambridge, MA: MIT, 1997), p. 30.

50 GA Resolution 47/191, par. 11.

51 Agenda 21 has earmarked roles for various major groups consisting of women, children and youth, indigenous people and their communities, non-governmental organizations, local authorities, workers and trade unions, business and industry, scientific and technological community as well as farmers; see Agenda 21, chapters 24 to 32.

52 The nine broad clusters are as follows: 1. Critical elements of sustainability (chapters 2–5) 2. Financial resources and mechanisms (chapter 33) 3. Education, science and technology (chapters 16 and 34–36) 4. Decision-making structures (chapters 8 and 37–40) 5. Role of major groups (chapters 23–32) 6. Health and human settlements (chapters 6–7 and 21) 7. Land, forests and biodiversity (chapters 10–15) 8. Atmosphere, oceans and freshwater (chapters 9 and 17–18) 9. Toxic chemicals and hazardous wastes (chapters 19–20 and 22).

The first five clusters are regarded as broadly cross-sectoral in nature, which could be reviewed annually. As regards the last four clusters, they are broadly sectoral in nature and, as such, reviewed in different years. The first comprehensive for the purpose was to be done in 1994 as well as covering all areas, along with sectoral, clusters, to be covered by 1996. The year 1997, five years after Rio, was to be used for an overall review prior to the UN General Assembly's Special Session scheduled in June 1997; see *ECOSOC*, Outline

programme of work for 1998–2002[53] with poverty as well as consumption and production patterns as overriding issues. This task is generally based upon national reports to be submitted by states. In fact, through reporting, states are required to provide their input for the annual session of CSD. However, as regards reports from all other entities, apart from the states, such as multilateral financial institutions, convention secretariats, international organizations, non-governmental organizations etc., *reporting* is voluntary. The CSD's experience with national reports during 1992–1997 has been varied.[54] Most of the states have been submitting reports as a voluntary exchange of information rather than any obligation *per se*.

(c) *GEF*

The roots of present day institutional structure of Global Environment Facility (GEF) lie in March 1990 Paris meeting convened by the World Bank, where 17[55] donor countries expressed their interest in setting up a "facility" to fund global environmental projects.[56] At the two subsequent meetings in July and

---

of a Multi-year Thematic Programme of Work for the Commission: Report of the Secretary-General, for the Commission on Sustainable Development's organizational session, 24–26 February 1993, UN Doc. E/CN.17/1993/2 of 19 February 1993.

53 The CSD Programme of Work covers *sectoral themes* on strategic approaches to freshwater management (1998), oceans and seas (1999), integrated planning and management of land resources (2000), atmosphere/energy (2001). The *cross-sectoral themes* would cover transfer of technology/capacity-building/education/science/awareness-raising (1998), consumption and production patterns (1999), financial resources/trade and investment/economic growth (2000) and information for decision-making and participation as well as international cooperation for an enabling environment (2001). The CSD 2002 session is slated for comprehensive review of the progress, which will also be tenth anniversary of the 1992 Rio Earth Summit; see UN, Earth Summit + 5: Programme for the Further Implementation of Agenda 21 (New York: UN, June 1997), Appendix, pp. 93–95.

54 The number of national reports received by CSD were as follows: 154 (1992), 53 (1994), 59 (1995), 41 (1996) and 97 (1997). The largest number of national reports came in the wake of organization of UNCED and there were no reports in 1993, as it was CSD's organizing year. It is quite revealing as to how seriously countries have been taking the reporting task to annual CSD meetings; for details see Farhana Yamin, "The CSD Reporting Process: A Quite Step Forward for Sustainable Development," *Yearbook of International Cooperation on Environment and Development*, 1998–1999, pp. 51–61 at 58.

55 These 17 donor countries were: Australia, Austria, Belgium, Canada, Denmark, Finland, France, Germany, Italy, Japan, Netherlands, Norway, Spain, Sweden, Switzerland, U.K., U.S., New Zealand joined at the second meeting.

56 As early as September 1989, the Development Committee of the World Bank asked it to assess the requirements for additional funding and potential interest from donor

September in 1990, seven developing countries including Brazil, China, India and Mexico, joined the deliberations. It gave the mandate to the World Bank to develop a framework for the proposed GEF. As a result, GEF took shape as a global environmental funding institution. Under a *pilot phase,* intended to examine its workability, several key details were worked out, especially concerning operational modalities, organizational arrangements and governance, size of the facility and funding modalities.[57] Its governance was entrusted to three entities – UNDP, UNEP and the World Bank – but it was housed within the World Bank. A concrete shape to the new funding entity was given following a resolution[58] adopted by the Executive Directors of the Bank. It sought to establish a Global Environment Trust Fund (GETF) to be administered by the Bank as a Trustee. The GETF initially comprised direct contributions (SDR 563.84 million) and co-financing arrangements (SDR 219.82 million). As per the provision of the resolution, the Bank entered into a Tripartite Agreement (1991)[59] for procedural arrangements among the three implementing institutions. This formalized the governance and operational mechanism of GEF. It also provided for administration of the Ozone Projects Trust Fund. Separate agreements were entered into among these three implementing agencies for this purpose[60] too.

---

countries for addressing global environmental concerns in developing countries. It in fact followed a specific request from France as well as a general proposal from Germany. The French proposal was for setting up of a *facility* to the order of SDR 1 billion, couple with an offer to contribute 900 million Francs. At subsequent discussions between the Bank and potential donors, four global environmental areas of ozone layer, greenhouse gases, biological diversity and international waters were identified as priority concerns. In fact the Bank was asked to bring in UNEP and UNDP too, under a tripartite arrangement to give concrete shape to the programme.

57 For details see the World Bank, *Establishment of the Global Environment Facility* (April 1991); 30 I.L.M. 1735, 1739–1757 (1991).

58 See Executive Director's Resolution 91–5 of 14 March 1991; see 30 I.L.M. 1758 (1991).

59 Procedural Arrangements Among the International Bank for Reconstruction and Development (World Bank), the United Nations Environment Programme and the United Nations Development Programme for Operational Cooperation under the Global Environment Facility. The agreement was signed between Lewis T. Preston, President of the World Bank, Mostafa K. Tolba, Executive Director of UNEP and William H. Draper III, the Administrator of UNDP on 28 October 1991; see 30 I.L.M. 1766 (1991).

60 Procedural Arrangements Among the International Bank for Reconstruction and Development, the United Nations Environment Programme and the United Nations Development Programme for *Cooperation and Assistance in Protecting the Ozone Layer in the Context of the Vienna Convention for the Protection of the Ozone Layer and Its Montreal Protocol on Substances that Deplete the Ozone Layer*. It came into effect on 12 March 1991; see 30 I.L.M. 1770 (1991).

A separate agreement[61] between the Bank and the Executive Committee of the Parties to the Montreal Protocol, which had set up a Multilateral Fund,[62] was also reached. In fact, subsequently GEF came to be identified as an *interim* financial mechanism both for the climate change[63] as well as biological diversity.[64]

The Pilot Phase (1991–1994) of GEF's life had a donor orientation and the World Bank had the final say on many mattes, especially concerning preparation of work programme as well as fund allocation. It was to organize the project identification, appraisal and supervision process with UNDP and UNEP participation. Its main focus was to be on subsidizing incremental costs of developmental activities which would result in global environmental benefits. During this phase, about 1.3 billion dollars was pledged to GEF. Primary contribution came from the GETF or core fund (860 million dollars), donated by 26 countries. This was supplemented by co-financing and parallel financing arrangements comprising loans and grants. In the four local areas identified initially, during the pilot phase, GEF funding was made available to the tune of US$733 million for a total of 116 projects.[65] All disbursements during the pilot phase to eligible member countries were to be done "in accordance with the rules of the Bank."[66] The Bank has had decisive leverage in the

61 *Ozone Projects Agreement* between the Executive Committee of the Interim Multilateral Fund for the Implementation of the Montreal Protocol and the International Bank for Reconstruction and Development. It came into effect on 19 June 1991; see 30 I.L.M. 1733 (1991).

62 Art. 10, Protocol on Substances that Deplete the Ozone Layer (Montreal), 16 September 1987; see 26 I.L.M. 1550 (1987).

63 Art. 21 (3) of the Framework Convention on Climate Change (1992), specifically referred to "interim arrangements" for financial mechanism. It identified the Global Environment Facility of UNDP, UNEP and the World Bank as the international entity (as per Article 8) entrusted with the operation of the financial mechanism on an interim basis; see 31 I.L.M. 849, 870 (1992).

64 Alike UNFCCC, Art. 39 of Convention on Biological Diversity (1992), also provided for interim financial arrangements. It also identified GEF as the institutional structure (as per Art. 21) on an interim basis for the purpose; see 31 I.L.M. 818, 837 (1992).

65 Gareth Porter, Raymond Clemencon, Waafas Ofosu-Amaah and Michael Philips, *Study of GEF's Overall Performance* (Washington D.C.: GEF, 1998), p. 1 (hereinafter "the GEF Study") This study came about at the instance of the GEF Council, which asked GEF Senior Monitoring and Evaluation Coordinator to undertake a study concerning GEF's overall performance. It was prepared in time for the First GEF Assembly Meeting held in New Delhi during 1–3 April 1998.

66 The constituent instrument for setting up of GEF-Pilot Phase explicitly intended it to be firmly part of the Bank itself. This is borne out by the wording: "The Bank will administer the Facility in accordance with the applicable provision of the Articles of Agreement,

functioning of GEF, being a Trustee of the GETF as well as an administrator of the Facility.

As compared to the magnitude of financial resources estimated,[67] in Agenda 21, for addressing global environmental problems, GEF has made available only a modest channel of funding. This too will be available only as new and additional funding, as *agreed incremental costs* of measures, to achieve agreed global environmental benefits. Most of the developing countries were quite sore over GEF practice and argued that it had donor bias. In fact, they consistently argued for GEF's democratic and transparent working. The UNCED provided a forum to articulate views for change in GEF's thrust, to make it broader, a funding mechanism for environmental agreements and developing countries too having effective say in its working. This came to be reflected in Agenda 21 too. In fact, the pilot phase experience of GEF was found to be grossly inadequate for ensuring participation as well as new obligations of developing countries under varied MEAs. In this context, the General Assembly resolution convening the UNCED did emphasise upon the need for "new and additional financial resources, particularly to developing countries"[68] in view of abnormal burden they now bear.

By-Laws, rules and decisions of the Bank, including this Resolution (rules of the Bank), any agreement made pursuant thereto, and such rules and regulations consistent therewith as the Bank may adopt as necessary or appropriate to achieve the purposes of the Facility. The Bank will exercise the same care in the discharge of its functions under this Resolution as it exercises with respect to its own affairs and will have no further liability in respect thereof"; see World Bank resolution 91–5/1991, Part A, par. 1, 30 I.L.M. 1758 (1991).

67 Agenda 21, Chapter 33, par. 18, see *Nicholas A. Robinson* (Ed.), Agenda 21: Earth's Action Plan (New York: Oceana, 1993), p. 552.

68 The General Assembly Resolution 44/228 provided that the UNCED should: "Identify ways and means of providing new and additional financial resources, particularly to developing countries, for environmentally sound development programmes and projects in accordance with national development objectives, priorities and plans and to consider ways of effectively monitoring the provision of such new and additional financial resources, particularly to developing countries, so as to enable the international community to take further appropriate action on the basis of accurate and reliable data;

Identify ways and means of providing additional financial resources for measures directed towards solving major environmental problems of global concern and especially of supporting those countries, in particular developing counties, for which the implementation of such measures would entail a special or abnormal burden, owing, in particular, to their lack of financial resources, expertise or technical capacity;

Consider various funding mechanisms, including voluntary ones, and examine the possibility of a special international fund and other innovative approaches, with a view to

In fact, UNCED faced the insurmountable task of meeting the expectations of developing countries and the equally non-committal position of most of the industrialized countries. However, Agenda 21 did aptly sum up the stark reality of costs of inaction, outweighing the financial costs of its implementation.[69] As such, it called for maximizing the availability of new and additional resources. In the particular case of GEF, it emphasized for restructuring,[70] which would bring about larger participation as well as ensure democratic and transparent functioning. Thus, UNCED did provide an opportunity for developing countries to voice their concerns on inadequate progress in mustering new and additional funding as well as prospect of using GEF as a funding mechanism for global environmental problems. Though it was argued that GEF was never intended to cover all international financial needs for the purpose, yet developing countries strove for hard bargaining on the issue.

To give effect to this growing chorus of demands for restructuring, representatives of 73 countries met in 1994 in Geneva to negotiate on the design of the new entity, on a permanent basis. The GEF participants' meet adopted the *Instrument for the Establishment of the Restructured Global Environment*

---

ensuring, on a favourable basis, the most effective and expeditious transfer of environmentally sound technologies to developing countries;

Quantify the financial requirements for the successful implementation of Conference decisions and recommendations and identify possible sources, including innovative ones, of additional resources."

69 The UNCED Secretariat had estimated an average annual cost (1993–2000) for implementation of Agenda 21 activities in the developing countries to the order of more than $600 billion. Out of this it expected that about $125 billion would be available on grant or concessional terms; see Agenda 21, Chapter 33, par. 18.

70 The perspective of *restructuring* envisaged in Agenda 21 was as follows: Encourage universal participation.

Have sufficient flexibility to expand its scope and coverage to relevant programme areas of Agenda 21, with global environmental benefits, as agreed:

Ensure a governance that it transparent and democratic in nature, including in terms of decision-making and operations, by guaranteeing a balanced and equitable representation of the interests of developing countries and giving due weight to the funding efforts of donor countries;

Ensure new and additional financial resources on grant and concessional terms, in particular to developing countries;

Ensure predictability in the flow of funds by contributions from developed countries, taking into account the importance of equitable burden-sharing;

Ensure access to and disbursement of the funds under mutually agreed criteria without introducing new forms of conditionality; see Agenda 21, Chapter 33 on "Financial Resources and Mechanisms," par. 14 (iii), Robinson, n. 67, p. 550–551.

Facility.[71] This restructured GEF retained the structure of having three implementing agencies as well as the World Bank being the Trustee for the GEF Trust Fund. In other respects, the GEF evolved as a facility for select focal areas only and not for global environment in general. In fact, varied factors[72] were responsible for pushing GEF in this direction.

The new structure of GEF has three organs, namely Assembly, Council and the Secretariat. The Assembly is to consist of all participants and has been entrusted with the task of reviewing the general policies, evaluating the operation as well as membership of the Facility and considering amendments to the GEF Instrument. Thus, functions of the Assembly are of overall review of performance. However, the Council possesses more substantive powers. The restructured Council now comprises 32 members, representing constituency groupings formulated and distributed. It appears to have been done keeping in view the need for balanced and equitable representation of all participants as well as due weight to the funding efforts of all donors. The total 32 constituencies comprise 18 recipient developing countries, including two for Central, Eastern Europe and former Soviet Union as well as 14 for non-recipient countries.[73] In practical terms, the Council wields real powers as compared to the Assembly. In fact, the very composition of the Council reflects a delicate balancing of interests of both recipient as well as non-recipient countries, as represented in constituencies. It is the supreme decision-making body for approving the work programs of projects. It has supervisory powers as regards

71 GEF, *Instrument for the Establishment of the Restructured Global Environment Facility* (Washington D.C.: GEF, 1994), pp. 1–39. Also see 33 I.L.M. 1273 (1994) (hereinafter the "GEF Instrument"). The GEF Instrument came into effect, after being adopted by the three Implementing Agencies "in accordance with their respective rules and procedural requirements" (Par. 1). The Executive Board of the United Nations Development Programme (UNDP) and of the UN Population Fund adopted the Instrument at a meeting on 13 May 1994 in New York (Doc. DP/1994/9). The Governing Council of the United Nations Environment Programme adopted the Instrument at a special meeting of the GC on 18 June 1994 in Nairobi (Res. SS.IV.1). In the case of the World Bank, the Instrument was adopted by the Executive Directors on 24 May 1994 in Washington D.C. (Res. No. 94–2) as well as by the Board of Governors on 7 July 1994 (Res. No. 487).

72 The Preamble to the *Instrument* for restructured GEF itself has acknowledged that Agenda 21, convention on Climate Change and Biological Diversity as well as GEF participant states and other states wishing to join it called for restructuring the Facility. Main concerns were to ensure transparent and democratic governance and to promote universality in its participation; see ibid., Preamble, p. 5.

73 For "Constituencies of the GEF Council," see the *GEF Instrument*, Annex E, Note 71, p. 33–34.

operation of the Facility, evaluation of policies, operational strategies and projects as well as availability and utilization of GEF funds. Both the Assembly and the Council are required to act *transparently* and adopt all decisions, as far as possible, by *consensus*. In the case of the Council, there is a provision to seek a *formal vote* if consensus does not materialize. In such cases, the Council decisions will be taken by a *double weighted*[74] majority.

The GEF Trust Fund is certainly not the all-encompassing *green fund* which was articulated by many developing countries earlier. The scope of the Trust Fund is limited in ambit, especially to the four focal areas identified in the GEF Instrument itself. It may also cover other areas having connection with the *focal areas* or other relevant activities under Agenda 21, having some relevance to them. Thus, the Trust Fund is quite focused in its application and criteria of eligibility for funding. The GETF replenishment depends upon *voluntary* contributions by the non-recipient donor countries. A country is eligible for GEF grants only if it is also eligible to borrow funds from the World Bank or is eligible to receive UNDP' technical assistance. Interestingly, the GEF remains decisively dependent upon the World Bank both for administrative purposes as well as operationalization of the Trust Fund. In fact, the Bank has been conferred with fiduciary responsibility[75] as a Trustee of the GEF Trust Fund and as such, is the *legal owner* of the Fund. The Bank's administration of the Trust Fund is to be governed by the GEF Instrument, decisions of the Council as well

---

74 The GEF Instrument, in Article 25(c), prescribes a formal voting mechanism, if consensus eludes any decision in the Council. The formal vote will follow the following criteria:

(i) Unless otherwise provided in this Instrument, decisions requiring a formal vote by the Council shall be taken by a double weighted majority, that is, an affirmative vote representing both a 60 percent majority of the total number of Participants and a 60 percent majority of the total contributions.

(ii) Each Member of the Council shall cast the votes of the Participant or Participants he/she represents. A Member of the Council appointed by a group of Participants may cast separately the votes of each Participant in the constituency he/she represents.

(iii) For the purpose of voting power, total contributions shall consist of the actual cumulative contributions made to the GEF Trust Fund as specified in Annex C (Attachment 1) and in subsequent replenishment of the GEF Trust Fund, contributions made under the GEF pilot program, or agreed with the Trustee, until the effective date of the GEF Trust Fund. Until the effective date of the GEF Trust Fund, advance contributions made under paragraph 7(c) of Annex C shall be deemed to be contributions to the GET"; see the *GEF Instrument*, n. 71.

75 For details of the World Bank's role as a Trustee of the Trust Fund, see the *GEF Instrument*, n. 71, Annex B, pp. 18–20.

as relevant provisions of the Bank's Articles of Agreement, by-laws, rules and decisions.

Regime Specific Institutions

It is rather difficult to think about a multilateral environmental agreement (MEA) without providing for some institutional form. The institutional form in such a case provides backbone to the agreement and ensures that the legal mechanism is implemented by the states parties to it. There are variations among different MEAs as regards the institutional structures laid down on the basis of requirement of the specific environment issue. The overarching umbrella is generally provided in the form of the Conference of the Parties (COP) as the supreme decision making body. The COP is an entity representing all the states and responsible for overall implementation. Though this entity is the key for final decision within an MEA, it is not regularly in session. Instead it meets generally once in a year or two years. There are some other subsidiary bodies which cater to various aspects of MEA's objectives. These include bodies such as Subsidiary Body on Implementation (SBI), Subsidiary Body on Science and Technology Advice (FCCC)/Committee on Science & Technology (CCD)/Scientific Council (CMS), Heritage Fund/ Multilateral Fund/Financial Mechanism and the Secretariat. Both subsidiary bodies as well as financial mechanisms may have different nomenclatures. In an interesting instance, a financial mechanism – Global Environment Facility – whose focal areas cover more than one sectoral environmental issues being dealt with by different MEAs.

(a) *Secretariats*

The Secretariat performs vital functions within an MEA. It is the only visible and permanent institutional form, which services both contracting states as well as maintains contacts with the outside world. It is a servicing arm subject to the control and supervision of the COP. The nature of functions assigned to a Secretariat of an MEA may vary in view of the special character of each such convention. A mere perusal of select ten MEAs reveals marginal variations in functions of Secretariats[76] as well as

76 The Secretariat is a permanent institution of an international environmental agreement. A comparative survey of ten important agreements shows a familiar pattern, with variations to cater to specific requirements of the convention. For example, see Art. 8, Convention on Wetlands of International Importance (1971), 11 I.L.M. 963 (1972); Art. 14,

their designations[77] and, in some cases, secretariat is housed by an international organization or another institution. UNESCO and the World Conservation Union (IUCN) and Economic Commission for Europe (ECE) have taken responsibility for the Heritage Convention, the Ramsar Convention and the LRTAP Convention respectively.

Moreover, UNEP holds the distinction in providing a basis for administration of Secretariats for five MEAs – Convention on International Trade in Endangered Species (CITES), Convention on Migratory Species of Wild Animals (CMS), Convention for the Protection of the Ozone Layer (Ozone), Convention on the Control of Transboundary Movements of Hazardous Wastes and their Disposal (Basel) and Convention on Biological Diversity (CBD). Each of these conventions explicitly provided that UNEP will arrange for carrying out secretariat functions, on an interim basis until decided by the first meeting of the COP.[78] The Secretariats of each of these five MEAs is permanently housed by UNEP but dispersed at different places like Bonn, Geneva, Montreal and Nairobi. The basic purpose of using facilities of an international environmental institution like UNEP is to take advantage of an established administrative structure. In such cases it leads to peculiar legal relationship between the COP of the concerned convention and UNEP. In such cases, UNEP is

---

Convention for the Protection of the World Cultural and Natural Heritage (1972), 11 I.L.M. 1385 (1972); Art. XII, Convention on International Trade in Endangered Species (1972), 12 I.L.M. 1055 (1973); Art. 11, Convention on Long-Range Transboundary Air Pollution (1979), 18 I.L.M. 1442 (1979); Art. IX, Convention on the Conservation of Migratory Species of Wild Animals (1979), 19 I.L.M. 15 (1980); Art. for the Protection of the Ozone Layer (1985), 26 I.L.M. 1529 (1987); Art. 16, Convention on the Control of Transboundary Movements of Hazardous Wastes and their Disposal (1989), 30 I.L.M. 775 (1991); Art. 8, Framework Convention on Climate Change (1992), 31 I.L.M. 849 (1992); Art. 24, Convention on Biological Diversity (1992), 31 I.L.M. 818 (1992); Art. 23, Convention to Combat Desertification in Those Countries Experiencing Drought and/or Desertification, Particularly in Africa (1994), 33 I.L.M. 1332 (1994).

77 The nomenclature of Conference of Parties (COP) is the norm for supreme decision-making body of an international environmental agreement. However, in some cases different names are given it. For instance the Bureau (Ramsar Convention), the World Heritage Committee (Heritage Convention) and the Executive Body (LRTAP Convention). In the case of the Secretariat, only Ramsar Convention has designated it as the *Bureau.*

78 The relevant provisions in this context can be found in: Art. IX Par. 2 of CITES, 12 I.L.M. 1055 (1973); Art. IX Par. 2 of CMS, 19 I.L.M. 15 (1980), Art. 7 Par. 2 of Ozone Convention, 26 I.L.M. 1529 (1987); Art. 16 Par. 2 of Basel Convention, 28 I.L.M. 657 (1989); Art. 23 Par. 1 and Art. 24 Par. 2 of CBD, 31 I.L.M. 818 (1992). The Secretariats of these five conventions are now provided on a permanent basis by UNEP. They are now located at Geneva (CITES and Basel), Bonn (CMS), Nairobi (Ozone) and Montreal (CBD).

answerable to the respective COPs for the limited purpose of ensuring smooth implementation of the conventions.

(b) *Conference of Parties*

It is the COP which reflects the political will of the contracting states. It not only can interpret the authority of the convention but also give effect to the in-built law-making process. Formal amendments to the convention or adoption of separate Protocol to the convention requires acceptance and/or ratification of the parties. All subsidiary bodies of an MEA report to and function under the supervision of the COP. Thus the institutional mechanism laid down under an MEA revolves under the COP and is designed to realize the objectives of the agreement as well as to help it keep pace with the changing requirements of the sectoral environmental issue.

The nature of the sectoral environmental challenge being dealt with by the COP also involves different approaches. In some cases, the primary task before the COP may be to only grapple with fixing the *threshold* limit of certain activities beyond which states would invite responsibility (e.g. UNFCCC) or protection of certain species and natural resources (e.g. CITES). In such cases, the COP has to constantly evaluate the performance and try to adapt the particular regime to the unfolding scientific evidence. In some other cases, the COP's primary preoccupation may be to focus on prohibition of certain state activities (e.g. Basel Convention) or phase-out of certain substances (e.g. Ozone Layer). In the latter cases, the COP does not attempt to find any "safe"[79] level, as has been the case with challenge of the ozone layer depletion. In the process, the COP employs different tools and techniques to attain its goals. The process turns out to be quite innovative and brings in new legal concepts and formulations. For instance, the ozone regime is understood to have "influenced the adoption of the principle of differentiated obligations"[80] for subsequent MEAs. Some states even try to put forward ideas which may act as subterfuges in the apportionment of funding contributions to affixing responsibility.

---

79 The ozone treaties, which include the 1985 Vienna Convention, 1987 Montreal Protocol as well as subsequent amendments and adjustments at London and Copenhagen, represent the first attempt to phase out the production and use of a group of chemical substances completely within a relatively very short period of time; see K.M. Sarma, "Innovation-The Key to Success" in Winfried Lang (Ed.) *Österreichische außenpolitische Dokumentation* (Wien, 1995), Special Issue on "The Ozone Treaties and their influence on the Building of International Environmental Regimes," p. 8.

80 Elizabeth Dowdeswell, "A Global Swing to Sustainable Development," ibid., p. 6.

The COP acts through an Executive Secretary to liaison and coordinate work with other MEAs concerning overlapping or related matters. The Executive Secretary is the chief executive officer of the Secretariat and also carries out the vital task of translating the political will of the contracting states as expressed in the COP. The work of the various institutional mechanisms under the conventions reveals that they evolve along with the evolution and development of the legal regime. In fact, these institutions can be regarded as vital in the entire process and provide a fine testimony to the institutionalized international environmental cooperation in actual practice.

Role of Multilateral Development Banks

One of the significant developments concerning IEIs is the sensitization of the multilateral development banks, whose primary aim is to provide lending for economic development. In this the World Bank group's initiation in bringing environmental perspective to lending operations originated at the top level, during Presidency of Robert McNamara. In a way, it brought environment as a "serious factor in economic planning and administrative practice."[81] Interestingly, the multilateral development banks derived their "inspiration" from Principle 25 of the Stockholm Declaration, which called upon "international organizations" to play a coordinated, efficient and dynamic role for the protection and improvement of the environment.[82] More than nine years after the Stockholm Conference, leading development banks as well as other international institutions supported the Stockholm mandate and adopted a seven point charter[83] to guide their future policies. The participant banks included the African Development Bank, the Arab Bank for Economic Development in Africa, the Asian Development Bank, the Caribbean Development Bank, the Inter-American Development Bank and the World Bank.

Among all developmental banks, the World Bank proceeded to establish an Environment Department in mid-1987 as well as beginning of preparation of

---

81 Kenneth Piddington, "The Role of the World Bank" in Andrew Hurrell and Benedict Kingsbury (Eds.), *The International Politics of the Environment: Actors, Interests and Institutions* (Oxford: Clarendon Press, 1992), p. 213.

82 See 11 I.L.M. 1421 (1972).

83 The New York Declaration was signed by Presidents of the six multilateral development banks on 1 February 1980. They were joined by heads of the Commission of the European Communities, the Organization of American States, the United Nations Development

"Environmental Issues Papers" for each borrower throughout the Bank.[84] The Bank, recognizing the need of time, proceeded to adopt special operational policies on environment. Some of these include Operation Manual Statement on Environmental Aspects of Bank Work (1984), Operational Directives on Environmental Assessment (1989 and 1991), Environment Policy for Dam and Reservoir Projects (1989), Involuntary Resettlement (1990), National Environmental Action Plans (1992) etc. It led the Bank to finance US$9 billion for 118 "free standing" or "primarily environmental projects."[85] Following the 1992 Rio Earth Summit, the World Bank sought to "mainstream environmental concerns into its whole portfolio and into all aspects of its work."[86] This effective change in landing gear appears to have come about following

---

Programme and the United Nations Environment Programme. They collectively undertook (to the best of their abilities, endeavour) to:

1. *Institute*, procedures for systematic examination of all development activities, including policies, programmes and projects, under consideration for financing to ensure that appropriate measures are proposed for compliance with section I (support for the principles and recommendations for action of the UNCHE) above;
2. *Enter* into cooperative negotiations with governments and relevant international organizations and agencies, to ensure integration of appropriate environmental measures in the design and implementation of economic development activities;
3. *Provide* technical assistance, including training, on environmental matters to developing countries, at their request, thus developing their indigenous capacity, and facilitating technical cooperation between developing countries;
4. *Give* active consideration and, if appropriate, support project proposals that are specially designed to protect, rehabilitate, manage or otherwise enhance the human environment, the quality of life, and resources thereto related;
5. *Initiate* and/or otherwise cooperate in research and studies leading to improvement or project appraisal, implementation and evaluation methodologies, including cost-benefit analysis, of environmental protection measures;
6. *Support* the training and informing of operational staff in the environmental dimension of economic development;
7. *Prepare*, publish and disseminate documentation and audio-visual material providing guidance on the environmental dimension of economic development activities.

See *Declaration of Environmental Policies and Procedures Relating to Economic Development*, New York, 1 February 1980 reproduced in *Philippe Le Prestre, The World Bank and the Environmental Challenge* (Selinsgrove: Susquehanna Uni. Press, 1989), Appendix A, pp. 208–209.

84 Piddington, n. 81, p. 216.

85 Ibrahim F.I. Shihata, *The World Bank in a Changing World*, vol. II (1996), p. 185.

86 In fact in order to "promote the objectives of UNCED and of Agenda 21 for environmentally sustainable development, the Bank is understood to have adopted a four-part programme: "(1) to ensure that potential adverse environmental impacts for Bank-financed activities are addressed; (2) to help member countries build upon the complementarities

realization of mistakes in the Bank's past approach. How this understanding has come to change is explained, by a vice-president of the Bank:

> (E)arlier Bank activities focused largely on massive infrastructure projects, often involving the dislocation of communities and damage to terrestrial and marine ecosystem, in recent years the Bank – along with the United Nations and other development agencies – has come to appreciate the critical importance of sustainable development...is now so much a part of the Bank's view of its mission that it is transforming the nature of our work.[87]

The recent stocktaking of the progress since the Earth Summit took note of the significance of financial resources as well as mechanisms in the implementation of Agenda 21. The nineteenth special session of the General Assembly explicitly underscored the need for *all sources of funding* to contribute to "economic growth, social development and environment protection" as well as funding by multilateral financial institutions through "concessional mechanisms" to attain objectives of Agenda 21.[88] In fact, in this context it has been argued that multilateral development banks have "responded to the emerging international consensus on 'sustainable development' as a new global paradigm by explicitly endorsing...their financial role in development activities."[89]

Conclusion

It goes without saying that in the international institutional landscape, the arrival of environmental institutions has been a significant development.

---

among poverty reduction, economic efficiency and environment protection; (3) to help member countries set priorities, build institutions and implement programs for sound environmental stewardship; and (4) to address global environmental challenges through participation in the Global Environment Facility; see ibid., "The World Bank's Contribution to the Development of International Environmental Law" in: Gerhard Hafner et al. (Eds.), *Liber Amicorum in Honour of Professor Ignaz Seidl-Hohenveldern* (Dordrecht: Kluwer Law International, 1998), pp. 631–658 at 632.

87 See *Preface* by Ian Johnson, Vice President for Environmentally and Socially Sustainable Development, *The World Bank in Environment Matters*, Annual Review (Washington D.C.: The World Bank, 1998), p. 3.

88 See *Programme for the Further Implementation of Agenda 21*, Adopted by Governments at Earth Summit + 5, Special Session of the United Nations General Assembly, 23–28 June 1997 (New York: United Nations, 1997), pp. 1–95, par. 76 and 78, at pp. 62–63.

89 Günther Handl, "The Legal Mandate of Multilateral Development Banks as Agents for Change Toward Sustainable Development," *AJIL*, vol. 92, no. 4, 1998, pp. 642–665 at 642.

It not only underscores the growing need for international environmental cooperation but also efforts in addressing global environmental challenges in various institutional frameworks. It appears that the pace as well as the content of these multilateral environmental regulatory efforts is gradually intensifying. It is generally taken for granted that environmental regulatory frameworks also throw up institutional mechanisms. In fact, there is a remarkable synergy in the growth of both multilateral environmental law-making and international environmental institution-building.

The role played by various specialized IEIs as well greening of other international institutions has, in a sense, created an institutional *clogging*. There is also considerable institutional fragmentation, which haunts states in terms of ensuring their coordination. The entry of various international institutions on the environmental scene has led to considerable "encroachment" upon UNEP's domain and, in turn, dilution of its authority as an entity which sets the global environmental agenda. A void has been generally felt as regards the need for a centralized environmental authority, which can lead the way and provide an overarching guidance to the states. As this issue still hangs in the balance and sharp differences exist on the matter, various international environmental institutions have a role cut out for them in their respective areas of work. In fact they have become a necessity to cater to a host of international environmental regulatory measures being regularly put into place.

PART 2

Efforts at Revitalization

CHAPTER 4

The Quest for a UN Specialized Agency for the Environment

Introduction

Concern about international environmental governance (IEG) gathered pace when the United Nations Environment Programme Governing Council (UNEP GC) decided to 'revitalise'[1] itself in 1997. Convinced that a strong, effective and revitalized UNEP was essential in efforts to reverse environmentally unsustainable trends, the Council declared: "...the United Nations Environment Programme has been and should continue to be the principal United Nations body in the field of the environment and we, the ministers and heads of delegation...are determined to play a stronger role...[The] United Nations Environment Programme is to be the global environmental authority that sets the global environmental agenda...and that serves as an authoritative advocate for the global environment..." After a series of reports, intergovernmental ministerial meetings and consideration at the UN General Assembly (UNGA) and the UNEP GC,[2] the matter received a sudden boost in January 2006 when the President of the UNGA, Jan Elliason, sought to follow up the 2005 World Summit Outcome.[3] It led to the launch of an Informal Consultative Process on the Institutional Framework for the United Nations Environmental Activities led by the Permanent Representatives of Mexico and Switzerland to the UN (see Appendices, p. 301).[4]

---

* Published in *The Round Table: The Commonwealth Journal of International Affairs* (Special Issue: Environmental Governance: Securing Our Common Wealth), vol. 101, no. 2, 2012, pp. 167–179.

1 Nairobi Declaration adopted by UNEP Council vide decision 19/1 of 7 February 1997. See http://www.unep.org/newyork/Portals/129/docs/1997_nairobi_declaration.pdf, accessed 19 December 2011.

2 Included Töpfer Task Force Report (1998); UNGA resolution 53/242 of 10 August 1999; Malmo¨ Ministerial Declaration (2000); Cartagena Report of the Open-ended Intergovernmental Group of Ministers or their Representatives on International Environmental Governance (2002).

3 UNGA resolution 60/1 (2005 World Summit Outcome) was adopted 16 September 2005; see UN Doc. A/RES/60/1, 24 October 2005, pp. 1–38.

4 http://www.un.org/ga/president/60/summitfollowup/index.html.

 | DOI 10.1163/9789004214552_005

Around the same time, the UN Secretary-General also announced the establishment of a High-level Panel on UN System-wide Coherence in the Area of Development, Humanitarian Assistance and the Environment (see Appendices, p. 309).[5] The panel emphatically recommended that 'UNEP should be upgraded and have real authority as the environmental policy pillar of the UN system, backed by normative and analytical capacity and with broad responsibility to review progress towards improving the global environment'.[6] Whether to upgrade UNEP or to replace it with a new specialized agency[7] for the environment has, however, remained contentious between governments, scholars and civil society. Decisions will be taken at the Rio+20 Conference, 20–22 June 2012, but at the time of writing the zero draft conference statement contains options for decisions on each side.[8]

The Issues

There are over 500 multilateral environmental agreements (MEAs) and specialized institutions grappling with governance of environmental problems ranging from loss of wetlands to ozone depletion, and climate change to persistent organic pollutants. In general these institutions have been established through ad hoc, diffuse and somewhat chaotic processes, generally following the essentially random emergence of environmental issues on to national and international political agendas.[9] Since the early 1970s a large number of MEAs in the areas of ocean, atmosphere, nature, waste, fisheries and chemicals have

---

5 In pursuance of the mandate of the 2005 World Summit Outcome, UN Secretary-General Kofi Annan communicated (on 15 February 2006) establishment of the High-level Panel, co-chaired by Prime Ministers of Norway, Pakistan and Mozambique (plus 12 others), to Jan Eliasson, President, UNGA.

6 United Nations, Delivering as One: Report of the Secretary-General's High-Level Panel on UN System-wide Coherence in the Areas of Development, Humanitarian Assistance and the Environment, 9 November 2006, New York, pp. 1–42 at p. 6.

7 The UN Charter has institutionalized a system of 'specialized agencies' established by an 'intergovernmental agreement and having wide international responsibilities, as defined in their basic instruments in economic, social, cultural, educational, health, and related fields' (Article 57). These agencies are brought into relationship with the UN in accordance with Article 63 of the UN Charter. Hence they are referred to as specialized agencies.

8 The Future We Want–Zero draft of the outcome document; available at, http://www.uncsd2012.org/futurewewant.html.

9 UNU Report, International Environmental Governance–The Question of Reform: Key Issues andProposals Preliminary Report (UNU/IAS, March 2002).

established institutional arrangements comprising a conference or a meeting of the parties (COP/MOP) with decision-making powers, a secretariat and specialised subsidiary bodies.[10] These institutions are regarded as 'treaty bodies' in the sense that they do not constitute traditional intergovernmental organisations (IGOs). Not only are they distinct both from the state parties to a particular agreement and the existing IGOs, but in many cases they also have their own law-making powers and compliance mechanisms.[11] These treaty organs have become international environmental institutions (IEIs), fulfilling a range of functions, including: awareness raising and agenda setting; collecting, processing and disseminating information; setting international standards and regulations; capacity building and provision of financial and technical assistance; and avoiding and settling disputes.[12]

There has been growing concern in the past decade over the proliferation of these legal and institutional arrangements. Most IEIs have earnestly sought to fulfil their mandates to protect the environment, but it is increasingly apparent that their fragmented and uncoordinated nature causes duplication and inefficiency, and renders them inadequate to meet the environmental challenges of the 21st century. The main concerns are lack of a functional framework for coordinated international action, and consequent inefficient use of the limited resources available for environmental protection.[13] This lack of coherence can be attributed to the complexities of the environmental issues involved, and to the sui generis nature of the international environmental law-making process. There is a growing acceptance that better governance could be achieved by establishing inter-linkages and synergies between multilateral institutions, and/or thc creation of new or reformed institutions. For example, Chapter 38 of Agenda 21 called for restructuring and revitalisation of the UN system to implement Agenda 21 and other conclusions of the UN Conference on Environment and Development (UNCED).[14]

---

10 Discussed by R.R. Churchill and Geir Ulfstein (2000) 'Autonomous institutional arrangements in multilateral environmental agreements: a little-noticed phenomenon in international law', *American Journal of International Law*, 94, pp. 623–659; V. Ro¨ ben (2000) 'Institutional developments under modern international environmental agreements', *Max Planck Yearbook of United Nations Law*, 4, pp. 363–443.

11 Churchill and Ulfstein (2000) at p. 623.

12 Jake Werksman (Ed.) (1996) *Greening International Institutions* (1996), London: Earthscan, pp. xiii–xvii.

13 United Nations, 'Report of the Secretary-General on Environment and Human Settlements', UNGA/A/RES/53/242, 105th plenary meeting, 28 July 1999, p. 28.

14 Bharat H. Desai (2000) 'Revitalizing international environmental institutions: the UN Task Force Report and beyond', *Indian Journal of International Law*, 40, pp. 455–504 at p. 471.

Quest for an Environmental Entity

As we raise a toast to the 40th anniversary (in June 2012) of UNEP, it is pertinent to consider its provenance and purpose. As a result of the 1972 Stockholm UN Conference on the Human Environment (UNCHE), the UNGA created UNEP as a new quasi-autonomous entity to serve as a focal point for environmental action and coordination within the United Nations system. Its mandate is to develop environmental policy consensus by keeping the global environment under review and bringing emerging issues to the attention of governments and the international community for action.[15] As it was designed as a programme, the enabling UNGA resolution described it merely as 'institutional and financial arrangements for international environmental cooperation'. The 58-member UNEP GC was given a mandate that includes promotion of 'international cooperation in the field of the environment' and to provide 'general policy guidance for the direction and coordination of environmental programmes within the United Nations system'.[16] The Stockholm mandate required UNEP to act as a coordinator of activities and programmes within the UN as well as a trigger for international environmental cooperation. It reports to the UNGA through the Economic and Social Council (ECOSOC) and, despite some success, UNEP has always been denied the status of a 'specialised agency' (as per Articles 57 and 63 of the UN Charter) on the specious ground that such an 'agency for the environment would result in duplication of activities and would compound already serious problems of coordination'.[17] Although UNEP lacks the legal status of an independent international organization, it does have some measure of international legal personality because it is required to fulfill certain tasks on the international plane (such as entering into headquarters agreement with Kenya, the host country).

Notwithstanding the creation of UNEP, international environmental organizations such as the Commission on Sustainable Development (CSD), specialized agencies, treaty-based organs, functional commissions, regional commissions and other programmes continued to multiply within the UN system, particularly after the 1992 Rio Earth Summit, which sought to 'green' the existing UN

---

15 UNEP's mandate and objectives emanate from UNGA resolution 2997 (XXVII), 15 December 1972 as amended at UNCED 1992, Nairobi Declaration on the Role and Mandate of UNEP, adopted at the 19th Session of UNEP GC and Malmo¨ Ministerial Declaration.

16 Report of the UN Conference on the Human Environment, UN Doc. A/CONF.48/14 (1972), Chapter III, Part II.

17 Richard N. Garder (1972) 'The role of the UN in environmental problems', *International Organization*, 26(2), p. 245.

system. Ironically, these have contributed to the dilution of UNEP's mandate and authority. This expansion might be testimony to the need for environmental action but, less helpfully, also reflects an instinct for survival. It has been argued that a number of UN agencies charged with aiding economic development felt threatened by the impact of the new interest in environmental protection, and this led them to reorganize their programmes in order to protect their budgets and preserve the integrity of their mandate.[18] It has also been argued that it made little sense to pursue an "organization of the impossible" and the task of the environment to be "left to a single agency".[19] As a result of these undercurrents within the UN system, UNEP was denied specialized agency status and it became an inexplicable exception for such a functional environmental organization.

Crisis of 'Environmental Conscience'

Over the four decades of its existence, UNEP seems to have 'attained considerable success in galvanizing action on international environmental concerns, and laying down the threshold of environmental behaviour'.[20] Even within the narrow confines of its mandate, UNEP has catalysed preparations for many MEAs, including two of the instruments adopted at the 1992 Rio Earth Summit: the Convention on Biological Diversity (CBD) and the UN Framework Convention on Climate Change (UNFCCC). At the behest of a resolution (1988) of the UNGA, UNEP and the World Meteorological Organisation (WMO) have also co-sponsored the Intergovernmental Panel on Climate Change (IPCC), and UNEP provided substantive support and expertise for the conclusion of the 1994 Convention to Combat Desertification (CCD). It possesses a 'jewel in the crown', known as the Regional Seas Programme, in which 18 regions manage a web of a staggering 50 instruments.[21] UNEP is the host institution for five MEAs, including the 1973 Convention on International Trade in Endangered Species of Wild Fauna and Flora (CITES), the 1979 Convention on the Conservation of Migratory Species of Wild Animals (the Bonn Convention), the 1985 Vienna Convention and the 1987 Montreal

---

18 Ernst B. Haas, Mary Pat Williams and Don Babi (1977) *Scientists and World Order* (Berkeley: University of California Press), p. 182.

19 For this argument, see generally, Konrad von Moltke, 'The organization of the impossible', *Global Environmental Politics*, vol. 1(1), 2001, pp. 23–28.

20 Bharat H. Desai (2000), n. 14, p. 462.

21 Bharat H. Desai (2006) 'UNEP: a global environmental authority?' *Environmental Policy & Law*, 36(3–4), pp. 137–157 at p. 139.

Protocol on the Depletion of the Ozone Layer, the 1989 Basel Convention on Transboundary Movements of Hazardous Wastes and their Disposal, and the CBD.

In spite of these achievements, it is widely felt that UNEP's ability to set the global environmental agenda is severely constrained by its organizational structure, unpredictable funding, institutional clogging of the environmental field and lack of political confidence of some key UN member states. The gradual inroads made into environmental matters by other agencies of the UN system, as a peripheral concern within their own functional jurisdiction, has also contributed to the dilution of UNEP's authority. In short, in the euphoria of the 1992 Rio Earth Summit, UNEP was relegated to the background and became a cog in the larger UN machine rather than an effective environmental conscience-keeper of the UN.

Efforts to Revitalize the UNEP

With this backdrop of a simmering environmental governance crisis, declining funding, erosion of authority and perception of weakness, serious efforts were made by the UNEP GC to revitalize UNEP. After the adoption of the 1997 Nairobi Declaration by the Council, a Töpfer Task Force was created by the UN Secretary – General in early 1998, which reported to the UNGA in June 1998 (see Appendices, p. 359).[22] The UNGA, through a landmark resolution[23] (see Appendices, p. 355), gave direction for a series of institutional steps both within the UN Secretariat as well as at the intergovernmental level. It brought into being two new arrangements, namely the Environmental Management Group (EMG) for inter-agency environmental coordination within the UN system (modelled on the UN Development Group) and the Global Ministerial Environment Forum (GMEF) for high-level policy dialogue. The GMEF was to be an extended UNEP GC meeting at ministerial level. Thus, the UNGA–like the conductor of a grand orchestra–provided overarching guidance to the entire process, coupled with crucial policy direction.

These policy initiatives were the culmination of a long-held view that any major change in UNEP's situation would require high-level ministerial

22 The UN Task Force on Environment and Human Settlements, Report to the Secretary-General, 15 June 1998 in UN Doc. A/53/463, Annex, pp. 11–28, 6 October 1998. Also see Doc. UNEP/GC.20/INF/13 of 6 January 1999.

23 UNGA resolution 53/242 on Report of the Secretary-General on Environment and Human Settlements; UN Doc. A/RES/53/242 of 10 August 1999.

intervention. The launch of the GMEF was a bold political initiative to revive the sagging fortunes of UNEP and an attempt to regain policy coherence in the field of the environment. In the post-Johannesburg Summit decade (2002–2012), states face a litmus test of their determination to grapple effectively with the problems afflicting environmental governance.

UNEP has largely driven these processes, but has nevertheless been criticised for its inability to address its mandate as a catalyst for international cooperation in addressing environmental issues. This problem can be largely attributed to the growing complexities of environmental problems, coupled with UNEP's small secretariat, inadequate and unpredictable funding, difficulties relating to location of its headquarters in Nairobi, perceived lower voice of its Executive Director in the UN Secretary-General's cabinet, the lower status of environmental matters in the over-crowded schedule of the Second Committee of the UN General Assembly, and duplication of its functions with other UN organs.[24] This diagnosis of the governance problems of the UN's premier environmental programme has thrown up a host of issues concerning the possible options and remedies to address the malaise.

Can there be a Specialized Agency?

In institutional terms, a reformed UNEP with universal membership could emerge as a global environmental forum to address governance problems and the expectations of UN member states. This vital reform, coupled with adequate, stable and predictable funding, could provide a natural route for elevating UNEP to the level of a UN specialized agency. Proposals on the table include a UN Environment Protection Organisation (UNEPO; favoured by this writer)[25] or UN Environment Organization (UNEO; favoured by the European Union). There are already strong undercurrents that favour such an upgrade of UNEP, as shown by deliberations at the UNEP GC Global Ministerial Environment Forum meetings in Nairobi (2007) as well as Monte Carlo (2008). The advantages and disadvantages of a specialized agency for environment protection

24 Paul C. Szasz (1992) Restructuring the International Organizational Framework, in E.B. Weiss (Ed.), *Environmental Change and International Law*, Tokyo: United Nations University Press, pp. 340–351.

25 UNEP, Summary of Selected Papers, Open-ended Intergovernmental Group of Ministers or their Representatives on International Environmental Governance, First Meeting, New York, 18 April 2001; Doc. UNEP/IGM/1/INF/2, 5 April 2001, pp. 1–11 at p. 10. For full details of UNEPO proposal, see Bharat H. Desai (2000), n. 14, pp. 495–498.

now need to be considered. The core question is whether to elevate UNEP's status or carve out a new global organization. The history of institution building not only shows how difficult and cumbersome it is to create a new entity (implicitly jettisoning the existing UNEP), but also reminds us that a brand new entity such as a World Environment Organization (WEO)[26] would not necessarily be more effective than UNEP.

UNEP's remarkable performance during 1972–1992, when many important treaties were agreed, shows how, in practical terms, it can almost work as a WEO. Nevertheless, to impart credibility and authority to this beleaguered entity in the midst of a perceived widening global environmental crisis, several elements are needed if UNEP is to emerge as a specialized agency. If form and perception are key factors in determining the authority of a robust international environmental institution amidst the multiplicity of actors, UNEP would qualify for that through the trappings of a UN specialized agency in the form of UNEPO. This model, devised in 1999, would provide UNEP with the effective institutional wherewithal to address global environmental problems. The UNEO model mooted by the European Union in 2005 has striking similarities (see Table 1).

There appears to be an urgent need to strengthen the UN's environmental institutional framework and augment coordination so as to avoid duplication and wastage of resources. UNEP–being UN's environmental conscience–has the best credentials to spearhead the process. Given the political will and emergence of consensus among key sovereign actors, there is strong justification–and growing support of more than 50 states–for UNEP's upgrade to a UN specialized agency. The exact structure would be drawn from experience and existing models, adjusted to meet the expectations of the sovereign states, supported by the necessary resources and structure.

The UNEPO proposal comprises a plenary body (General Conference/ Council), subsidiary organs such as a Science and Technology Council, Environmental Policy & Law Council, Environmental Emergencies Relief Council and a Bureau, as well as a Secretariat headed by a Director-General (see Figure 1). For practical reasons, UNEPO could be established through an upgrade of UNEP, agreed by a resolution of the UNGA, or an intergovernmental treaty. Nairobi should remain the location of the headquarters, this being the only such major UN entity in a developing country. Its funding contributions would follow the UN scale of assessments or the current pattern of a voluntary indicative scale of assessment.

---

26 For legal analysis of the WEO model, see Ole Kristian Fauchald (2010) *International Environmental Governance: A Legal Analysis of Selected Options* (Lysaker, Norway: Fridtjof Nansens Institutt), pp. 1–57 at pp. 11–13.

TABLE 1 *Comparison of Proposals on a UN 'specialized agency' for the environment.*

Proposal/ recommendation	Name	Structure	HQ location	Mandate	Funding
Bharat H. Desai (1999) [Originally made on 15 January 1999 at the World Bank, D.C.; revised 2000]	United Nations Environment Protection Organization (UNEPO) • by elevating UNEP • Specialized Agency	– General Conference – Science & Technology Council – Envir'l Policy & Law Council – Environmental Emergencies Relief Council – Bureau and Secretariat with D-G	Developing country; Nairobi could continue as HQ	– A truly global environmental forum that reflects the wishes and expectations of all members of the United Nations. – Lawmaking, scientific assessment, environmental emergencies relief	Adequate, stable and predictable funding based on voluntary indicative scale of assessment
Eropean Union (2005) [Contribution to UN General Assembly Informal Consultation Co-Chairs; 20 April 2007]	United Nations Environment Organization (UNEO) • by upgradation of UNEP • Specialized Agency	– Plenary Body with open membership to UN member – Executive organ – Secretariat, headed by D-G – Regional Offices – Consultative Boards	Nairobi to be the first UN specialized agency headquar-tered in a developing country	– Environmental Pillar of the UN with a revised and strength-ened mandate – Authoritative body on the global environment	Adequate, stable and predictable resources as well as ability to respond to environmental emergencies. Execute priority programmes through core budget

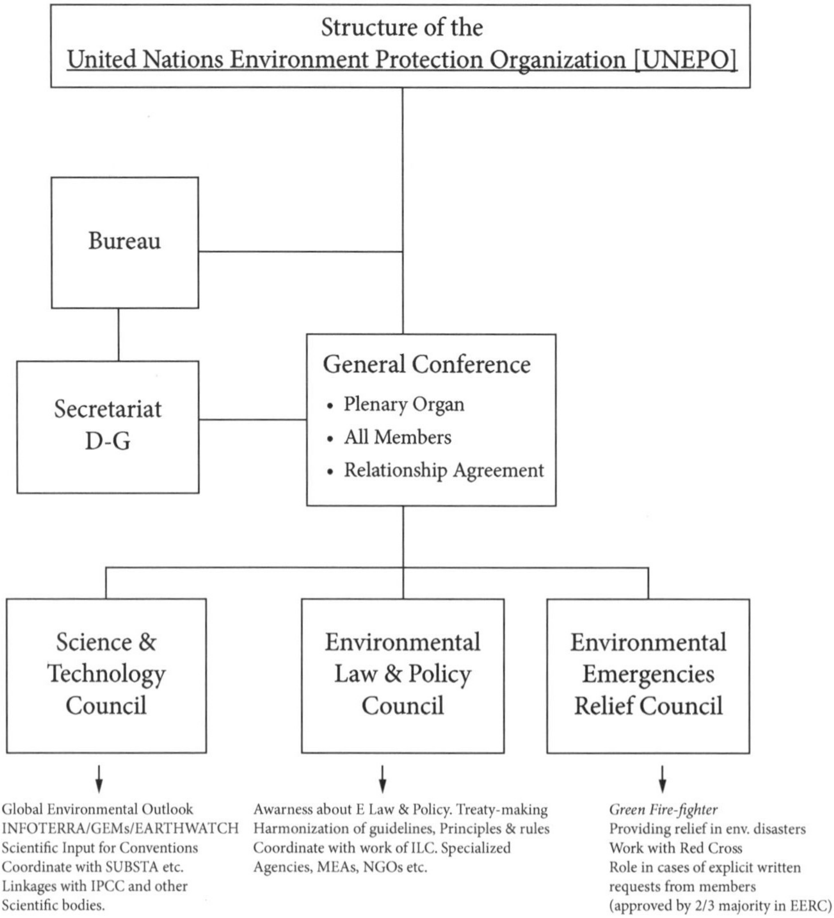

FIGURE 1 *Structure of the United Nations Environment Protection Organisation.*

Any such exercise will need to remain within the UN system for credibility and wider acceptability. The process, content and range of subsequent institutional restructuring will depend upon the political will of the sovereign states. Certainly, efficiencies could be obtained through mergers of some existing UN environmental departments and programmes with the new specialized agency. Future direction will be dictated more by the political will of States, how far they wish to go in the process, how best they want to translate their international environmental commitments into action, and how much they are willing to allow transparency in the functioning of different international institutional structures in order to address the global environmental challenge.

Whither International Environmental Governance?

As today's architects of reform seek to improve the complex system of global environmental governance, they face the task of rethinking the existing structures to address global environmental problems. While the scope and scale of environmental concerns have changed and actors in the environmental field have proliferated, the crux of the debate remains the same–how does the international system implement an effective environmental policy that takes into account the concerns of developed and developing countries? In this regard, the contemporary process of consultations among governments is actively searching for innovative ways to reform the governance architecture for the environment.

Two reform initiatives for the global environmental governance architecture are currently under way at the United Nations: (1) the implementation phase of the recommendations of the High-level Panel on UN System-wide Coherence; and (2) the informal consultations on international environmental governance held under the auspices of the UN General Assembly. These policy debates seek to outline an optimal institutional form and function for the global environmental governance system.

The UN General Assembly President mandated an Informal Consultation Process (co-chaired by UN Permanent Representatives of Mexico and Switzerland) to carry out extensive consultation with UN member states as well as other institutions and experts. This has enabled them to produce (14 June 2007) an options paper on key issues. The said paper in fact sought to analyze weaknesses of the existing system and suggested seven 'building blocks' for a strengthened international environmental governance system. The co-chairs also proposed that by the end of the 62nd session of the UN General Assembly, terms of reference could be decided for formal negotiations on 'transformation' of the IEG system.

The proposal for UNEP's upgrade to a specialized agency (UNEPO) as well as a wide range of issues coming within the rubric of international environmental governance was presented by the author before the co-chairs on 26 November 2007 in New York. The presentation recommended a central environmental institutional structure (UNEP), improved synergies and interlinkages between MEAs, and an environmental 'supervisory' organ at the UN headquarters (e.g. revival of the Trusteeship Council). In addition, a detailed presentation was made on this writer's 1999 proposal for an upgrade of UNEP into a UN specialized agency to be called UN Environment Protection Organization (UNEPO). It emphasized the necessity of carving out an institutional structural for environmental governance, and presented UNEP's challenges, including misconceptions about its role, 'dwarfing' of UNEP, difficulties in coordinating the UN's environment-related institutional structures, and declining voluntary financial contributions to UNEP by member states in the post-1992 Rio Earth Summit period. In this context the Global Ministerial Environmental Forum/Tenth Special Session of UNEP GC at Monaco (2008) provided some support for strengthening IEG as rooted in the Cartagena Package of 15 February 2002[27] and the 'need for and modalities of a possible resolution by the UN General Assembly'. It was expected that the informal consultation co-chairs would provide input for the proposed General Assembly resolution that could set the format for future talks. It seems, however, that in spite of best efforts, many of the key states were wary of such a move. As such the co-chairs had to abandon their effort and seek further political guidance. In fact, noticing that an 'attempt to find a decision increased the difficulties in finding consensus', the co-chairs in a sense of exasperation declined to call for further consultations and presented their final report (10 February 2009).[28]

In the aftermath of this disappointment, the UNGA mandated an informal consultation process and the baton was passed back to UNEP GC, which adopted decision 25/4 (20 February 2009)[29] and decision SS. XI/1 (26 February 2010)[30] to establish a regionally representative Consultative Group of Ministers or High-level Representatives. It met in Nairobi (7–9 July 2010) and in Espoo (21–23 November 2010) with the participation of 58 and 44 countries, respectively (see Appendices, p. 296).[31]

The churning that took place during this tortuous process emphatically endorsed the consensus that in reforming international environmental governance, form must follow the function. The suggestions on the table include: enhancing UNEP; establishing a UN specialized agency; and enhancing institutional reforms and streamlining existing structures. It was suggested that incremental changes could be considered alongside more fundamental reforms. The outcome of the process was expected to feed into the work of the 26th UNEP GC, 65th UN General Assembly session and the Prep-Com for the UN Conference on Sustainable Development (Rio+20). Thus, the concerted intergovernmental deliberations have continued, but they are yet to lead to a way out of the impasse.

27 See, http://www.unep.org/gc/GCSS-VII/Reports.htm.

28 See, http://www.un.org/ga/president/63/PDFs/ReportIEG100209.pdf.

29 See, http://www.unep.org/gc/gc25/proceedings-docs.asp.

30 See, http://www.unep.org/gc/GCSS-XI/proceeding_docs.asp.

31 See, http://www.unep.org/environmentalgovernance/Portals/8/NairobiHelsinkifinalout come.pdf.

Conclusion

There is an urgent need to strengthen the UN's environmental institutional and governance framework as well as to augment coordination in order to address global environmental challenges, while avoiding duplication and waste of resources. UNEP–being UN's environmental conscience–has the best credentials to spearhead this vital process. Given the political will and consensus among key sovereign actors, there appears to be strong justification–and the growing support of more than 50 states–for UNEP's upgrade to a UN specialized agency. While building on past experience, the proposed structure will need to be *sui generis* in view of the nature and uniqueness of this functional area. The contours of the new entity must emerge on the basis of expectations of the sovereign states.

As the plenary organ of the UN, the General Assembly will need to step in to address the complexity of the institutional dimensions of international environmental governance. It remains to be seen whether the Rio+20 (UNCSD) triggers this process, and provides a way forward in the jigsaw of environmental governance for our common future in the 21st century.

The general aversion to creation of new international institutions is partly due to the criticism of UN bureaucracy and funding implications. It has been felt that an autonomous character of the institution would be able to make it more efficient as well as result-oriented and not merely a talk shop or a turf for politicking. There have also been apprehensions over the voting method, as anything less than one-state – one-vote would be regarded as undemocratic and jeopardize wider political support among states. Some the developing countries have, however, expressed concern that institutionalizing global environmental governance will result in 'stricter environmental standards (green protectionism)'.

The powerful states favor strong international institutions especially if their decision-making structures are either based upon weighted voting or are likely to help in maintaining their interests. The system of specialized agencies within the UN has occasionally come under severe strain in view of the clash of interests of states. In fact powerful states, contributing substantial sums to budgets, felt exasperated and withdrew from some institutions since they could not have their view prevail, as it happened in the case of UNESCO. Some of the specialized agencies have come under pressure to undergo 'restructuring', including change of chief executive officers.

Under these circumstances, the merits and demerits of having a specialized agency for environment protection will need to be considered in terms of possibility of improvement over the existing situation. The core issue in the matter revolves over the desirability of enhancing UNEP's status or carving out a new organization altogether. The institution-building history shows that it is difficult to negotiate wholly a new international organization. Therefore, enhancing UNEP's status through an international agreement could be a preferred option. The process of institutional restructuring will depend upon the political will of the states, which may reflect in a merger of some other UN departments and programmes in the new organization with UNEP at its core.

New Structure

Various suggestions have been put forward on nomenclature of the new organization, ranging from an international (world) environmental organization to world environment and development organization. It appears that the primary purpose of such a specialized agency could be to enhance the UNEP's status and authority. Thus, any sculpting of a new institution would comprise UNEP at its core. The question of merger of other existing organs and programmes (such as CSD, UNDP etc.) would depend upon the extent to which states prefer to make the exercise ambitious.

At the minimum level, a new institutional structure should result in an enhancement of UNEP's status from a UN programme to that of a specialized agency. It would be ideal if the Millennium General Assembly meet seriously reviews the requirements for a 'really strengthened institutional structure for international environmental governance', as called upon by the first meeting of the GMEF. It would be appropriate if the Assembly decides this issue and provides mandate for the purpose. The mandate could be assigned to an intergovernmental negotiating committee on revitalizing international environmental institutions. The INC can work on a draft of constituent instrument for a new specialized agency. The constituent instrument could be adopted at a conference of plenipotentiaries. It can give shape to a United Nations Environment Protection Organization (UNEPO), wherein the existing UNEP could merge.

The new organization's constituent instrument could provide for a plenary organ which may be known as the General Conference (GC) and a Bureau, apart from other functional organs such as Science & Technology Council (STC), Environmental Law and Policy Council (ELPC), Environmental Emergencies Council (EERC) as well as a Secretariat headed by the Director-General (see Figure I). In the case of the GC, it will be the plenary organ and it membership can comprise all the members of the organization. It will be the supreme decision-making body of the UNEPO and based upon the one-state – one-vote principle. The GC would constitute a small Executive Committee or Bureau of about ten states and act under the authority delegated by it. In respect of membership of other functional organs, they may comprise a limited number of member states, which may vary between 24 to 60. The election of members of these organs can be by rotation, with one-third members retiring every two years. The STC and ELPC can be technical bodies, consisting of experts, who can be nominated by the states. The STC may be designed to address science and technology issues. It can maintain crucial interaction with bodies such as Subsidiary Body for Science and Technology Advice (SBSTA) of convention secretariats as well as professional bodies like the Intergovernmental Panel on Climate Change (IPCC).

The STC can provide vital scientific input on which decisions of policy-making organs can rest. Such input will also be crucial for the in-built law-making processes of the Conference of Parties (COPs) of various convention secretariats. Similarly, the ELPC's primary task can consist of maintaining coherence in the progressive development of international environmental law. It can launch new initiatives for environmental law awareness, supervise developments in soft law and examine the need for appropriate hard instruments from time to time. The ELPC's role will be crucial in imparting planned development of international environmental law in consonance with changing needs.

The third functional organ EERC's main task can be to address environmental emergencies. As such, it can perform the task of international green firefighters. It can rush assistance to victims of environmental catastrophes, such as oil pollution disasters, forest fires, transfrontier pollution (air, water, radiation etc.), major industrial accidents and natural disasters (earthquakes, cyclones, floods etc.). It can maintain close liaison with the International Committee of the Red Cross (ICRC) to provide succor to the victims of such emergencies. However, the EERC can act only subject to the explicit written request from the affected member state as well as approval by two-thirds of EERC's total members. The representatives of members of the EERC will be accessible at very short notice to facilitate quick decisions in such cases. In order to prevent any possible misuse, the work of the EEC will need to be strictly confined to redressing the environmental calamity with its expertise as well as providing relief (such as relocation, rehabilitation) to the affected people. It will not go into the issues of liability and compensation, which must necessarily be dealt separately within the framework of international instruments. The Director-General would head a small and efficient secretariat to cater to the needs of the UNEPO.

The funding of the new organization can be worked out on the same pattern of scale of contributions of the United Nations and other specialized agencies. The predetermined allocation of members' contributions will ensure stability in the functioning of UNEPO, as compared to the voluntary Environment Fund of UNEP.

CHAPTER 5

UNEP

A Global Environmental Authority?

Introduction

It is evident that the growth of law and institutions keeps pace with the changing needs of international society. The need for global regulatory efforts has been mooted, in addition to efforts at the national level, to address environmental problems with global dimensions.[1] This has, in turn, put to test the traditional rules and principles of international law. It is now well recognized that the underpinnings of the current drive for the legal protection of the global environment remain embedded in the general principles of international law.[2] In recent years, however, the increasing reliance upon Multilateral Environmental

---

* Published in *Environmental Policy and Law*, vol. 36, no. 3–4, 2006, pp. 137–157.

** This article is a revised and updated version of the author's Bonn Open Lecture of 26 October 2005 at United Nations University's Institute for Environment and Human Security (Bonn, Germany). It has substantially revised, updated and taken forward the analysis and submissions made by the author (especially concerning UNEP's change into a 'specialized agency' to be known as the United Nations Environment Protection Organization (UNEPO)) in his *Fourth Sarah and Gilbert Kerlin Lecture* delivered at Pace University School of Law (White Plains, New York) on 27 October 2003 as well as other previous lecture seminars he has delivered on the subject, especially at the Free University of Berlin on 10 July 2003, the Max-Planck Institute of Comparative Public and International Law (Heidelberg) on 9 March 1999 and the Environment and International Law Unit at Legal Department of the World Bank (Washington, DC) on 15 January 1999.

1 For writings on this issue see, generally, Peter H. Sand, 'Lessons Learned in Global Environmental Governance' in Commission on Global Governance (ed.), *Issues in Global Governance* (1995), pp. 1–60; Peter M. Haas, *Global Environmental Governance,* ibid, pp. 333–369; Rahmatullah Khan, 'The Thickening Web of International Law', *in* Commission on Global Governance, ibid, pp. 249–262; Peter M. Haas and Ernst B. Haas, *Learning to Learn: Some Thoughts on Improving International Governance of the Global Problematique, in* Commission on Global Governance, ibid, pp. 295–331; Bharat H. Desai, 'Global Accords and Quest for a New International Ecological Order: From Law of Indifference to Common Concern', *Business and the Contemporary World* (John Wiley, New York), vol. 9, no. 3, 1997, pp. 545–572; Hilary French, 'Strengthening Global Environmental Governance' in *Vanishing Borders: Protecting the Planet in the Age of Globalisation* (New York: W.W. Norton & Company, 2000), pp. 144–162; Bharat H. Desai, 'Mapping the Future of International Environmental Governance', *Yearbook of International Environmental Law,* vol. 13, 2002, pp. 43–61.

2 Ian Brownlie's leading textbook on international law does not consider the need for a separate branch to address environmental problems and did not even have, until recently,

 | DOI 10.1163/9789004214552_006

Agreements (MEAs)[3] as a pivotal mode of international environmental law-making has long-term implications for the process of centralized legalization on environmental issues as well as for the body of international law itself.

Since the establishment of the United Nations, international institutions have provided useful forums for international cooperation on a variety of issues. The growth of functional international organizations (specialized agencies), functional commissions and regional commissions as well other programmes within the UN system provide living testimony to the craving for *institutionalization* of international cooperation. The web of institutionalization is also growing in the field of international environmental law.[4] In fact, the recent World Summit on Sustainable Development (WSSD) was expected to give attention to the debate on strengthening the institutional architecture for international environmental governance (IEG). The debate in this respect, however, is not confined to the UN's environment programme (UNEP). It has drawn the attention of States, intergovernmental organizations and civil society.

---

a separate section on the subject. For the first time, in the 1998 (fifth) edition of the book, Brownlie devoted a six-page section (Chapter XIII) to the subject, which was entitled 'Legal Aspects of the Protection of the Environment'. As a 'generalist', in this context, Brownlie has argued that '[t]he fact is environmental concerns have for long been reflected in general international law and the relevant categories include the law of the sea, state responsibility, space law, the legal regime of Antarctica, and the non-navigational uses of international watercourses'; see Ian Brownlie, *Principles of Public International Law* (5th edition, 1998), pp. 283–288 at 283.

3 These MEAs are institutionalized forms of intergovernmental cooperation. In a way, this form of governance is *sui generis* as it has all the trappings of an international organization without formally being one. As a matter of fact, these forms of governance cater to the requirement for *ad hoc* bodies based upon multilateral treaties akin to functional international organizations. Their existence is determined by the political will of the contracting states and tailored to the need to address a specific global problem. MEAs have also created a new institutionalized form of intergovernmental cooperation to respond to new and complex challenges as they arise. In a way, this form of governance is *sui generis,* as it has trappings of an international organization without formally being one. MEAs cater to the need for *ad hoc* and autonomous arrangements that are tailored to address a specific global environmental issue. In view of the very nature of this institutional arrangement, a MEA is expected to be 'wound up' as and when its desired objectives are met. Its autonomous nature is determined by the political will of the contracting states as reflected through the decisions of the Conference (or Meeting) of the Parties of the MEA. Many questions are raised by the widening web of these regimes, such as the role of 'catalysts' who initiate the law-making process, their regulatory contribution, inherent complexities, flexibility, large participation of states, role of non-state actors and issues of implementation and compliance.

4 For a detailed study of this trend of 'institutionalization' in the field of international environmental law, see Bharat H. Desai, *Institutionalizing International Environmental Law* (New York: Transnational Publishers, 2004).

As a plenary organ of the United Nations, the General Assembly has provided crucial guidance to the whole process even as the technique of 'global conferencing' has become more popular. In the environmental arena, the General Assembly has acted as 'conductor of a grand orchestra' that provides political guidance to States, notwithstanding the inbuilt Charter limitation that it can only make 'recommendations' through its resolutions.[5] In the environmental arena, the Assembly provides guidance to its member States through its subsidiary organ, UNEP. This entity has acted as a catalyst for the environmental law-making process. This again presents an anomalous situation because for such initiatives, another subsidiary organ of the Assembly – International Law Commission – has been sidestepped. The Assembly has adopted, often without a vote, resolutions comprising constituent instruments for specialized environmental institutions such as UNEP and the Commission on Sustainable Development (CSD). In this context, the focus of this article is on UNEP's birth, mandate, contribution in the development of international environmental law, its post-Rio political neglect, intergovernmental efforts at 'revitalization' as well as its future direction in the context of the current debate on 'international environmental governance' (IEG), among others, within the UN system, governments and civil society.

Premier Environmental Entity

UNEP was established by the UN General Assembly in 1972 as a follow-up to the first UN Conference on Human Environment (UNCHE)[6] to meet the

5 There has been a great debate concerning the nature and legal effect of the resolutions of the UN General Assembly. It has been observed that the records of the United Nations Conference on International Organization (UNCIO) at San Francisco do not provide an authoritative interpretation of what exactly was envisaged by the use of the word 'recommendations' in Articles 10 to 14 of the Charter; see F. Blaine Sloan, 'The Binding Force of a 'Recommendation' of the General Assembly of the United Nations', *British Yearbook of International Law* (BYIL), vol. 25, 1948, pp. 7, 10. Also see Rosalyn Higgins, 'The Development of International Law by the Political Organs of the United Nations', ASIL *Proceedings,* vol. 59, 1965, p. 117; *Preface* by Wolfgang Friedmann in Obed Y. Asamoah, *The Legal Significance of the Declarations of the General Assembly of the United Nations* (The Hague: Martinus Nijhoff, 1966), p. v; Stephen M. Schwebel, 'The Effect of Resolutions of the UN General Assembly on Customary International Law', ASIL *Proceedings,* vol. 73, 1979, p. 301.

6 See Report of the United Nations Conference on the Human Environment, *UN Doc. A/CONF.48/14, pp. 2–65 and Corr. 1* (1972). Also see *International Legal Materials* (ILM), vol. 11, 1972, p. 1416. UNCHE became a major milestone for international environmental cooperation. It came out with a charter of principles in the form of the *Stockholm Declaration on*

'urgent need for a permanent institutional arrangement within the United Nations system for the protection and improvement of the environment.'[7] The General Assembly gave a mandate to the UNCHE to lay down guidelines for action, by national governments as well as international organizations, on broad topics of significance. Being the first major UN effort to diagnose global environmental problems, the UNCHE was expected to address both legal and institutional responses to the environmental challenge. Thus the Stockholm Conference may well be regarded as a major milestone and catalyst in heralding the process of 'greening' of international law.

UNEP's constituent instrument *per se* does not mention its role in international environmental law-making. This, it seems, has now come to be regarded as its 'cornerstone'.[8] The innovative exercise of such 'implied power' gives latitude to the institution as well as facilitates in actual governance by giving effect to such a mandate. Most institutions come across a situation during their lifespan when they are required to exercise certain powers or functions so as to "effectuate the general purposes for which [they have been] created, though [their] constitutive instrument does not expressly provide for such a specific power or function".[9]

State practice shows that, for maximum clarity, States do try to put things in the written form. However, many of the things that are not clarified in the constituent instrument can be presumed, if they are essential for its *raison d'être*. Therefore, the theory of 'implied power' has come to be widely accepted. This was affirmed by the International Court of Justice (ICJ) in the *Reparations* case in this much-quoted passage:

> Under international law, the Organization must be deemed to have those powers which, though not expressly provided in the Charter, are

---

Human Environment as well as an *Action Plan* for protection of the environment comprising 109 recommendations on a wide array of issues.

7 UNGA Resolution 2997 on Institutional and Financial Arrangements for International Environmental Cooperation; see A/RES/2997 (XXVII) of 15 December 1972 in *United Nations General Assembly Official Records,* 27th Session, Supp. No. 30, 1972, p. 43. Also see *Yearbook of the United Nations,* vol. 26, 1972, pp. 331–333; *ILM,* vol. 12, 1973, pp. 433–438.

8 Elizabeth Dowdeswell, 'Implementation: Enhancing the Effectiveness of International Environmental Law' in Scandinavian Seminar College, *Implementing Environmental Conventions,* Papers from the Second High-level Nordic Policy Seminar, Copenhagen (Denmark), 28 October 1994, p. 39.

9 See Rahmatullah Khan, *Implied Powers of the United Nations* (New Delhi: Vikas Publications, 1970), p. 3.

> conferred upon it by necessary implication as being essential to the performance of its duties. This [is a] principle of law.[10]

An exercise of such a power may depend upon several factors, such as the intention of the parties involved, the scope of the law's objectives and purposes, the ambit of its expressed powers, the historical background and the need to adapt to changing times. In the specific case of UNEP, the attitude of States, especially in the Governing Council, can act as a barometer of endorsement for the exercise of such implied powers. In this sense, as creatures of institutionalized cooperation, international environmental institutions (IEIs) evolve as dictated by the interests and expectations of the sovereign States.

Thus the successful carving out of such a role by UNEP is a manifestation of innovative exercise of implied power. The drafters of UNEP's constituent instrument (General Assembly resolution 2997/XXVII) might have envisaged such a role but left it as amorphous, probably so as not to cause panic among other high-profile 'specialized agencies' (some of which were already dealing with environmental issues). It seems to have been tacitly understood and accepted, at the time of adoption of this resolution, that UNEP would undertake such a role. Such an implicit role for UNEP could have been necessary, especially due to moves to deny status of a specialized agency to UNEP, efforts at the time to establish an environmental agency outside the UN system, as well as concerns and suspicions of a large number of developing countries regarding practical implications of conceding such a role to a UN programme. It seems that the subsequent attitude and State practice has come to accept the role that UNEP has performed under its *Montevideo Programme* in view of an absence of any other institutional actor that can undertake such a role.

'Catalyst' for Law-Making

An important characteristic of IEIs is that they stem from international *instruments* (not necessarily creating 'legal' obligations for the States). Once formed, they contribute to the law-making process itself. This process happens in a

10 The ICJ provided a rationale for this interpretation as: 'In the opinion of the Court, the Organization was intended to exercise and enjoy, and is in fact exercising and enjoying, functions and rights which can only be explained on the basis of the possession of a large measure of international personality and the capacity to operate on the international plane'; see *Reparations for the Injuries* case, ICJ Reports, 1949, pp. 179 and 182. Also see *Effect of Awards,* ICJ Reports, 1954, p. 56.

subtle way. In the absence of a supra-legislature at the international level, States inevitably come to rely upon an IEI to provide an institutionalized platform and, in turn, facilitate international cooperation. Such international institutions, especially in the environmental field, have come to play the role of a catalyst in the law-making process. As one of the former Executive Directors of UNEP observed:

> To be able to catalyze action, an organization must have full command of relevant information, the capacity to interpret data in the development of knowledge and the ability to translate that knowledge and wisdom which informs policy development. These, together, form the intellectual basis of an 'organization's authority' for management of environmental disputes.[11]

The precise nature of the role played by an IEI will depend upon the mandate in its constituent instrument, the exigencies of situation and the expectation of sovereign States from it. Interestingly, if States are willing to place their confidence in it, the lack of an explicit mandate for the purpose may not *per se* remain a handicap for an IEI. In UNEP's case, it has exercised roles that were both its as well as in conjunction with other intergovernmental institutions. The launching of an ambitious *Montevideo Programme*[12] has served as an

---

11 The significance of the catalytic role for an IEI such as UNEP has been explained in terms of bringing about a real and measurable improvement in the quality of the world's environment; see Elizabeth Dowdeswell, Keynote Address on 'The Global Conventions & Key Regional Initiatives' at MIT; see Symposium Report, *Global Accords for Sustainable Development* (Cambridge, M A: MIT, 1997), p. 63.

12 *Montevideo Programme I* was prepared by the *Ad Hoc* Meeting of Senior Government Officials Expert in Environmental Law, held at Montevideo (Uruguay), 28 October–7 November 1981. The Meeting's report (UNEP/GC.10/5/Add.2 & Add.2/Corr. 1, 2) outlined a draft programme for the development and periodic review of environmental law. After more than a decade, another Meeting of Senior Government Officials Expert in Environmental Law met in November 1991 and September 1992. The Meeting sought to identify programme areas as well as their respective objectives, strategies and activities for action by UNEP, especially in the light of experience and new developments including Agenda 21. On the basis of the report of the Meeting, the Governing Council of UNEP adopted Decision 17/25 on 21 May 1993, which has come to be known as Montevideo Programme II. The Programme for the Development and Periodic Review of Environmental Law for the 1990s defined a broad strategy for UNEP activities in the field of environmental law for the 1990s. See *Yearbook of the United Nations,* vol. 36, 1982, p. 1030 and *Yearbook of the United Nations,* vol. 47, 1993, pp. 820–821. For an overview see, Alexandre S. Timoshenko, 'Development and Periodic Review of Environmental Law in

important part of UNEP's initiatives for a coherent programmatic approach to law-making on sectoral environmental issues.

The Governing Council of UNEP, whose decisions have also provided an impetus to the States to carry out intergovernmental negotiations, has duly supervised this process. That is also scrutinized by the General Assembly while considering the annual reports of the Governing Council. It has resulted in a fine collection of soft law instruments containing principles, rules, guidelines and recommendations, as well as initiating and contributing to negotiations and the adoption of several MEAs. Such a task performed by an IEI such as UNEP underscores its vital role in enhancing international environmental cooperation as well as acting as a catalytic agent for international environmental law-making.

UN's Environmental Conscience

UNEP may be regarded as having *locus classicus* as regards institutionalized international environmental cooperation. It is the product of the United Nations Conference on Human Environment (Stockholm, 1972), which was attended by 113 nations. Many of the States had doubts about the first global effort to address international environmental problems. As such, UNEP became the first major UN environmental institution, in spite of proposals to 'bypass the United Nations in favor of an environmental agency run by the developed countries of the world'.[13] The birth of UNEP at the Stockholm

---

the 1990s: UNEP Programmmatic Approach' in Alexandre Kiss and Francoise Burhenne-Guilmin (Eds) *A Law for the Environment: Essays in Honour of Wolfgang E. Burhenne* (Gland: IUCN, 1994), pp. 17–20. The Governing Council of UNEP has now launched the third phase of the Montevideo Programme. At its 20th Session, the Governing Council adopted Decision 20/3, on 3 February 1999, authorising the UNEP Executive Director to continue to use the current Programme (II) for the Development and Periodic Review of Environmental Law as strategic guidance for the work of UNEP, until a new programme is adopted by the Council. Accordingly, a meeting of Senior Government Officials Expert in Environmental Law was convened by the Executive director in from 23–27 October 2000 in Nairobi. This meeting adopted Montevideo Programme III on 27 October 2000 as the *Draft Programme for the Development and Periodic Review of Environmental Law for the First Decade of the Twenty-First Century,* comprising 20 subject areas, for presentation to the Twenty-First Session of the Governing Council to be held in February 2001. The Governing Council Decision 21/23 adopted the Montevideo Programme III at the 21st Session of the Governing Council of UNEP on 9 February 2001; available at www.unep.org.

13 For example, George F. Keenan disfavored the UN forum because it works on the basis of 'universal, or near-universal, governmental consensus' and favored the initiative being

Conference, as a part of the UN system, followed the realization that 'there are problems in using the UN for environmental action; the problems in bypassing it in favour of other institutions would be more serious still'.[14]

In the post-Stockholm era, UNEP has generally been the centerpiece of the UN's efforts to protect the global environment. At the institutional level, UNEP has simply been *a programme,*[15] a subsidiary organ of the UN General Assembly. Though its legal status is not that of an independent international organization, it does not appear to have deprived this UN body of some measure of international legal personality as it is required to fulfill certain tasks on the international plane (such as entering into headquarters agreement with the host country as well as other international agreements and arrangements as host institution), as per the criteria laid down by the International Court of Justice in the *Reparations*[16] case. In the preparatory stage, there was

taken by a small group of advanced nations. He put forward rationale for the setting up of an institution called the International Environmental Agency by a small group of leading industrial and maritime countries as: 'It is they whose economies produce, in the main, the problem of pollution. It is they, again, who have the means to correct it. It is they, finally, who have the scientific and other resources to analyze the problem and to identify the most promising lines of solution. The devastation of the environment is primarily, though not exclusively, a function of advanced industrial and urban society. The correction of it is primarily a problem for the advanced nations'; see George F. Keenan, 'To Prevent a World Wasteland: A Proposal', *Foreign Affairs,* Vol. 48, No. 3, April 1970, pp. 401–413 at 410.

14 Richard N. Gardner, 'The Role of the UN in Environmental Problems', *International Organisation,* vol. 26, No. 2, 1972, p. 238.

15 It was established by virtue of the General Assembly's Resolution 2997 (XXVII) of 15 December 1972, which set out the institutional and financial arrangements for the launching of UNEP. Its establishment was again reaffirmed by the General Assembly Resolution 32/112 of 16 December 1976. UNEP comprises the institutional machinery of the Governing Council (now comprising 58 members) of the United Nations Environment Programme, the Environment Secretariat headed by the Executive Director of the Programme, the Environment Fund and the Environment Coordination Board (now disbanded). By virtue of the decision 19/32 of 4 April 1997 of the Governing Council (GC), the Committee of Permanent Representatives (COPR) has been formally established and strengthened as a subsidiary organ of the GC. For the composition, functions and responsibilities of the GC and the COPR see www.unep.org/governingbodies. Also see UNEP, Annual Report 2002 (Nairobi: UNEP, 2002), p. 2.

16 In this landmark advisory opinion, the International Court of Justice (ICJ), with reference to the legal competence of the United Nations, observed: 'It is at present the supreme type of international organization, and it could not carry out the intentions of its founders if it was devoid of international personality. It must be acknowledged that its Members, by entrusting certain functions to it, with the attendant duties and responsibilities, have

considerable caution regarding the creation of a new international institution. The UN Secretary-General' s Report to the Preparatory Committee stated that:

(a) Any organizational arrangement should be based first on agreement about what needs to be done. Until this is reached, no firm decision can be made on the ways and means to be adopted.
(b) All functions that can best be performed by existing organizations should be assigned to those organizations, international and national, most capable of carrying them out effectively. *No unnecessary new machinery should be created.*
(h) The United Nations should be the principal centre for international environmental cooperation.
(i) The organization of environmental activities within the United Nations should be so designed as to strengthen and reinforce the entire United Nations system (emphasis added).[17]

Thus, the institutional structure thrown up by UNCHE was the result of a need within the UN system to have a specialized entity to promote international cooperation in the field of the environment. UNEP was designed to perform a vital role in the entire process. This new quasi-autonomous entity of Environment Secretariat within the UN, headed by the Executive Director, was carved out to serve as *a focal point for environmental action and coordination within the United Nations system.*[18] Since it was decided to be merely a *programme* within the UN, the enabling General Assembly resolution described it merely as 'institutional and financial arrangements for international environmental cooperation'. Its 58-member Governing Council[19] was given a mandate that includes the following primary functions:

---

clothed it with the competence required to enable those functions to be effectively discharged'; see *ICJ Reports* (1949), p. 179.

17 See *Report of the Secretary-General to the Third Session of the Preparatory Committee,* UN Doc.A/CONF.48/PC.11, 30 July 1971, p. 222.

18 See the General Assembly Resolution A/RES/2997(XXVII) of 15 December 1972, part II, p. 3 in *United Nations General Assembly Official Records,* 26th Session, Supp. No. 30, p. 43.

19 The 58 members of the UNEP Governing Council are elected by the UN General Assembly, for a period of three years on the following basis: (a) Sixteen seats for African States; (b) Thirteen seats for Asian States; (c) Six seats for Eastern European States; (d) Ten seats for Latin American States; (e) Thirteen seats for Western European and other States; see UNGA Res.2997, Part I, para. 1.

(a) To promote international cooperation in the field of the environment and to recommend, as appropriate, policies to this end;
(b) To provide general policy guidance for the direction and coordination of environmental programmes within the United Nations system;[20]
The Stockholm mandate required UNEP to act as a main fulcrum, both in terms of coordinating activities and programmes within the UN system as well as in terms of triggering international environmental cooperation. As a UN programme, in terms of hierarchy, it is responsible and reports to the General Assembly through the Economic and Social Council.[21]

As discussed earlier, even prior to setting up UNEP, several specialized and related agencies used to deal with environment-related functions. These included agencies such as Food and Agriculture Organization (FAO), United Nations Educational, Scientific and Cultural Organization (UNESCO), International Labour Organization (ILO), World Bank (IBRD) World Health Organization (WHO), World Meteorological Organization (WMO), International Maritime Organization (IMO) and International Atomic Energy Agency (IAEA). However, the creation of a specialized environmental programme underscored the need for a hub or focal point within the UN system. In fact, UNEP has been regarded, in the words of the UN Secretary-General, as the 'environmental conscience of the United Nations'.[22] It was basically a reflection of the consensus that:

> (T)he key international environmental institutions should be intergovernmental in character. Governments are not prepared to surrender authority to a supranational agency that could bind them to act against their will. Governments may, however, be willing to delegate authority to international entities to act in carefully prescribed areas under norms and policies already agreed upon ... the central machinery for environmental cooperation should be within the framework of the United Nations ... as the central world institution for global cooperation.[23]

20 Ibid, Part I, para. 2 (a) and (b).

21 The enabling resolution requires that 'the Governing Council shall report annually to the General Assembly through the Economic and Social Council, which will transmit to the Assembly such comments on the report as it may deem necessary, particularly with regard to questions of coordination and to the relationship of environmental policies and programmes within the United Nations system to overall economic and social policies and priorities'; see UNGA Res.2997, Part I, para. 3.

22 Kofi A. Annan, 'An Indispensable Contribution', *Our Planet,* Vol. 9, No. 1, 1997, p. 4.

23 Gardner, n. 14, pp. 244–245.

Thus the UN, which represented mankind's needs and aspirations, became the natural rallying point in intergovernmental efforts for institutionalized environmental cooperation.

Contribution to Law-Making

Keeping these goals in view, UNEP appears to have achieved considerable success in galvanizing international environmental concerns.[24] In turn, it propelled intergovernmental efforts to lay down a threshold of environmental behaviour of States on various issues of global concern. As a follow-up to the Stockholm Declaration[25] and the Action Plan, the Governing Council of UNEP asked the Executive Director, in its very first session (1973) to stimulate international and regional agreements for the control of all forms of pollution of the marine environment with a special focus on particular bodies of water.[26] One of the important achievements of UNEP – regarded as its 'jewel in the crown' – was the Regional Seas Programme (RSP),[27] which brought together regional seas conventions and Action Plans. The current web of 18 RSPs

24 For a detailed account of UNEP's contribution in this context see, generally, Mostafa K. Tolba and Iwona Rummel-Bulska, *Global Environmental Diplomacy: Negotiating Environmental Agreements for the World 1973–1992 (Cambridge, Mass.: MIT Press, 1998)*.

25 Principle 7 of the Stockholm Declaration provides: 'States were to take all possible steps to prevent pollution of the seas by substances that were liable to create hazards to human health, to harm living resources and marine life, to damage amenities or to interfere with other legitimate uses of the sea'; see *Yearbook of the United Nations,* vol. 26, 1972, p. 320. Also see the *Action Plan for the Human Environment,* Recommendations 86–94, *ILM,* vol. 11, 1972, and pp. 1454–1457.

26 The Governing Council Decision 1 (I), 22 June 1973; see UN *General Assembly Official Records* (GAOR), vol. 28, 1973, Supp. 25 (A/9025), p. 42. Also see Decision 8 (II), 21 March 1974; *GAOR,* vol. 29, Supp. 25 (A/9625), p. 63.

27 The Regional Seas Programme (RSP) has been regarded as one of UNEP's greatest achievements. The RSP was launched in 1974. The first of the RSP was developed in the Mediterranean with an Action Plan (1975), followed by a Convention (1976). Following the success of the RSP for the Mediterranean region, RSPs were developed for other regions. The Governing Council of UNEP has consistently endorsed a regional approach to the control of marine pollution, management of marine and coastal resources and development of regional Action Plans for the purpose. From the first Action Plan adopted in the Mediterranean (1975), to the most recent Convention for the Caspian Sea (2003), the RSPs have multiplied to cover the marine environment of more than 150 of the world's coastal countries.

comprise a staggering number of 50 instruments that includes 12 regional conventions, 2 special regional mechanisms and 4 action plans[28] as well as

---

28 The 18 regional seas programmes are: 1. Antarctic: Convention on the Conservation of Antarctic Marine Living Resources (1980), entered into force 7 April 1982; 2. Arctic: Protection of the Arctic Marine Environment (PAME) established by the Arctic Council Ministers in Nuuk, Greenland, September 1993; 3. Baltic Sea: The Convention on the Protection of the Marine Environment of the Baltic Sea Area, 1992, entered into force on 17 January 2000; 4. Black Sea: The Convention on the Protection of the Black Sea Against Pollution was signed in Bucharest in April 1992, and ratified by all six legislative assemblies of the Black Sea countries at the start of 1994; 5. Caspian Sea: Framework Convention for the Protection of the Marine Environment of the Caspian Sea (Tehran, 4 November 2003); 6. East Africa: Convention for the Protection, Management and Development of the Marine and Coastal Environment of the Eastern African Region (1985); 7. East Asian Seas: Action Plan for the Protection and Development of the Marine Environment and Coastal Areas of the East Asian Seas Region (1981); 8. Mediterranean: The Barcelona Convention for the Protection of the Mediterranean Sea against Pollution (1976, as amended in 1995; entered into force 9 July 2004); 9. North-East Atlantic: Convention for the Protection of the Marine Environment of the North-East Atlantic (OSPAR Convention, 1992); entered into force 25 March 1998; 10. North-East Pacific: Convention for Cooperation in the Protection and Sustainable Development of the Marine and Coastal Environment of the Northeast Pacific (Antigua Convention, 2002); 11. North-West Pacific: Action Plan for the Protection, Management and Development of the Marine and Coastal Environment of the North-West Pacific Region (1994); 12. South Pacific: Noumea Convention for the Protection of Natural Resources and Environment of the South Pacific Region (1986). SPREP is the secretariat for the Apia Convention 1976, the SPREP (or Noumea) Convention 1986 and the Waigani Convention 1995; 13. Red Sea and Gulf of Aden: Regional Convention for the Conservation of the Red Sea and Gulf of Aden (1982); entry into force 20 August 1985; 14. ROPME Sea Area: Action Plan for the Protection and Development of the Marine Environment and the Coastal Areas, the Kuwait Regional Convention for Cooperation on the Protection of the Marine Environment from Pollution, and the Protocol concerning Regional Cooperation in Combating Pollution by Oil and Other Harmful Substances in Cases of Emergency adopted in 1978; 15. South Asian Seas: S ASP is a cooperative partnership, formally adopted in 1995 for the protection and management of the shared marine waters and associated coastal ecosystems of five maritime SACEP countries (Bangladesh, India, Maldives, Pakistan and Sri Lanka); 16. South-East Pacific: Permanent Commission for the South Pacific (CPPS) is the appropriate Regional Maritime Organisation responsible for the coordination of the maritime policies of its Member States: Colombia, Chile, Ecuador and Peru. The Organisation was established on 18 August 1952, as a result of the 'Declaration on the Maritime Zone' subscribed at Santiago by the Governments of Chile, Ecuador andPeru. Colombia joined the CPPS on 9 August 1979; 17.West & Central Africa: Abidjan Convention for Cooperation in the protection and Development of the Marine and Coastal Environment of the West and Central African Region (Abidjan Convention, 1981); entered into force 5 August 1984; Action Plan for the protection and Development

32 protocols.[29] Out of these, UNEP provides secretariat services for six RSPs, seven others are non-UNEP administered and five are independent

---

of the Marine Environment and Coastal Areas of the West and Central African Region (1981); entered into force 5 August 1984; 18. Wider Caribbean Region: Cartagena Convention for the Protection and Development of the Marine Environment of the Wider Caribbean Region (1983); see www.unep.org/regionalseas (as at 18 May 2006).

29 The cumulative list of these protocols, region wise, includes the following: Mediterranean: (1) Protocol for the Prevention of Pollution in the Mediterranean Sea by Dumping from Ships and Aircraft (Dumping Protocol); adopted 16 February 1976, entered into force 12 February 1978; (2) Protocol for the Prevention and Elimination of Pollution in the Mediterranean Sea by Dumping from Ships and Aircraft or Incineration at Sea; adopted 10 June 1995, not yet in force; (3) Protocol on the Protection of the Mediterranean Sea against Pollution from Land-Based Sources (LBS Protocol); adopted 17 May 1980, in force 17 June 1983; (4) Protocol for the Protection of the Mediterranean Sea against Pollution from Land-Based Sources and Activities; adopted 7 March 1996, not yet in force; (5) Protocol Concerning Specially Protected Areas and Biological Diversity in the Mediterranean (SPA and Biodiversity Protocol); adopted 10 June 1995, in force 12 December 1999; (6) Protocol Concerning Cooperation in Preventing Pollution from Ships and, in Cases of Emergency, Combating Pollution of the Mediterranean Sea (Prevention and Emergency Protocol); adopted 25 January 2002, in force 17 March 2004; (7) Protocol for the Protection of the Mediterranean Sea against Pollution Resulting from Exploration and Exploitation of the Continental Shelf and the Seabed and its Subsoil (Offshore Protocol); adopted 14 October 1994, not yet in force; (8) Protocol on the Prevention of Pollution of the Mediterranean Sea by Transboundary Movements of Hazardous Wastes and their Disposal (Hazardous Wastes Protocol); adopted 1 October 1996, not yet in force; ROPME Sea Area (9) Protocol concerning Regional Cooperation in Combating Pollution by Oil and other Harmful Substances in Cases of Emergency; adopted 24 April 1978, in force 1 July 1979; (10) Protocol concerning Marine Pollution resulting from Exploration and Exploitation of the Continental Shelf; adopted 1989, in force 17 February 1990; (11) Protocol for the Protection of the Marine Environment against Pollution from Land-Based Sources; adopted 1990, in force 2 January 1993; (12) Protocol on the Control of Marine Transboundary Movements and Disposal of Hazardous Wastes and other Wastes; adopted 17 March 1998, not yet in force. West and Central Africa: (13) Protocol Concerning Cooperation in Combating Pollution in Cases of Emergency; adopted: 1981, into force 5 August 1984; South-East Pacific: 14) Agreement on Regional Cooperation in Combating Pollution in the South East Pacific by Hydrocarbons and other Harmful Substances in cases of Emergency; signed: 12 November 1981, participating countries: Chile, Colombia, Ecuador, Peru and Panama; (15) Complementary Protocol on the Agreement for Regional Cooperation in Combating Pollution in the South East Pacific by Hydrocarbons and other Harmful Substances in Cases of Emergency; adopted 22 July 1983, in force 1987; (16) Protocol for the Protection of the South East Pacific Against Pollution from Land-Based Sources; adopted 1983, in force 1986; (17) Protocol for the Conservation and Management of Protected Marine and Coastal Areas of the South East

programmes.[30] Furthermore, five regional organizations[31] have also come into being to implement and administer their respective RSP. At the Second Global

---

Pacific; adopted 1989, in force 1984; (18) Protocol for the Protection of the South East Pacific from Radioactive Pollution; adopted 21 September 1989, in force 1995; (19) Protocol on the regional program for the study of the El Niño phenomenon in the South East Pacific (ERFEN); adopted 6 November 1992, participating countries: Chile, Colombia, Ecuador and Peru. Red Sea and Gulf of Aden: (20) Protocol Concerning Regional Cooperation in Combating Pollution by Oil and Other Harmful Substances in Cases of Emergency; adopted 14 February 1982, into force 1985; Wider Caribbean: (21) The Protocol Concerning Cooperation in Combating Oil Spills; adopted 1983, in force 11 October 1986; (22) The Protocol Concerning Specially Protected Area and Wildlife (SPAW); adopted 1990, in force 18 June 2000; (23) The Protocol Concerning Pollution from Land-Based Sources and Activities (LBS); adopted 6 October 1999, not yet in force. Eastern Africa: (24) Protocol Concerning Protected Areas and Wild Fauna and Flora in the Eastern African Region; adopted 21 June 1985, in force 30 May 1996; (25) adopted for the following programmes Protocol Concerning Cooperation in Combating Marine Pollution in Cases of Emergency in the Eastern African Region; adopted 1985, in force 30 May 1996. South Pacific: (26) Protocol for the Prevention of Pollution of the South Pacific Region by Dumping; adopted 1986, in force 1990; (27) Protocol Concerning Cooperation in Combating Pollution Emergencies in the South Pacific Region; adopted 1986, in force 1990. Antarctic: (28) Protocol on Environmental Protection to the Antarctic Treaty; adopted 1991, in force 14 January 1998. Black Sea: (29) Protocol on Protection of the Black Sea Marine Environment Against Pollution from Land Based Sources; adopted 1992, in force 15 January 1994; (30) Protocol on Cooperation in Combating Pollution of the Black Sea Marine Environment by Oil and Other Harmful Substances in Emergency Situations; adopted 1992, in force 15 January 1994; (31) Protocol on The Protection of the Black Sea Marine Environment Against Pollution by Dumping; adopted 1992, in force 15 January 1994; (32) Black Sea Biodiversity and Landscape Conservation Protocol; adopted 2003, not yet in force; see www.unep.org/ regional seas (as at 18 May 2006).

30 This division is as follows: I. UNEP-Administered Programmes (6) Caribbean Region, East Asian Seas, Eastern Africa Region, Mediterranean Region, North-West Pacific Region and West and Central Africa Region II. Non-UNEP Administered Programmes: (7) Black Sea Region, North-East Pacific Region, Red Sea and Gulf of Eden, ROPME Sea Area, South Asian Seas, South-East Pacific Region, South Pacific Region III. Independent Programmes: (5) Arctic Region, Antarctic Region, Baltic Sea, Caspian Sea and North-East Atlantic Region; see www.unep.org/regionalseas.

31 These regional organizations for RSP are: 1.Regional Organization for the Protection of the Marine Environment (ROMPE). It comprises Bahrain, Iran, Iraq, Kuwait, Oman, Qatar, Saudi Arabia and United Arab Emirates. 2. Programme of Environment for the Red Sea and the Gulf of Eden (PERSGA). It comprises Egypt, Jordan, Palestine, Saudi Arabia, Somalia, Sudan and Yemen 3. Permanent Commission of the South Pacific (CPPS). It comprises Chile, Colombia, Ecuador, Panama and Peru. 4. South Pacific Regional Environment Programme (SPREP). Its members are Australia, Cook Islands, Federated States of Micronesia, Fiji, France, Kiribati, Marshall Islands, Nauru, New Zealand, Niue,

Meeting of Regional Seas Conventions and Action Plans,[32] convened by UNEP in July 1999, a call was made for close links between RSP and the newly established Global Programme of Action for the Protection of the Marine Environment from Land-Based Activities (GPA).[33]

It is expected that in the current (third phase) of the Montevideo Programme, special emphasis will be placed on the 'effective implementation and compliance with environmental law at the national and international level including aspects of enforcement and liability'.[34] Under the mandate of this programme, UNEP has contributed, directly and indirectly, to the evolution of several MEAs and produced a body of soft law[35] comprising principles, standards and

---

Palau, Papua New Guinea, Soloman Islands, Tonga, Tuvalu, United Kingdom, United States of America, Vanuatu and Western Samoa. 5. South Asian Cooperative Environment Programme (SACEP). It comprises Bangladesh, India, Maldives, Pakistan and Sri Lanka; see www.unep.org/regionalseas (as at 18 May 2006).

32 See 'A regional seas renaissance' in UNEP, *Annual Report 1999* (Nairobi: UNEP, 1999), p. 33.

33 The Global Programme of Action was officially launched in November 1995 by 108 countries and the European Union at an intergovernmental conference in Washington D.C. to preserve and protect the marine environment from harmful effects of land-based activities. It also invited UNEP to act as the GPA Secretariat. In 1996, the GPA Implementation Plan was presented to the Commission on Sustainable Development (CSD-4) and the General Assembly adopted resolution 51/189 on the institutional arrangements for the implementation of the GPA. At the 19th Session of UNEP Governing Council decision 19/14 was adopted on global and regional GPA implementation, which led to establishment and operationalization of the UNEP/GPA Coordination Office in The Hague, the Netherlands; see www.gpa.unep.org (as at 26 May 2006).

34 See UNEP, *Report on the Implementation of the Decisions adopted at the 21st Session of the Governing Council/Global Ministerial Environment Forum,* for the Seventh Special Session of the Governing Council, Cartagena, Columbia, 13–15 February 2002; Doc. UNEP/GCSS. VII/4 of 14 November 2001, p. 12, para 36.

35 These non-binding or soft instruments have been adopted by the UNEP GC or intergovernmental meetings convened by UNEP. They include: Principles of Conduct in the Field of the environment for the Guidance of States in the Conservation and Harmonious Utilisation of Natural Resources Shared by Two or More States; Conclusions of the Study of Legal Aspects concerning the Environment Related to Offshore Mining and Drilling within the Limits of National Jurisdiction; Montreal Guidelines for the Protection of the Marine Environment Against Pollution from Land-Based Sources; Cairo Guidelines and Principles for the Environmentally Sound Management of Hazardous Wastes; Goals and Principles of Environmental Impact Assessment; London Guidelines for the Exchange of Information on Chemicals in International Trade; Code of Ethics on the International Trade in Chemicals; Global Programme of Action for the Protection of the Marine Environment from Land-Based Activities; International Technical Guidelines for Safety in Biotechnology.

guidelines. It has also contributed to the development of environmental law and policy at the national level.

Some of the important MEAs, to which UNEP has contributed in various degrees, include the 1979 Convention on Migratory Species of Wild Animals (Bonn Convention),[36] the 1985 Vienna Convention, the 1987 Montreal Protocol for the Protection of the Ozone Layer[37] and the 1989 Basel Convention on the Control of Transboundary Movements of Hazardous Wastes and their Disposal.[38] During the preparatory process for the 1992 United Nations Conference on Environment and Development (UNCED), UNEP played an important role in the framing of the Convention on Biological Diversity.[39] The recent Rotterdam Convention on Prior Informed Consent Procedure (PIC) for Certain Hazardous Chemicals and Pesticides in International Trade (1998, jointly with FAO)[40] is an example of a different genre of environmental issues being brought under a multilateral regulatory umbrella.

Negotiations were also spearheaded by UNEP to have an International Legally Binding Instrument for Implementing International Action on Certain Persistent Organic Pollutants (POP).[41] The aim was to reach an agreement to

36 Convention on the Conservation of Migratory Species of Wild Animals (Bonn), 1979. It came into force on 1 November 1983; see *I.L.M.,* Vol. 19, 1980, p. 15.

37 Convention for the Protection of the Ozone Layer (Vienna), 1985. It came into force on 22 September 1988. The Protocol on Substances that Deplete the Ozone Layer (Montreal), 1987. It came into force on 1 January 1989; see *I.L.M.,* Vol. 26, 1987, pp. 1529 and 1550 respectively. The UNEP headquarters in Nairobi houses the Secretariat of the Ozone Regime.

38 Convention on the Control of Transboundary Movement of Hazardous Wastes and Their Disposal (Basel), 1989. It came in to force on 24 May 1992; see *I.L.M.,* Vol. 28, 1989, p. 657.

39 Convention on Biological Diversity (Rio de Janeiro), 1992. It came into force on 29 December 1993; see *I.L.M.,* Vol. 31, 1992, p. 822.

40 The Convention on the Prior Informed Consent Procedure for Certain Hazardous Chemicals and Pesticides in International Trade was adopted at Rotterdam on 10 September 1998. It seeks to curtail the $1.5 trillion trade in hazardous pesticides and chemicals; see UNEP, *Annual Report 1998* (Nairobi: UNEP, 1998), p. 7 and 21. For text of the Rotterdam PIC Convention see UNEP/FAO/PIC/CONF.5 of 17 September 1998. Also see www.pic.int.

41 The first session of the Intergovernmental Negotiating Committee (INC) for an international legally binding instrument for implementing international action on certain persistent organic pollutants (POPs) took place in Montreal in June 1998. At the INC-3 in Geneva, during 6–11 September 1999, an agreement was reached on proposals favoring the elimination of intentionally produced POPs. While the pesticides *aldrin, endrin* and *toxaphene* are slated for elimination without any exemptions; other POPs like *chlordane, dieldrin, heptachlor, mirex* and *hexachlorobenzene* are to be eliminated with country-specific exemptions. UNEP Secretariat has played an important role for the environmental management of chemicals as well as negotiations on a convention on POPs.

reduce and/or eliminate 12 specific POPs and to establish scientific criteria and a process for identifying additional pollutants for future international action. At the fifth session of the Intergovernmental Negotiating Committee, the final text[42] of the instrument was reached in December 2000. The POPs agreement, which was formally adopted[43] at a diplomatic conference in Stockholm (May 2001), may be able to help in minimizing and eliminating some of the most toxic chemicals mankind has produced.

Moreover, UNEP provided substantive support and expertise for the development of the UN Framework Convention on Climate Change (1992)[44] and the UN Convention to Combat Desertification in those Countries Experiencing Serious Drought and/or Desertification, particularly in Africa (1994).[45] It has also provided assistance to the African governments in the development of the Harare Agreement on the Action Plan for the Environmentally Sound Management of the Common Zambezi River System (1987)[46] and the Lusaka Agreement on Cooperative Enforcement Operations Directed at Illegal Trade in Wild Fauna and Fauna (1994).[47] As a sequel to the process for ensuring

The fourth round of negotiations took place in Bonn, during 20–25 March 2000, when a draft text of the instrument was prepared; see UNEP/POPS/INC. 4/5, 25 March 2000.

42 The fifth and final session of the Intergovernmental Negotiating Committee (INC5), held in Johannesburg (South Africa), 122 countries finalized the text of a legally binding treaty. It set out control measures covering the production, import, export, disposal and use of POPs. It requires the governments to promote the best available technologies and practices for replacing the existing POPs, while preventing the development of new POPs; see Report of the Intergovernmental Negotiating Committee for an International Legally Binding Instrument for Implementing International Action on Certain Persistent Organic Pollutants, Fifth Session, Johannesburg, 4–9 December 2000; Doc. UNEP/POPs/INC.5/7, 26 December 2000. Also see UNEP Press Release 00/138 of 10 December 2000 at http://www.unep.org/documents/default.asp.documentid=186&articleid=2712.

43 The Conference of Plenipotentiaries on the Stockholm Convention on Persistent Organic Pollutants was held during 22–23 May 2001 in Stockholm (Sweden). The POPs Convention was formally adopted on 22 May 2001. It was to remain open for 'signature' at the United Nations Headquarters until 22 May 2002. As on 16 May 2006, the Convention was signed by 151 states and ratified by 124 states; see www.pops.int.

44 See *International Legal Materials* (ILM), vol. 31, 1992, p. 849.

45 See *ILM,* vol. 33, 1994, p. 1328.

46 See ILM, vol. 27, 1987, p. 1109.

47 The Lusaka Agreement has made stricter provisions by strengthening implementation of the CITES in Eastern and Southern African countries. For the text of the agreement see UNEP, *Handbook of Environmental Law,* pp. 156–63, quoted in Elisabeth M. Mrema, 'The Role of International Organisations in the Development of International Environmental

implementation of the CBD and Basel Convention, UNEP has helped in the adoption of the Basel Protocol on Liability and Compensation for Damage Resulting from Transboundary Movements of Hazardous Wastes and their Disposal (1999)[48] as well as the Cartagena Protocol on Biosafety (1999)[49] respectively. UNEP even provides secretariat[50] services for five of the global conventions, namely the Convention on International Trade in Endangered

---

Law: The Case of UNEP", paper presented at the International Conference titled *Towards an Effective Role of Law in the UAE Environment Protection and Development*, 2–4 May 1999 (on file with the author), p. 36.

48 The Basel Protocol on Liability and Compensation for Damage resulting from Transboundary Movements of Hazardous Wastes and Their Disposal was adopted by the Fifth Conference of Parties meeting of the Basel Convention. The objective of the Protocol is to provide for a comprehensive regime for liability as well as adequate and prompt compensation for damage resulting from the transboundary movement of hazardous wastes and other wastes, including incidents occurring due to illegal traffic in those wastes. For text of the Protocol, see Report of the Conference of the Parties to the Basel Convention, Fifth Meeting, 6–10 December 1999; UNEP/CHW.5/29, 10 December 1999, Annex III, pp. 88–111. Also see www.basel.int.

49 The Protocol seeks to protect biological diversity from the potential risks posed by living modified organisms resulting from modern biotechnology. It establishes an advance informed agreement (AIA) procedure for ensuring that countries are provided with the information necessary to make informed decisions before agreeing to the import of such organisms into their territory. The Protocol contains reference to a precautionary approach and reaffirms the precaution language in Principle 15 of the Rio Declaration on Environment and Development. The Protocol also establishes a Biosafety Clearing-House to facilitate the exchange of information on living modified organisms and to assist countries in the implementation of the Protocol. As of 16 May 2006, 132 instruments of ratification or accession were deposited with the UN Secretary-General. For text of the protocol see www.biodiv.org/biosafety (as at 26 May 2006).

50 Whenever an international institution accepts responsibility for providing secretariat facilities for an international convention, relevant provisions of the convention govern their relationship. Essentially, a convention secretariat is a body of the convention created to implement the functions assigned to it by the convention and is subject to the authority of the Conference of Parties (COP) as far as those specific functions of the convention are concerned. As UNEP is a subsidiary body of the UN General Assembly, 'it is obliged to abide by the preconceived rules and regulations of the UN in its administration, including the administration of the Convention secretariats. By requesting UNEP to provide these services, the Conventions acknowledge this, and in fact rely on the established structure of administration provided by the UN system'; see UNEP, 'The Relationship Between the Executive Director of UNEP and the Conventions Regarding the administration of their Secretariats', Doc. UNEP/DEP/Coord.4/3/COR.1, 4 January 1996, pp. 1–7 at 3.

Species (CITES),[51] Convention on the Conservation of Migratory Species of Wild Animals (CMS),[52] Ozone, Basel and CBD. Another remarkable work, which has not been widely publicized, is the administration of 'trust funds'. As of December 2001, UNEP administered almost 100 trust funds,[53] out of which 73 directly supported the programme of work of UNEP, 22 trust funds were for the MEAs and regional seas and five were for special accounts.

Dilution of Authority

From its inception, UNEP was set on the course of addressing ambitious goals, without commensurate structure or even stature, with the help of just a voluntary[54] Environment Fund. It seems, primarily, that the Programme was

51 Convention on International Trade in Endangered Species of Wild Fauna and Fauna, Washington, 3 March 1973. It came into force on 1 July 1975; see ILM, vol. 12, 1973, p. 1085.

52 Convention on the Conservation of Migratory Species of Wild Animals, Bonn, 23 June 1979. It came into force on 1 November 1983; see *ILM,* vol. 19, 1980, p. 15.

53 UNEP managed 43 trust funds in 1992, which rose to 81 in 1998, 92 in 1999 and 100 in 2001. In 1998–99 biennium, the total expenditure from trust funds was $ 329.17 million. Out of this, however, the Multilateral Fund (Ozone) alone accounted for $ 202.23 million (70%) and GEF's share was $ 26.50 million. In the 2000–2001 biennium, the projected income and expenditures were $816.86 million and $650.71 million respectively. The detailed break-up of the 86 UNEP administered trust funds (1998–99) was: (a) Direct Support to UNEP (68): General Trust Funds (17), Technical Cooperation Trust Funds: General (28), Technical Cooperation Trust Funds: Personnel (23); (b) Conventions/Protocols/Regional Seas Programmes (15): General Trust Funds (12), Technical Cooperation Trust Funds: General (1), Technical Cooperation Trust Funds: Personnel (2); (c) Special Accounts and Trust Funds (3): Multilateral Fund for the Montreal Protocol (1), UN International Partnership Trust Fund (1), GEF (1); see UNEP, *Report of the Executive Director on Activities of the United Nations Environment Programme* for the Sixth Special Session of the Governing Council, Malmö, 29–31 May 2000, Doc. UNEP/GCSS.VI/6 of 11 April 2000, pp. 45 and 63. Also see UNEP, *Status of the Environment and other Sources of Funding for the United Nations Environment Programme: Information Note by the Executive Director* (Report on the Implementation of the Decisions of the Twenty-first Session of the Governing Council/Global Ministerial Environment Forum), Seventh Special Session of the Governing Council, Cartagena, 13–15 February 2002; Doc. UNEP/GCSS.VII/INF/8 of 6 February 2002.

54 The UN General Assembly established this fund in 1972 to provide financing for environmental programmes. However, in view of the voluntary character of this fund, total of 174 UN member countries (average 88 donor countries per year) are said to have made at least *one* contribution to the Environment Fund during the period 1973 to 2005. The fact that mere 13 countries (Botswana, Finland, India, Japan, Mexico, Netherlands, New Zealand, Norway, Singapore, Spain, Sweden, United Kingdom and United States) thought it fit to

designed to coordinate and promote action rather than initiate concrete operations by itself. It did, however, generate high expectations. But anyone who expected that 'UNEP' would itself solve all the problems of the environment, or fund others for the job, was bound to be disappointed'.[55] Even the often-repeated use of the term 'catalyst' for UNEP's law-making role has been regarded by some as a camouflage as:

> Calling UNEP's task a 'catalytic function' simply masked the fact that it was supposed to work with other agencies, which would never view it as an equal. In effect, UNEP was given an impossible assignment. It was also provided with inadequate staff, minimal funding, and a location far from the decision-making centres of the UN system.[56]

The birth of UNEP was a product of special circumstances. It emerged in the midst of deep suspicion among most of the participants at the Stockholm Conference. If developing countries were concerned about any global framework being used to restrict their legitimate developmental goals, industrialized countries were not in favour of a powerful environmental watchdog. This did not help in giving UNEP teeth. It was left to be just one of the UN programmes, having been denied even the status of a 'specialized agency' (as per Article 57 and 63 of the UN Charter) for 'environmental' purposes on the specious ground that such an 'agency for the environment would result in duplication of activities and would compound already serious problems of coordination'.[57] It was also argued that it made 'no sense to remove these activities from existing specialized agencies and place them in a new agency'.[58] There was an undercurrent within the UN system pushed by some of the specialized agencies that were not in favour of a new agency specially designed for environment protection. Thus, it appears, that:

---

make regular annual contribution during this entire period, speaks volumes for the voluntarism at work; see www.unep.org/rmu (as at 12 May 2006).

55 UNEP, *UNEP: What It Is What It Does? How It Works,* quoted in P.M. Dupuy, 'United Nations Environment Programme' in Rudolf Bernhardt (Ed.), *Encyclopedia of Public International Law* (Amsterdam: North-Holland, 1983), p. 321.

56 Konrad von Moltke, 'Why UNEP Matters', *Green Globe Yearbook of International Cooperation on Environment and Development,* 1996, pp. 55–64 at 57. Also see Konrad von Moltke, 'The Organisation of the Impossible' in *Global Environmental Politics,* vol. 1, no. 1, 2001, pp. 23–28 at 24.

57 Gardener, n. 14, p. 245.

58 Said Mahmoudi, 'The United Nations Environment Programme: An Assessment', *Asian Yearbook of International Law* (AsYIL), vol. 5, 1995, pp. 175–198 at 184.

> (I)ts creation was at best somewhat half-hearted reflecting on the one hand a lack of conviction on the part of the most powerful decision-makers about the importance and urgency of environmental issues (many of which were recognized only dimly or not at all in those more innocent times) and on the other the opposition of certain less-developed States that perceived a contradiction between the then emerging environmental demands and the requirements of rapid development.[59]

As a result of this, UNEP's ability to set the global environmental agenda came to be severely constrained by its organizational structure and unpredictable funding. Such inherent weakness could be a product of half-hearted political support to this international environmental institution. Cumulatively, it could not but have compromised the 'clout of UNEP both among States and among organizations'.[60]

With the help of a small secretariat and a voluntary Environment Fund, this UN environment programme, in addition to promoting international cooperation and coordination of environmental programmes, was required to be a focal point to undertake new environmental initiatives (including the Action Plan for the Human Environment).[61] Even within the UN system, as a part of the complex web of functioning of a general political organization of States, environmental matters were being dealt with peripherally in the General Assembly as 'a small part of the crowded schedule of the over-burdened Second (Committee)',[62] as compared to other high-profile issues that had their exclusive committees. The cumulative effect of these structural inadequacies was accentuated by UNEP's gradual political neglect by the States, especially in the post-Rio Earth Summit period.

In spite of this, however, it seems no mean achievement that UNEP could contribute significantly in terms of development of both hard law and soft law. The gradual inroads made by other agencies of the UN system in environmental matters, as a peripheral concern within their own functional jurisdiction, also appear to have contributed to the dilution of UNEP's authority. Ironically, the very centralized regulatory approach (through development of sectoral multilateral environmental agreements) promoted by UNEP, has also

---

59 Paul C. Szasz, 'Restructuring the International Organisational Framework' in Edith Brown Weiss (Ed.), *Environmental Change and International Law: New Challenges and Dimensions* (Tokyo: United Nations University Press, 1992), pp. 351–352.

60 Ibid, p. 351.

61 See the UNGA Res.2997 (XXVII), Part II at para 1 and Part III at para 1–2.

62 Szasz, n. 59, p. 353.

contributed in a 'weakening of UNEP's oversight'.[63] Thus, once these MEAs come into force, they tend to take their own orbit without any 'control' from UNEP. At best UNEP can make an effort, like chasing a mirage, to 'coordinate' – if possible – their work. Earlier efforts of the UNEP Executive Director towards coordination meetings of MEAs have also now been assigned to an Environment Management Group (EMG). The EMG (created by a resolution of the General Assembly), is also to be chaired by the UNEP Executive Director. It aims at coordinating the environmentally related work of all relevant UN agencies, commissions and programmes.

It is not widely known that the World Commission on Environment and Development (Brundtland Commission)[64] came to be established at the recommendation of the UNEP Governing Council.[65] As a sequel to it, one of the recommendations of the WCED led to the convening of the 1992 United Nations Conference on Environment and Development (UNCED) by the General Assembly.[66] Ironically, the 'expert 'watchdog'[67] and environmental conscience of the UN was not even assigned with the task of 'preparation of the follow-up conference to Stockholm'.[68] It seems that, in the euphoria of the Rio Earth Summit, UNEP was not paid any prominent attention. It was relegated to the background. In a way the unchallenged position of UNEP suffered a severe jolt; it became just a cog in the machine instead of emerging as an effective environmental conscience-keeper. Moreover, the gradual

63 On UNEP' promotion of international legal instruments, Cutajar and Osafo have observed: 'One of the consequences of UNEP's success in promoting international legal instruments as a means of advancing the international environmental agenda has been a dissipation of governmental and secretariat energies in different institutional frameworks and thus, paradoxically, weakening of UNEP's oversight'; see Michael Zammit Cutajar and Seth Osafo, 'International Legal Instruments: a Means of Raising Awareness and Engaging Action for the Global Environment' in Ahmad K. Hegazy (Ed.), *Environment 2000 and Beyond* (Cairo: Horus, 1999), pp. 365–378 at 374–75.

64 The World Commission on Environment and Development (WCED), headed by the former Norwegian Prime Minister Gro Harlem Brundtland was established pursuant to the UNEP Governing Council decision UNEP/GC.11/3 on 23 May 1983. The WCED report *Our Common Future* (published by Oxford Uni. Press, Oxford, 1987) was endorsed by the UN General Assembly Resolution A/RES/42/187 on 11 December 1987.

65 UNEP Governing Council Decision 15/3 of 25 May 1989 on a UN Conference on Environment and Development; see General Assembly Official Records, Forty-forth Session, Supp no. 25 (A/44/25), annex I.

66 See the UN General Assembly Resolution 43/196 (1988). Also see the General Assembly Resolution 44/228 of 22 December 1989, Part I, para 1.

67 Kofi A. Annan, 'An Indispensable Contribution', *Our Planet,* vol. 9, no. 1, 1997, p. 4.

68 Szasz, n. 59, p. 352.

FIGURE 2 *Prof. Janos J. Bogardi, Director UNU-EHS, introducing Prof. Desai to the audience;* Courtesy: UNU-EHS.

institutional clogging of the environmental field and emergence of other high-profile actors contributed to the gradual dwarfing of UNEP. The multiplicity of environmental institutions has also had a negative effect on UNEP's role in the development of international environmental law.

UNEP Tightens its Belt

During the first two decades of its existence, UNEP appears to have had a salutary effect in terms of setting the global environmental agenda and catalyzing international environmental initiatives. This period saw the recognition of UNEP's role as a leading global environmental agency. As seen earlier, the imprint of its actions could be seen and its presence felt globally as well as in the development of environmental policies and legislations at the national level. At the 1992 UNCED, which marked the twentieth anniversary of the Stockholm Conference, Agenda 21 recognized a 'need for an enhanced and strengthened role for UNEP and its Governing Council'.[69] Curiously, however,

69 Agenda 21, Chapter 38, para 21; see Nicholas A. Robinson (Ed.), *Agenda 21: Earth's Action Plan: Annotated,* IUCN Environmental Policy & Law Paper No. 27 (New York: Oceana, 1993), p. 612. Also available at www.unep.org.

the Governing Council (GC) of UNEP was asked to continue to play its role (policy guidance and coordination in the field of the environment) with an added dimension of the development perspective and underlined the priority areas[70] on which it was asked to concentrate.

In order to ensure an effective follow-up to the Conference, UNCED carved out a new institutional structure. A high-level Commission on Sustainable

70 Agenda 21 has prescribed 14 such *priority areas* as follows: '(a) Strengthening its catalytic role in stimulating and promoting environmental activities and considerations throughout the United Nations system; (b) Promoting international cooperation in the field of environment and recommending, as appropriate, policies to this end; (c) Developing and promoting the use of such techniques as natural resource accounting and environmental economics; (d) Environmental monitoring and assessment, both through improved participation by the United Nations system agencies in the Earthwatch programme and expanded relations with private scientific and non-governmental research institutes; strengthening and making operational its early warning function; (e) Coordination and promotion of relevant scientific research with a view to provide a consolidated basis for decision-making; (f) Dissemination of environmental information and data to Governments and to organs, programmes and organizations of the United Nations system; (g) Raising general awareness and action in the area of environmental protection through collaboration with the general public, non-governmental entities and intergovernmental institutions; (h) Further development of international environmental law, in particular the international conventions and guidelines, promotion of its implementation, and coordinating functions arising from an increasing number of international legal agreements, *inter alia,* the functioning of the secretariats of the Conventions, taking into account the need for the most efficient use of resources, including possible co-location of secretariats established in the future; (i) Further development and promotion of the widest possible use of environmental impact assessment, including activities carried out under the auspices of specialised agencies of the United Nations system, and in connection with every significant economic development project or activity; (j) Facilitation of information exchange on environmentally sound technologies, including legal aspects, and provision of training; (k) Promotion of sub-regional and regional cooperation and support to relevant initiatives and programmes for environmental protection, including playing a major contributing and coordinating role in the regional mechanisms in the field of environment identified for the follow-up to the conference; (l) Provision of technical, legal and institutional advice to Governments, upon request in establishing and enhancing their national legal and institutional frameworks, in particular, in cooperation with UNDP capacity-building efforts; (m) Support to Governments, upon request, and development agencies and organs in the integration of environmental aspects into their development policies and programmes, in particular through provision of environmental, technical and policy advice during programme formulation and implementation; (n) Further developing assessment and assistance in cases of environmental emergencies'; see Agenda 21, Chapter 38, para 22, ibid, pp. 612–14.

Development (CSD) was established in accordance with Article 68[71] of the UN Charter. This is in agreement with the Charter scheme wherein all principal UN organs have been conferred with powers to create their own subsidiary organs. As such, the new CSD, as a functional commission, was placed under the supervision of the ECOSOC.[72]

The creation of this new UN environmental institution appears to have indirectly contributed to dilution in the authority of UNEP as regards institutionalized international environmental cooperation. UNCED's negative implication, for UNEP as well as the setting up of CSD, has been viewed as ineffective for the environmental agenda:

> In hindsight, Rio indirectly contributed to UNEP's weakness while adding a CSD that failed to raise the profile of the international environmental agenda. The implications of this institutional weakness have become increasingly apparent while the state of much of the environment has kept on deteriorating. The proliferation of environmental secretariats for individual conventions, located in different parts of the world, has highlighted the lack of a forceful central institution. Fragmentation and lack of coordination grew, rather than the integrated approach, which has rightly become the hallmark of the modern environmental paradigm.[73]

In fact, CSD's mandate hints that:

> To monitor progress in the implementation of Agenda 21 and activities related to the integration of environmental and developmental goals throughout the United Nations system through *analysis and evaluation of reports from all relevant organs, organizations, programmes and institutions of the United Nations system* dealing with various issues of

71 Article 68 of the UN Charter provides: 'The Economic and Social Council shall set up commissions in economic and social fields and for the promotion of human rights, and such other commissions as may be required for the performance of its functions'.

72 It is, generally, understood that in setting up of commissions no questions have been raised regarding the type of such subsidiary organs, since the ECOSOC's competence in this respect is not confined to Article 68 alone. It can also flow from Article 7(2), which permits 'such subsidiary organs as may be found necessary may be established in accordance with the present Charter'. As compared to the regional economic commissions set up by the ECOSOC, the functional commissions like CSD are designated for a specialized purpose such as follow-up to the 1992 UNCED.

73 Rudolf Dolzer, 'Time for Change', *Our Planet* (UNEP), vol. 9, no. 1, 1997, p. 19.

> environment and development, including those related to finance (emphasis added).[74]

Thus it requires reporting from UNEP to CSD. It presents an interesting legal situation when a subsidiary organ of the General Assembly is required to report to another subsidiary organ created by ECOSOC. It may not be a coincidence that international institutional arrangements under Agenda 21 first deal with the mandate and structure of CSD, followed by recognizing the need for an 'enhanced and strengthened role for UNEP and its Governing Council'.[75] It seemed to signify that during the Rio process and its aftermath, States have shown less confidence in UNEP than in the higher-profile CSD. A cursory look at the steep decline from 1994–1995 to 1998–1999[76] of 35.5 per cent in the Governing Council approved biennium appropriations as well as a decline of 26 per cent, 35 per cent and 11 per cent (in the three biennia respectively) in the

---

74 The General Assembly resolution 47/191, para 3 (a); see *Yearbook of the United* Nations, vol. 46, 1992, p. 676. Also see Agenda 21, Chapter 38, para 13 (a).

75 Ibid, para 11 to 13 and para 21 to 23.

76 The Environment Fund of UNEP has been consistently faced with shrinking contributions in these four bienniums As compared to the budgets approved by the Governing Council during 1994–95, 1996–97, 1998–99 and 2000–2001 at 166.8, 137, 107.5 and 119.23 million US dollars, the Fund received merely 124, 88.82, 95.41 and 84.80 million US dollars respectively. Cumulatively, it shows that, between 1994–95 and 2000–2001, there has been approx. 28.5% decline in the Governing Council approved appropriation and approx. 31% decline (26%, 35%, 11% and 29% in the four biennium since 1994–95) in the actual contributions received from the states. For the biennium 2002–2003, the amount of actual contribution projected to receive is 95.0 million US dollars as compared to GC approved appropriation of 119.9 million US dollars. The actual contribution received for 2002 is 48.30 million US dollars; see Opening Address by the Executive Director of the UNEP to the Fifth Special Session of the Governing Council held during 20–22 May 1998; *General Assembly Official Records* (GAOR), 53rd Session, Supplement No. 25 (A/53/25), p. 40–42; *Report of the Executive Director,* Global Ministerial Environment Forum, Sixth Special Session of the GC (Malmo, 29–31 May 2000), Annex I (Status of the Environment Fund); *Report of the Executive Director on the Implementation of the Decisions adopted at the 21st Session of the GC/GMEF,* Seventh Special Session of the GC/GMEF, Cartegena, 13–15 February 2002, Doc.UNEP/GCVII/4 of 14 November 2001; Report of the Executive Director, Twenty-second Session of the Governing Council/GMEF, Nairobi, 3–7 February 2003, UNEP/Gc.22/6/Add.1, 26 November 2002; UNEP, *Annual Report 2002* (Nairobi: UNEP, 2002), pp. 60–61. For an interesting and detailed analysis of year-wise, country-wise and region-wise contributions to the Environment Fund, see (as at 12 May 2006):http://www.unep.org/rmu/en/Financing_of_UNEP/Environment_Fund/index.asp.

contributions received for UNEP's Environment Fund underscores this trend (see Table 2).[77]

As per the UNEP constituent instrument (GA Resolution 2997 (XXVII) of 15 December 1972), the cost of servicing the Governing Council and providing the secretariat is to be borne by the regular budget of the United Nations whereas operational programme costs, programme support and administrative costs of the Environment Fund are to be borne by the Fund. Thus the Environment Fund, based upon voluntary contributions from States, and supplemented by trust funds and a small allocation from the regular UN budget, is designed to provide funding for UN's environmental programme (UNEP), including new environmental initiatives.[78] UNEP mainly uses this Fund to cater to its environmental mandate.The erosion in the status and authority of UNEP is best reflected in the drastic decline in UNEP's voluntary Environment Fund. The funding figures reveal that on the one hand annual paid contributions have shown a marginal increase from US$44.05 million (1997) to 45.91 million (1998) to 49.50 million (1999), while the number of contributing countries, on the other hand, has

77 In terms of funding (Governing Council-approved appropriation), UNEP has witnessed a drastic decline from US $166.8 million in 1994–95 to US $107.5 million in 1998–99. See UNEP, *Report of the Governing Council,* 5th Special Session, 20–2 May 1998, www.unep.org/governingbodies; *Address of the Executive Director,* UN GAOR, 53rd Sess., Supp. 25, at 40–2, UN Doc. A/53/25; *Policy Statement of the Executive Director to 20th Session of the UNEP Governing Council,* 1 February 1999, www.unep.org/governingbodies ; *Report of the Executive Director, at the Global Ministerial Environment Forum,* 6th Special Session, 31 May 2000, www.unep.org/governingbodies, at Annex I (status of the Environment Fund); Governing Council Decision 21/31, 21st Session, 9 February 2001; available at www.unep.org/gc_21/Documents; and *Report on the Implementation of the Decisions of the Twenty-First Session of the Governing Council/GMEF,* 6 February 2002, Doc.UNEP/GCSS.VII/INF/8, at 4–7. Also see http://www.unep.org/rmu/en/Financing_of_UNEP/Environment_Fund/index.asp (as at 12 May 2006).

78 See UNEP, *Report of the Governing Council,* Fifth Special Session, 20–22 May 1998, Opening Address of the Executive Director; *General Assembly Official Records,* 53rd Session, Supplement 25 (A/53/25), pp. 40–42; Policy Statement of the Executive director to 20th Session of the UNEP Governing Council, 1 February 1999; *Report of the Executive Director,* Global Ministerial Environment Forum, Sixth Special Session of the GC, Malmö, Doc.UNEP/GCSS.VI/6, 11 April 2000, Annex I (Status of the Environment Fund). The Governing Council Decision 21/31 of 9 February 2001, Twenty-first Session of the UNEP Governing Council (Second Global Ministerial Environment Forum) at http://www.unep.org/decisions; *Report of the Executive Director on the Implementation of the Decisions adopted at the 21st Session of the GC/GMEF,* Seventh Special Session of the GC/GMEF, Cartagena, 13--15 February 2002, Doc.UNEP/GCVII/4 of 14 November 2001; *Report of the Executive Director,* Twenty-second Session of the Governing Council/GMEF, Nairobi, 3–7 February 2003, UNEP/Gc.22/6/Add.1, 26 November 2002.

TABLE 2 *Decline in UNEP's environment fund*[79]

Biennium	GC Approved Appropriation	Actual Contributions	Shortfall	
			Amount	Percentage
1994–1995	166.8	124.00	42.80	26%
1996–1997	137.0	88.82	48.18	35%
1998–1999	107.5	95.41	12.09	11%
2000–2001	119.23	85.60	33.63	28%
2002–2003	116.60	95.00 (*Projected*)	21.60	18%
2004–2005	130.00 (*Proposed*)	115.00 (*Projected*)		

(*Amounts in millions of US$*)

declined from 88 (1997) to 73 (1998) to 66 (1999) to 56 (2000) to 34 (2001).[80] However, neither the number of countries nor the amount of contributions pledged and paid for in 2001 had reached 1998/1999 levels. During the biennium 2000–2001, the bulk of contributions to the Environment Fund of $84.8 million came from a group of some 15 countries that contributed 92 per cent of the total to the Fund. UNEP's 2002 Annual Report provides graphic details of figures indicating the downward slide and shrinking base. It provides a list of 34 countries (which includes 22 countries making six-digit and above contributions) making a total contribution of US$40.9 million in 2001. It is projected that this will increase (on the basis of pledges made) to contributions by 52 countries (with 25 countries making six-digit and above contribution) to the sum of US$48.41 million. Thus funding as well as the donor funding base for the Environment Fund has shown a sharp negative trend that speaks for the funding 'health' of this UN environmental entity.

At the Seventh Special Session of the Governing Council/Global Ministerial Environment Forum at Cartagena (February 2002), a proposal was mooted by the Executive Director for the introduction, on a pilot basis, of a voluntary indicative scale of contributions (VISC) to broaden the base as well as make more predictable the contributions to the Environment Fund. To

79 UNEP, *Report of the Executive Director on Activities of the United Nations Environment Programme,* Sixth Special Session of the Governing Council, Malmö, 29–31 May 2000; see Doc. UNEP/GCSS.VI/6, 11 April 2000, p. 43.

80 United Nations, *Basic Facts about the United Nations* (New York: UN, 1998), and p. 39.

address the 'current unsatisfactory [funding] situation',[81] UNEP decided to introduce ISC from 2003,[82] on the basis of feedback received from all 191 UN member States. This may help in slightly improving the funding situation as, on the basis of actual contributions and pledges (as at 3 February 2006), UNEP is likely to receive funds to the tune of US$52.72 (2003), 58.99 (2004)

FIGURE 3 *Global environmental conference initiatives by the UN General Assembly.*

81 UNEP, *International Environmental Governance: Report of the Executive Director,* Global Ministerial Environment Forum, Seventh Special Session of the Governing Council, Cartagena, Columbia, 13–15 February 2002, Doc.UNEP/GCSS.VII/2 of 27 December 2001, p. 27, para 122.

82 See UNEP, *Annual Report 2002* (Nairobi: UNEP, 2002), p. 60.

and 58.96 (2005) million.[83] It has been predicted that this expected increase in funding will be contributed by a wider donor base of 127, 126 and 128 countries respectively.

Ironically, a large number of countries appearing in the donor list have been contributing insignificant or token amounts to the fund. The fact that a mere 13 countries have maintained their regular annual contributions, during the period 1973 to 2005, shows the precarious basis of the voluntary contributions. Moreover, a comparative region-wise picture for the years 1995 and 2005 shows that contributions from Africa ($300,628 and $136,880) and Asia-Pacific ($6,318,106 and $4,364,768) have decreased and those from Latin America & Caribbean ($233,401 and $246,283) and West Asia ($225,250 and $343,186) have increased. However, most noticeable are the consistency and increase in European contribution ($34,014,781 and $45,811,588) as compared to the sharp decline in the North American contribution ($16,214,492 and $8,058,894).[84] It remains to be seen how VISC will be able to bring about any material change in the uncertainties surrounding the Environment Fund.

Institutional Proliferation

By 1998, as a part of the overall effort to reform the UN system, the UN Secretary-General established a Task Force on Environment and Human Settlements, which was headed by UNEP's then Executive Director, Klaus Töpfer (see Appendices, p. 359).[85] The Töpfer task force identified a 'proliferation'[86] of environmental

---

83 See www.unep.org/rmu.

84 Ibid.

85 In early 1998, the UN secretary-general set up a high-level twenty-one-member United Nations Task Force on Environment and Human Settlements. It comprised ministers, government advisors, and members of the civil society as well as representatives from the UN Secretariat. It was headed by Klaus Töpfer, who was the executive director of UNEP. The task force presented its report to the secretary-general on 15 June 1998. See UN Task Force on Environment and Human Settlements, *Report to the Secretary-General,* 15 June 1998 [on file with the author]. See also UN, *Report of the Secretary-General 'Environment and Human Settlements,'* 6 October 1998, Doc. A/53/463, Annex, at 11–28; and UN, *Report of the Secretary-General on Environment and Human Settlements, Presented to the UNGA at Its Fifty-Third Session,* 20th Session, 6 January 1999, Doc.UNEP/GC.20/INF/13 (hereinafter *Task Force Report*).

86 There has been proliferation of environmental institutions in the post-UNCED period, including the Commission on Sustainable Development [hereinafter CSD], the Inter-Agency Committee on Sustainable Development, and the Global Environment Facility.

institutions that had changed the UN's environmental structure as well as led to the creation of institutional structures parallel to UNEP. In the view of the Töpfer task force, this proliferation had given rise to 'substantial overlaps, unrecognized linkages and gaps'.[87] The task force expressed the concern that:

> These flaws are basic and pervasive. They prevent the UN system from using its scarce resources to best advantage in addressing problems that are crucial to the human future; harm the credibility and weight of the United Nations in the environmental arena; and damage the UN's working relationship with its partners in and outside of Government.[88]

A variety of reasons can be found for this multiplicity of institutions, including the growth in *ad hoc,* piecemeal and sectoral environmental law-making, which was represented by the MEAs; periodic efforts at 'global conferencing'[89] on the environment and sustainable development, represented by the Rio and Johannesburg summits; as well as the creation of more permanent structures with mandates that overlap with UNEP's existing or potential mandate, such as the Global Environment Facility (GEF) and the Commission on Sustainable Development (CSD). In the environmental arena, as noted earlier, the UN General Assembly has provided crucial political guidance to States, acted as a catalyst for the law-making process, and adopted resolutions comprising constituent instruments for some of the specialized environmental institutions including UNEP and the CSD (see Figure 3, p. 125).

The role that is being played by these institutions has often resulted in overlapping of jurisdictions, working at cross-purposes, turf wars and resources

---

Similarly, considerable 'greening' of other development-oriented international institutions can be seen within the UN system, such as World Health Organisation, the World Meteorological Organisation, the Food and Agriculture Organisation, the United Nations Educational, Scientific and Cultural Organisation [hereinafter UNESCO] as well as the UN's regional economic commissions (the Economic Commission for Africa, the Economic Commission for Europe, the Economic Commission for Latin America and the Caribbean, the Economic and Social Commission for Asia and the Pacific, and the Economic and Social Commission for Western Asia).

87 See UN Task Force on Environment and Human Settlements, *Report to the Secretary-General,* 15 June 1998 (on file with the author), pp. 29–30 (hereinafter the *Task Force Report*). Also see UN, *Report of the Secretary-General 'Environment and human settlements',* Doc. A/53/463, Annex, pp. 11–28, 6 October 1998 at 85.

88 Ibid.

89 For details of a series of UN convened recent global conferences, see United Nations, *The World Conferences: Developing Priorities for the 21st Century* (New York: UN, 1997).

being wasted. Cumulatively, they have not helped in efficiently and effectively realizing the goal of institutionalized international environmental cooperation. At the same time, the multiplicity of institutions has also made the task of coordination very difficult. In fact, lack of coordination has emerged as one of the major challenges of international environmental governance. Recent academic studies have concluded that the current system of IEG is 'not only too complicated, but it is also steadily getting worse'.[90] This institutional proliferation has taken a particularly heavy toll on the role, effectiveness and authority of UNEP.

It is difficult to pinpoint exact reasons for the downward trend in the Environment Fund. It appears that UNEP has relied heavily over the years on the leadership of its Executive Directors who set the direction for the organization and lead efforts at resource mobilization. The first UNEP Executive Director was Maurice Strong of Canada, who served from 1972 to 1975. He was succeeded by Mostafa K. Tolba of Egypt, who held the position for seventeen years (1975–1992), until Elizabeth Dowdeswell of Canada was elected in December 1992. Klaus Töpfer of Germany held the post from 1998 to (31 March) 2006. During Dowdeswell's tenure, it seems, the fund seems to have experienced an exceptional decline (paid contributions came down to just US$88.82 million). As a result, UNEP insiders claim, it is during her tenure that most of UNEP's reserve funds fell to their lowest point.

In the course of discussions with Dowdeswell, however, the author was given the impression that a 'refusal to toe the line pushed by some States' might have resulted in UNEP being isolated and, in turn, jeopardized pledges to the Environment Fund. The situation improved to some extent (with paid contributions reaching US$95.41 million in 1998–1999) when Töpfer, former German federal environment minister, took over as Executive Director. However, during the following biennium, paid contributions reached the lowest ever level of US$85.60 million. Even the high profile initiatives and diplomatic blitzkrieg of Töpfer, especially through the Global Ministerial Environment Forum (GMEF), could only do so much to avert further decline. It appears to have shown a slight increase in the Environment Fund during the last two years of Töpfer's tenure, possibly due to the introduction of voluntary indicative scale of assessment.

90 See United Nations University, *International Sustainable Development Governance: the Question of Reform: Key Issues and Proposals,* Final Report 10 (Tokyo: UNU/IAS, 2002), pp. 4–48.

Several factors could be considered responsible for the 'lack of interest' in UNEP of the key developed and developing countries. It could have been the result of fatigue from the seventeen-year-long Tolba era, a simple disdain for an entity engaged in subjects that are only of interest to the poorest countries, or the prospect of funding ambitious proposals that might address 'unattractive' issues such as unsustainable production and consumption patterns as well as profligate lifestyles. It is possible that some of the developing countries making regular contributions to the Environment Fund found it difficult to sustain the level of previous years as a result of the funding contributions required by a growing number of MEAs and other parallel structures that have emerged in the post-1992 Rio summit period. Small and developing countries, for whom UNEP matters most in terms of support for a series of programmes, including scientific assessments and capacity building, might have reduced or stopped contributions to the fund in response to a genuine funding crunch and/or the growing cost of participation in intergovernmental environmental initiatives.

The most worrying outcome of this process is the extent to which the funding base itself has shrunk and UNEP's reliance on an ever-smaller number of countries has increased. Implicit in this state of affairs is the message that, at least for some of the leading donor countries, UNEP matters much less than it did in the pre-Rio period or that these countries are using the funding squeeze to put pressure on UNEP to marginalize it. Arguments have been heard in the corridors of the World Bank on the 'mainstreaming' of the environment and whether there is any need for UNEP. Moreover, reports churned out by some of the institutions intending to propagate a brand new Global Environmental Organization (GEO) or World Environmental Organization (WEO) or World Environmental and Sustainable Development Organization (WESDO) were mainly premised upon inconvenient location, connectivity and security related problems in Nairobi. Implied in these arguments was the effort to uproot UNEP from there, being the seat of the only UN entity located in a developing country. It was also not surprising that the Töpfer task force report emphatically stated that the UN Office in Nairobi (UNON) was not given the same attention and resources as other UN offices in New York, Geneva and Vienna. It seems the developing countries, sensing a hidden move to take UNEP to a 'greener' location in Europe, thwarted any such move. By the time of the UNEP Governing Council meeting in 2003, it was interesting to notice a prominent banner on the stage that boldly read: 'Nairobi: Environment Capital of the World'!

Revitalizing UNEP

UNEP's Governing Council has responded to declining resources and eroding authority by seeking to reassert the programme's pre-eminence in the field of the environment. With the adoption of the 1997 Nairobi Declaration by the Governing Council, serious efforts were launched to 'revitalize' UNEP (see Appendices, p. 398). It was explicitly emphasized that:

> (UNEP) has been and should *continue to be the principal United Nations body in the field of the environment...* the role of the United Nations Environment Programme is to be the leading global environmental authority that sets the global environmental agenda, that promotes the coherent implementation of the environmental dimension of sustainable development within the United Nations system and that *serves as an authoritative advocate for the global environment* (emphasis added).[91]

Although, as has been seen, these assertions have not been reflected in States' willingness to commit to UNEP financially, some modest efforts have been made to transform this mandate into an institutional reality. The Nairobi Declaration was followed by the inauguration of the Töpfer task force by the Secretary-General, as mentioned earlier in this article. The task force's report was duly examined by the General Assembly[92] (see Appendices, p. 355), which, in turn, gave direction for a series of institutional steps both within the UN Secretariat as well as at the intergovernmental level.[93] It brought into being two

---

91 See the Nairobi Declaration on the Role and Mandate of the United Nations Environment Programme, in Governing Council Resolution 19/1, UN GAOR, 52nd Sess., Supp. 25, 7 February 1997, and Doc. A/52/25, at annex [emphasis added]. See also UNEP, Annual Report 1998, 5 (1998); and 7 Bulletin of Environmental Law 4–5 (June 1997).

92 The UNGA considered the *Report of the Secretary-General on Environment and Human Settlements* and the report of the UN task force (annexed to it) at its fifty-third session in 1999 (see UNGA Resolution 53/242, 10 August 1999, Doc. A/RES/53/242, available at http://www.un.org/earthwatch/about/docs/ga53_242.htm and *Task Force Report,* n. 85). It also took cognizance of the decision of the Governing Council (Decision 20/17 of 5 February 1999 (available at www.unep.org/Documents. Also see A/54/25, annex 1) and the resolution of the Commission on Human Settlements (Resolution 17/6 of 14 May 1999, www.chs.org as well as the need to strengthen the institutions of the United Nations in the field.

93 For a comprehensive discussion on this issue, see Bharat H. Desai, *Revitalizing International Environmental Institutions: The UN Task Force Report and Beyond, Indian Journal of International Law* (ISIL), vol. 40, no. 3, 2000, pp. 455–504; ibid, 'Mapping the Future of International Environmental Governance', *Yearbook of International*

intra-institutional and inter-governmental forums, namely the Environmental Management Group (EMG),[94] for inter-agency environmental coordination within the UN system, and the Global Ministerial Environment Forum (GMEF),[95] for high-level policy dialogue at the intergovernmental level. The UN General Assembly has provided an overarching guidance to the entire process, coupled with the crucial policy direction contained in UNGA Resolution 53/242.

Through EMG,[96] the UNEP Executive Director chairs coordination meetings of all the UN system-wide institutions working in the field of environment. Early reports have not been very encouraging. Furthermore, the UNEP Executive Director has been periodically chairing the coordination meetings of secretariats of MEAs. The process for crafting many of these MEAs was actually initiated by UNEP, pursuant to its mandate to catalyze the development of international environmental law,[97] and a number of MEA secretariats are

---

Environmental Law (OUP), vol. 13, 2002, pp. 43–62 and ibid, *Institutionalizing International Environmental Law* (New York: Transnational Publishers, 2004), Chapter 6, pp. 221–270.

94 UNGA Resolution 53/242, n. 92, supported the proposal of the secretary-general on the establishment of an environment management group [herein after EMG] for the inter-agency coordination in the field of environment and human settlements. It asked the secretary-general to develop the mandate, terms of reference, criteria for membership, working methods, and so on in consultation with the member states and the Administrative Committee on Coordination. Its membership comprises the specialized agencies, programs, and organs of the United Nations system, including the secretariats of multilateral environment agreements (hereinafter MEAs).

95 The first meeting of the GMEF was at held in Malmö, Sweden; *see Notification by the Executive Director, Global Ministerial Environment Forum,* 6th Special Session, 9 March 2000, www.unep.org/governingbodies. The notification stated that the forum was being convened pursuant to Governing Council Decision 20/17 of 5 February 1999, n. 92, and the General Assembly Resolution 53/242 of 28 July 1999, n. 92, and in accordance with Rules 5 and 6 of the Rules of Procedure of the Governing Council.

96 The EMG came to be set up, following the recommendation of the Töpfer task force report (*Task Force Report, supra* note 89, at para. 22) in order to have better coordination and joint action by replacing the Inter-Agency Environmental Coordination Group. The new institution, headed by the UNEP executive director, comprises at its core all the leading UN entities in the field of environment and human settlements as well as other UN entities, financial institutions, and organizations outside the UN system, including MEA secretariats whenever required. See GA Resolution 53/242, n. 92.

97 Under the Montevideo Programme I (1981) and II (1993), UNEP has organized and coordinated its environmental law activities through a series of ten-year programs for the development and periodic review of environmental law. For two decades, this program provided UNEP with strategic guidance in the field. Now the UNEP Governing Council has launched, through Decision 21/23 of 9 February 2001, the third phase of the Montevideo Programme for the Development and Periodic Review of Environmental

administratively housed within UNEP. However, as has been mentioned, MEA secretariats and conferences of the parties are not accountable to UNEP since their destiny is decided by their own parties and by their constituent treaty rules and procedures.

Ministerial Forums

It was recognized early on in the discussion on IEG reform that any major change in UNEP's situation, or in IEG more generally, would require high-level ministerial intervention. Thus, the launching of the GMEF represented a bold political initiative to revive the sagging fortunes of UNEP. It was also an attempt to regain policy coherence in the field of the environment, which, as has been described earlier in this article, suffered from the fragmentation of the environmental agenda as well as from the multiplicity of institutions.[98]

These efforts received further momentum from the initiative taken by the Malmö Ministerial Declaration[99] (see Appendices, p. 349) and the twenty-first meeting of the UNEP Governing Council (Decision 21/21), which decided to establish the Open-ended Intergovernmental Group of Ministers or their Representatives on International Environmental Governance (IGM) (see Appendices, p. 335). The IGM was given a mandate to make a comprehensive assessment of existing institutional weaknesses as well as the future needs and options for strengthened international environmental governance. In the course of its marathon work, the IGM held six meetings, in addition to

---

Law for the First Decade of the Twenty-First Century. For the text of the Montevideo Programme I and II, see 36 Yearbook of the United Nations 1030 (1982) and 47 Yearbook of the United Nations 820–1 (1993). For the GC Decision 21/23, see www.unep.org/gc_21/Documents.

98 Bharat H. Desai, 'UNEP: Coming out of Coma', *Down To Earth*, 9(20), 2001, p. 49. See also ibid, "Towards WSSD: Future of International Environmental Governance", Woodrow Wilson International Centre for Scholars (Washington D.C.), *ECSP Report*, 8th issue, 2002, pp. 42–43.

99 The Malmö Ministerial Declaration stresses that '(g)overnments and UNEP have a major role in the preparation for the 2002 review of UNCED at the regional and global levels ... The 2002 conference should review the requirement for a greatly strengthened institutional structure for international environmental governance based on an assessment of future needs for an institutional architecture that has the capacity to effectively address wide-ranging environmental threats in a globalised world. UNEP's role in this regard should be strengthened and its financial base broadened and made more predictable'; see Malmö Ministerial Declaration, Global Ministerial Environment Forum, 31 May 2000, Doc. UNEP/GCSS.VI/L.3, available at www.unep.org.

carrying out consultations with civil society and experts.[100] The negotiations were tortuous, and the IGM saw its final meeting gaveled to a close in Cartagena on 15 February 2002 (see Appendices, p. 315). The main focus in the course of the debate was on the structural aspects of IEG and, in particular, on the role of UNEP and of the MEAs. The IGM was expected to come out with concrete proposals for the GMEF as well as to revitalize international environmental governance in general and UNEP in particular.

An agreed starting point for this effort was, to the greatest possible extent, to avoid the creation of new institutions. In view of the large number of institutions active in the field of the environment, this aspect of the exercise was significant. As a corollary, the IGM was to address issues of overlapping jurisdiction, wastage of resources and turf wars, which have marred the performance of many of the existing institutional structures and, in particular, have helped to reduce UNEP's effectiveness.

The IGM discussions confirmed that in the three decades since the establishment of UNEP in 1972, the number of IEG structures has multiplied. This growth has raised fundamental concerns about overlap and conflict in both structure and substance. These governance structures have been produced through the State-centric process and work of the UN system, along with

100 In order to ensure the cost-effectiveness of the work of the Open-Ended Intergovernmental Group of Ministers or Their Representatives on International Environmental Governance [hereinafter IGM] and to maximize the attendance by ministers, IGM meetings were held on the margins of ministerial meetings already scheduled to take place. The IGM meetings and consultations were held as follows: (1) IGM-1 took place on 18 April 2001, immediately prior to the high-level segment of the ninth session of the CSD; (2) IGM-2 was held on 17 July 2001 in Bonn, Germany, on the margins of the resumed sixth Conference of the Parties to the UN Framework Convention on Climate Change; (3) IGM-3 was held on 9–10 September 2001 in Algiers, Algeria; (4) IGM-4 was held from 29 November to 1 December 2001 in Montreal, Canada, after the conclusion of the Intergovernmental Review Meeting on the Implementation of the Global Programme of Action for the Protection of the Marine Environment from Land-Based Activities; (5) IGM-5 took place in New York, United States, on 25 January 2002, prior to the second session of the Preparatory Committee for the WSSD from 28 January to 8 February 2002; and (6) IGM-6 took place on 12 February 2002 in Cartagena, Colombia, immediately prior to the seventh special session of the UNEP Governing Council and the third GMEF on 13–15 February 2002. The IGM also benefited from the Civil Society Consultations, which were held in Nairobi on 22–3 May 2001 as well as the Expert Consultation in Cambridge on 28–9 May 2001. At its seventh special session, the Governing Council/GMEF adopted the report of the IGM; see *Report of the Open-Ended Intergovernmental Group of Ministers or Their Representatives on International Environmental Governance,* 15 February 2002, UNEP GC Decision SS.VII/1, at annex, available at www.unep.org/GoverningBodies.

several multilateral regimes that are regarded as treaty bodies having their own institutional standing under international law. Cumulatively, they have made the puzzle of IEG more complicated than ever before. The resulting effect has even been dubbed as 'organization of the impossible'.[101]

Since many international institutions have entered the environmental scene, the role and authority of UNEP as an entity that is expected to set the global environmental agenda has diminished. As such, there has been an intensive debate in the post-Rio period on the 'needs and options' concerning IEG. In fact, the complex web of IEG affects the fate of not only UNEP but also the future effectiveness of other structures and multilateral processes, agreements and consultative mechanisms that address the environment and environment-related issues.

The substantive role of MEAs, as well as their coordination[102] and coherence,[103] remain the second part of the challenge of IEG. Linkages, synergy and coordination of the work of MEAs were an important focus of the IGM process. On the one hand, these MEAs have set in motion independent international institutional structures to cater to the need for international cooperation on numerous sectoral issues. The majority fall within the broad categories of regional seas (marine pollution); biodiversity, such as the Convention on Wetlands of International Importance Especially as Waterfowl Habitat,[104] the Convention for the Protection of the World Cultural and Natural Heritage,[105] the Convention on International Trade in Endangered Species of

---

101 For details of this argument, see Konrad von Moltke, "The Organization of the Impossible", *Global Environmental Politics,* vol. 1(1), 2001, pp. 23–28.

102 In this respect, it needs to be noted that the task of 'coordination' is a part of a process of governance on multilateral environmental issues. It seems the task of coordination of various MEAs has become difficult especially due, *inter alia,* to their different mandates, different membership, their dispersal in various parts of the world, and the location of these MEAs within some 'host institution,' such as UNEP, the IUCN, UNESCO, and so on). The task of coordination is still defying a clear solution, despite UNEP holding coordination meetings of convention secretariats, and it gets further complicated in the absence of an effective central overarching institution. For a detailed assessment of this issue, see generally IGM, *Proposal for a Systematic Approach to Coordination of Multilateral Environmental Agreements,* 4 July 2001, Doc. UNEP/IGM/2/5. See also UNEP, 'Improving International Environmental Governance among Multilateral Environmental Agreements: Negotiable Terms for Further Discussion,' 4 July 2001, Doc. UNEP/IGM/2/4.

103 *See Earth Negotiations Bulletin,* 16(24), 18 February 2002, p. 6.

104 Convention on Wetlands of International Importance Especially as Waterfowl Habitat, 2 February 1971; in force 21 December 1975; see 22 *ILM 698* (1982).

105 Convention for the Protection of the World Cultural and Natural Heritage, 16 November 1972; in force 17 December 1975; see 11 *ILM* 1358 (1972).

Wild Fauna and Flora (CITES),[106] the Convention on the Conservation of Migratory Species of Wild Animals (CMS),[107] and the Convention on Biological Diversity (CBD);[108] chemicals and hazardous wastes-related (International Labour Organization (ILO) conventions on occupational hazards, transboundary movements of hazardous wastes,[109] chemicals in international trade,[110] and persistent organic pollutants[111]) and atmosphere-related instruments (such as ozone depletion[112] and climate change[113]).[114] MEAs generally bring into being a separate set of institutional structures, including a conference of parties, subsidiary bodies (on implementation, science and technology, etc.), a funding mechanism and a secretariat.

Through the creation of these new and autonomous institutions, each new MEA contributes to the increasing fragmentation of the environmental agenda. Each of these MEAs comes into being due to different 'trigger events', responsible factors and convergence of State interests (especially of the main actors). Moreover, they are also dispersed in different countries (and different continents) and have differing administrative links to the UN system (such as UNEP, UNESCO, IMO, ILO, IAEA and so on) as well as other organizations such as the World Conservation Union (IUCN).

106 Convention on International Trade in Endangered Species of Wild Fauna and Flora, 3 March 1973; in force 1 July 1975; see 993 *UNTS* 243 (1973).

107 Convention on the Conservation of Migratory Species of Wild Animals, 23 June 1979; in force 1 November 1983; see 19 *ILM 15* (1980).

108 Convention on Biological Diversity, 5 June 1992; in force 29 December 1993; see 31 *ILM* 322 (1992).

109 Convention on the Control of Transboundary Movements of Hazardous Wastes and Their Disposal (Basel), 1989; in force 24 May 1992; see 28 *ILM* 657 (1989).

110 Convention on the Prior Informed Consent Procedure for Certain Hazardous Chemicals and Pesticides in International Trade (Rotterdam), adopted at Rotterdam, 10 September 1998. It entered into force on 24 February 2004. As on 28 March 2006, there were signatories: 73, Parties: 106; see www.pic.int.

111 Convention on Persistent Organic Pollutants (Stockholm) adopted on 22 May 2001 and entered into force on 17 May 2004. As on 17 May 2006, there were 151 signatories and 124 parties. For the text of the convention, see www.pops.int.

112 Convention for the Protection of the Ozone Layer (Vienna), 1985, in force 22 September 1988 and the Protocol on Substances that Deplete the Ozone Layer (Montreal), 1987, in force 1 January 1989; see 26 *ILM* 1529 and 1550 (1987).

113 United Nations Framework Convention on Climate Change (Rio de Janeiro), 1992, 31 *ILM* 849 (1992) and the Protocol to the Convention on Climate Change (Kyoto), 1997, see www.unfccc.int.

114 IGM, *Multilateral Environmental Agreements: A Summary,* 30 March 2001, UN Doc. UNEP/IGM/1/INF/1.

Parallel to the work of the IGM, UNEP's Executive Director prepared a report[115] on IEG. It served as a 'living document', which took into account deliberations of the IGM and sought to identify the emerging consensus. The Executive Director's report sought to synthesize the gamut of issues concerning IEG and included a section on the 'needs and options' that underscored alternatives for strengthening the institutional architecture as well as achieving coordination, synergy and linkages among the MEAs. A further UNEP document listed a summary of selected papers[116] that contained outlines of various proposals put forward by governments, institutions and eminent experts. The main thrust of these proposals has been that the existing architecture of IEG needs to be strengthened, in order to better address the emerging environmental challenges as well as to better meet the expectations of the member States.

In the specific case of UNEP, as a principal UN environment programme, several elements were flagged in the IGM discussion, such as the need to build the political confidence of States in the effectiveness of UNEP's institutional mandate as well as to provide more reliable funding. Resolving these issues will ultimately hold the key to the emergence of a concrete blueprint to strengthen UNEP. In this context, the various options and proposals put forward have been seen as 'building blocks'[117] for the IEG process. These options included providing a new mandate for the UN Trusteeship Council on environment protection and global commons; launching a new world environment organization (which may be called WEO or GEO); enhancing the status of UNEP from a UN programme to a UN specialized agency (which may be called UNEPO[118] or UNEO), or continuing the existing UNEP, but with more secure and predictable funding.

---

115 IGM, *International Environmental Governance: Report of the Executive Director,* 16 November 2001, UN Doc. UNEP/IGM/4/3.

116 IGM, *Summary of Selected Papers,* 5 April 2001, UN Doc. UNEP/IGM/1/INF/2.

117 IGM, *Report of the Chair,* 27 December 2001, UN Doc. UNEP/IGM/4/6, at 3.

118 On the proposal for a 'specialised agency' and detailed blueprint of the structure for such an agency to be called United Nations Environment Protection Organisation (UNEPO), see lecture seminar by Bharat H. Desai, "Revitalising International Environmental Institutions: The UN Task Force Report and Beyond" at Environment and International Law Unit of the World Bank, Washington D.C., on 15 January 1999 and its revised and updated version published in *Indian Journal of International Law,* vol. 40, no. 3, 2000, pp. 455–504. It was short listed and circulated at the First Meeting (New York, 18 April 2001) of the UNEP constituted *Open-ended Intergovernmental Group of Ministers or their Representatives on International Environmental Governance.* Its summary was included in UNEP Doc. 'Summary of Selected Papers', UNEP/IGM/1/INF/2 of 5 April 2001 at page 10. Also see, ibid, *Institutionalizing International Environmental Law* (New York: Transnational Publishers, 2004), Chapter 6.

The IGM discussions fed into the sessions of the GMEF, which began in Malmö in May 2000. The GMEF, in turn, sought to set an agenda for World Summit on Sustainable Development (Johannesburg, 2002). In fact, the GMEF explicitly stated, through the Malmö Ministerial Declaration, that:

> The 2002 conference [WSSD] should review requirements for a greatly strengthened institutional structure or IEG based on an assessment of future needs for an institutional architecture that has the capacity to effectively address wide-ranging environmental threats in a globalizing world. UNEP's role in this regard should be strengthened and its financial base broadened and made more predictable.[119]

By the final session of the IGM in Cartagena (February 2002), the positions of the main negotiating blocs were clear, and many of the ambitions that had launched the IEG process had been fully explored. The Group of 77 (G-77) and China supported 'strengthening UNEP within its current mandate' and emphasized that the 'proposals on MEAs must respect the autonomy of the COPs'.[120] This support can be explained, in part, by developing countries' long-standing concern that the strengthening of environmental institutions will undermine a development-focused agenda. The idea of enhancing UNEP's status into a specialized agency was not favoured by the G-77 and China, the United States or Russia.[121] The European Community (EC) had earlier called for strengthening the IEG based on the existing structures, in particular, UNEP, but had indicated the need to adapt these structures to the new requirements leading, ultimately, to a world environment organization.[122] The idea of creating a new world environment organization did not, however, find favour with delegations, particularly the United States.

Thus the outcomes of the IGM process can be crystallized as follows:

1. The GMEF has been established as a high-level deliberative forum of environmental ministers with *universal participation* (as compared to membership), raised ministerial awareness, and support for the need to expand participation in UNEP's governance structures, including the possibility of expanding the Governing Council membership beyond its current fifty-eight members. For UNEP, which is a mere programme and

119 See the Malmö Ministerial Declaration n. 99, para. 23.

120 *See Earth Negotiations Bulletin,* n. 103, p. 5.

121 See *Earth Negotiations Bulletin,* ibid

122 *See Earth Negotiations Bulletin,* ibid, p. 6.

a subsidiary organ of the General Assembly, universal membership could be a significant advance.

2. UNEP's Executive Director has begun to coordinate meetings of the secretariats of MEAs. The effectiveness of this role, generally, remains limited to the secretariats for which UNEP acts as a 'host'. Currently, the Executive Director has a say in the functioning of five such secretariats (CITES, the CMS, Ozone Layer, the Basel Convention and the CBD). However, such a coordinating role is limited even with respect to these secretariats as they report to their own conferences of the parties.
3. UNEP's financial position has been a matter of great debate, especially following the sharp decline it has witnessed in the past few years. During the IGM process, controversy surrounded how best to make funding of UNEP adequate, stable and predictable, which is essential to avoid large gaps between pledges made and actual contributions received from States. As such, the Executive Director mooted the idea of having an 'indicative' scale of assessment by States. It is expected that this move might make States accountable for providing the funds committed by them, and could impart certainty to the budget of UNEP.
4. In view of the proliferation of MEAs, it is essential to have proper coordination and coherence in the work of these MEAs. Various ideas that have been put forward include *co-location* of the secretariats to take advantage of cost-effective common administrative facilities and other support services (following the examples set by the co-location of secretariats of the climate change (UNFCCC), desertification (UNCCD),[123] and the migratory species (CMS) conventions located at the UN premises in Bonn or the co-location of the secretariats to CITES and the Basel Convention at the International Environment House in Geneva). Proposals have also been mooted as regards clustering of convention secretariats that have close interests or are in the same field (such as biodiversity-related conventions, atmosphere-related conventions, or chemicals and hazardous wastes-related conventions). An important element that has emerged from the IGM process is the recognised need to enhance the synergies and linkages between MEAs with comparable areas of focus or of a regional character keeping in view their respective mandates. The UNEP Governing Council has asked the Executive Director to continue his efforts to enhance policy coherence and synergy among

123 United Nations Convention to Combat Desertification in Those Countries Experiencing Serious Drought and/or Desertification, particularly in Africa (Rio de Janeiro); see 33 *ILM* 1328 (1994).

international legal instruments related to the environment and sustainable development at both the inter-agency and intergovernmental levels.[124]

5. The issue of coordination within the UN system is as old as the UN itself. With increasing fragmentation of the environmental agenda and proliferations of institutions working in the field, it has been felt that there is a need to have an effective mechanism for the purpose of coordination. General Assembly Resolution 53/242 brought into being the EMG. The EMG is chaired by the UNEP Executive Director and follows an issue-management approach. This approach facilitates the establishment of issue-management groups in order to address specific issues within a fixed time frame. It is now being felt that the EMG, among others, needs to have senior-level participation by member institutions, transparency in its work, and adequate funding.

In a way, the recommendations of the IGM process have laid the road map for realizing the possibility of a greatly strengthened environmental institutional structure. It seems that both at the intergovernmental level in general, as well as within UNEP in particular, a step-by-step approach is preferred to radical changes. In view of the cautious approach of most States as well as their preference for strengthening existing institutions rather than adding to 'clogging' of institutions, a clearer picture could emerge in the coming years depending on interests and consensus among the key players on the scene. In judging the outcome, one will need to look at the *content* rather than at the institutional form that may finally emerge.

Expectations at the Johannesburg Summit

The deliberations and recommendations of the IGM process provided a basis for discussion as well as some concrete proposals during the third (25 March to 2 April in New York) and fourth (27 May to 7 June in Bali) meetings of the Commission on Sustainable Development (CSD), which served as the preparatory body for the WSSD.[125] Among the issues that came to the fore at the Johannesburg Summit, two had significant implications for the future of UNEP as well as setting a precedent within the UN system. They include a

124 UNEP GC Decision 21/20, 9 February 2001; see www.unep.org/gc_21/Documents.

125 See *Earth Negotiations Bulletin*, 22(19), 11 February 2002. Also see www.johannesburg summt.org/html/prep_process.

proposal for the universal membership of the Governing Council of UNEP as well as a means for providing stable and predictable funding for the Environment Fund. In this respect, the Johannesburg Plan of Implementation called upon States to:

> [f]ully implement the outcomes of the decision on international environmental governance adopted by the Governing Council of the United Nations Environment Programme at its seventh special session and invite the General Assembly at its fifty-seventh session to consider the important but complex issue of establishing universal membership for the Governing Council/Global Ministerial Environment Forum.[126]

As a follow-up to the Plan of Implementation, the General Assembly adopted resolution 57/251,[127] which invited governments to submit written comments on universal membership of the UNEP Governing Council. Several of the issues surrounding the IEG debate were considered and discussed at the twenty-second session of the UNEP Governing Council, which coincided with the fourth meeting of the GMEF, which was held in February 2003.[128] The Governing Council, in turn, invited governments to submit their written comments concerning both the subject of universal membership of the Governing Council (especially its legal, political, institutional, financial and system-wide implications) as well as the pilot phase for a voluntary indicative scale of assessment for the Environment Fund.[129]

In the post-Johannesburg period, States are facing a litmus test of their sincerity to grapple effectively with the problems afflicting IEG. The test of

126 WSSD, Plan of Implementation, chapter XI (on institutional framework for sustainable development), para. 140 (d); see www.johannesburgsummit.org.

127 General Assembly Resolution 57/251 has required comments from the governments to be sent by 31 October 2003. The executive director of UNEP has been asked to submit a report on the matter for the consideration of the eighth special session of the Governing Council/GMEF in 2004. See UNGA Resolution 57/251, 20 December 2002, Doc. A/RES/57/251; available at www.un.org.

128 For a detailed discussion on these issues, see *Report of the Executive Director on 'Implementing Outcome of the World Summit on Sustainable Development: International Environmental Governance,'* 22nd Session, 16 December 2002, Doc. UNEP/GC.22/4.

129 UNEP Governing Council Decision 22/17, 7 February 2003; see www.unep.org/GoverningBodies/GC22/Document/GC 22_GMEF_decisions.doc. Also see *Summary of the 22nd Session of the UNEP Governing Council and the Fourth Global Ministerial Environment Forum 3–7 February 2003, Earth Negotiations Bulletin,* 16(30), pp. 1–14 at 9 (10 February 2003); www.unep.org/governingbodies.

sincerity was also pointed out by Achim Steiner, the then Director-General of the IUCN (current UNEP Executive Director), in his presentation at the IGM's final session in Cartagena:

> The world has become weary and cynical about grand policy statements and new institutions being touted as the answer to our environmental problems. The world today is calling out for delivering on commitments and this has been clearly acknowledged through the IEG process.[130]

This observation, to some extent, underscores the problems that lie at the base of IEG discourse. The IEG process has dealt with a large number of issues

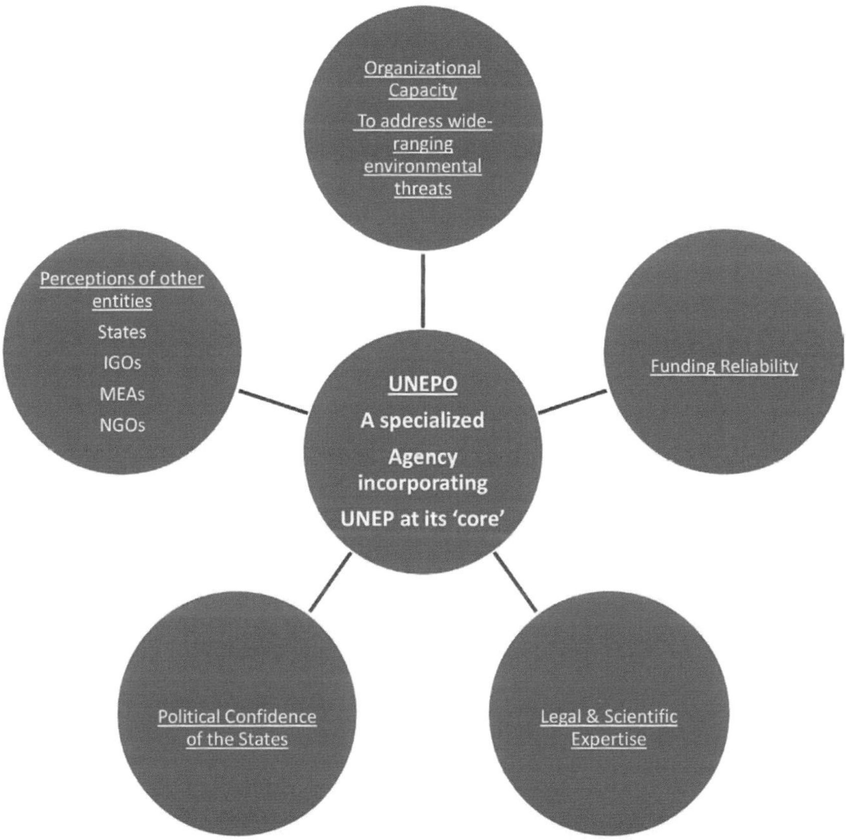

FIGURE 4 *Essential elements for UNEP to become global environmental authority.*

130 Achim Steiner, *Intervention at the Global Ministerial Forum, Cartegena, Columbia, 12–15 February 2002,* 1–5 at 3 (paper on file with the author).

during its work, which has spanned six meetings and numerous consultations. The deliberations at the Johannesburg summit, true to the nature of UN global conferences, did not provide any clear mandate for this purpose. It appears that it is the UN General Assembly, as demonstrated in resolution 57/251 that will finally need to provide concrete political guidance to solve the jigsaw of IEG.

UNEP has been the focus of the IEG process (though not being 'UNEP-centric'). If the main policy options that emerged from the process, including universal membership and a secured funding base, could be achieved, its cumulative effect will be profound for the future of UNEP. It is expected that universal membership, as compared to mere participation, will bring about more legitimacy as well as more authority to the work of the Governing Council of UNEP. It may also contribute to widening the funding base. Since the Environment Fund is voluntary, States that are currently not among the fifty-eight elected members of the Governing Council may not feel the same obligation to commit funding, as discussed earlier.

UN General Assembly resolution 53/242 did not decide to establish GMEF as a 'new organ'.[131] However, in institutional terms, a UNEP with a Governing Council of universal membership could formally emerge as a truly global environmental forum that reflects the wishes and expectations of all the members of the United Nations. This reform, coupled with adequate, stable and predictable funding, could provide, in due course, a basis for elevating UNEP to the level of a UN specialized agency (which could be designated as UNEPO). It remains to be seen if States take this course of action in the coming years. Similarly, the challenge for attaining synergy, linkages and coordination of MEAs will be a long process and will necessitate accommodating the convention secretariats in order to prevent turf wars, as each MEA seeks to guard its sectoral interests. MEA host institutions will also need to minimize control while providing a secretariat for the purpose and will need to work out clear relationship agreements to avoid potential conflicts. Similarly, if co-location is to be achieved, some current host countries will have to forgo the benefits of hosting a major multilateral institution. Such accommodations will demonstrate that States are indeed willing to address the challenges of global environmental problems widely regarded as 'common concerns of mankind'.

131 General Assembly Resolution 53/242 in fact stated that an arrangement was needed at a 'ministerial level' to provide a forum 'in which participants can gather to review important and emerging policy issues in the field of environment ... and that the Governing Council of UNEP should constitute such a forum'; see UNEP, *Legal Status of the Global Ministerial Environment Forum,* 1 December 2001, Doc.UNEP/IGM/4/INF/5/Rev.1, at 2.

UNEP: A Global Authority?

There is general aversion to the creation of new international institutions, especially due to the criticism of the UN bureaucracy as well as its funding implications. However, it has been felt that making the institution autonomous in character would make it more efficient and result-oriented, not merely a talk shop or a turf for politicking. Several of the issues concerning the institution-building process such as implications on the sovereign capacity of the States, membership, legal personality, internal law, coordination, contribution of the parties as well as the decision-making process are relevant in this context.

There have been apprehensions regarding the decision-making method (voting), as anything less than 'one State, one vote' would be regarded as undemocratic and jeopardize wider political support among States. It seems that powerful States favour strong international institutions, especially if their decision-making structures are either based upon weighted voting or can be used by them to further their own interests to the detriment of weaker States. On the other hand, such States abhor institutions which act on the basis of majority principle (one State, one vote) and may not be willing to serve their interests or follow their dictates, due to being made up of a majority of small and weak States (such as the UN General Assembly). The system of specialized agencies within the UN has occasionally come under severe strain due to clashes of interests of States. Often, powerful States, contributing substantial sums to their budgets, have withdrawn funding, as in the case of UNESCO.[132] As a consequence, the UN and some specialized agencies have in the past come under severe pressure to undergo so-called 'restructuring', including changing of chief executive officers.

In spite of the general dislike for any expansion in the ranks of the specialized agencies, they have performed a salutary role in the UN system. In fact the

132 Three states – USA, UK and Singapore – withdrew from UNESCO in the mid-eighties on the ground of their perceived grievances against it. In this context, in a seminal work on the Specialized agencies, Douglas Williams has tried to explain two main sources of strain on the system: (i) 'First, the developing countries feel that the Agencies of the United Nations have proved inadequate both in the major task of stimulating and organizing the changes they seek in international economic arrangements (changes commonly summed up in the demand for a New International Economic Order) and in the more practical enterprise of providing them efficiently with the technical and financial resources they need' and (ii) 'the view of some Western governments that the Agencies have been misused to promote debates on issues outside, or only marginally related to, their proper function'; see Douglas Williams, *The Specialised Agencies and the United Nations: The System in Crisis* (London: C.Hurst & Company, 1987), p. xiii.

functional institutions have brought about a specialized approach in dealing with issues under their jurisdiction. In the economic and social fields, many of the agencies have become almost indispensable for generating scientific and technical data and its dissemination among States as well as extending assistance to the States to build their capacity.

The advantages and disadvantages of having a specialized agency for environment protection will need to be considered in terms of the possibility of improvement over the existing situation. The core issue in the matter remains the question of elevating existing UNEP's status or carving out a *de novo* global environmental organization. The history of institution building shows that it is difficult and cumbersome to create a new organization. Moreover, it would be a fallacy to presume that a brand new entity such as a world environment organization (WEO) would be more effective than UNEP. It is also important not to lose sight of the argument that 'UNEP is still the closest we have come to a WEO'.[133] It worked as such during the first two decades of its existence. Still, to impart credibility and authority to this beleaguered entity, several elements (see Figure 4) could be considered necessary.

In this respect, however, an agreement on the 'content' should precede any discussion about the 'form', including maintaining the *status quo* – backed by the strong political will of UN member States – that may be considered suitable for UNEP. Following the establishment of the Global Ministerial Environment Forum (GMEF), with universal participation (instead of 58 members), the Governing Council (GC) of UNEP has attained a unique status. Moreover, the preparatory process for the World Summit on Sustainable Development (WSSD) indicated a possibility for making membership of the GC itself universal[134] (as compared to the GC's role as GMEF in a year when it does not meet; as it meets once in two years).

Universal membership could enhance the stakes of all UN member States in strengthening the mandate and role of UNEP in addressing global

133 Konrad von Moltke, "The Organisation of the Impossible", *Global Environmental Politics,* vol. 1, no. 1, 2001, pp. 23–28 at 27.

134 The *Draft Plan* shows agreement among the states to 'Fully implement the outcomes of UNEP's Governing Council Seventh Special Session, Decision I: International Environment Governance, and invite the General Assembly at its 57th Session to consider the important but complex issue of establishing universal membership for the Governing Council/ Global Ministerial Environment Forum'; see *Draft Plan of Implementation for the World Summit on Sustainable Development,* Commission on Sustainable Development acting as the preparatory committee for the World Summit on Sustainable Development: Fourth session; Bali, 27 May – 7 June 2002 (12 June 2002), para 122 (h); available at www.johannesburgsummit.org.

environmental problems. The General Assembly has called upon the Executive Director of UNEP to seek States' views on universal membership of the UNEP Governing Council. This development (if it materializes) would take UNEP closer to being a 'specialized agency', perhaps to be called the United Nations Environment Protection Organization (UNEPO; see Figure 1, p. 90).

Some of the reasons cited for disliking UNEP emanate from its perceived 'inconvenient' location (Nairobi in the African continent, as compared to privileged locations in Europe) where not many would prefer to work. No other compelling argument has been advanced by those favouring closure of UNEP in favour of a brand new WEO. UNEP has, in actual practice, generally performed all those essential functions, except actual operational work, which would ordinarily be done by a specialized agency. Many criticisms of UNEP would also be equally applicable to any other existing specialized agencies. Therefore, it seems that most of the reasons given for UNEP's inadequacies are due to the extraneous and subjective (external) factors such as dislike for locating important multilateral institutions in developing countries, States' lack of political confidence in it, failure of States to provide stable and predictable funding, encroachment upon UNEP's areas of work by other high-profile actors in the field as well as turf wars or 'politics of institutions'[135] which are so endemic within the UN system.

Thus, it seems that in the process of revitalizing UNEP, it is the prior determination and consensus on the 'content' – based on expectations of States as well as specialized functions that could reasonably be undertaken by the entity on the basis of available adequate resources -that will help in defining the 'form' of the new organization.[136] Still, if the 'form' and 'perceptions' are key factors in determining authority of an environmental institution, especially in view of multiplicity of actors, UNEP would qualify for that through the trappings of a UN 'specialized agency' (UNEPO). For the reasons described earlier, any such exercise will need to remain within the UN system for credibility and wider acceptability among States. The process, content and range of institutional restructuring within the UN system for this purpose will depend upon the political will of States, which may consist of mergers of some existing UN departments and programmes in the new specialized agency with UNEP at its core (UNEPO).

---

135 Achim Steiner, n. 130.

136 For instance, see United Nations University Report on *International Environmental Governance: the Question of Reform: Key Issues and Proposals* (UNU/IAS, March 2002), pp. 1–40 at 9. Also see LEAD Report on *Reflections on International Institutions for Environment and Development*, No. 1, (LEAD International, 2001), pp. 1–104, 94 and 95.

Elevating UNEP to a specialized agency appears to be a pragmatic course of action compared to creating a brand new organization with a new bureaucracy, which may jettison UNEP. Such a course of action is not favoured by most countries, especially developing ones.[137] This was shown in the deliberations of the Open-ended Intergovernmental Group of Ministers or their Representatives on International Environmental Governance (IGM) that was instituted by the Governing Council of UNEP.[138]

Interestingly, an initiative of the French President recently called for a United Nations Environment Organization (UNEO). This has been, it seems, endorsed by the European Union. Its basic ingredients appear akin to the suggestion made by this author for UNEPO (initially at a lecture at the Legal Department of the World Bank, Washington DC, on 15 January 1999). A process has now been initiated within the UNGA to look at the institutional framework for the UN's environment work. The President of the General Assembly has begun informal consultations through a letter on 26 January 2006. Moreover, as mandated by the 2005 World Summit Outcome,[139] the UN Secretary-General has constituted a High-level Panel on System-wide Coherence on Development, Humanitarian Assistance and the Environment[140] (see Appendices, p. 309) (co-chaired by the Prime Ministers of Norway, Pakistan and Mozambique). These processes are likely to look at issues of both institutional structures in the environmental field

137 For details, see Summary of the Seventh Special Session of the UNEP Governing Council/ Third Global Ministerial Environment Forum and Final Open-ended Intergovernmental Group of Ministers or their Representatives on International Environmental Governance, 12–15 February 2002 in *Earth Negotiations Bulletin,* vol. 16, no. 24, 18 February 2002, p. 5.

138 See UNEP Governing Council adopted a Decision 21/21 on 9 February 2001 on 'International Environmental Governance'. It decided 'to establish an open-ended Intergovernmental Group of Ministers or their representatives, with the Executive Director as an ex-officio member, to undertake a comprehensive policy-oriented assessment of existing institutional weaknesses as well as future needs and options for strengthened international environmental governance, including the financing of the United Nations Environment Programme, with a view to presenting a report containing analysis and options to the next session of the Governing Council/Global Ministerial Environment Forum'; see for the text www.unep.org/governingbodies.

139 The General Assembly resolution 60/1 of 16 September 2005, paragraph 169, pp. 1–38 at pp. 36–37; available at www.un.org/ga/resolutions.

140 See communications from the Secretary-General to the General Assembly President Jan Eliasson (dated 29 November 2005 and 15 February 2006) as well as from President Jan Eliasson (dated 30 September 2005 and 31 March 2006) to all Permanent Representatives and Permanent Observers to the United Nations, New York; available at http://www.un.org/News/ossg; http://www.un.org/News/Press/docs/2006/sgsm10349.doc.htm; and http://www.globalpolicy.org/reform/initiatives/panelindex.htm#coherence.

and system-wide environmental coordination. They should generate suggestions that may lead to a long and arduous road ahead to ensure that all pieces of the jigsaw fall into place.

Conclusion

In the course of the final deliberations of the IGM in Cartagena, several States, including the United States, Russia, the G-77 and China, expressed reservations about the proposals for a world environment organization and even about the conversion of UNEP into a specialized agency. However, if States sincerely wish to realize the ambitious objectives expressed in the 1997 Nairobi Declaration as well as in the 2000 Malmö Ministerial Declaration, they will need to move forward in an incremental manner. Some of the steps that have already been taken, including the GMEF, will serve as the 'building blocks' of a revitalized IEG. Moreover, when the Governing Council of UNEP meets as the GMEF – a deliberative global environmental forum with universal participation – and UNEP is provided with adequate, stable and predictable funding, it will gain far greater institutional legitimacy and authority. UNEP could be just a step away from elevation into a specialized agency that could be designated as the United Nations Environment Protection Organization (UNEPO). It could directly address the crisis of perception as well as legitimacy that UNEP currently faces from UN member States, specialized agencies, the secretariats of MEAs, international governmental and non-governmental organizations.

If States are unable to effectively 'revitalize' UNEP (as mandated by the 1997 Nairobi Declaration) then, it seems, the key goal in the immediate future could be to upgrade environment protection within the UN system through UNEP and strengthen its location in Nairobi. The process will be evolutionary. Similarly, considering the manner in which MEAs have progressed as sectoral legal restraints upon the behaviour of States, it would be difficult either to dismantle them or to bring them under the control of a single entity or even expect that UNEP would be in a position to effectively coordinate work of the different MEAs. Depending upon how it is designed, given effect to and how much consensus could be attained among the parties to various MEAs, co-location or clustering could be considered. However, that will need to respect the autonomous legal status of MEAs. As such, the future direction of IEG will be dictated more by the political will of States – how far they wish to go in the process, how best they want to translate their international environmental commitments into action, and how much they are willing to allow transparency in the functioning of different institutional structures – in order to address the global environmental challenge.

CHAPTER 6

Mapping the Future of International Environmental Governance

Introduction

Have the institutions entrusted with international environmental governance (IEG) kept pace with the changing needs of the international community? Multidimensional challenges to the human environment have necessitated responses in kind, both in terms of legal instruments as well as effective institutional structures. International regulatory efforts are required, in addition to efforts at the national level, to address environmental problems with global dimensions.[1] While it is well recognized that the legal underpinnings of the current drive to protect the global environment remain embedded in the general principles of international law,[2] states are increasingly reliant upon treaty

---

* Published in *Yearbook of International Environmental Law*, vol. 13, 2002, pp. 43–61.

1 For writings on this issue, see generally Peter H. Sand, *Lessons Learned in Global Environmental Governance* 1–60 (1990); Peter M. Haas, *Global Environmental Governance, in* Commission on Global Governance (ed.), *Issues in Global Governance* 333–69 (1995).; Rahmatullah Khan, The Thickening Web of International Law, *in* Commission on Global Governance, *supra* note 1, at 249–62; Peter M. Haas and Ernst B. Haas, *Learning to Learn: Some Thoughts on Improving International Governance of the Global Problematique, in* Commission on Global Governance, *supra* note 1, at 295–331; Bharat H. Desai, "Global Accords and Quest for a New International Ecological Order: From Law of Indifference to Common Concern", *Business and the Contemporary World* (John Wiley, New York), vol. 9, no. 3, 1997, pp. 545–72; Hilary French, "Strengthening Global Environmental Governance" in *Vanishing Borders: Protecting the Planet in the Age of Globalization* (New York: W.W.Norton & Company, 2000), pp.144–162.

2 Ian Brownlie's leading textbook on international law does not consider the need for a separate branch to address environmental problems and did not have, until recently, even a separate section on the subject. For the first time, in the 1998 (fifth) edition of the book, Brownlie has devoted just a six-page section (chapter XIII) to the subject, which is entitled "Legal Aspects of the Protection of the Environment." As a "generalist" in this context, Brownlie has argued that "[t]he fact is environmental concerns have for long been reflected in general international law and the relevant categories include the law of the sea, state responsibility, space law, the legal regime of Antarctica, and the non-navigational uses of international watercourses"; see Ian Brownlie, Principles of Public International Law 283–8 at 283 (5th edition, 1998).

 | DOI 10.1163/9789004214552_007

law, in the form of multilateral environmental agreements (MEAs), to respond to new and complex challenges as they arise. MEAs have also created a new institutionalized form of intergovernmental cooperation. In a way, this 'form' of governance is *sui generis,* as it has many of the trappings of an international organization without formally being one. MEAs cater to the need for *ad hoc* and "autonomous"[3] arrangements that are tailored to address a specific global challenge. In view of the very nature of this institutional arrangement, a MEA is expected to be 'wound up' as and when its desired objectives are met. Its autonomous nature is determined by the political will of the contracting states as reflected through the decisions of the Conference (or Meeting) of the Parties of the MEA. Although the continued growth of these institutional arrangements suggests that states have developed some confidence in their effectiveness, questions have been raised about whether their *ad hoc* and disjoined nature can have a long-term and coherent impact on global environmental problems. Indeed, recent academic studies have concluded that the current system of IEG is "not only too complicated, but it is also steadily getting worse."[4]

This article chronicles one recent effort to bring MEAs and other aspects of IEG into a more coherent and stable institutional framework–the work of the Open-Ended Intergovernmental Group of Ministers or Their Representatives on International Environmental Governance (IGM on IEG) and the follow up to this work at the World Summit on Sustainable Development (WSSD).[5] The IGM was established by the Governing Council of the United Nations

3 Robin Churchill and Geir Ulfstein have preferred to describe these institutional arrangements as "autonomous." The autonomous character of the MEA institutions emanates from their in-built law making powers as well as respective compliance mechanisms. See Robin R. Churchill and Geir Ulfstein, *Autonomous Institutional Arrangements in Multilateral Environmental Agreements: A Little-noticed Phenomenon in International Law,* 94(4) Am. J. Int'l L. 623–59 at 623 (2000).

4 See Institute of Advanced Studies of the United Nations University, *International Sustainable Development Governance: The Question of Reform: Key Issues and Proposals,* Final Report (2002).

5 The twenty-first session of the UNEP Governing Council adopted Decision 21/21 on 9 February 2001 on international environmental governance [hereinafter IEG]. It decided "to establish an open-ended Intergovernmental Group of Ministers or their representatives, with the Executive Director as an ex-officio member, to undertake a comprehensive policy-oriented assessment of existing institutional weaknesses as well as future needs and options for strengthened international environmental governance, including the financing of the United Nations Environment Programme, with a view to presenting a report containing analysis and options to the next session of the Governing Council/Global Ministerial Environment Forum." The text of this decision is available at www.unep.org/gc_21/Documents.

Environment Programme (UNEP) to "undertake a comprehensive policy-oriented assessment of existing institutional weaknesses as well as future needs and options for strengthened international environmental governance including financing of the United Nations Environment Programme."[6] The IGM's work focused, in particular, on the changing fortunes and future role of UNEP in a constantly shifting landscape of global conferences and international negotiations. The IGM's recommendations were fed into the WSSD,[7] which was held in Johannesburg from 26 August to 4 September 2002. The WSSD sought to take stock of the progress during the ten years since the UN Conference on Environment and Development (Rio Earth Summit) and had the explicit mandate to address "ways of strengthening the institutional framework for sustainable development." Therefore, it was expected that the WSSD would give attention to a decision on concrete action on the institutional architecture for IEG. As will be seen, the results of this process were inconclusive, but the process itself has helped to identify the range of what is both theoretically and politically possible at this stage in the evolution of strengthened architecture of IEG.

The "Proliferation" of Institutions

UNEP was established by the UN General Assembly in 1972 to meet the "urgent need for a permanent institutional arrangement within the United Nations

6 The 21st Session of the UNEP Governing Council adopted a Decision 21/21 on 9 February 2001 on "International Environmental Governance". It decided "to establish an open-ended Intergovernmental Group of Ministers or their representatives, with the Executive Director as an ex-officio member with a view to presenting a report containing analysis and options to the next session of the Governing Council/Global Ministerial Environment Forum"; see for the text www.unep.org/governingbodies.

7 At its fifty-fifth session, the UN General Assembly [hereinafter UNGA] decided to organize a ten-year review of progress achieved in the implementation of the outcome of the United Nations Conference on Environment and Development [hereinafter UNCED] in 2002 at the summit level to "reinvigorate the global commitment to sustainable development." UNGA by a Resolution [A/RES/55/199 of 20 December 2000] decided that the focus of the proposed review at World Summit on Sustainable Development [hereinafter WSSD] should be on the identification of accomplishments and areas where further efforts were needed to implement Agenda 21 and other outcomes of UNCED. It also decided to focus on "action-oriented decisions in areas where further efforts are needed to implement Agenda 21, address, within the framework of Agenda 21, new challenges and opportunities, and result in renewed political commitment and support for sustainable development, consistent, *inter alia,* with the

system for the protection and improvement of the environment."[8] By 1998, as part of the overall effort to reform the UN system, the UN secretary-general established a Task Force on Environment and Human Settlements, which was headed by UNEP's executive director, Klaus Toepfer.[9] The Toepfer task force identified a "proliferation"[10] of environmental institutions that had altered the UN's environmental structure as well as led to the creation of institutional structures parallel to UNEP. In the view of the Toepfer task force, this proliferation had given rise to "substantial overlaps, unrecognized linkages and gaps."[11] The task force expressed grave concern that

> [t]hese flaws are basic and pervasive. They prevent the UN system from using its scarce resources to best advantage in addressing problems that

principle of common but differentiated responsibilities." See UNGA Resolution A/RES/55/199 of 20 December 2001, 31(1) Envtl, Pol. & L. 63–4 (2001).

8 UNGA Resolution 2997 on Institutional and Financial Arrangements for International Environmental Cooperation; see A/RES/2997 (XXVII) of 15 December 1972 in *United Nations General Assembly Official Records*, 27th Session, Supp. No. 30.

9 In early 1998, the UN secretary-general set up a high-level twenty-one-member United Nations Task Force on Environment and Human Settlements. It comprised ministers, government advisors, and members of the civil society as well as representatives from the UN Secretariat. It was headed by Klaus Toepfer, who was the executive director of UNEP. The task force presented its report to the secretary-general on 15 June 1998. See UN Task Force on Environment and Human Settlements, *Report to the Secretary-General,* 15 June 1998 [on file with the author]. See also UN, *Report of the Secretary-General "Environment and Human Settlements,"* 6 October 1998, Doc. A/53/463, Annex, at 11–28; and UN, *Report of the Secretary-General on Environment and Human Settlements, Presented to the UNGA at Its Fifty-Third Session,* 20th Sess., 6 January 1999, Doc.UNEP/GC.20/INF/13 [hereinafter *Task Force Report*].

10 In the post-UNCED proliferation of environmental institutions, including the Commission on Sustainable Development [hereinafter CSD], the Inter-Agency Committee on Sustainable Development, and the Global Environment Facility. There has also been considerable "greening" of other development-oriented international institutions within the UN system, such as World Health Organization, the World Meteorological Organization, the Food and Agriculture Organization, the United Nations Educational, Scientific and Cultural Organization [hereinafter UNESCO] as well as the UN's regional economic commissions (the Economic Commission for Africa, the Economic Commission for Europe, the Economic Commission for Latin America and the Caribbean, the Economic and Social Commission for Asia and the Pacific, and the Economic and Social Commission for Western Asia).

11 See UN Task Force on Environment and Human Settlements, *Report to the Secretary-General,* 15 June 1998 (on file with the author), pp.29–30 (hereinafter the *Task Force Report*). Also see UN, R*eport of the Secretary-General "Environment and human settlements"*, Doc.A/53/463, Annex, pp. 11–28, 6 October 1998 at 85.

> are crucial to the human future; harm the credibility and weight of the United Nations in the environmental arena; and damage the UN's working relationship with its partners in and outside of Government.[12]

A variety of reasons can be found for this multiplicity of institutions, including the growth in ***ad hoc***, piecemeal, and sectoral environmental law-making, which was represented by the MEAs; periodic efforts at "global conferencing"[13] on environment and sustainable development, which was represented by the Rio and Johannesburg summits; as well as the creation of more permanent structures with mandates that overlap with UNEP's existing or potential mandate, such as the Global Environment Facility (GEF) and the Commission on Sustainable Development (CSD). In the environmental arena, the General Assembly has also provided crucial political guidance to states, acted as a catalyst for the law-making process, and adopted resolutions comprising constituent instruments for some of the specialized environmental institutions including UNEP and the CSD (see Figure 3, p. 125).

The role that is being played by these institutions has often resulted in overlapping jurisdictions, working at cross-purposes, turf wars, and a waste of resources. Cumulatively, they have not helped in efficiently and effectively realizing the goal of institutionalized international environmental cooperation. At the same time, the multiplicity of institutions has also made the task of 'coordination' very difficult. In fact, lack of coordination has emerged as one of the major challenges of international environmental governance.

UNEP under Stress

This institutional proliferation has taken a particularly heavy toll on the role, effectiveness, and authority of UNEP. The erosion in the status and authority of UNEP is best reflected in the drastic decline in UNEP's voluntary Environment Fund. Although the core costs of servicing UNEP's Governing Council and its "small secretariat" are borne by the regular budget of the United Nations, operational program costs and program support were intended to be funded

12 Ibid.

13 For details of a series of UN convened global conferences in recent years, see United Nations, The World Conferences: Developing Priorities for the 21st Century (1997).

by voluntary contributions to the Environment Fund (see Table 2, p. 124).[14] Similarly, the funding base, in terms of the number of countries making contributions, has declined from eighty-eight countries in 1997, to seventy-three countries in 1998, to sixty-six countries in 1999, and then to fifty-six countries in 2000,[15] making it a clear barometer of the state of this premier UN environmental institution. Even in 2001 (as of 31 December 2001), of the pledges given by seventy-three countries (for an amount of US $43.53 million), only sixty-five countries had paid what they owed (US $41.64 million).[16] In the biennium 2000–1, the bulk of the contributions to the Environment Fund, which totalled US $ 85.6 million, came from a group of just fifteen countries, which contributed 92 per cent of the total funds. However, neither the number of countries nor the amount of contributions pledged and paid for in 2001 had reached the levels of 1998 and 1999.

It is difficult to pinpoint exact reasons for the downward trend in the Environment Fund. UNEP has relied heavily over the years on the leadership of its executive directors who set the direction for the organization and lead efforts at resource mobilization. The first UNEP executive director was Maurice Strong of Canada, who served from 1972 to 1975. He was succeeded by Mostafa K. Tolba of Egypt, who held the position for seventeen years,

14 For Table 1, see Chapter 5 at p. 111. In terms of funding (Governing Council-approved appropriation), UNEP has witnessed a drastic decline from US $166.8 million in 1994–5 to US $107.5 million in 1998–9. See UNEP, *Report of the Governing Council*, 5th Special Session, 20–2 May 1998, www.unep.org/governingbodies *Address of the Executive Director*, UN GAOR, 53rd Sess., Supp. 25, at 40–2, UN Doc. A/53/25; <this citation is in perfect form. If you could supply all of this information for each one it would be great. Consistency is best. If you can't, please supply the date for this one to make it consistent with the others> *Policy Statement of the Executive Director to 20th Session of the UNEP Governing Council*, 1 February 1999, <UN Document number? www.unep.org/governingbodies >; *Report of the Executive Director, at the Global Ministerial Environment Forum*, 6th Special Session, 31 May 2000, <UN Document number?> www.unep.org/governingbodies, at Annex I (status of the Environment Fund); Governing Council Decision 21/31, 21st Sess., 9 February 2001; available at www.unep.org/gc_21/Documents <UN Document number?>; and *Report on the Implementation of the Decisions of the Twenty-First Session of the Governing Council/GMEF*, 6 February 2002, Doc.UNEP/GCSS.VII/INF/8, at 4–7.

15 Global Ministerial Environment Forum [hereinafter GMEF], *International Environmental Governance: Report of the Executive Director*, 7th Special Session, 27 December 2001, Doc. UNEP/GCSS VII/2, at 26.

16 *Report on the Implementation of the Decisions of the Twenty-First Session of the Governing Council/Global Ministerial Environment Forum: Status of the Environment Fund and Other Sources of Funding for the United Nations Environment Programme*, 7th Special Session, 6 February 2002, Doc.UNEP/GCSS.VII/INF/8, at 4.

until Elizabeth Dowdeswell of Canada was elected in December 1992. Klaus Toepfer of Germany has held the post since 1997. During Dowdeswell's tenure, the fund seems to have experienced an exceptional decline (paid contributions came down to just US $88.82 million). In the course of discussions with her, the author was given the impression that a "refusal to toe the line pushed by some of the states" might have jeopardized pledges to the Environment Fund. The situation improved to some extent (with paid contributions reaching US $95.41 million in 1998–9) when Toepfer, former German federal environment minister, took over as executive director. However, even during the biennium that followed, the actual amount of paid contributions reached the lowest level ever of US $85.60 million. Thus, even recent efforts to build the political confidence of states in UNEP did not achieve a quantum leap.

Considering the attitudes of some of the powerful developed countries, it could have been the result of fatigue from the seventeen – year-long Tolba era, a simple disdain for an entity that has been engaged in down-to earth-subjects that are only of interest to the poorest countries, or the prospect of funding ambitious proposals that might address issues such as unsustainable production and consumption patterns as well as profligate lifestyles. Even the high-profile initiatives and diplomatic blitzkrieg of Toepfer's era could only arrest the sharp decline, and the annual amount that is now made available to the fund hovers around US $43–5 million.

It is possible that some of the developing countries making regular contributions to the Environment Fund found it difficult to sustain the level of previous years as a result of the funding contributions required by a growing number of MEAs and other parallel structures that have emerged in the post-1992 Rio summit period. Small and developing countries, for whom UNEP matters most in terms of support for a series of programs, including scientific assessments and capacity building, might have reduced or stopped contributions to the fund in response to a genuine funding crunch and/or growing cost of participation in intergovernmental meetings taking place throughout the year.

The most worrying outcome of this process is the extent to which the funding base itself has shrunk and UNEP's reliance on an ever-smaller number of countries has increased. Implicit in this problem is the message that, at least for some of the leading donor countries, UNEP matters less than it did in the pre-Rio period or that these countries are using the funding squeeze to put pressure on UNEP. As the Toepfer task force report emphatically stated, the UN office in Nairobi did not get the same attention and resources as other UN offices in New York, Geneva, and Vienna.

UNEP Fights Back

UNEP's Governing Council has responded to declining resources and eroding authority by seeking to reassert the program's pre-eminence in the field of the environment. Serious efforts began in 1997, when the Governing Council's Nairobi Declaration asserted that the institution has been and should *continue to be the principal United Nations body in the field of the environment* ... the role of the United Nations Environment Programme is to be the leading global environmental authority that sets the global environmental agenda, that promotes the coherent implementation of the environmental dimension of sustainable development within the United Nations system and that *serves as an authoritative advocate for the global environment.*[17] Although, as has been seen, these assertions have not been reflected in states' willingness to commit to UNEP financially, some modest efforts have been made to transform this mandate into an institutional reality.

The Nairobi Declaration was followed by the inauguration of the Toepfer task force by the UN Secretary-General, as mentioned earlier in this article. The task force's report was duly examined by the General Assembly,[18] which, in turn, gave direction for a series of institutional steps both within the UN Secretariat as well as at the intergovernmental level.[19] It brought into being two distinct forums, namely the Environmental Management Group (EMG),[20]

---

17 See the Nairobi Declaration on the Role and Mandate of the United Nations Environment Programme, in Governing Council Resolution 19/1, UN GAOR, 52nd Sess., Supp. 25, 7 February 1997, and Doc. A/52/25, at annex [emphasis added]. See also UNEP, Annual Report 1998, 5 (1998); and 7 Bulletin of Environmental Law 4–5 (June 1997).

18 The UNGA considered the *Report of the Secretary-General on Environment and Human Settlements* and the report of the UN task force (annexed to it) at its fifty-third session in 1999 (see UNGA Resolution 53/242, 10 August 1999, Doc. A/RES/53/242, available at <www.un.org> and *Task Force Report, supra* note 11). It also took cognizance of the deci sion of the Governing Council (Decision 20/17 of 5 February 1999 (available at www.unep .org/Documents. Also see A/54/25, annex 1) and the resolution of the Commission on Human Settlements (Resolution 17/6 of 14 May 1999, www.chs.org as well as the need to strengthen the institutions of the United Nations in the field.

19 For a comprehensive discussion on this issue, see Bharat H. Desai, *Revitalizing International Environmental Institutions: The UN Task Force Report and Beyond*, 40(3) Indian J. Int'l L. 455–504 (2000).

20 UNGA Resolution 53/242, n.18, supported the proposal of the secretary-general on the establishment of an environment management group [hereinafter EMG] for the inter-agency coordination in the field of environment and human settlements. It asked the secretary-general to develop the mandate, terms of reference, criteria for membership, working methods, and so on in consultation with the member states and the

for inter-agency coordination within the UN system, and the Global Ministerial Environment Forum (GMEF),[21] for high-level policy dialogue at the intergovernmental level. The UN General Assembly has provided an overarching guidance to the entire process, coupled with the crucial policy guidance contained in UNGA Resolution 53/242.

Through the EMG,[22] the UNEP executive director chairs the coordination meeting of all UN system-wide institutions working in the field of environment. It remains to be seen how much headway the EMG will make. Early reports have not been very encouraging. Furthermore, the UNEP executive director has been periodically chairing the coordination meetings of secretariats of MEAs. The process for crafting many of these MEAs was actually initiated by UNEP, pursuant to its mandate to catalyze the development of international environmental law,[23] and a number of MEA secretariats are administratively housed within UNEP. However, as has been mentioned, MEA secretariats and their conferences of the parties are not accountable to UNEP

Administrative Committee on Coordination. Its membership comprises the specialized agencies, programs, and organs of the United Nations system, including the secretariats of multilateral environment agreements [hereinafter MEAs].

21 The first meeting of the GMEF was at held in Malmo, Sweden; see *Notification by the Executive Director, Global Ministerial Environment Forum*, 6th Special Session, 9 March 2000, www.unep.org/governingbodies The notification stated that the forum was being convened pursuant to Governing Council Decision 20/17 of 5 February 1999,n.18, and the General Assembly Resolution 53/242 of 28 July 1999,n. 18, and in accordance with Rules 5 and 6 of the Rules of Procedure of the Governing Council.

22 The EMG came to be set up, following the recommendation of the Toepfer task force report (*Task Force Report,* n. 11,at Para. 22) in order to have better coordination and joint action by replacing the Inter-Agency Environmental Coordination Group. The new institution, headed by the UNEP executive director, comprises at its core all the leading UN entities in the field of environment and human settlements as well as other UN entities, financial institutions, and organizations outside the UN system, including MEA secretariats whenever required. See GA Resolution 53/242, n.18.

23 Under the Montevideo Programme I (1981) and II (1993), UNEP has organized and coordinated its environmental law activities through a series of ten-year programs for the development and periodic review of environmental law. For two decades, this program provided UNEP with strategic guidance in the field. Now the UNEP Governing Council has launched, through Decision 21/23 of 9 February 2001, the third phase of the Montevideo Programme for the Development and Periodic Review of Environmental Law for the First Decade of the Twenty-First Century. For the text of the Montevideo Programme I and II, see 36 Yearbook of the United Nations 1030 (1982) and 47 Yearbook of the United Nations 820–1 (1993). For the GC Decision 21/23, see www.unep.org/gc_21/Documents.

since their destiny is decided by their own parties and by their constituent treaty rules and procedures.

The GMEF and the IGM/IEG

It was recognized early on in the discussion on IEG reform that any major change in UNEP's situation or in IEG more generally, would require high-level ministerial intervention. Thus, the launching of the GMEF represented a bold political initiative to revive the sagging fortunes of UNEP. It was also an attempt to regain policy coherence in the field of environment, which, as has been described earlier in this article, has suffered from the fragmentation of the environmental agenda as well as from the multiplicity of institutions.[24]

These efforts received further momentum from the initiative taken by the Malmö Ministerial Declaration[25] and the twenty-first meeting of the UNEP Governing Council, which decided to establish the IGM. The IGM was given a mandate to make a comprehensive assessment of the existing institutional weaknesses as well as the future needs and options for strengthened international environmental governance. In the course of more than one year of marathon work, the IGM held six meetings, in addition to carrying out consultations with civil society and experts.[26] The negotiations were tortuous, and the IGM

24 Bharat H. Desai, *UNEP: Coming Out of Coma*, 9(20) Down To Earth 49 (2001). See also Bharat H. Desai, *Towards WSSD: Future of International Environmental Governance*, ECSP Report 2002 42–43 (8th issue, 2002).

25 The Malmö Ministerial Declaration stresses that "[g]overnments and UNEP have a major role in the preparation for the 2002 review of UNCED at the regional and global levels … The 2002 conference should review the requirement for a greatly strengthened institutional structure for international environmental governance based on an assessment of future needs for an institutional architecture that has the capacity to effectively address wide-ranging environmental threats in a globalised world. UNEP's role in this regard should be strengthened and its financial base broadened and made more predictable." See Malmö Ministerial Declaration, Global Ministerial Environment Forum, 31 May 2000, Doc. UNEP/GCSS.VI/L.3; available at www.unep.org.

26 In order to ensure the cost-effectiveness of the work of the Open-Ended Intergovernmental Group of Ministers or Their Representatives on International Environmental Governance [hereinafter IGM] and to maximize the attendance by ministers, IGM meetings were held on the margins of ministerial meetings already scheduled to take place. The IGM meetings and consultations were held as follows: (1) IGM-1 took place on 18 April 2001, immediately prior to the high-level segment of the ninth session of the CSD; (2) IGM-2 was held on 17 July 2001 in Bonn, Germany, on the margins of the resumed sixth Conference of the Parties to the UN Framework Convention on Climate Change; (3) IGM-3 was held on 9–10

saw its final meeting gavelled to a close in Cartagena on 15 February 2002. The main focus in the course of the debate was on the structural aspects of IEG and, in particular, on the role of UNEP and of the MEAs. The IGM was expected to come out with concrete proposals for the GMEF as well as to revitalize international environmental governance, in general, and UNEP, in particular.

An agreed starting point for this effort was, to the extent possible, to avoid the creation of new institutions. In view of the large number of institutions that are active in the field of environment, this aspect of the exercise was significant. As a corollary, the IGM was to address issues of overlapping jurisdiction, waste of resources, and 'turf wars', which have marred the performance of many of the existing institutional structures and, in particular, have reduced UNEP's effectiveness.

The IGM discussions confirmed that in the last three decades since the establishment of UNEP in 1972, the number of IEG structures has grown many fold. This growth has raised fundamental concerns about overlap and conflict in both structure and substance. These governance structures have been produced through the state-centric process and work of the UN system, along with several multilateral regimes that are regarded as "treaty bodies" having their own "autonomous,"[27] institutional standing under international law. Cumulatively, they have made the puzzle of IEG more confusing and difficult to grapple with than ever before. The resulting effect has even been dubbed the "organization of the impossible."[28]

September 2001 in Algiers, Algeria; (4) IGM-4 was held from 29 November to 1 December 2001 in Montreal, Canada, after the conclusion of the Intergovernmental Review Meeting on the Implementation of the Global Programme of Action for the Protection of the Marine Environment from Land-Based Activities; (5) IGM-5 took place in New York, United States, on 25 January 2002, prior to the second session of the Preparatory Committee for the WSSD from 28 January to 8 February 2002; and (6) IGM-6 took place on 12 February 2002 in Cartagena, Colombia, immediately prior to the seventh special session of the UNEP Governing Council and the third GMEF on 13–15 February 2002. The IGM also benefited from the Civil Society Consultations, which were held in Nairobi on 22–3 May 2001 as well as the Expert Consultation in Cambridge on 28–9 May 2001. At its seventh special session, the Governing Council/GMEF adopted the report of the IGM. See *Report of the Open-Ended Intergovernmental Group of Ministers or Their Representatives on International Environmental Governance*, 15 February 2002, UNEP GC Decision SS.VII/1, at annex; available at www.unep.org/GoverningBodies.

27 Churchill and Ulfstein have described these as "autonomous" since they have their own built-in law-making process, in addition to the fact that the institutional building is *sui generis*; see Churchill and Ulfstein; n. 3, at 623–59.

28 For details of this argument, see Konrad von Moltke, *The Organization of the Impossible*, and 1(1) Global Envtl. Pol. 23–8 (2001).

Since many international institutions have entered the environmental scene, the role and authority of UNEP as an entity that is expected to set the global environmental agenda has diminished. As such, there has been in the post-Rio period an intensive debate on the "needs and options" concerning IEG. In fact, the complex and thickening web of IEG affects the fate of not only UNEP but also the future effectiveness of other structures and multilateral processes, multilateral agreements, and consultative mechanisms that address environment and environment-related issues.

The substantive role of MEAs, as well as their coordination[29] and coherence[30] remain the second part of the challenge of IEG. Linkage, synergy, and coordination of the work of MEAs were an important focus of the IGM process. On the one hand, these MEAs have set in motion independent international institutional structures to cater to the need for international cooperation on numerous sectoral issues. Among these MEAs, a majority fall within the broad categories of regional seas[31] (marine pollution); biodiversity, such as the Convention on Wetlands of International Importance Especially as Waterfowl Habitat,[32] the Convention for the Protection of the World Cultural and Natural

29 In this respect, it needs to be noted that the task of "coordination" is a part of a process of governance on multilateral environmental issues. It seems the task of coordination of various MEAs has become difficult especially due, *inter alia*, to their different mandates, different membership, their dispersal in various parts of the world, and the location of these MEAs within some "host institution," such as UNEP, the IUCN, UNESCO, and so on). The task of coordination is still defying a clear solution, despite UNEP holding coordination meetings of convention secretariats, and it gets further complicated in the absence of an effective central overarching institution. For a detailed assessment of this issue, see generally IGM, *Proposal for a Systematic Approach to Coordination of Multilateral Environmental Agreements*, 4 July 2001, Doc. UNEP/IGM/2/5. See also UNEP, "Improving International Environmental Governance among Multilateral Environmental Agreements: Negotiable Terms for Further Discussion," 4 July 2001, Doc. UNEP/IGM/2/4.

30 See 16(24) Earth Negotiations Bulletin 6 (18 February 2002).

31 The regional seas conventions are regarded as the "jewel in the crown" for UNEP and represent a regional approach to environmental problems at work. The regional seas program (RSP) has so far covered fourteen regions with 150 coastal states participating, through a network of nine regional conventions, three action plans as well as twenty-seven protocols. The fourteen regions so far covered under the RSP include the Mediterranean, Kuwait region, west and central Africa, southeast Pacific, south Pacific, Red Sea and Gulf of Aden, wider Caribbean, eastern Africa, Black Sea, East Asian Seas, east-central Pacific, northwest Pacific, south Asian Seas, and southwest Atlantic. Out of these fourteen RSPs, nine have full regional conventions, three have action plans, and two have cooperative programs that are under development; see www.unep.org/regionalseas.

32 Convention on Wetlands of International Importance Especially as Waterfowl Habitat, 2 February 1971, in force 21 December 1975; see 22 ILM 698 (1982).

Heritage,[33] the Convention on International Trade in Endangered Species of Wild Fauna and Flora (CITES),[34] the Convention on the Conservation of Migratory Species of Wild Animals (CMS),[35] and the Convention on Biological Diversity (CBD);[36] and chemicals and hazardous wastes-related (International Labour Organization (ILO) conventions on occupational hazards, transboundary movements of hazardous wastes,[37] chemicals in international trade,[38] and persistent organic pollutants[39]) and atmosphere-related instruments (such as ozone depletion,[40] and climate change[41]).[42] The MEAs generally bring into being a separate set of institutional structures, including a conference of parties, subsidiary bodies (on implementation, science and technology, so on), a funding mechanism, and a secretariat. Through the creation of these new and autonomous institutions, each new MEA can contribute to the increasing fragmentation of the environmental agenda. Each of these MEAs comes into being due to different factors and the converging interests of various states. Moreover, they also are dispersed in different countries (and continents) and have differing administrative links to the UN system (such as UNEP, the UN Educational, Scientific, and Cultural Organization, the International Maritime Organization, the ILO, the International Atomic Energy Association, and so on) and other entities such as the World Conservation Union (IUCN).

---

33 Convention for the Protection of the World Cultural and Natural Heritage, 16 November 1972, in force 17 December 1975, 11 ILM 1358 (1972).

34 Convention on International Trade in Endangered Species of Wild Fauna and Flora, 3 March 1973, in force 1 July 1975, 993 UNTS 243 (1973).

35 Convention on the Conservation of Migratory Species of Wild Animals, 23 June 1979, in force 1 November 1983, 19 ILM 15 (1980).

36 Convention on Biological Diversity, 5 June 1992, in force 29 December 1993, 31 ILM 322 (1992).

37 Convention on the Control of Transboundary Movements of Hazardous Wastes and Their Disposal (Basel), 1989, in force 24 May 1992, 28 ILM 657 (1989).

38 Convention on the Prior Informed Consent Procedure for Certain Hazardous Chemicals and Pesticides in International Trade (Rotterdam), 1998, see www.irptc/pic/incs/dipcom/finale.htm#convention.

39 Convention on Persistent Organic Pollutants (Stockholm), 2001, not in force, see www.pops.int.

40 Convention for the Protection of the Ozone Layer (Vienna), 1985, in force 22 September 1988 and the Protocol on Substances that Deplete the Ozone Layer (Montreal), 1987, in force 1 January 1989, 26 ILM 1529 and 1550 (1987).

41 United Nations Framework Convention on Climate Change (Rio de Janeiro), 1992, 31 ILM 849 (1992) and the Protocol to the Convention on Climate Change (Kyoto), 1997, not in force, see www.unfccc.int.

42 IGM, *Multilateral Environmental Agreements: A Summary,* 30 March 2001, UN Doc. UNEP/IGM/1/INF/1.

Parallel to the work of the IGM, UNEP's executive director prepared a report[43] on IEG. It served as a "living document," which took into account the deliberations of the IGM and sought to identify an emerging consensus. The executive director's report basically sought to synthesize the entire gamut of issues concerning IEG and included a section on the "needs and options" that underscored alternatives for strengthening the institutional architecture as well as achieving coordination, synergy, and linkages among the MEAs. A further UNEP document listed a summary of selected papers[44] that contained outlines of various proposals put forward by governments, institutions, and eminent experts. The main thrust of these proposals has been that the existing architecture of IEG needs to be strengthened, in order to better address the emerging environmental challenges as well as to better meet the expectations of the member states.

In the specific case of UNEP, as a principal UN environment program, several elements were flagged in the IGM discussion, such as the need to build the political confidence of states in the effectiveness of UNEP's institutional mandate as well as to provide more reliable funding. Resolving these issues will ultimately hold the key to the emergence of a concrete blueprint to strengthen the existing UNEP. In this context, the various options and proposals put forward were seen to be "building blocks"[45] for the IEG process. These options included providing a new mandate for the UN Trusteeship Council on environment protection and global commons; launching a new world environment organization; enhancing the status of UNEP from a UN program to a UN "specialized agency," or continuing the existing UNEP, but with more secure and predictable funding.[46]

The IGM discussions fed into the three sessions of the GMEF, which began in May 2000. The GMEF, in turn, sought to set an agenda for WSSD, which was scheduled to be held in Johannesburg in 2002. In fact, the GMEF explicitly stated, through the Malmö Ministerial Declaration that

> [t]he 2002 [WSSD] conference should review requirements for a greatly strengthened institutional structure of IEG based on an assessment of future needs for an institutional architecture that has the capacity to effectively address wide-ranging environmental threats in a globalizing

43 IGM, *International Environmental Governance: Report of the Executive Director,* 16 November 2001, UN Doc. UNEP/IGM/4/3.

44 IGM, *Summary of Selected Papers,* 5 April 2001, UN Doc. UNEP/IGM/1/INF/2.

45 IGM, *Report of the Chair,* 27 December 2001, UN Doc. UNEP/IGM/4/6, at 3.

46 See Desai, n. 19, pp. 28–29, para 136–137.

> world. UNEP's role in this regard should be strengthened and its financial base broadened and made more predictable.[47]

By the final session of the IGM in Cartagena in early 2002, the positions of the main negotiating blocs were clear, and many of the ambitions that had launched the IEG process had been fully explored. The Group of 77 (G-77) and China supported "strengthening UNEP within its current mandate" and emphasized that the "proposals on MEAs must respect the autonomy of the COPs."[48] This support can be explained, in part, by the developing countries' long-standing concern that the strengthening of environmental institutions will undermine a development-focused agenda. The idea of enhancing UNEP's status into a specialized agency was not favoured by the G-77 and China, the United States, or Russia.[49] The European Community had earlier called for strengthening the IEG based on the existing structures, in particular, UNEP, but had indicated the need to adapt these structures to the new requirements leading, ultimately, to a world environment organization.[50] The idea of creating a new world environment organization did not, however, find favour with delegations, particularly not with the United States.

The outcomes of the IGM process can be distilled as follows:

- The GMEF has been established as a high-level deliberative forum of environmental ministers with universal membership, raised ministerial awareness, and support for the need to expand participation in UNEP's governance structures, including the possibility of expanding the Governing Council membership beyond its current fifty-eight members. For UNEP, which is a mere "program" and subsidiary organ of the General Assembly, universal membership would be a significant advance.
- UNEP's executive director has begun coordinating meetings of the secretariats of MEAs. The effectiveness of this role generally remains limited to the secretariats for which UNEP acts as a "host." Currently, the executive director has an important say in the functioning of five secretariats (CITES, the CMS, Ozone Layer, the Basel Convention, and the CBD) – citations for these are given above coordinating role is, however, limited even with respect to these secretariats as they are primarily responsible to their own conferences of the parties.

47 See the Malmö Ministerial Declaration n.26, Para 24.

48 See Earth Negotiations Bulletin, n. 31, p. 5.

49 See Earth Negotiations Bulletin, ibid.

50 See Earth Negotiations Bulletin, ibid, p. 6.

- UNEP's financial position has been a matter of great debate, especially following the sharp decline it has witnessed in the past few years. During the IGM process, controversy surrounded how best to make funding of UNEP adequate, stable, and predictable, which will be essential to avoid large gaps between pledges made and actual contributions received from the states. Therefore, the executive director has now mooted the idea of having an 'indicative' scale of assessment by the states. This move will make states accountable for providing the funds committed by them and would impart certainty to the budget of UNEP.
- In view of the proliferation of MEAs, it is essential to have proper coordination and coherence in the work of these MEAs. Various ideas that have been put forward include the co-location of the secretariats to take advantage of cost-effective common administrative facilities and other support services (following the examples set by the co-location of secretariats of the UNFCCC (climate change), desertification,[51] and CMS (migratory species) treaties at the UN premises in Bonn or the co-location of the Secretariats to CITES and the Basel Convention at the Geneva Executive Centre in Geneva). Proposals have also been mooted in regard to the "clustering" of convention secretariats that have close interests or are in the same field (such as biodiversity-related conventions, atmosphere conventions, or chemicals and hazardous wastes-related conventions). An important element that has emerged from the IGM process is the recognized need to enhance the synergies and linkages between MEAs with comparable areas of focus or of a regional character keeping in view their respective mandates. UNEP Governing Council has asked the executive director to continue efforts to enhance policy coherence and synergy among international legal instruments related to environment and sustainable development at both the inter-agency and intergovernmental levels.[52]
- The issue of coordination in the UN system is as old as the UN itself. With the fragmentation of the environmental agenda and the proliferations of institutions working in the field, it has been felt that there is a need to have an effective mechanism for the purpose of coordination. General Assembly Resolution 53/242 brought into being the EMG. The EMG is chaired by the UNEP executive director and follows an issue-management approach. This approach facilitates the establishment of issue-management groups in

---

51 United Nations Convention to Combat Desertification in Those Countries Experiencing Serious Drought and/or Desertification, particularly in Africa (Rio de Janeiro), 33 ILM 1328 (1994).

52 UNEP GC Decision 21/20, 9 February 2001; available at www.unep.org/gc_21/Documents.

> order to address specific issues within a fixed time frame. It is now being felt that the EMG, among others, needs to have senior-level participation by member institutions, transparency in its work, and adequate funding.

In a way, the recommendations of the IGM process set the tone for realizing the goal of a greatly strengthened environmental institutional structure in due course. It seems that both at the intergovernmental level generally, as well as within UNEP in particular, a step-by-step approach are being preferred to radical changes. In view of the cautious approach of most of the states as well as their preference for strengthening existing institutions, a clearer picture may emerge in the next few years. In judging the outcome, one will need to look at the content rather than at the form that finally emerges.

The IEG at the WSSD and the UN General Assembly

The deliberations and recommendations of the IGM process provided a basis for discussion as well as some concrete proposals during the third (25 March to 2 April in New York) and fourth (27 May to 7 June in Bali) meetings of the Commission on Sustainable Development (CSD), which served as the preparatory body for the WSSD.[53] Among the issues that came to the fore at the Johannesburg summit, two stand apart as being significant for their implications for the future of UNEP as well as being a precedent within the UN system. They include a proposal for the universal membership of the Governing Council of UNEP as well as a means for providing stable and predictable funding for the Environment Fund.

In this respect, the Johannesburg Plan of Implementation has called upon the states to:

> fully implement the outcomes of the decision on international environmental governance adopted by the Governing Council of the United Nations Environment Programme at its seventh special session and invite the General Assembly at its fifty-seventh session to consider the important but complex issue of establishing universal membership for the Governing Council/Global Ministerial Environment Forum.[54]

53 See 22(19) Earth Negotiations Bulletin (11 February 2002). See also <www.johannesburgsummt.org/html/prep_process>.

54 WSSD, Plan of Implementation, available at <http://www.johannesburgsummit.org>, at chapter XI (on institutional framework for sustainable development), Para. 140 (d).

As a follow-up to the Plan of Implementation, the General Assembly adopted Resolution 57/251,[55] which invites governments to submit written comments on the universal membership of the UNEP Governing Council. Several of the issues surrounding the IEG debate were considered and discussed at the twenty-second session of the UNEP Governing Council, which coincided with the fourth meeting of the GMEF, which was held in February 2003.[56] The Governing Council has invited the governments to submit their written comments concerning both the subject of universal membership of the Governing Council, especially its legal, political, institutional, financial, and system-wide implications, as well as on the pilot phase for a voluntary indicative scale of assessment for the Environment Fund.[57]

In the post-Johannesburg period, states are facing a crucial litmus test of their sincerity to grapple effectively with the problems afflicting IEG. The test of sincerity was also pointed out by Achim Steiner, the director-general of the IUCN, in his presentation at the IGM's final session in Cartagena:

> The world has become weary and cynical about grand policy statements and new institutions being touted as the answer to our environmental problems. The world today is calling out for delivering on commitments and this has been clearly acknowledged through the IEG process.[58]

This observation, to some extent, underscores the problems that lie at the base of IEG discourse. It is the states that possess the key to deliver on this matter. The IEG process has dealt with a large number of issues during its work spanning six meetings and numerous consultations. However, the states will be

55 General Assembly Resolution 57/251 has required comments from the governments to be sent by 31 October 2003. The executive director of UNEP has been asked to submit a report on the matter for the consideration of the eighth special session of the Governing Council/GMEF in 2004. See UNGA Resolution 57/251, 20 December 2002, Doc. A/RES/57/251; available at <www.un.org>.

56 For a detailed discussion on these issues, see *Report of the Executive Director on "Implementing Outcome of the World Summit on Sustainable Development: International Environmental Governance,"* 22nd Sess., 16 December 2002, Doc. UNEP/GC.22/4.

57 See UNEP Governing Council Decision 22/17, 7 February 2003; available at <www.unep.org/GoverningBodies/GC22/Document/GC22_GMEF_decisions.doc>. See also *Summary of the 22nd Session of the UNEP Governing Council and the Fourth Global Ministerial Environment Forum 3–7 February 2003*, 16(30) Earth Negotiations Bulletin, 1–14 at 9 (10 February 2003). See also <www.unep.org/governingbodies>.

58 Achim Steiner, *Intervention to the Global Ministerial Forum, Cartegena, Columbia, 12–15 February 2002*, 1–5 at 3 (paper on file with the author).

facing a test of their sincerity in regard to the broad outline proposed in the report of the IGM? The deliberations at the Johannesburg summit, true to the nature of UN global conferences, did not provide any clear mandate for this purpose. It appears that it is the UN General Assembly, as demonstrated in Resolution 57/ 251 that will finally need to provide concrete political guidance to solve the jigsaw puzzle of IEG.

UNEP has been the focus of the IEG process. If the main policy options that emerged from the process, including universal membership and a secured funding base, are achieved, the cumulative effect will be profound for the future of UNEP. Providing universal membership, as compared to mere "participation," will bring about more legitimacy as well as more authority to the work of the Governing Council of UNEP. It may also contribute to widening the funding base. Since the Environment Fund is voluntary, states that are currently not among the fifty-eight elected members of the Governing Council may not feel the same obligation to commit funding.

UN General Assembly Resolution 53/242 did not decide to establish a "new organ."[59] However, in institutional terms, a UNEP with a Governing Council of universal membership could formally emerge as a truly global environmental forum that reflects the wishes and expectations of all the members of the United Nations. This reform, coupled with adequate, stable, and predictable funding, could be a prelude to elevating UNEP to the level of a UN "specialized agency." It remains to be seen if the states take such a course of action in the coming years.

Similarly, the challenge for attaining synergy, linkages, and coordination of MEAs will be a long process and will necessitate accommodating the convention secretariats in order to prevent turf wars, as each MEA seeks to guard its sectoral interests. MEA host institutions will also need to minimize control over "administering" secretariats and will need to work out clear relationship agreements to avoid potential conflicts. Similarly, if co-location is to be achieved, some current host countries will have to forgo benefits of hosting a major multilateral institution. Such accommodations will demonstrate that states are indeed willing to address the challenges of some of the global environmental problems widely regarded as 'common concerns of humankind'.

59 The General Assembly Resolution 53/242 in fact stated that an arrangement was needed at a "ministerial level" to provide a forum "in which participants can gather to review important and emerging policy issues in the field of environment ... and that the Governing Council of UNEP should constitute such a forum; see UNEP, *Legal Status of the Global Ministerial Environment Forum*, 1 December 2001, Doc.UNEP/IGM/4/INF/5/Rev.1, at 2.

Conclusion

In the course of the final deliberations of the IGM in Cartagena, several states, including the United States, Russia, as well as the G-77 and China, expressed reservations about the proposals for a world environment organization and even about the conversion of UNEP into a specialized agency. However, if states sincerely wish to realize the ambitious objectives expressed in the 1997 Nairobi Declaration as well as in the 2000 Malmö Ministerial Declaration, they will need to move forward in an *incremental* manner. Some of the steps that have already been taken, including the GMEF, will serve as the "building blocks" of a revitalized IEG. Moreover, when the Governing Council of UNEP meets at the GMEF–a deliberative global environmental forum with universal participation–and UNEP is provided with adequate, stable, and predictable funding, UNEP will gain far greater institutional legitimacy and authority. UNEP will be just one step away from elevation into a specialized agency, which will directly address the crisis of perception as well as legitimacy that UNEP currently faces from UN member states, specialized agencies, and the secretariats of MEAs and non-governmental organizations.

In view of the nature of intergovernmental deliberations so far on IEG, no dramatic results were expected to emerge at the WSSD. The indications of the views of the states, which were confirmed by the twenty-second Governing Council of UNEP, show that at last there seems to be a felt need to confront the core issues in the IEG debate. It seems that the key goal in the immediate future will be to *upgrade* environment protection within the UN system through UNEP and to strengthen its location in Nairobi, which hosts the only major UN institution in the developing world. The process will be evolutionary. Similarly, considering the manner in which MEAs have progressed as sectoral legal restraints upon the behaviour of states, it would be difficult either to dismantle them or to bring them under the control of a single entity. It would be prudent to find better ways to coordinate the work of different MEAs, preferably through the "clustering" approach, while respecting their autonomous legal status. As such, the future direction of IEG will be dictated more by the political will of the states–how far they wish to go in the process, how much they want to translate their international environmental commitments into action, and how willing they are to allow transparency into the functioning of different institutional structures–in order to address the global environmental challenge.

CHAPTER 7

Revitalizing International Environmental Institutions

Introduction

We live in an era of momentous changes and global environmental challenges. It is no doubt a great testing period for the human species on this small planet. History shows that the humans – as one of nature's finest creatures – have time and again shown a remarkable ability to survive within the means dictated by the finite resources of the Earth. But as Gandhi underscored *"Earth provides enough to satisfy everyone's need but not anybody's greed"*. In fact defining and respecting the thresholds of *need* is the principal source of humankind's dilemma. The problem is, we are upsetting the delicate balance which the nature designed for us. The human endeavor to restore that balance is evidenced by the array of measures to prevent the frightening prospect of *ecocide*. The effort has warranted international environmental cooperation cutting across nation-states. International environmental institutions have been employed as tools for the protection of the environment and natural resources. A set of principles and rules of international law have evolved in the process to provide a basis for international environmental regulatory efforts. This paper seeks to focus upon some of the challenges faced by international environmental institutions (IEI) in the creation and working of multilateral environmental regimes. In this context, it seeks to focus on the United Nations Environment

---

* Published in *Indian Journal of International Law*, vol. 40, no. 3, July–Sept. 2000, pp. 455–504.

** The paper is an enlarged and revised version of the author's Seminar organized by Environment and International Law Unit of the Legal Department of the World Bank, Washington D.C. on 15 January 1999. The revised version was presented at the Max-Planck Institute for Comparative Public Law and International Law, Heidelberg on 9 March 1999. The author would like to acknowledge with thanks Niles Blokker, Jutta Brunnee, Rudolf Dolzer, David Freestone, Rahmatullah Khan, Daniel Navid, C.S.R. Murthy and Edith Brown Weiss for their helpful comments on an earlier draft of this paper as well as Thomas Buß, Nitin Desai, Gerhard Löibl, Thomas Mensah, Janos Pasztor, Lee Kimball and Nicholas Robinson for spending time for discussion on the subject. The views expressed are those of the author only.

 | DOI 10.1163/9789004214552_008

Programme (UNEP), as the premier institution established by the United Nations Conference on Human Environment (UNCHE).[1] It analyses the mandate and mixed contribution of this environment programme of the UN. The on-going effort to revitalize UNEP is sought to be addressed, with special reference to the 1998 UN Task Force Report. An effort has also been made to explore possibilities of an expanded structure and a new mandate under the Trusteeship Council.

International Environmental Institutions

It is evident that the growth of both law and institutions keeps pace with the changing needs of the international society. The multidimensional challenges to the human environment have necessitated responses in kind, both in terms of legal instruments as well as effective institutional structures. Mankind's ill-advised drive to conquer nature has brought it to the present brink, as threats to the global environment essentially emanate from human activities in almost every sector.[2] It may not be an exaggeration to say that we may be even facing a serious crisis of survival of the human species "if we are not prepared to reconsider and change our traditional modes of life and production".[3] The notion of environment protection thus tantamount to the protection of the very basis of life on this small planet.

The need for international regulatory efforts has been mooted, in addition to efforts at the national level, especially to address environmental problems having global dimensions. This has, in turn, put to test the traditional rules and principles of international law. It is now well recognized that legal underpinnings[4] of the current drive for the protection of the global environment remain

1 *Report of the U.N. Conference on the Human Environment, U.N. Doc.* A/CONF.48/14(1972). Also see *I.L.M.*, Vol. 11, 1972, p. 1416.

2 For a detailed study on this, see Bharat H. Desai, "Threats to the World Eco-system: A Role for the Social Scientists", *Social Science & Medicine* (Oxford), Vol. 35, No. 4, pp. 589–596. Also see, ibid, "Destroying the Global Environment", *International Perspectives* (Ottawa), Nov./Dec. 1986, pp. 27–29.

3 Lothar Gundling, "Environment, International Protection" in Rudolf Bernhardt(Ed.), *Encyclopedia of Public International Law, Vol. 2* (Amsterdam: North-Holland, 1995), p. 96.

4 Brownlie's leading textbook on international law does not consider the need for a separate branch to address environmental problems and did not have, till recently, even a separate section on the subject. For the first time, in the 1998 (fifth) edition of the book Brownlie has devoted just a six-page section (chapter XIII) entitled: 'Legal Aspects of the Protection of the Environment'. As a 'generalist' in this context, Brownlie has argued that: "The fact is

embedded in the general principles of international law. Environmental concerns, especially in the last quarter of this century, have forced the international community move towards an increasingly complex web of international legal as well as institutional structures. It has contributed not only to the study of international environmental law as a separate branch[5] of international law but also to the emergence of specialized international environmental institutions, and to the gradual 'greening' of the other multilateral institutions. We have also witnessed a plethora of multilateral environmental agreements (MEAs) on a wide range of environmental issues. In spite of all this, the UNEP's first (1997) *Global Environment Outlook* (GEO) report, observed that a "sense of urgency"[6] is still lacking at international level. The *GEO 2000* has again warned that continuation of grave imbalances in productivity and the distribution of goods and services due to "unsustainable progression of extremes of wealth and poverty"[7] pose a grave threat to the global environment.

Since the formation of the UN, there has been a remarkable proliferation in the number of 'new' states on the international scene. This has put its own pressure in terms of addressing the problems of the burgeoning humanity. The economic and social field, of which environment forms part, is one of the most hard pressed. Veritable institutional forms have provided useful forums for international cooperation. The growth of functional international organizations (specialized agencies), functional commissions, and regional economic commissions as well as other programmes, as a part of the UN system,[8] provide

---

environmental concerns have for long been reflected in general international law and the relevant categories include the law of the sea, state responsibility, space law, the legal regime of Antarctica, and the non-navigational uses of international watercourses"; see Ian Brownlie, *Principles of Public International Law*, 5th edition (Oxford: Clarendon Press, 1998), pp. 283–288 at 283.

5 In the past decade or so, teaching as well as research in the field of International Environmental Law has grown rapidly. Views, however, differ on what forms part of this nascent branch of international law. Different writers have sought to give different treatment in their writings on the subject. See, generally: Alexander C. Kiss and Dinah Shelton, *International Environmental Law* (New York: Transnational, 1991) and 1994 Supplement; Patricia W.Birnie and Alan E.Boyle, *International Law & the Environment* (Oxford: Clarendon Press, 1992) and Philippe Sands, *Principles of International Environmental Law, Vol. 1* (Manchester: Manchester Uni. Press, 1995); Ved P. Nanda, *International Environmental Law & Policy* (New York: Transnational, 1995).

6 United Nations Environment Programme (UNEP), *Global Environment Outlook* (Oxford: Oxford Uni. Press, 1997), p. 3.

7 UNEP, *Global Environment Outlook 2000* (Nairobi: UNEP, 2000), *Overview*, p. 2.

8 The Economic and Social Council (ECOSOC) has been assigned the task of bringing various *functional* organizations, established under intergovernmental agreements, into

a living testimony to the craving for institutional forms of international cooperation.

Most of the major institutional responses have understandably emerged within the UN system. The specialized agencies, of course, did not have environment protection as a part of their original mandate. Their responses in this context, therefore, show remarkable adaptability to the *greening* process. Before the advent of the specialized environmental institutions such as UNEP, the Commission on Sustainable Development (CSD), the Inter-Agency Committee on Sustainable Development (IACSD) and the Global Environment Facility (GEF), it is the specialized agencies which played a role, to some extent, on environmental issues as part of their respective functional mandates. Among the specialized environmental institutions, UNEP has since the Stockholm Conference, been UN's conscience keeper in the field. However, UNEP's institutional space has been gradually shrinking in view of emergence of other actors on the scene.

The growth in the number of MEAs has contributed to a new set of institutional forms such as conference of parties, subsidiary bodies, financial mechanisms and secretariats. The legal regime under various MEAs revolves around these institutional forms. Furthermore, a number of multilateral development banks, including the World Bank, also adopted the New York Declaration (1980),[9] to accommodate environmental concerns in their lending operations. Some other intergovernmental (IGO) and non-governmental (NGO) actors, such as the World Conservation Union (IUCN) and the World Wide Fund for Nature (WWF), have also made a remarkable contribution in the field.

---

relationship with the UN, under Article 63 of the Charter. There are 18 such specialized international organizations [ILO, FAO, UNESCO, WHO, IBRD, IDA, IFC, MIGA, IMF, ICAO, UPU, ITU, WMO, IMO, WIPO, IFAD, UNIDO and WTO having cooperative arrangements and practices]. The ECOSOC also has power to establish *subsidiary* organs [Article 7(2) and 72] for the discharge of its functions. As such the ECOSOC has set up so far 8 functional commissions and 5 regional economic commissions. For further details of the UN's institutional structure see UN, *Basic Facts About the United Nations* (New York: UN, 1998), pp. 22–23.

9 The New York Declaration was signed by the Presidents of the six multilateral development banks, namely the African Development Banks, the Arab Bank for Economic Development in Africa, the Asian Development Bank, the Caribbean Development Bank, the Inter-American Development Bank and the World Bank on 1 February 1980. They were joined by heads of the Commission of the European Communities, the Organization of American States, the United Nations Development Programme and the United Nations Environment Programme; see *Declaration of Environmental Policies and Procedures Relating to Economic Development*, New York, 1 February 1980, *reproduced* in Philippe Le Prestre, *The World Bank and the Environmental Challenge* (Selinsgrove: Susquehanna Univ. Press, 1989), Appendix A, pp. 208–209.

The main thrust of intergovernmental environmental cooperation, however, stems from the precincts of the UN system. Interestingly, the UN General Assembly has from time to time taken initiatives in the field of international environmental cooperation, primarily through the technique of 'global conferencing'. The establishment of both UNEP as well as CSD followed the two landmark global conferences (UNCHE and UNCED) convened by the Assembly. The Assembly has over the years emerged as a primary force in international environmental institution-building.

The emergence of IEIs as a specialized set of structures has been, in a sense, a logical corollary to the growth of international environmental law. In fact the organic linkage between "substantive law and institutions"[10] in this rapidly growing field has been regarded as very close as compared to any other field of international law. It has been often almost taken for granted that an MEA needs to be equipped with a corresponding institution. Thus, generally speaking, IEIs have been the tools employed to translate goals of MEAs into action. Consequently, institutionalized international environmental cooperation includes entities like intergovernmental commissions, intergovernmental panels or negotiating committees, conference of parties and intergovernmental organizations. They operate both within the United Nations system and outside it. The most notable IEI is United Nations Environment Programme. A brief look at the emergence as well as contribution of this premier IEI will be useful in understanding the current debate about its reform and revitalization.

United Nations Environment Programme

Mandate and Role

The UNEP may be regarded as having *locus classicus* in the field of institutionalized international environmental cooperation. It is the product of the UNCHE (Stockholm, 1972), which was attended by 113 nations. Many of the states had doubts about that maiden global effort to address international environmental problems. Nonetheless the UNEP became the first major UN environmental institution, overruling proposals to bypass the United Nations in favor of an environmental agency run by the developed countries of the

10 See the remarks by the Chair Said Mahmoudi in the Panel Discussion on "Environment: New Institutional Challenges", *American Society of International Law Proceedings* (90th Annual Meeting), Vol. 90, 1996, p. 488.

world.[11] The birth of the UNEP at the Stockholm Conference was partly in keeping with the realization that "there are problems in using the UN for environmental action, the problems in bypassing it in favor of other institutions would be more serious still".[12]

Although conceived as the centre-piece of the UN system for the protection of the global environment, UNEP was born as just a *programme,*[13] a subsidiary organ of the UN General Assembly. Though its legal status is not that of an independent international organization, it does not seem to be deprived of "international legal personality since it is required to fulfill certain tasks on the international plane".[14] This appears to be in consonance with the Advisory Opinion of the International Court of Justice in the *Reparations*[15] case. In the

11 For example, George F. Keenan disfavored the UN forum especially since it works on the basis of "universal or near-universal, governmental consensus" and favored initiative being taken by a small group of advanced nations. He put forward rationale for the setting up of an institution called International Environmental Agency by such a small group of leading industrial and maritime countries as: „It is they whose economies produce, in the main, the problem of pollution. It is they, again, who have the means to correct it. It is they, finally, who have the scientific and other resources to analyze the problem and to identify the most promising lines of solution. The devastation of the environment is primarily, though not exclusively, a function of advanced industrial and urban society. The correction of it is primarily a problem for the advanced nations"; see George F. Keenan, "To Prevent a World Wasteland: A Proposal", *Foreign Affairs*, Vol. 48, No.3, April 1970, pp. 401–413 at 410.

12 Richard N. Gardner, "The Role of the UN in Environmental Problems", *International Organization*, Vol. 26, No.2, 1972, p. 238.

13 It was established by virtue of the General Assembly's Resolution 2997 (XXVII) of 15 December 1972, which set out the institutional and financial arrangements for launching the UNEP. Its establishment was again reaffirmed by the General Assembly Resolution 32/112 of 16 December 1976. The UNEP comprises the institutional machinery of the Governing Council (now 58 members) of the United Nations Environment Programme, the Environment Secretariat headed by the Executive Director of the Programme, the Environment Fund and the Environment Coordination Board (now disbanded).

14 Patricia W. Birnie and Alan E. Boyle, *International Law and the Environment* (Oxford: Clarendon Press, 1992), p. 35.

15 In this landmark Opinion, the International Court of Justice (ICJ), with reference to the legal competence of the United Nations, observed: "In the opinion of the Court, the Organization was intended to exercise and enjoy, and is in fact exercising and enjoying, functions and rights which can only be explained on the basis of the possession of a large measure of international personality and the capacity to operate upon an international plane. It is at present the supreme type of international organization, and it could not carry out the intentions of its founders if it was devoid of international personality. It must be acknowledged that its Members, by entrusting certain functions to it, with the

preparatory stage, there was considerable caution as regards creation of a new set of international institutions. In fact, the UN Secretary-General's Report to the Preparatory Committee, did underscore this:

(a) Any organizational arrangement should be based first on agreement about what needs to be done. Until this is reached, no firm decision can be made on the ways and means to be adopted.
(b) All functions that can best be performed by existing organizations should be assigned to those organizations, international and national, most capable of carrying them out effectively. *No unnecessary new machinery should be created.*

....

(h) The United Nations should be the principal centre for international environmental co-operation.
(i) The organization of environmental activities within the United Nations should be so designed as to strengthen and reinforce the entire United Nations system (emphasis added).[16]

Therefore, the institutional structure set up by the UNCHE was the result of a clear felt need within the UN system to have an exclusive entity to cater to the requirement for international environmental cooperation. UNEP was in fact designed to perform a very vital catalytic role in the entire process. This new quasi-autonomous entity of Environment Secretariat within the UN and headed by the Executive Director, was carved out to serve as a *focal point for environmental action and co-ordination within the United Nations system.*[17] Since it was decided to be a *programme* within the UN, the enabling General Assembly Resolution did not carry the name of the new entity as its title, which was described as "Institutional and financial arrangements for international environmental co-operation". Its 58 member Governing Council[18] has been given the mandate which includes the following primary functions:

---

attendant duties and responsibilities, have clothed it with the competence required to enable those functions to be effectively discharged"; see *ICJ Reports* (1949), p. 179.

16 See *Report of the Secretary-General to the Third Session of the Preparatory Committee*, U.N.Doc.A/CONF.48/PC.11, 30 July 1971, p. 222.

17 See *Report of the UNCHE*, n.1, Ch.III, part II. Also see the General Assembly Resolution *A/RES/2997(XXVII)* of 15 December 1972, part II, p. 3 in *United Nations General Assembly Official Records*, 26th Session, Supp. No.30, p. 43.

18 The 58 members of the UNEP Governing Council are to be elected by the UN General Assembly, for a period of three years on the following basis: (a) sixteen seats for African states; (b) thirteen seats for Asian states; (c) six seats for Eastern European states; (d) ten

(a) To promote international co-operation in the field of the environment and to recommend, as appropriate, policies to this end;
(b) To provide general policy guidance for the direction and co-ordination of environmental programmes within the United Nations system[19];

Therefore, the Stockholm mandate required UNEP to act as a *catalyst* of activities and programmes within the UN system and promote international environmental co-operation, rather than "initiating or mandating environmental programmes on its own account".[20] Since it is one of the UN's own programmes, it is responsible to and reports to the General Assembly through the Economic and Social Council.[21]

Contribution

The UN system had, even prior to the setting up of UNEP, several specialized and related agencies which were dealing with environment-related functions in their own functional jurisdictions. This included agencies such as Food and Agriculture Organization (FAO), International Labor Organization (ILO), United Nations Educational, Scientific and Cultural Organization (UNESCO), World Bank (IBRD) World Health Organization (WHO), World Meteorological Organization (WMO), International Maritime Organization (IMO) and International Atomic Energy Agency (IAEA). In spite of it, the fact that a specialized environmental programme was created, underscored the need for a hub or focal point within the UN system. In fact it has been regarded, in the words of the UN Secretary-General, as the "environmental conscience of the United Nations".[22] It was in a way reflection of the consensus that:

seats for Latin American states; (e) thirteen seats for Western European and other states; see UNGA Res.2997, Part I, para 1.

19 *Ibid*, Part I, para 2 (a) and (b).

20 Patricia W. Birnie and Alan E. Boyle, *International Law and the Environment* (Oxford: Clarendon Press, 1992), p. 42.

21 The enabling resolution requires that the Governing Council shall report annually to the General Assembly through the Economic and Social Council, which will transmit to the Assembly such comments on the report as it may deem necessary, particularly with regard to questions of co-ordination and to the relationship of environmental policies and programmes within the United Nations system to overall economic and social policies and priorities; see UNGA Res.2997, Part I, para 3.

22 Kofi A. Annan, "An Indispensable Contribution", *Our Planet*, Vol. 9, No.1, 1997, p. 4

> [T]he key international environmental institutions should be intergovernmental in character. Governments are not prepared to surrender authority to a supranational agency that could bind them to act against their will. Governments may, however, be willing to delegate authority to international entities to act in carefully prescribed areas under norms and policies already agreed upon…the central machinery for environmental cooperation should be within the framework of the United Nations…as the central world institution for global cooperation.[23]

Given these goals and operational constraints, UNEP seems to have attained considerable success in galvanizing action on international environmental concerns, and in laying down the *threshold* limits of environmental behavior. As a follow-up to the Stockholm Declaration and the Action Plan,[24] the Governing Council asked the Executive Director, in its very first session (1973) to stimulate international and regional agreements for the control of all forms of pollution of the marine environment with a special focus on particular bodies of water.[25] One of the important achievements, regarded as a 'jewel in the crown', of the UNEP has been the Regional Seas Programme (RSP),[26] which has facilitated crystallization of agreements as well as regional action plans. The RSP has expanded to cover 14 regions (with 150 of the coastal states

23 Gardner, n.12, pp. 244–245.

24 Principle 7 of the Stockholm Declaration provides: "States were to take all possible steps to prevent pollution of the seas by substances that were liable to create hazards to human health, to harm living resources and marine life, to damage amenities or to interfere with other legitimate uses of the sea"; see *Yearbook of the United Nations*, vol. 26, 1972, p. 320. Also see the Action Plan for the Human Environment, Recommendations 86–94, *ILM*, vol. XI, 1972, pp. 1454–1457.

25 The Governing Council Decision 1(I), 22 June 1973; see UN *General Assembly Official Records* (GAOR), vol. 28, 1973, Supp.25 (A/9025), p. 42. Also see Decision 8 (II), 21 March 1974; *GAOR*, vol. 29, Supp.25 (A/9625), p. 63.

26 The Regional Seas Programme (RSP) has been regarded as one of the greatest achievements of UNEP. The RSP was launched in 1974. The first of the RSP was developed in the Mediterranean with an Action Plan (1975), followed by a Convention (1976). Following success of the RSP for the Mediterranean region, RSP for other regions were developed. The UNEP Governing council has, in fact, consistently endorsed a regional approach to the control of marine pollution, management of marine and coastal resources and development of Action Plans for the purpose at the regional level. From the first Action adopted in the Mediterranean (1975), to the most recent for the North-West Pacific (2000), the RSP have multiplied to cover the marine environment of more than 150 of the world's coastal countries.

participating) with 9 conventions and 3 action plans[27] as well as their 27 protocols.[28] Out of these, UNEP provides secretariat services for 8 RSPs[29] and 1 RSP (Black Sea) has an independent secretariat. Moreover, 5 regional

---

27 The 14 regions so far covered include the Mediterranean, Kuwait region, West and Central Africa, South-East Pacific, South Pacific, Red Sea and Gulf of Aden, Wider Caribbean, Eastern Africa, Black Sea, East Asian Seas, East-Central Pacific, North-West Pacific, South Asian Seas and South-West Atlantic. Out of these 14 RSPs, 9 have full regional conventions, 3 have Action Plans and 2 cooperative programmes are under development. The 9 respective main regional conventions are: 1.The Barcelona Convention for the Protection of the Mediterranean Sea Against Pollution (1976, as amended in 1995); 2.The Kuwait Convention for Cooperation on the Protection of the Marine Environment from Pollution (1978); 3.The Abidjan Convention for Cooperation in the Protection and Development of the Marine and Coastal Environment of the West and Central African Region (1981); 4.The Lima Convention for the Protection of the Marine Environment and Coastal Areas of the Southeast Pacific (1981). Also Agreement on Regional Cooperation in Combating Pollution of the South-East Pacific by Hydrocarbons or Other Harmful Substances in Case of Emergency (1981); 5.The Noumea Convention for the Protection of Natural Resources and Environment of the South Pacific Region (1986); 6. The Jeddah Regional Convention for the Conservation of the Red Sea and Gulf of Aden Environment (1982); 7.The Cartagena Convention for the Protection and Development of the Marine Environment of the Wider Caribbean Region (1983); 8.The Nairobi Convention for the Protection, Management and Development of the Marine and Coastal Environment of the Eastern African Region (1985) and 9.The Bucharest Convention on the Protection of the Black Sea Against Pollution (1992). Three RSPs having only Action Plans are: 1. Action Plan for the Protection and Development of the Marine Environment and Coastal Areas of the East Asian Seas Region 2. Action Plan for the Protection and Management of the Marine and Coastal Environment of the South Asian Seas Region 3. Action Plan for the Protection, Management and Development of the Marine and Coastal Environment of the Northwest Pacific Region. The RSPs for the protection and management of the marine and coastal environment in 2 regions – Southwest Atlantic and East-Central Pacific- are under development. Three more partner programmes are: 1.Convention on the Protection of the Marine Environment of the Baltic Sea Area (Helsinki), signed 1974 (in force 1980) and revised 1992 (in force 2000) 2. The Convention for the Protection of the Marine Environment of the North-East Atlantic (Oslo and Paris), signed 1974. Both the conventions were revised and combined into OSPAR Convention, 1992 (in force 1998) and 3. The Arctic Ministers on the Arctic Environmental Protection Strategy (AEPS) established the Working Group on Protection of the Arctic Marine Environment (PAME) in Nuuk (Greenland), September 1993. The Arctic Council member countries are: Canada, Denmark, Finland, Iceland, Norway, Russia, Sweden and the USA See *http://www.unep.ch./seas/main/lconlist.html*

28 The 27 protocols so far adopted for RSPs are: Mediterranean (6), Kuwait Region (4), West and central Africa (1), South-East Pacific (5), Red Sea and Gulf of Aden (1), Wider Caribbean (3), Eastern Africa (2), South Pacific (2) and Black Sea (3). *See http:://www.unep .ch/seas/main/hconlist.html* . Also see Elizabeth Maruma Mrema, "The Role of

organizations[30] have come into being to implement and administer their respective RSPs. The Governing Council of UNEP has now endorsed the establishment of regional seas programme for the East Central Pacific region.[31] In July 1999, the second Global Meeting of Regional Seas Conventions and Action Plans was convened by UNEP,[32] which called for close linkage between RSP and the newly established Global Programme of Action for the Protection of the Marine Environment from Land-based Activities (GPA).[33]

International Organizations in the Development of International Environmental Law: The Case of UNEP", paper presented at the International Conference titled "Towards an Effective Role of Law in the UAE Environment Protection and Development", 2–4 May 1999 (on file with the author). Also see Donald Kaniaru, "UNEP's Development and Implementation of Environmental Law", paper presented at Southeast Asian Regional Symposium on the Judiciary and Law in the Field of sustainable Development, Manila, 4–7 March 1999 (on file with the author).

29 The 8 RSPs for which UNEP currently provides permanent/interim secretariat services are: Mediterranean Action Plan; West and Central African Region; Caribbean Environment Programme; Eastern African Region, East Asian Seas; Northwest Pacific Region; Southwest Atlantic Region and East-Central Pacific.

30 These regional organizations for RSPs are: 1.Regional Organization for the Protection of the Marine Environment (ROMPE). It comprises Bahrain, Iran, Iraq, Kuwait, Oman, Qatar, Saudi Arabia and United Arab Emirates. 2. Programme of Environment for the Red Sea and the Gulf of Eden (PERSGA). It comprises Egypt, Jordan, Palestine, Saudi Arabia, Somalia, Sudan and Yemem. 3. Permanenet Commission of the South Pacific (CPPS). It comprises Chile, Colombia, Ecuador, Panama and Peru. 4. South Pacific Regional Environment Programme (SPREP). Its members are Australia, Cook Islands, Federated states of Micronesia, Fiji, France, Kiribati, Marshall Islands, Nauru, New Zealand, Niue, Palau, Papua New Guinea, Solomon Islands, Tonga, Tuvalu, United Kingdom, United States of America, Vanuatu and Western Samoa. 5. South Asian Cooperative Environment Programme (SACEP). It comprises Bangladesh, India, Maldives, Pakistan and Sri Lanka. See *http://www.unep.ch/earthw/Pdepwat.htm*

31 The twentieth session of the Governing Council in fact invited the Governments of Costa Rica, El Salvador, Guatemala, Honduras, Mexico, Nicaragua and Panama to endorse the proposed Meeting of High-Level Government-Designated Experts to Review the Proposals for a Convention and Plan of Action for the Protection of the Marine and Coastal Environment of the East Central Pacific region; see UNEP GC Decision 20/20 of 4 February 1999 at *http://www.unep.org/Documents.*

32 See "A regional seas renaissance" in UNEP, *Annual Report 1999* (Nairobi: UNEP, 1999), p. 33.

33 The Global Programme of Action was officially launched in November 1995 by 108 countries and the European Union at an intergovernmental conference in Washington D.C. to preserve and protect the marine environment from harmful effects of land-based activities. It also invited UNEP to act as the GPA Secretariat. In 1996, the GPA Implementation Plan was presented to the Commission on Sustainable Development (CSD-4) and the

UNEP has also effectively translated its catalyst role into action through an ambitious Montevideo Programme I (1981) and II (1993).[34] The Governing Council of UNEP has called for convening a meeting of senior government experts in environmental law in the year 2000, for the "preparation of a new programme for the development and periodic review of environmental law".[35] Under this ambitious programme, UNEP has contributed directly or indirectly to the development of several multilateral environmental agreements and produced a body of *soft law*[36] consisting of principles, standards and guidelines, as well as contributed in the development of environmental law and policy at the national level. Some of the important MEAs which were negotiated under auspices of UNEP were the Vienna Convention (1985) and Montreal Protocol for the Protection of the Ozone Layer (1987)[37] and the Basel Convention on the

---

General Assembly adopted resolution51/189 on the institutional arrangements for the implementation of the GPA. At the 19th Session of UNEP Governing Council decision 19/14 was adopted on global and regional GPA implementation, which led to establishment and operationalization of the UNEP/GPA Coordination Office in the Hague, the Netherlands; see *http://www.gpa.unep.org/about/default.htm.*

34 See *Report of the Ad Hoc Meeting of Senior Government Officials Experts in Environmental Law*, UNEP/GC 10/5/Add.2, Annex, Ch.11 (1981) and UNEP, *Programme for the Development and Periodic Review of Environmental Law for the 1990s* (Nairobi, June 1993), pp. 1–17. Also see *Yearbook of the United Nations*, vol. 36, 1982, p. 1030 and *Yearbook of the United Nations*, vol. 47, 1993, pp. 820–21.

35 UNEP GC Decision 20/3 of 3 February 1999 on "Programme for the Development and Periodic Review of Environmental Law beyond the year 2000". This Decision has authorized the Executive Director of UNEP to use the current Programme (1993) as "strategic guidance" for the work of UNEP in the field of environmental law until a new programme is adopted by the Council; see 20th Governing Council Decisions at *http://www.unep.org/Documents.*

36 These non-binding or soft instruments have been adopted by the UNEP GC or intergovernmental meetings convened by UNEP. They include: Principles of Conduct in the Field of the environment for the Guidance of States in the Conservation and Harmonious Utilization of Natural Resources Shared by Two or More States; Conclusions of the Study of Legal Aspects concerning the Environment Related to Offshore Mining and Drilling within the Limits of National Jurisdiction; Montreal Guidelines for the Protection of the Marine Environment Against Pollution from Land-Based Sources; Cairo Guidelines and Principles for the Environmentally Sound Management of Hazardous Wastes; Goals and Principles of Environmental Impact Assessment; London Guidelines for the Exchange of Information on Chemicals in International Trade; Code of Ethics on the International Trade in Chemicals; Global Programme of Action for the Protection of the Marine Environment from Land-Based Activities; International Technical Guidelines for Safety in Biotechnology.

37 Convention for the Protection of the Ozone Layer (Vienna), 1985. It came into force on 22 September 1988. The Protocol on Substances that Deplete the Ozone Layer (Montreal),

Control of Transboundary Movements of Hazardous Wastes and their Disposal (1989),[38] Convention on Biological Diversity (1992)[39] and the recent Rotterdam Convention on Prior Informed Consent Procedure(PIC) for Certain Hazardous Chemicals and Pesticides in International Trade (1998, jointly with FAO).[40] Both UNEP and Food and Agriculture Organization (FAO), pending final decision by the COP of the Convention, are to jointly provide an interim secretariat[41] facility for the purpose. Negotiations are also under way to have an International Legally Binding Instrument for Implementing International Action on Certain Persistent Organic Pollutants (POPs).[42] The aim has been to reach an agreement in the year 2000 on a treaty to reduce and/or eliminate 12 specific POPs and to establish scientific criteria and a process for identifying additional pollutants for future international action. Moreover, UNEP provided substantive support and expertise for the development of UN Framework Convention on Climate Change (1992)[43] and UN Convention to Combat

---

1987. It came into force on 1 January 1989; see *I.L.M.*, Vol. 26, 1987, pp. 1529 and 1550 respectively. The UNEP headquarters in Nairobi houses the Secretariat of the Ozone Regime.

38 Convention on the Control of Transboundary Movement of Hazardous Wastes and Their Disposal (Basel), 1989. It came in to force on 24 May 1992; see *I.L.M.*, Vol. 28, 1989, p. 657.

39 Convention on Biological Diversity (Rio de Janeiro), 1992. It came into force on 29 December 1993; see *I.L.M.*, Vol. 31, 1992, p. 822.

40 The Convention on the Prior Informed Consent Procedure for Certain Hazardous Chemicals and Pesticides in International Trade was adopted at Rotterdam on 10 September 1998. It seeks to curtail the $1.5 trillion trade in hazardous pesticides and chemicals; see UNEP, *Annual Report 1998* (Nairobi: UNEP, 1998), p. 7 and 21. For text of the Rotterdam PIC Convention see UNEP/FAO/PIC/CONF.5 of 17 September 1998. Also see *http://www.irptc/pic/incs/dipcom/finale.htm#convention.*

41 See UNEP GC Decision SS.V/5 of 22 May 1998 as well as Decision 20/22 of 4 February 1999; available at *www.unep.org/Documents.*

42 The first session of the Intergovernmental Negotiating Committee (INC) for an international legally binding instrument for implementing international action on certain persistent organic pollutants (POPs) took place in Montreal in June 1998. At the INC-3 in Geneva, during 6–11 September 1999, an agreement was reached on proposals favoring the elimination of intentionally produced POPs. While the pesticides *aldrin, endrin* and *toxaphene* are slated for elimination without any exemptions, other POPs like *chlordane, dieldrin, heptachlor, mirex* and *hexachlorobenzene* are to be eliminated with country-specific exemptions. UNEP Secretariat has played an important role for the environmental management of chemicals as well as negotiations on a convention on POPs. The fourth round of negotiations took place in Bonn, during 20–25 March 2000, when a draft text of the instrument was prepared; see UNEP/POPS/INC.4/5, 25 March 2000. This may be given a final shape at INC5, tentatively scheduled to be held in November 2000 in South Africa.

43 See *International Legal Materials* (ILM), vol. 31, 1992, p. 849.

Desertification in those Countries Experiencing Serious Drought and/or Desertification, particularly in Africa (1994).[44] It has also provided assistance to the African governments in the development of Harare Agreement on the Action Plan for the Environmentally Sound Management of the Common Zambezi River System (1987)[45] and Lusaka Agreement on Cooperative Enforcement Operations Directed at Illegal Trade in Wild Fauna and Fauna (1994).[46] As a sequel to the process for ensuring implementation of CBD and Basel Convention, UNEP has helped in the adoption of Basel Protocol on Liability and Compensation for Damage Resulting from Transboundary Movements of Hazardous Wastes and their Disposal (1999)[47] as well as Cartagena Protocol on Biosafety (1999)[48] respectively. UNEP even provides secretariat[49] services for five of the global conventions, namely Convention on

44 See *ILM*, vol. 33, 1994, p. 1328.

45 See *ILM*, vol. 27, 1987, p. 1109.

46 The Lusaka Agreement has made stricter provisions by strengthening the implementation of the CITES in Eastern and Southern African countries. For the text of the agreement see UNEP, *Handbook of Environmental Law*, pp. 156–63, quoted in Elisabeth M. Mrema, n. 28, p. 36.

47 The Basel Protocol on Liability and Compensation for Damage resulting from Transboundary Movements of Hazardous Wastes and Their Disposal was adopted by the Fifth Conference of Parties meeting of the Basel Convention. For text of the Protocol see Report of the Conference of the Parties to the Basel Convention, Fifth Meeting, 6–10 December 1999; UNEP/CHW.5/29, 10 December 1999, Annex III, pp. 88–111.

48 The Protocol on Biosafety to the Convention on Biological Diversity was adopted by the First Extraordinary Meeting of the Conference of the Parties to the Convention on Biological Diversity, Cartagena, 22–24 February 1999 and Montreal 24–29 January 2000. See Decision EM-I/3 as well as Annex in UNEP/CBD/ExCOP/1/3, 20 February 2000 at pp. 38 and pp. 42–65. The Protocol opened for signature at UN Office at Nairobi during the Fifth Meeting of the Conference of the Parties from 15 May to 26 May 2000.

49 Whenever an international institution accepts responsibility for providing secretariat facilities for an international convention, their relationship is governed by relevant provisions of the convention. Essentially, a convention secretariat is a body of the convention created to implement the functions assigned to it by the convention and is subject to the authority of the Conference of Parties (COP). As UNEP is a subsidiary body of the UN General Assembly, "it is obliged to abide by the preconceived rules and regulations of the UN in its administration, including the administration of the Convention secretariats. By requesting UNEP to provide these services the Conventions acknowledge this, and in fact rely on the established structure of administration provided by the UN system"; see UNEP, "The Relationship Between the Executive Director of UNEP and the Conventions Regarding the administration of their Secretariats", Doc. UNEP/DEP/Coord.4/3/COR.1, 4 January 1996, pp. 1–7 at 3.

International Trade in Endangered Species (CITES),[50] Convention on the Conservation of Migratory Species of Wild Animals (CMS),[51] Ozone, Basel and CBD. Another remarkable work, which has not much come into limelight, is administration of 'trust funds'. At the end of December 1999, UNEP administered 92 trust funds,[52] out of which 73 directly supported the UNEP programme of work and other 19 covered trust funds for conventions, protocols, regional seas action plans.

Dilution of Authority

It has been time and again emphasized, at least within the UN system, that the UNEP is the fulcrum of the world organization's international environmental actions. It seems that from its inception this Programme was set on the course of addressing ambitious goals, without a commensurate structure or stature or financing (given *voluntary* nature of the Environment Fund). The primary task of the Programme was designed to coordinate and to promote action rather than to initiate concrete operations by itself. However, it did generate a lot of expectations but "anyone who expected that UNEP would itself solve all the problems of the environment, or fund others for the job, was bound to be disappointed".[53]

50 Convention on International Trade in Endangered Species of Wild Fauna and Fauna, Washington, 3 March 1973. It came into force on 1 July 1975; see *ILM*, vol. 12, 1973, p. 1085.

51 Convention on the Conservation of Migratory Species of Wild Animals, Bonn, 23 June 1979. It came into force on 1 November 1983; see *ILM*, vol. 19, 1980, p. 15

52 UNEP managed 43 trust funds in 1992, which rose to 81 in 1998 and 92 in 1999. The total expenditure from trust funds in 1998–99 biennium was $ 329.17 million. Out of this, however, the Multilateral Fund alone accounted for $ 202.23 million (70%) and GEF's share was $ 26.50 million. The detailed break-up of the 86 UNEP administered trust funds in 1998–99 was: A. Direct Support to UNEP (68): General Trust Funds (17), Technical Cooperation Trust Funds: General (28), Technical Cooperation Trust Funds: Personnel (23); B. Conventions/Protocols/Regional Seas Programmes (15): General Trust Funds (12), Technical Cooperation Trust Funds: General (1), Technical Cooperation Trust Funds: Personnel (2); C. Special Accounts and Trust Funds (3): Multilateral Fund for the Montreal Protocol (1), UN International Partnership Trust Fund (1), GEF (1); see UNEP, *Report of the Executive Director on Activities of the United Nations Environment Programme* for the Sixth Special Session of the Governing Council, Malmö, 29–31 May 2000, Doc. UNEP/GCSS.VI/6 of 11 April 2000, pp. 45 and 63.

53 UNEP, *UNEP: What It Is, What It Does. How It Works*, quoted in P.M.Dupuy, "United Nations Environment Programme" in Rudolf Bernhardt (Ed.), *Encyclopedia of Public International Law* (Amsterdam: North-Holland, 1983), p. 321.

The birth of UNEP was a product of special circumstances of the 1972 UNCHE. It emerged in the midst of deep suspicion among most of the participants in the Stockholm Conference. If the developing countries were concerned about any international action being used to restrict their legitimate developmental goals, the industrialized countries were not in favor of a powerful environmental watchdog. This was one of the reasons why no teeth were given to the nascent body. It was also left to be just one of the UN's programmes, having been denied the status of a specialized environmental agency on the specious ground that such an "agency for the environment would result in duplication of activities and would compound already serious problems of coordination".[54] It is, however, perceived that UNEP "lacks teeth and has no executive authority".[55] As a result, it is felt that:

> [I]ts creation was at best somewhat half-hearted-reflecting on the one hand a lack of conviction on the part of the most powerful decision makers about the importance and urgency of environmental issues (many of which were recognized only dimly or not at all in those still more innocent times) and on the other the opposition of certain less-developed states that perceived a contradiction between the then emerging environmental demands and the requirements of rapid development.[56]

The net result of this maiden effort at the creation of a global environmental institution was that UNEP's ability to set the global environmental agenda has been severely constrained by its organizational structure and unpredictable funding which, in turn, is a product of half-hearted political support to this international environmental institution. Cumulatively, these cannot but have compromised the "clout"[57] of UNEP both among states and among organizations. With the help of a small secretariat and a voluntary Environment Fund, this UN programme, in addition to promoting international co-operation and co-ordination of environmental programmes, was required to act as a focal point for new environmental initiatives (including the Action Plan for the Human Environment).[58] Even within the UN system, as a part of the complex

54 Gardener, n. 12, p. 245.

55 Geoffrey Palmer, "New Ways to Make International Environmental Law", *AJIL*, vol. 86, no. 2, 1992, p. 261.

56 Paul C. Szasz, "Restructuring the International Organizational Framework" in Edith Brown Weiss (Ed.), *Environmental Change and International Law: New Challenges and Dimensions* (Tokyo: United Nations Uni. Press, 1992), pp. 351–352.

57 Ibid, p. 351.

58 See the UNGA Res.2997(XXVII), Part II at para 1 and Part III at para 1–2.

web of a general political organization of states, environmental matters were being dealt with in the General Assembly as "a small part of the crowded schedule of the over-burdened Second [Committee]",[59] as compared to other high profile issues having their exclusive committees. The cumulative effect of this was accentuated by gradual political neglect by the states.

It is, however, no mean achievement that UNEP has contributed significantly in terms of development of both hard law and soft law during more than a quarter century of its existence. The so-called gradual greening of other members of the UN system has generally come at the expense of UNEP and can be said to have contributed in diluting UNEP's authority. It is noteworthy that the World Commission on Environment and Development (Brundtland Commission)[60] came to be established by the General Assembly, on the basis of a recommendation of the UNEP Governing Council.[61] Following the work of the WCED (during 1983–87), its report was accepted by the General Assembly. On the basis of WCED recommendation, the Assembly decided to convene[62] a United Nations Conference on Environment and Development (UNCED). However, the "expert 'watchdog'"[63] of the UN was not even assigned with the

59 Szasz, n. 56, p. 353.

60 The World Commission on Environment and Development (WCED), headed by the former Norwegian Prime Minister was established pursuant to the UNEP Governing Council decision UNEP/GC.11/3 on 23 May 1983. The WCED report *Our Common Future* (published by Oxford Uni. Press, Oxford, 1987) was endorsed by the UN General Assembly Resolution A/RES/42/187 on 11 December 1987.

61 The UNEP governing Council took up the question of preparing an environmental perspective to the year 2000 and beyond. It also considered a report [UNEP/GC.10/2/Add.5 & Corr.1] of the Executive Director on the perspective's desirability, feasibility and financing. At a Special Session of the Governing Council on 18 May 1982, it adopted a resolution [A/37/25, II], which invited the GC to recommend at its Tenth regular session to recommend to the General Assembly to establish a "voluntarily financed special commission to propose environmental strategies to the year 2000 and beyond". The Executive Director in his report [UNEP/GC.11/3/Add.3] again summed up government views on the creation of an independent commission of eminent persons representing all regions to report on global environment perspectives and on establishing an intergovernmental process. This 'special commission' propounded by UNEP came to adopt the name World Commission on Environment and Development. The General Assembly, in fact approved UNEP GC Decision 11/3 of 23 May 1983, in its resolution 38/161 (adopted without vote) of 19 December 1983; see *Yearbook of the United Nations*, vol. 36, 1982, p. 1000 and *Yearbook of the United Nations*, vol. 37, 1983, pp. 771–72. Also see *Yearbook of the United Nations*, Vol. 41, 1987, p. 661 [GA resolution 42/186 of 11 December 1987].

62 See the UN General Assembly Resolution 43/196 (1988).

63 Kofi A. Annan, n. 22, p. 4.

"preparation of the follow-up conference to Stockholm".[64] When the first UN environmental conference was convened in 1972, there was no specialized environmental institution. However, during the second UN conference, there was no such institutional vacuum. As such there did not appear to be any compelling reason in denying UNEP the task of at least supervising the UNCED preparatory process, which came to be assigned to a specially set up Prep COM. In the euphoria of the Earth Summit, UNEP did not even find any prominent attention.

Revitalizing UNEP

The existence of UNEP, however, appears to have had a salutary effect to some extent in setting the global environmental agenda and crystallizing international environmental initiatives. In fact the pre-UNCED period witnessed recognition of UNEP's role as a leading global environmental agency. As seen earlier, the imprint of its actions and its presence has been felt throughout the international environmental spectrum, which also culminated in a series of measures at the national level. However, this specialized UN environment programme did not emerge stronger following the UNCED (which marked the twentieth anniversary of the Stockholm Conference) in spite of Agenda 21 recognizing a "need for an enhanced and strengthened role for UNEP and its Governing Council".[65] In fact the Governing Council (GC) was asked to continue to play its role (policy guidance and coordination in the field of the environment) with an added dimension of the development perspective and underlined the priority areas[66] on which it should concentrate.

---

64 Szasz, n. 56, p. 352.

65 Nicholas A. Robinson (Ed.), *Agenda 21: Earth's Action Plan: Annotated*, IUCN Environmental Policy & Law Paper No.27 (New York: Oceana, 1993), p. 612.

66 Agenda 21 has prescribed 14 such *priority areas* as follows:
"(a) Strengthening its catalytic role in stimulating and promoting environmental activities and considerations throughout the United Nations system; (b) Promoting international cooperation in the field of environment and recommending, as appropriate, policies to this end; (c) Developing and promoting the use of such techniques as natural resource accounting and environmental economics; (d) Environmental monitoring and assessment, both through improved participation by the United Nations system agencies in the Earth watch programme and expanded relations with private scientific and non-governmental research institutes; strengthening and making operational its early warning function; (e) Coordination and promotion of relevant scientific research with a view to provide a consolidated basis for decision-making; (f) Dissemination of environmental

UNCED specifically carved out a new institutional structure in order to ensure an effective follow-up to the Conference. A high-level Commission on Sustainable Development (CSD)[67] was established in accordance with Article 68[68] of the UN Charter. This is squarely in consonance with the Charter scheme wherein all principal UN organs have been conferred with power to create

information and data to Governments and to organs, programmes and organizations of the United Nations system; (g) Raising general awareness and action in the area of environmental protection through collaboration with the general public, non-governmental entities and intergovernmental institutions; (h) Further development of international environmental law, in particular the international conventions and guidelines, promotion of its implementation, and coordinating functions arising from an increasing number of international legal agreements, *inter alia* , the functioning of the secretariats of the Conventions, taking into account the need for the most efficient use of resources, including possible co-location of secretariats established in the future; (i) Further development and promotion of the widest possible use of environmental impact assessment, including activities carried out under the auspices of specialized agencies of the United Nations system, and in connection with every significant economic development project or activity; (j) Facilitation of information exchange on environmentally sound technologies, including legal aspects, and provision of training; (k) Promotion of sub-regional and regional cooperation and support to relevant initiatives and programmes for environmental protection, including playing a major contributing and coordinating role in the regional mechanisms in the field of environment identified for the follow-up to the conference; (l) Provision of technical, legal and institutional advice to Governments, upon request in establishing and enhancing their national legal and institutional frameworks, in particular, in cooperation with UNDP capacity-building efforts; (m) Support to Governments, upon request, and development agencies and organs in the integration of environmental aspects into their development policies and programmes, in particular through provision of environmental, technical and policy advice during programme formulation and implementation; (n) Further developing assessment and assistance in cases of environmental emergencies"; see Agenda 21, Chapter 38, para 22, ibid, pp. 612–14.

67 CSD was established as a *functional* commission of the Economic and Social Council (ECOSOC) by its Decision 1993/207. The functions of CSD are set out in the General Assembly resolution 47/191 of 22 December 1992. CSD is composed of 53 members elected for a period of three years. It holds an annual meeting (mostly in April) for a period of two to three weeks and receives substantive and technical services from the Department of Economic and Social Affairs/Division for sustainable Development. The Commission reports to the Economic and Social Council and, through it, to the Second Committee of the UN General Assembly.

68 Article 68 of the UN Charter provides: "The Economic and Social Council shall set up commissions in economic and social fields and for the promotion of human rights, and such other commissions as may be required for the performance of its functions".

their own subsidiary organs. As such the new CSD, as a functional commission, was placed under the supervision of the ECOSOC.[69]

The creation of this new UN environmental institution appears to have indirectly contributed in diluting the authority of UNEP in the field of institutionalized environmental cooperation. For instance, Rudolf Dolzer has veiwed UNCED's negative implication for UNEP and setting up of CSD as non-effectual for the environmental agenda:

> In the hindsight, Rio indirectly contributed to UNEP's weakness while adding a CSD which failed to raise the profile of the international environmental agenda. The implications of this institutional weakness have become increasingly apparent while the state of much of the environment has kept on deteriorating. The proliferation of environmental secretariats for individual conventions, located in different parts of the world, has highlighted the lack of a forceful central institution. Fragmentation and lack of coordination grew, rather than the integrated approach which has rightly become the hallmark of the modern environmental paradigm.[70]

The mandate of CSD also provides a hint to this effect:

> To monitor progress in the implementation of Agenda 21 and activities related to the integration of environmental and developmental goals throughout the United Nations system through *analysis and evaluation of reports from all relevant organs, organizations, programmes and institutions of the United Nations system* dealing with various issues of environment and development, including those related to finance (emphasis added).[71]

Thus CSD's mandate requires reporting from UNEP. It presents an interesting legal situation where one subsidiary organ of the General Assembly is required

69 It is generally understood that in setting up of commissions no questions have been raised regarding the type of such subsidiary organs, since the ECOSOC's competence in this respect is not confined to Article 68 alone. It can also flow from Article 7(2), which permits „such subsidiary organs as may be found necessary may be established in accordance with the present Charter„. As compared to the regional economic commissions set up by the ECOSOC, the functional commissions like CSD are designated for a specialized purpose such as follow-up to the 1992 UNCED.

70 Rudolf Dolzer, "Time For Change", *Our Planet*, Vol. 9, No.1, 1997, p. 19.

71 Agenda 21, Chapter 38, para 13(a).

to report to another subsidiary organ created by ECOSOC. Moreover, international institutional arrangements envisaged by Agenda 21 first dealt with the mandate and structure of the CSD, followed by recognizing the need for an "enhanced and strengthened role for UNEP and its Governing Council".[72] In a sense it signified that during the Rio process and its aftermath, states have shown less confidence in UNEP and thereby its political neglect as compared to the high profile CSD. A cursory look at the steep decline[73] from 1994–95 to 1998–99 of 35.5% in the approved biennium appropriations as well as decline of 26%, 35% and 11% (in the three biennium's respectively) in the actual contributions received for UNEP's Environment Fund underscores this trend (see Table 3).

TABLE 3 *Decline in UNEP's Environment Fund (US $ millions)*

Biennium	GC Approved Appropriation	Actual Contributions	Shortfall	
			Amount	Percentage
1994–1995	166.8	124.00	42.8	26%
1996–1997	137.0	88.82	48.18	35%
1998–1999	107.5	95.41	12.09	11%
2000–2001	119.23	98.70 (Projected)	20.53	17%
2002–2003	120.0 (Proposed)			

Source: UNEP, Report of the Governing Councll, Fifth Special Session, 20-22 May 1998, Opening Address of the Executive Director: General Assembly Official Records, 53rd Session. Supplement 25 (A/53/25), pp.40-42; Policy Statement of the Executive Director to 20th Session of the UNEP Governing Council. 1 February 1999: Report of the Executive Director. Global Ministerial Environment Forum. Sixth Special Session of the GC (Malmo.29-31 May 2000), Annex I (Status of the Environment Fund).

72 Ibid, para 11 to 13 and para 21 to 23.

73 The Environment Fund of UNEP has been faced with shrinking contributions in last three bienniums. As compared to the budgets approved by the Governing Council during 1994–95, 1996–97 and 1998–99 at 166.8, 137 and 107.5 million US dollars, the Fund received merely 124, 90 and 87.1(projected) respectively. Cumulatively it shows since 1994–95, 35% decline in the Governing Council approved budget and 30% decline in the actual contributions received from the states in the post-UNCED period; see Opening Address by the Executive Director of the UNEP to the Fifth Special Session of the Governing Council held during 20–22 May 1998, *General Assembly Official Records* (GAOR), 53rd Session, Supplement No.25 (A/53/25), p. 40–42.

As per UNEP's constituent instrument [GA Resolution 2997 (XXVII) of 15 December 1972], the costs of servicing the Governing Council and providing the small secretariat is to be borne by the regular budget of the United Nations whereas operational programme costs, programme support and administrative costs of the Environment Fund are to be borne by the Fund. Thus the Environment Fund, based upon voluntary contributions from states, and supplemented by *trust* funds and a small allocation from the regular UN budget, is designed to provide funding for UNEP's environmental programmes, including new environmental initiatives.[74] In fact UNEP has only the Fund to bank on to cater to its environmental mandate. The funding figures reveal that on the one hand annual paid contributions have shown marginal increase from 44.05 million (1997) to 45.91 million (1998) to 49.50 million (1999), the number of contributing countries have, on the other hand, have declined from 88 (1997) to 73 (1998) to 66 (1999).[75] Thus the base for contributions to the Environment Fund has not shown improvement. For instance, in 1999, the Japanese contribution alone accounted for almost one-fifth of total contribution to the Environment Fund.

The Nairobi Mandate

In the backdrop of the growing feeling about marginalization of UNEP, the nineteenth session of the GC came out with a renewed mandate in the Nairobi Declaration,[76] aiming at the role and mandate of the UNEP in the changing context. Taking cognizance of the continuing deterioration of the global environment as well as increasing complexity and fragmentation of the institutional responses, the GC underlined the need for a strong, effective and revitalized UNEP. The political consensus reflected in the Declaration, through the ministers and heads of delegation, has impliedly sought to address the growing encroachment upon the UNEP's mandate on account of not only new institutional structures but also 'greening' of the existing international

74 See, UN, *Basic Facts*, n. 8, p. 39.

75 UNEP, *Report of the Executive Director on Activities of the United Nations Environment Programme*, Sixth Special Session of the Governing Council, Malmö, 29–31 May 2000; see Doc. UNEP/GCSS.VI/6, 11 April 2000, p. 43.

76 For the text of the Nairobi Declaration, see Annex to the Governing Council Resolution 19/1 of 7 February 1997 in *GAOR*, 52nd Session, Supp.No.25 (A/52/25), and annex. Also see UNEP, *Annual Report 1998* (Nairobi: UNEP, 1998), p. 5 and UNEP, *Bulletin of Environmental Law*, Vol. 7, June 1997, pp. 4–5.

institutions within and outside the UN system, in their respective functional jurisdictions. Accordingly, it declared that:

> [T]he United Nations Environment Programme has been and should *continue to be the principal United Nations body in the field of the environment* ...the role of the United Nations Environment Programme is to be the leading global environmental authority that sets the global environmental agenda, that promotes the coherent implementation of the environmental dimension of sustainable development within the United Nations system and that *serves as an authoritative advocate for the global environment* (emphasis added).[77]

In fact the GC put forward a six-point plan[78] in the Declaration for the revitalization and strengthening of the UNEP. The Declaration also seeks to improve the governance structure of UNEP especially in terms of making it a world forum for ministers and high-level government officials. However, it did not propose any basic changes in the composition of UNEP GC to facilitate this. It also remains a moot point as to what extent the ministers in charge of environment matters would consider UNEP's political influence and weight attractive

77 Ibid, para 1–2.

78 The GC has defined the 'core elements' for this as follows:

(a) To analyze the state of the global environment and assess global and regional environmental trends, provide policy advice, early warning information on environmental threats, and to catalyze and promote international cooperation and action , based on the best scientific and technical capabilities available;

(b) To further the development of its international environmental law aiming at sustainable development, including the development of coherent interlink ages among existing international environmental conventions;

(c) To advance the implementation of agreed international norms and policies, to monitor and foster compliance with environmental principles and international agreements and stimulate cooperative action to respond to emerging environmental challenges;

(d) To strengthen its role in the coordination of environmental activities in the United Nations system in the field of the environment, as well as its role as an Implementing Agency of the Global Environment Facility, based on its comparative advantage and scientific and technical expertise;

(e) To promote greater awareness and facilitate effective cooperation among all sectors of society and actors involved in the implementation of the international environmental agenda, and to serve as an effective link between the scientific community and policy makers at the national and international levels;

(f) To provide policy and advisory services in key areas of institution-building to Governments and other relevant institutions; ibid, para 3.

enough to do so. In fact the core elements put forward in the Declaration also do not go a long way, except in reaffirming the current functions of UNEP, to impart it the stature essential to provide it requisite visibility as an authoritative advocate for the global environment.

As a sequel to the Nairobi Declaration, the nineteenth special session of the General Assembly specifically addressed the issue of international institutional arrangements in the broader context of implementation of Agenda 21. The Assembly, accepting the role of UNEP as the principal UN body in the field of environment and its role as a catalyst, reproduced almost *verbatim* the second para of the Nairobi Declaration.[79] The notion of *revitalization*, mooted by the Nairobi Declaration has been duly endorsed by the Assembly, calling for "adequate, stable and predictable funding".[80] The Assembly underlined the need for strengthening the funding capability of UNEP, notwithstanding the grim situation of drastic curtailment in the official development assistance (ODA) in the post-UNCED period.[81]

The UN Secretary-General has also addressed the issue of revitalization of UNEP as a part of the wider UN reform agenda. Extending his support to the substance of the Nairobi Declaration for strengthening of UNEP, the Secretary-General observed:

> UNEP is the environmental voice of the United Nations and the principal source of the environmental input into the work of the Commission on Sustainable Development. High priority must be given to according to it

79 See the resolution S/19–2 entitled "Programme for the Further Implementation of Agenda 21" of 28 June 1997, adopted on the Report of the Ad Hoc Committee of the Whole of the Nineteenth Special Session of the General Assembly; *GAOR*, A/S-19/29, para 123, p. 32. Also see United Nations, *Earth Summit +5: Programme for the Further Implementation of Agenda 21* (New York: UN, 1997), pp. 1–95.

80 Ibid, para 124, p. 33.

81 The General Assembly took a grim note of significant negative trend in respect of the ODA, far away from the target set by the UNCED. It observed:
"Most developed countries have still not reached the United Nations target, reaffirmed by most countries at the United Nations Conference on Environment and Development, of committing 0.7 per cent of their gross national product to official development assistance or the United Nations target, as agreed, of committing 0.15 per cent of gross national product as official development assistance to the least developed countries. Regrettably, on average, official development assistance as a percentage of the gross national product of developed countries has drastically declined in the post-Conference period from 0.34 per cent in 1992 to 0.27 per cent in 1995…"; see ibid, para 18, p. 9.

> the status, strength and access to resources it requires to function effectively as the environmental agency of the world community.[82]

As a first and immediate step to strengthen and restructure UNEP as well as Centre for Human Settlements (Habitat),[83] the Secretary-General proposed to develop "new measures"[84] for the purpose. One such measure was the setting up of a special Task Force to examine the issue and provide recommendations on such measures.

The UN Task Force Report

A high-level 21 member[85] United Nations Task Force on Environment and Human Settlements was set up early 1998. It comprised ministers, government advisors, members of the civil society as well as representatives from the

---

82 The Report of the Secretary-General on *Renewing the United Nations: A Programme for Reform*, UN General Assembly 51st Session, Doc.A/51/950, 14 July 1997, para 176, p. 58.

83 The United Nations Centre for Human Settlements (Habitat) was set up by the General Assembly Resolution 32/162 in 1978, pursuant to the United Nations Conference on Human Settlements held in Vancouver, Canada during 31 May to 11 June 1976. The second Habitat Conference (Habitat II), held in Istanbul, Turkey (June 1996), adopted the Habitat Agenda (principles, commitments and the plan of action) as well as the Istanbul Declaration which called for the "universal goals of ensuring adequate shelter for all and making human settlements safer, healthier and more livable, equitable, sustainable and productive". The 15 para Istanbul Declaration commits governments to address unsustainable consumption and production patterns, particularly in industrialized countries, unsustainable population changes, homelessness, unemployment, inadequate resources, lack of basis infrastructure and services, growing insecurity and violence and increased vulnerability to disasters; see Report of the United Nations Conference on Human Settlements (Habitat II), Istanbul, 3–14 June 1996 [UN pub. Sales No.E.97.IV.6]. The UN General Assembly has decided (resolution 53/180, para 2) that the Special Session for overall review and appraisal of the implementation of the Habitat Agenda (Istanbul+5) will be held in June 2001. The Commission on Human Settlements will serve as the Prep COM for the GA Special Session; see *http://www.istanbul5.org/background* and *http://www.unchs.org*.

84 See n. 82, para 179, Action 12, p. 59.

85 The Task Force Members were: Klaus Töpfer (the UNEP Executive Director, Chair-Germany), Christina Amoako-Nuama (Ghana), Julia Carabias Lillo (Mexico), Lars-Goran Engfeldt (Sweden), and Jean-Pierre Halbwachs (Asstt. Secretary-General/Controller UN Office of Programme Planning, Budget and Accounts), Ashok Khosla (Development Alternatives, India), Maria Julia Alsogaray (Argentina), John Ashe (Antigua and Barbuda),

UN Secretariat and was headed by the Executive Director of UNEP. During the period of ten weeks of its work (April to June), the Task Force examined a wide range of issues especially focusing upon the work of UNEP and Habitat as well as the United Nations Office in Nairobi (UNON), all three of which have a common head. The mandate of the Task Force was formulated in the following Terms of Reference (TOR):

> To *review existing structures and arrangements* through which environment and environment-related activities are carried out within the United Nations, with particular reference to those departments, Funds and Programmes which report to the Secretary-General, but *taking into account also the relevant programmes and activities of the specialized agencies*;
>
> In this respect to focus particularly on the distinctive functions of policy, development of norms and standards, programme development and implementation and financing as well as relationships amongst these functions;
>
> *To evaluate the efficacy and effectiveness of existing structures and arrangements* and make recommendations for such changes and improvements as will *optimize the work and effectiveness of the United Nations environmental work at the global level and of UNEP as the leading environmental organization or "authority"* as well as the role of UNEP as the principal source of environmental input into the work of the Commission on Sustainable Development;

Nitin Desai (Under Secretary-General, UN Department of Economic and Social Affairs), Guro Fjellanger (Norway), Martin Holdgate (UK), Martin Khor (Third World Network, Malaysia), Tommy Koh (Singapore), James Gustave Speth (Administrator, UNDP), Mostafa K. Tolba (Inter. Centre for Environment & Development, Egypt), Makarim Wibisono (Indonesia), Michael Zammait Cutajar (Executive Secretary, Climate Change Secretariat), Julia Marton LeFevre (Lead International, USA), Maurice Strong (Special Advisor to the Secretary-General), Joseph Tomusange (Uganda) and Timothy E. Wirth (United Nations Foundation). Peter Thacher and Eileen Claussen were Advisors to the Task Force. The Secretariat comprised of Per Bakken, Donatus Okpala, Thomas Stoel, Donald Kanairu and Lesly Puyol.

See UN Task Force on Environment and Human Settlements, *Report to the Secretary-General*, 15 June 1998 (on file with the author), pp. 29–30). Also see UN, *Report of the Secretary-General "Environment and human settlements"*, Doc.A/53/463, Annex, pp. 11–28, 6 October 1998 and Report of the Secretary-General on environment and human settlements, presented to the General Assembly at its fifty-third session, Twentieth Session of the UNEP Governing Council, Nairobi, 1–5 February 1999, Doc. UNEP/GC.20/INF/13, 6 January 1999 (hereinafter the *Task Force Report*).

> To prepare proposals, for consideration by the Secretary-General and subsequent submission to the General Assembly, on reforming and strengthening UN activities in the environmental and human settlement areas (emphasis added).[86]

The broad mandate of the Task Force was to enable it to address the *existing structures and arrangements* concerning the environment and human settlement areas. The Task Force was expected to cover within the ambit of its work all environment and environment-related work of relevant departments, Funds and Programmes within the UN system, including that of the specialized agencies. The work and effectiveness of UNEP is central to this mandate.

In a brief report, submitted to the fifty-third session of the GA (through the Secretary-General), the Task Force restricted itself to UNEP's work and its relationship to other UN agencies and programmes, as well as multilateral environmental convention secretariats. The Task Force pointedly noted to the proliferation of environmental institutions established in the post-UNCED period, such as Commission on Sustainable Development (CSD),[87] Inter-Agency Committee on Sustainable Development (IACSD)[88] and Global

86 *The Task Force Report*, Doc. A/53/463, Appendix II, p. 28.

87 The CSD was set up pursuant to the UN General assembly Resolution 48/191 of 22 December 1992, which was adopted without a vote, as a functional commission of the Economic and Social Council (ECOSOC). CSD's very ambitious mandate comprises of, among others, monitoring implementation of Agenda 21 as well as promoting incorporation of the Rio Declaration on Environment and Development. For the text of the GA Resolution see *Yearbook of the United Nations*, Vol. 46, 1992, pp. 676–680; *ILM*, vol. 31, 1993, pp. 254–262. Also see Patricia W. Birnie and Alan Boyle, *Basic Documents on International Law and the Environment* (Oxford: Clarendon Press, 1995), pp. 658–665.

88 The IACSD is a Standing Committee of the United Nations' Administrative Committee on Coordination (ACC). The role of IACSD, set up in 1993, is to identify major policy issues relating to the follow-up to UNCED by the UN system. It has sought to bring together relevant UN bodies as well as coordinates their work. It also advises ACC on ways and means of addressing these issues in order to ensure effective system-wide cooperation and coordination in the implementation of Agenda 21, the Programme of Action for the Sustainable Development of Small Island Developing States (SIDS) and other outcomes of UNCED and their follow-up. IACSD meets twice a year and reports to ACC. The ACC Sub-Committee on Oceans and Coastal Areas and the ACC Sub-Committee on Water Resources report to IACSD. The Chairman of the Committee is Nitin Desai, Under-Secretary-General, Department of Economic and Social Affairs (DESA). Since 1993, fifteen sessions of IACSD have been held, the last one being held in New York during 24–25 January 2000.

Environment Facility (GEF),[89] and observed that the new structures had not only altered the UN's environmental structure but also led to parallel institutional structures to the UNEP. The Task Force also referred to the so-called 'greening' of other development-oriented international institutions within the UN system, such as World Health Organization (WHO), World Meteorology Organization (WMO), Food and Agriculture Organization (FAO), United Nations Educational, Scientific and Cultural Organization (UNESCO) and United Nations Industrial Development Organization (UNIDO) as well as the UN's Regional Economic Commissions (RECs).[90] The work of these specialized agencies, as well as RECs, has, in its view, led to what a commentator called "treaty congestion",[91] and, in the view of the Task Force, to the problem of "substantial overlaps, unrecognized linkages and gaps".[92] But the Task Force, refrained itself from categorically pointing out that the cumulative effect of these developments had diluted UNEP's ambit of work or its authority.

A review of recent developments did prompt the Task Force to underline the need for "reformed structures and new methods"[93] in order to optimize their effectiveness:

> [T]he *UN system needs a strong and respected UNEP as its leading environmental organization*...needs to be given adequate financial, staff and information capacities. In particular, it should be the recognized centre

89 The GEF is a special funding mechanism carved out to address specific environmental areas, such as climate change, ozone depletion, international waters and desertification. It is jointly being administered by the World Bank, UNDP and UNEP. An Instrument for Establishing the Restructured Global Environment Facility was adopted at Geneva on 16 March 1994; see GEF, *Instrument for the Establishment of the Restructured Global Environment Facility* (Washington D.C.: GEF, 1994), pp. 5–34; *I.L.M.*, vol. 33, 1994, p. 1273.

90 There are five such regional economic commissions: Economic Commission for Africa (ECA), Economic Commission for Europe (ECE), Economic Commission for Latin America and the Caribbean (ECLAC), Economic Commission foe Asia and the Pacific (ESCAP) and Economic and Social Commission for Western Asia (ESCWA); see UN, *Basic Facts*, n.74, p. 23.

91 Edith Brown Weiss, "International Environmental Law: Contemporary Issues and the Emergence of a New world Order", *Georgetown University Law Journal*, Vol. 81, no.3, 1993, p. 675.

92 It has in fact expressed grave concern that: "These flaws are basic and pervasive. They prevent the UN system from using its scarce resources to best advantage in addressing problems that are crucial to the human future; harm the credibility and weight of the United Nations in the environmental arena; and damage the UN's working relationship with its partners in and outside of Government"; see the *Task Force Report*, para 20.

93 Ibid, para 16.

> of a network of information, monitoring, assessment, and early warning, and should play to the full its role as an implementing agency of the GEF (emphasis added).[94]

The Report made 24 recommendations, covering coordination, UNEP's location, its relationship with the environmental convention secretariats, as well as with CSD and GEF. It did not go into the issue of making substantial changes in the very structure and status of UNEP within the UN system (that of the *programme* level). Its recommendations fall into two main categories, namely action required at the secretariat level and the inter-governmental level and can be broadly covered under four heads.

(i) Environmental Monitoring Group

The Report has noted that institutional fragmentation, characterized by substantial overlaps, unrecognized linkages and gaps within the UN system, has undermined UN's role in the environmental arena. It nevertheless suggested the creation of one more institution – Environmental Management Group (EMG)[95] – to achieve better coordination and joint action, replacing the existing Inter-Agency Environmental Coordination Group (IAECG). The new institution, to be headed by the UNEP Executive Director, was to comprise at its core all the leading UN entities in the field of environment and human settlements as well as other UN entities, financial institutions and organizations outside the UN system, including the convention secretariats whenever required. While requiring the EMG to report to the UN Secretary-General (who also chairs the Administrative Committee on Coordination) and assisting UNEP Governing Council and Commission on Human Settlements (CHS), the Task Force did not want it to produce for the UN a unified environmental programme. Therefore, all the institutions within the UN system, working in the field of environment, will continue to carry out their respective tasks. Interestingly, the Task Force did not prefer to recognize or commend UNEP's pivotal and lead role in the entire process. As such UNEP becomes just one of the environmental institutions dealing with environmental issues within the UN system, to be coordinated by the proposed EMG, rather than work as a principal institution. The mandate of the proposed EMG transferred to it the task of coordination among convention secretariats currently being carried

94 Ibid, para 19.

95 Ibid, para 22, Recommendation 1.

out by UNEP,[96] which will further contribute to UNEP's gradually shrinking space within the UN system.

(ii) UNEP and Other Entities

The Task Force has primarily sought to address the issue of UNEP's structure as well as its role in the rapidly changing international environment within a very limited context. This mainly concerns UNEP's relationship with post-Rio environmental institutions (especially CSD and GEF) as well as the environmental convention secretariats,[97] some of which are in fact UNEP-administered (CITES, CMS, Ozone, Basel and CBD). The setting up of the high-profile CSD appears to have diminished UNEP's international stature, in as far as CSD has been placed in charge of the implementation of Agenda 21 (UNCED mandate) and activities related to the integration of environmental and developmental goals throughout the UN system through analysis and evaluation of reports from "all relevant organs, organizations, programmes and institutions of the UN system".[98]

96 See, for instance, UN Doc. UNEP/ELI/Coord.2/5 of 30 April 1995.

97 A multilateral environmental convention secretariat is an administrative instrument, which is product of an agreement under international law. The international agreement between states parties creates a legal regime in a particular sectoral environmental area. The Conference of Parties (COP) is the supreme decision-making body for such a convention. Almost every environmental convention establishes a small secretariat to service the work to be done under it. The nature of powers conferred upon the convention secretariats may defer from one area to another. The COP is also considered to have the legal capacity, within the limits of its mandate, to enter into agreements and other arrangements with entities such as states, intergovernmental and non-governmental organizations and bodies, which also have the authority to do so. However, the fact remains that a convention secretariat is a subsidiary body of the convention and directly answerable, through its head, to the COP. For details see "The Relationship between the Executive Director of UNEP and the Conventions Regarding the Administration of their Secretariats", UNEP Doc. UNEP/DEP/Coord.4/3/COR.1, 4 January 1996. Also see "Memorandum to the Executive Secretary of the Framework Convention on Climate Change from the UN Under Secretary-General for Legal Affairs", Inter-office Memorandum, UN Office of Legal Affairs, New York, 4 November 1993, which is available at *http://www.jura.uni-muenchen .de/tel/cases/cop.html*.

98 See CSD's 'constituent instrument', the General Assembly resolution 47/191 (para 3) of 22 December 1992 on "Institutional arrangements to follow-up the United Nations Conference on Environment and Development"; *Yearbook of the United Nations*, vol. 46, 1992, pp. 676–680 and *ILM*, vol. 31, 1993, pp. 254–262.

The Report has proposed that the UNEP Governing Council should host an annual, ministerial-level, global environmental forum, which will review and revise the whole UN environmental agenda. This suggestion has been made on the ground of inadequacy of direction forthcoming from existing intergovernmental forums.[99] It is also suggested that the membership of the GC should be made universal,[100] instead of restricting it to 58 members as at present. This internal restructuring of the UNEP GC, however, is sought to be done within the existing *programme* level. In fact, if implemented, such universal membership for the governing council of a UN programme would be unique in the UN system. UNEP GC is also expected to continue providing input into the CSD's yearly meetings. It is difficult to find a clear demarcation of respective roles of UNEP and the CSD. As a creature of UNCED, CSD will still be calling the shots, especially on the implementation of the UNCED mandate. It remains to be seen as to what extent the universal membership of the UNEP GC, unaided by a commensurate international institutional status, will help in making it an 'environmental authority' of the UN system. A logical step, generally, could have been to upgrade it into one of the UN specialized agencies.

UNEP has been playing an important role as a *catalyst* not only in terms of initiating guidelines/principles but also in subsequent development of conventions to address specific environmental issues, apart from providing secretariats for some of the conventions. The relationship between UNEP and such convention secretariats is governed by the relevant provisions of the conventions (MEAs). The Task Force has suggested, in addition to integrating convention secretariats and convention-related issues in the work of the EMG, a framework[101] which can govern UNEP's relationship with the

---

99 Explaining the rationale for setting up of such a global ministerial environmental forum (GMEF) due to inadequate guidance from the existing forums, the Task Force has observed: "These forums, consisting primarily of the UNEP Governing Council, the Commission on Sustainable Development, and meetings of the conferences of parties of leading conventions, are scattered as to time and place. They are attended by different constellations of ministers. They differ in their outcomes: some are decision-making bodies, whereas others serve primarily as forums for policy debates, consensus-building, review of United Nations activities and plans, and exchanges with major groups. Ministers have expressed dissatisfaction because attendance at so many meetings on different subjects makes it hard for participants to get the 'big picture' perspective that is important for setting global priorities"; see the *Task Force Report*, para 45–47 and Recommendation 13.

100 *The Task Force Report*, para 47, Recommendation 13.

101 It has been suggested, among others, that UNEP should provide substantive support to global and regional conventions, the Executive Director should continue to sponsor joint meetings of heads of secretariats as well as address the issue of operational inefficiencies

convention secretariats. It has also opined that effort should be made to co-locate new conventions linking with institutions having a particular affinity as well as promoting cooperation among the secretariats within each cluster.

Interestingly, the issue of UNEP's location in Nairobi also figured prominently. The Task Force has taken due cognizance of the sensitivity of developing countries on this issue, as Nairobi remains the only location of a major UN office in a developing country. It has expressed concern over the genuine problems of communication, as well as physical security. The Report endorsed the UN Secretary-General's decision for a common head for UNEP, Habitat and UN Office in Nairobi (UNON).[102] The fact that it has felt constrained to observe that UNON "should have arrangements in keeping with its status", shows its neglect by the UN headquarters, as compared to other, better-placed UN offices in New York, Geneva and Vienna.

(iii) Major Groups

The Task Force took cognizance of the growing role for elements outside government in actions and decisions affecting environmental and human settlements, including activities and decisions of the UN system. In fact Agenda 21 recognizes the role of a wide constituency which it described as "major groups".[103] Taking a cue from it, the Task Force has proposed that, as per NGOs participation in the work of the CSD, the UNEP GC and the CHS should facilitate participation of major groups.[104] This would enablc these groups to play an influential role in the entire process together with the states.

---

and costs arising from geographical dispersal of convention secretariats ; see ibid, para 29–31 and Recommendation 2.

102 Ibid, para 32–34 and Recommendations 5 – 6. The decision of the UN Secretary-General as well as its endorsement by the Task Force has been rejected by the General Assembly. The Assembly did endorse increased cooperation and strengthened coordination of activities of UNEP and Habitat, but wanted to them maintain their separate programmatic and organizational identities as well as their separate Executive Directors; see GA resolution A/RES/53/242 of 10 August 1999, para 4, p. 3.

103 Chapters 24 to 32 of Agenda 21 recognize roles of major groups, including women, youth, indigenous people, NGOs, local authorities, trade unions, business and industry, scientific and technological community and farmers in the implementation of this action plan.

104 *The Task Force Report*, para 53–60 and Recommendations 18–23.

(iv) Concept of Trusteeship

The Task Force was expected to examine the suggestion made by the Secretary-General on this issue in his Report, as well as his Note to the General Assembly.[105] The idea of *trusteeship* was put forward by the Secretary-General to address the issue of integrity of the global environment and the global commons (such as oceans, atmosphere and outer space). At the basis of the notion of holding them in "trust"[106] lies the view that they are common repository of the humankind as a whole and so need to be taken beyond the control of the nation states. It is somewhat akin to the idea inherent in the international trusteeship system[107] under chapters XII and XIII of the UN Charter, the supervision of which was assigned to the General Assembly and, under its authority, the Trusteeship Council. Since all of the 11 original trust territories[108]

105 The Secretary-General observed in his Report that: "Member States appear to have decided to retain the Trusteeship Council. The Secretary-General proposes, therefore, that it be reconstituted as the forum through which Member states exercise their collective trusteeship for the integrity of the global environment and common areas such as the oceans, atmosphere and outer space. At the same time, it should serve to link the united Nations and civil society in addressing these areas of global concern, which require the active contribution of public, private and voluntary sectors"; see "Renewing the United Nations: A Programme for Reform", UN Doc.A/51/950, 14 July 1997, para 84–85.
He made a further reference to it in his *Note* on "A New Concept of Trusteeship" that: "The Task Force (set up in line with Action 12 of above report) will have an opportunity to elaborate further on the Secretary-General's proposals for a new concept of trusteeship, as its terms of reference include, *inter alia*, the preparation of proposals, for consideration by the Secretary-General and subsequent submission to the General Assembly, on reforming and strengthening United Nations activities in the environmental and human settlement areas. Based on the work of the Task Force, it is envisaged that the proposal will be reviewed by the General Assembly at a later date"; see UN Doc.A/52/849, 31 March 1998, para 1–3.

106 Scholars like Edith Brown Weiss have articulated the concept of *intergenerational equity*, which argues that as members of the present generation, we hold the earth in "trust" for future generations; for details see, generally, Edith Brown Weiss, "Our Rights and Obligations to Future Generations for the Environment" *American Journal of International Law*, Vol. 84, 1990, pp. 198–207. Also see, ibid, *In Fairness to Future Generations: International Law, Common Patrimony and Intergenerational Equity* (Tokyo and Dobbs Ferry: UNU and Transnational, 1989).

107 Article 75 of the UN Charter committed the UN to the establishment "under its authority of an international trusteeship system for the administration and supervision of such territories as may be placed hereunder by subsequent individual agreements…".

108 In 1994 the UN Security Council terminated the UN Trusteeship Agreement for the last Trust Territory of the Pacific Islands (Palau), which was administered by the United States.

have now attained self-government or independence, the Trusteeship Council – as one of the six principal organs of the UN – is now without business. Therefore, it has been suggested that the Trusteeship Council may now be assigned a new mandate for the global environment, especially the global commons.

It is in this context that the Secretary-General had proposed the concept of 'collective trusteeship' for further examination and had called upon the Task Force to elaborate further on the concept of trusteeship, as a part of its proposals regarding "reforming and strengthening United Nations activities in the environmental and human settlement areas".[109] The Task force, in its wisdom thought not to express any definite opinion on the concept of trusteeship and a mandate for the Trusteeship Council. Instead, it chose to assign this task to an environment forum, to be held at the time of the UNEP GC's meeting in 1999.[110]

The Task Force did acknowledge that institutional fragmentation and loss of policy coherence, as a result of the number of separate environment-related intergovernmental processes, had resulted in a loss of effectiveness in the work of the United Nations. It, however, has sought to address its mandate in the TOR for review of the existing institutional structures, without providing any innovative and bold institutional overhauling. This may be due to lack of consensus among members of the Task Force. The recommendations for defining UNEP's role in the climate of institutional fragmentation (concerning environmental issues) within the UN system do not go a long way in revitalizing as well as enhancing UNEP's status as the principal UN institution for environment protection. It certainly does not help UNEP in overcoming the problems[111] or its political neglect, as well as its *dwarfing* by other high-profile environmental institutional structures. The gradual encroaching upon UNEP's jurisdiction by several agencies within the UN system has affected its stature, besides aggravating the problem of co-ordination. While UNEP does need to address some of the pressing issues of its existing structure and functioning, it will need to come out of the morass of the *programme* level structure in which it is entrapped.

Palau became 185th member of the UN on 15 December 1994, after attaining self-government in 1993, followed by full independence in 1994; see UN, *Basic Facts*, n. 133, p. 276.

109 See Note A/52/849 of 31 March 1998.

110 *The Task Force Report*, para 61–64 and Recommendation 24.

111 See Editorial Comment on "Review of Existing Structures" in *Environmental Policy and Law*, vol. 28, no.5, 1998, p. 215.

Decision of the General Assembly

As a sequel to the report of the Task Force, the UN Secretary-General submitted his *Report on Environment and Human Settlements,*[112] as promised earlier, at the 53rd Session of the General Assembly. It termed the recommendations of the Task Force report as the "beginning of a process designed to equip the United Nations to concretely address the pressing environmental and sustainable development problems currently facing the international community".[113] The Secretary-General's report was also circulated in a Note[114] by the Executive Director at the 20th Session of the UNEP Governing Council. The GC meeting appears to have demonstrated restored faith in UNEP as the prominent UN agency with the responsibility for the environment and supported the general thrust of actions proposed to be taken by the Secretary-General and the Executive Director at the UN Secretariat level, including establishment of an EMG and convening of an annual ministerial-level global environmental forum, along with regular biennial and special sessions of the UNEP Governing Council.[115]

The General Assembly considered the Report of the Secretary-General on Environment and Human Settlements (A/53/463) and the Report of the UN Task Force (annexed to it) at its 53rd session in 1999. It also took cognizance of the decision (20/17 of 5 February 1999) of the Governing Council and the resolution (17/6 of 14 May 1999) of Commission on Human Settlements as well as the need to strengthen the institutions of the UN in the field. The main components of the resolution[116] can be summarized as follows:

1. The Assembly requested the Secretary-General to strengthen the UN office in Nairobi (UNON), being the only UN headquarters located in a developing country. This can be done through the provision of requisite

112 Agenda Item 30 on "United Nations reform: measures and proposals" Fifty-third Session of the UN General Assembly; *Doc. A/53/463* of 6 October 1998.

113 Ibid, p. 4.

114 Note by the Executive Director on „Report of the Secretary-General on Environment and Human Settlements, presented to the General Assembly at its Fifty-third Session„; Item 6 of the Provisional Agenda at 20th Session of UNEP Governing Council, Nairobi, 1–5 February 1999; see Doc. *UNEP/GC.20/INF/13*, 6 January 1999.

115 See UNEP GC Decision 20/17 of 5 February 1999, para 1(e) and (g) at www.unep.org/Documents . Also see A/54/25, annex I; *Official Records of the General Assembly*, Fifty-fourth Session, Supp. No.25. Also see *Earth Negotiations Bulletin*, Vol. 16, no.6, 8 February 1999, pp. 1–24 at 15.

116 The General Assembly resolution 53/242 on *Report of the Secretary-General on environment and human settlements*; see Doc. A/RES/53/242 of 10 August 1999.

support and stable, adequate and predictable financial resources, including provision for additional support from regular UN budget.

2. It called upon both UNEP and the UN Centre for Human Settlements (Habitat) to increase cooperation and to strengthen coordination of their activities. In this respect, the Assembly underscored their different mandates and separate programmatic and organizational identities. In calling for separate Executive Directors for both UNEP and Habitat, the Assembly appears to have not favored the current practice of the same head for both of them.
3. It supported the proposal of the Secretary-General on the establishment of an Environment Management Group (EMG) for the purpose of interagency coordination in the field of environment and human settlements. The Secretary-General was asked to develop the mandate, terms of reference, criteria for membership and working methods etc. in consultation with the member states and the Administrative Committee on Coordination (ACC).
4. It endorsed the proposal for instituting an annual global ministerial environment forum (GMEF). This forum is to meet along with the regular biennium sessions of the UNEP Governing Council; and in alternate years, take the form of a special session of the Governing Council. The forum is to ensure effective and efficient functioning of the governance mechanisms of UNEP. It will not affect role of the CSD as the main forum for high-level policy debate on sustainable development.
5. It supported the need for enhancing linkages and coordination within and among environmental and environment-related conventions. UNEP is expected to perform this task with the help of adequate resources for the purpose.
6. The involvement, participation and constructive engagement of major groups active in the field of environment and human settlements were favored.
7. It underscored the need for strengthening the capacity and capability of UNEP and Habitat in the areas of information, monitoring and assessment of global and regional environmental and human settlements trends and early warning information on environmental threats.
8. The Assembly did not favor UNEP's involvement in conflict identification, prevention or resolution.
9. It emphasized the need to ensure institutional strengthening in developing countries as well as research and scientific studies in the field of environment and human settlements.
10. It also underscored the need to enhance further the role of UNEP as an implementing agency of Global Environment Facility.

It will require concerted efforts to follow-up on other measures suggested by the Assembly, including the 1997 Nairobi Declaration on the Role and Mandate of UNEP. The Secretary-General presented his Report[117] to the 54th session of the General Assembly giving an account of the various follow-up measures taken on international institutional arrangements related to environment and development.

Global Ministerial Environment Forum

In response to the General Assembly recommendations, some steps have been taken at the secretariat level, especially in instituting Global Ministerial Environment Forum (GMEF). The first meeting of GMEF took place in Malmö in May 2000, as 6th Special Session of the UNEP Governing Council.[118] The Forum became the first meeting of its kind in the ministerial segment of all 58 members of the Governing Council. Convened as a follow-up to the 20th GC decision (20/17) as well as the General Assembly resolution (53/242), and regarded as 'Töpfer's baby', GMEF became a modest political initiative, to revive sagging fortunes of this premier UN environment institution... The coming together of environment ministers on such a platform represented an attempt to regain policy coherence in the field of environment, which has been witnessing fragmentation as well as 'clogging' by multiplicity of institutions.

The GMEF provided an opportunity to environment ministers to grapple with strategic policy discussions on major global environmental challenges[119]

117 United Nations, *Report of the Secretary-General: International institutional arrangements related to environment and development*, Fifth-fourth Session of the General Assembly; see UN Doc. A/54/468 of 15 October 1999.

118 See *Notification by the Executive Director*, Global Ministerial Environment Forum, Sixth Special Session of the Governing Council of the United Nations Environment Programme, Malmö (Sweden), 9 March 2000. The Notification stated that the Forum was being convened in pursuance of Governing Council decision 20/17 of 5 February 1999, entitled "Views of the Governing Council on the report of the Secretary-General on environment and human settlements", and General Assembly resolution 53/242 of 28 July 1999, entitled "Report of the Secretary-General on environment and human settlements", and in accordance with rules 5 and 6 of the rules of procedure of the Governing Council.

119 See Discussion Papers presented by the Executive Director, *Major environmental challenges in the new century*, Global Ministerial Environment Forum, Sixth Special Session of the Governing Council, Malmö, 29–31 May 2000; Doc. UNEP/GCSS.VI/8, 10 May 2000. Also see *Report of the Executive Director on Activities of the United Nations*

in the next century as well as on how to turn of existing commitments into action. It was to make recommendations on policy responses to address such issues to the 55th session of the General Assembly – the Millennium Assembly – in September 2000. The Malmö Declaration,[120] drafted by a Committee of the Whole, has been a fine act of balancing and a belated effort to bring UNEP back to the centre-stage of global environmental agenda. The Malmö Declaration has sought to confer legitimacy on UNEP, and many delegates from developing countries[121] did stress the central role UNEP, in taking reins of preparations for the Rio+10 summit:

> Governments and UNEP have a major role in the preparation for the 2002 review of UNCED at the regional and global levels...The 2002 conference should review the requirement for a greatly strengthened institutional structure for international environmental governance based on an assessment of future needs for an institutional architecture that has the capacity to effectively address wide-ranging environmental threats in a globalize world. UNEP's role in this regard should be strengthened and its financial base broadened and made more predictable.[122]

It appears to be good omen for UNEP to assume a major role in the preparation for the ten year review of the 1992 UNCED, especially since it was denied such a role in the preparation for convening of the UNCED. Moreover, it provides enough hints for strengthening the international environmental institutional structure. What shape this may finally take, for environmental governance in general and UNEP in particular, will depend upon political will on the part of states.

Beyond the Task Force: An Assessment

The report of the Task Force in a sense belied expectations on the institutional revitalization of UNEP. At the threshold of the new millennium, and 28 years after its establishment, UNEP is still faced with the challenge of equipping itself to deliver results. The root cause of UNEP's problems is lack of confidence

Environment Programme, Global Ministerial Environment forum, Sixth Special Session of the Governing Council; Doc. UNEP/GCSS.VI/6, 11 April 2000.

120 Global Ministerial Environment Forum, *Malmö Ministerial Declaration*; Doc. UNEP/GCSS.VI/L.3, 31 May 2000 (hereinafter the *Malmö Declaration*).

121 See *Earth Negotiations Bulletin*, vol. 16, no.10, 2 June 2000, p. 8.

122 The Malmö Declaration, para 22 and 24.

of member states of the UN. A whole series of processes, including centralized decision-making, poor management and problems of communication (due to location) are considered responsible for the lack of confidence and for the gradual diminishing of political support, the decline in funding, and for states turning away from UNEP to other actors on the international scene. In the post-UNCED period, developments both within the UN system as well as without it have contributed to the undermining UNEP's authority. The fact remains that no international institution can be ever fit enough to face all challenges in the rapidly changing global society. Institutions must be able to adapt to the changing needs and expectations of the international community.

The necessity for an effective and efficient international environmental institutional structure capable enough to handle the global environmental agenda in the twenty-first century is generally appreciated. Moreover, there appears to be considerable political consensus on according UNEP the status of an "environmental conscience"[123] or "leading global environmental authority".[124] The basic question is that, in the emerging scheme of things, where does UNEP stand in the institutional structure as it is today? Can this UN environmental programme rest on its past laurels? The UN Task Force was expected to suggest a workable blueprint, to revitalize and strengthen UNEP. It did not live up to that expectation. One hopes the forthcoming Millennium Assembly in September 2000 will be able take some concrete steps as the following:

---

123 See Kofi A. Annan, n.22, p. 4.

124 For instance, see UNEP Governing council Decision 19/1 of 7 February 1997, para 2 in UNEP, *Annual Report 1998* (Nairobi: UNEP, 1998), p. 5. Also see Agenda 21, Chapter 38, para 23 in Nicholas A. Robinson (Ed.), *Agenda 21: Earth's Action Plan* (New York: Oceana, 1993), p. 614.

The recent Nineteenth Special Session of the UN General Assembly (Earth Summit + 5) again reiterated political consensus, existing at least on paper if not action, concerning role of UNEP to be: "T)he leading global environmental authority that sets the global environmental agenda, promotes the coherent implementation of the environmental dimension of sustainable development within the United Nations system, and serves as an authoritative advocate for the global environment"; see UN, *Programme for the Further Implementation of Agenda 21,* Adopted by governments at Earth Summit + 5, Special Session of the United Nations General Assembly, 23–28 June 1997, New York (New York: UN, 1997), pp. 1–95 at 82. The 53rd Session of the General Assembly also reiterated that UNEP's role is to be the "leading global environmental authority that sets the global environmental agenda"; see GA resolution 53/187 of 15 December 1998 in Report of the Executive Director to the Twentieth Session of the UNEP Governing Council, Doc.UNEP/GC.20/14, 24 December 1998, p. 9 and doc. A/RES/53/187 of 12 February 1999.

(i) Enhancing UNEP's Status

The shortcomings of the existing international institutional structure in the environmental field have been catalogued. The choice generally presented, is between a global centralized[125] institutional structure and a "non-functioning status quo".[126] It has been often underscored that "action-oriented institutions are urgently needed"[127] in the place of rhetorical camouflage or noble-sounding but ill-defined environmental institutions. In view of the fragmented nature of environmental institutional structure, an upward change in UNEP's gear would be appropriate. This could restore to UNEP a primary role in the environmental arena, in consonance with the goal of making it a global environmental authority. A multi-pronged approach would need to be followed if UNEP is to be seen, both by states as well as other international institutions, as an 'authority' which can set the global environmental agenda.

The need for a stronger institutional structure, however, with requisite resources and paraphernalia would "help [states] negotiate treaties, implement them, settle disputes over their terms and dispense the financial and technological assistance required to make them work".[128] The idea of an institutional entity with a broader mandate and authority would be preferable as compared to multiple actors working at cross purposes to a situation, which may characterize an institutional anarchy. It would be necessary to do the stocktaking by states as to which structures will need to be jettisoned or merged in an existing institutional entity or a new cohesive entity, which would become an international organization. The existence of such an entity

125 Hilary French has argued that there could be advantages to centralizing the process, especially to take benefit of economies of scale as well as taking a broader view of law-making and institution-building; see Hilary French, "Strengthening International Environmental Governance", *Journal of Environment & Development*, vol. 3, no.1, 1994, pp. 59–69 at 67.

126 Daniel C. Esty, "The Case for a Global Environmental Organization" in Peter B. Kenen (Ed.), *Managing the World Economy: Fifty Years After Bretton Woods* (Washington D.C.: Institute for International Economics, 1994), p. 304.

127 Mostafa Tolba argued, in the Third Baer-Huxley Memorial Lecture (Budapest, 25 April 1990), that since more than 10,000 international organizations already exist, we "cannot be awash in institutions that repeat old mistakes"; see Mostafa k. Tolba, "Building an Environmental Institutional Framework for the Future", *Environmental Conservation*, vol. 17, no.2, 1990, p. 105.

128 Hilary F. French, *After the Earth Summit: The Future of Environmental Governance*, World watch Paper 107 (Washington D.C.: World watch Institute, 1992), p. 31.

within the UN system[129] would be generally preferable, especially in view of the principle of sovereign equality of states (one state one vote). It has been argued, for instance, that it would be an easier choice to establish a new specialized agency as:

> Many nations reshape and reorganize their domestic agencies periodically. Such an effort ought to be made at the UN level. If the position is taken that the total outlay for bureaucratic resources must not exceed what it is now, great and beneficial restructuring could be achieved. It would involve cutting away existing overlaps in international agencies. Without a new institution, progress will be too slow and unsystematic. How much better it would be to have a coherent set of procedures and institutions for creating the norms. The ability to respond to the global challenges we face will be greatly reduced unless a new organization with clean lines of jurisdiction and new powers is created.[130]

The 1989 Hague Declaration, in fact, did hint at a possibility for developing, within the framework of the United Nations, such an institutional authority, either by strengthening existing institutions or by creating a new institution. Surprisingly, it went to the extent of propounding decision-making procedures which may be effective even if, on occasion, "unanimous agreement has not been achieved".[131] Moreover, such a world organization has also been favored on the grounds of higher status for global environment and development policy, improved implementation and strengthened capacity for action as compared to only a "*minimalist* strategy of efficiency improvement".[132] As a corollary to the growing clout of World Trade Organization (WTO) and the

---

129 The developing countries in the South prefer to rely upon the UN, where one-country, one-vote system gives them prominence whereas the industrialized countries in the North prefer the Bretton Woods institutions. See, for instance, Peter M. Haas, "Global Environmental Governance" in Commission on Global Governance, *Issues in Global Governance* (London: Lower International, 1995), and p. 344.

130 The former New Zealand Prime Minister's put forward his thesis for institutional restructuring just prior to the 1992 Rio Earth Summit, which argued the states due to be gathered there could use the opportunity for the purpose; see Geoffrey Palmer, "New Ways to Make International Environmental Law", *AJIL*, Vol. 86, no.2, 1992, p. 282.

131 See Hague Declaration on the Environment, The Hague, 11 March 1989 in *ILM*, vol28, 1989, pp. 1308–1310 at para (a), p. 1309.

132 Biermann and Simonis have suggested setting up of a World Environment and Development Organization, with the integration of at "the very least UNEP, CSD and relevant convention secretariats": see Frank Biermann and Udo E. Simonis, *Needed Now: A World Environment and Development Organization*, FS II 98–408, A Report to the

consequent increase in trade and environment related disputes, there appears to be an institutional vacuum for a serious dialogue partner for environment. Interestingly, this idea came to be endorsed by the former WTO director-general Renato Ruggiero himself as:

> If we want to strengthen the bridge between trade and the environment then this bridge needs two pillars. This will not be the case as long as responsibility for environmental issues is scattered among a multitude of organizations and agreements...I would suggest that we need a similar multilateral rules-based system for the environment – a World Environment Organization to also be the *institutional and legal counterpart to the World Trade Organization* (emphasis added).[133]

The general aversion to creation of new international institutions is partly due to the criticism of UN bureaucracy and funding implications. It has been felt that an autonomous character of the institution would be able to make it more efficient as well as result-oriented and not merely a talk shop or a turf for politicking. There have also been apprehensions over the voting method, as anything less than one-state-one-vote would be regarded as undemocratic and jeopardize wider political support among states. Some the developing countries have, however, expressed concern that institutionalizing global environmental governance will result in "stricter environmental standards (green protectionism)".[134]

The powerful states favor strong international institutions especially if their decision-making structures are either based upon weighted voting or are likely to help in maintaining their interests. The system of specialized agencies within the UN has occasionally come under severe strain in view of the clash of interests of states. In fact powerful states, contributing substantial sums to budgets, felt exasperated and withdrew from some institutions since they could not have their view prevail, as it happened in the case of UNESCO.[135] Some of the specialized agencies have come under pressure to undergo 'restructuring', including change of chief executive officers.

Development and Peace Foundation Bonn (Berlin: Wissenschaftszentrum Berlin für Sozialforschung gGmbH, 1998), pp. 1–26 at 7 and 11.

133 The then WTO Director-General Renato Ruggiero made these observation in his opening remarks at a High Level Symposium on Trade and the Environment on 15 March 1999. These observations were made, interestingly, in the presence of the UNEP Executive Director Klaus Töpfer as well as IUCN Director-General Maritta Koch-Weser. See *http://www.wto.org/wto/hlms/dgenv.htm.*

134 For instance, see *Down To Earth*, 31 March 2000, p. 45.

135 Three states-USA, UK and Singapore- withdrew from UNESCO in the mid-eighties on the ground of their perceived grievances against it. In this context, in a seminal work on the

Under these circumstances, the merits and demerits of having specialized agency for environment protection will need to be considered in terms of possibility of improvement over the existing situation. The core issue in the matter revolves over the desirability of enhancing UNEP's status or carving out a new organization altogether. The institution-building history shows that it is difficult to negotiate wholly a new international organization. Therefore, enhancing UNEP's status through an international agreement could be a preferred option. The process of institutional restructuring will depend upon the political will of the states, which may reflect in a merger of some other UN departments and programmes in the new organization with UNEP at its core.

New Structure

Various suggestions have been put forward on nomenclature of the new organization, ranging from an international (world) environmental organization to world environment and development organization. It appears that the primary purpose of such a specialized agency could be to enhance the UNEP's status and authority. Thus, any sculpting of a new institution would comprise of UNEP at its core. The question of merger of other existing organs and programmes (such as CSD, UNDP etc.) would depend upon the extent to which states prefer to make the exercise ambitious.

At the minimum level, a new institutional structure should result in an enhancement of UNEP's status from a UN *programme* to that of a *specialized agency*. It would be ideal if the Millennium General Assembly meet seriously reviews the requirements for a "reatly strengthened institutional structure for international environmental governance", as called upon by the first meeting of the GMEF. It would be appropriate if the Assembly decides this issue and provides mandate for the purpose. The mandate could be assigned to an intergovernmental negotiating committee on revitalizing international environmental

---

Specialized agencies, Douglas Williams has tried to explain two main sources of strain as: (i) "first, the developing countries feel that the Agencies of the United Nations have proved inadequate both in the major task of stimulating and organizing the changes they seek in international economic arrangements (changes commonly summed up in the demand for a New International Economic Order) and in the more practical enterprise of providing them efficiently with the technical and financial resources they need" and (ii) "the view of some Western governments that the Agencies have been misused to promote debates on issues outside, or only marginally related to, their proper function", see Douglas Williams, *The Specialized Agencies and the United Nations: The System in Crisis* (London: C.Hurst & Company, 1987), p. xiii.

institutions. The INC can work on a draft of constituent instrument for a new specialized agency. The constituent instrument could be adopted at a conference of plenipotentiaries. It can give shape to a United Nations Environment Protection Organization (UNEPO), wherein the existing UNEP could merge.

The new organization's constituent instrument could provide for a plenary organ which may be known as the General Conference (GC) and a Bureau, apart from other functional organs such as Science & Technology Council (STC), Environmental Law & Policy Council (ELPC), Environmental Emergencies Council (EERC) as well as a Secretariat headed by the Director-General (see Figure 5). In the case of the GC, it will be the plenary organ and it membership can comprise *all* the members of the organization. It will be the supreme

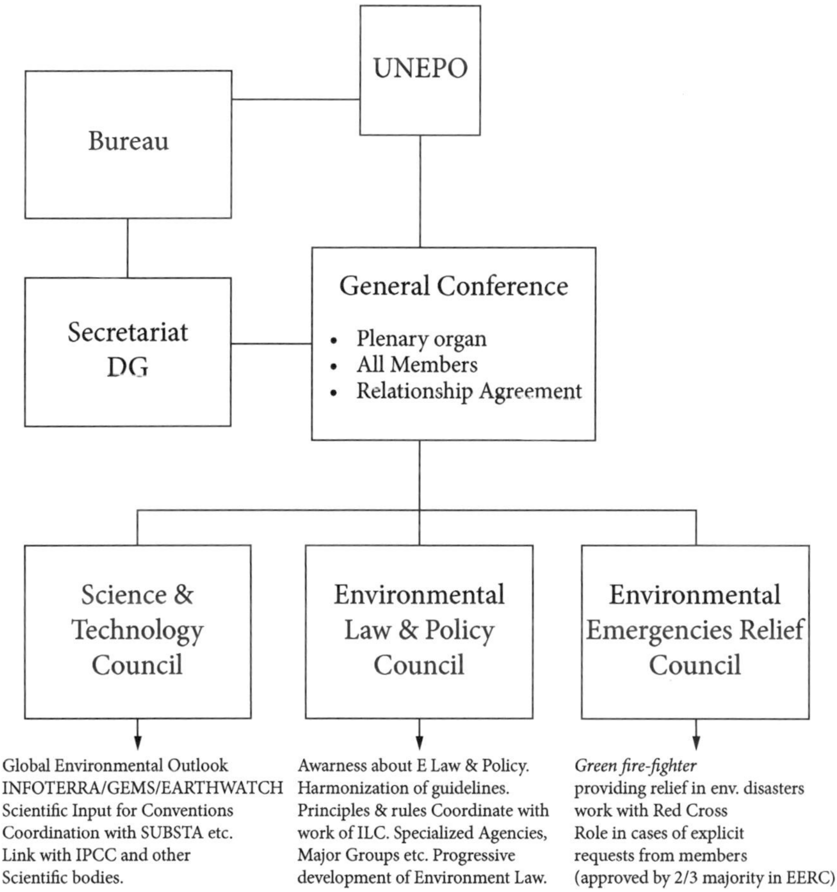

FIGURE 5 *Structure of the United Nations Environment Protection Organization* (*UNEPO*)

decision-making body of the UNEPO and based upon the one-state-one-vote principle. The GC would constitute a small Executive Committee or Bureau of about ten states and act under the authority delegated by it. In respect of membership of other functional organs, they may comprise a limited number of member states, which may vary between 24 to 60. The election of members of these organs can be by rotation, with one-third members retiring every two years. The STC and ELPC can be technical bodies, consisting of experts, who can be nominated by the states. The STC may be designed to address science and technology issues. It can maintain crucial interaction with bodies such as Subsidiary Body for Science and Technology Advice (SBSTA) of convention secretariats as well as professional bodies like the Inter-governmental Panel on Climate Change (IPCC).

The STC can provide vital scientific input on which decisions of policy-making organs can rest. Such input will also be crucial for the in-built law-making processes of the Conference of Parties (COPs) of various convention secretariats. Similarly, the ELPC's primary task can consist of maintaining coherence in the progressive development of international environmental law. It can launch new initiatives for environmental law awareness, supervise developments in *soft* law and examine the need for appropriate hard instruments from time to time. The ELPC's role will be crucial in imparting planned development of international environmental law in consonance with changing needs.

The third functional organ EERC's main task can be to address environmental emergencies. As such, it can perform the task of international *green* firefighters. It can rush assistance to victims of environmental catastrophes, such as oil pollution disasters, forest fires, transfrontier pollution (air, water, radiation etc.), major industrial accidents and natural disasters (earthquakes, cyclones, floods etc.). It can maintain close liaison with the International Committee of the Red Cross (ICRC) to provide succor to the victims of such emergencies. However, the EERC can act only subject to the explicit written request from the affected member state as well as approval by two-thirds of EERC's total members. The representatives of members of the EERC will be accessible at very short notice to facilitate quick decisions in such cases. In order to prevent any possible misuse, the work of the EERC will need to be strictly confined to redressing the environmental calamity with its expertise as well as providing relief (such as relocation, rehabilitation) to the affected people. It will not go into the issues of liability and compensation, which must necessarily be dealt separately within the framework of international instruments. The Director-General would head a small and efficient secretariat to cater to the needs of the UNEPO.

The funding of the new organization can be worked out on the same pattern of scale of contributions of the United Nations and other specialized agencies. The predetermined allocation of members' contributions will ensure stability in the functioning of UNEPO, as compared to the voluntary Environment Fund of UNEP.

(ii) New Mandate for the UN Trusteeship Council:

The UN Trusteeship Council (TC) inherited the legacy of the *mandate* system of the erstwhile League of Nations. It was entrusted with the responsibility of most of those mandate territories. The TC, as one of the main organs of the UN, was assigned responsibility to supervise the administration of the 11 original Trust Territories and their progress towards self-government or independence. As all the 11 Trust Territories have since then either become independent states or voluntarily associated themselves with a state, the TC is understood to have fulfilled its historical mission.[136] Therefore, time and again it has been suggested that the TC can be assigned with a new responsibility within the framework of the overall goals of the United Nations.

In view of the global environmental challenge, it is proposed that the TC could be entrusted with the task of overall supervision of global environmental protection as well as common areas. The UN Secretary-General's recent suggestion, in his Report to the 51st session of the General Assembly, has again revived the issue. Since the member states of the UN appear to have decided to retain the Trusteeship Council, the Secretary-General proposed that:

> [I]t be reconstituted as the forum through which Member States exercise their *collective trusteeship for the integrity of the global environment and common areas* such as the oceans, atmosphere and outer space. At the same time, it should serve to link the United Nations and civil society in

136 The 11 original Trust Territories and their Administering States were: Britain (Togoland, Cameroons and Tanganyika), Italy (Somaliland), France (Togoland and Cameroons), Belgium (Ruanda-Urundi), New Zealand (Western Samoa), Australia (Nauru and New Guinea) and United States (Pacific Islands – Federated States of Micronesia, Republic of the Marshall Islands, Commonwealth of the Northern Mariana Islands and Palau). In 1994 the UN Security Council terminated the *last* Trusteeship Agreement for the Trust Territory of the Pacific Islands (Palau), which was administered by the United States. Palau chose self-government in 1993 through plebiscite, became independent in 1994 as well as 185th member state of the UN; see United Nations, *Basic Facts*, n.8, pp. 276 and 299–300.

> addressing these areas of global concern, which require the active contribution of public, private and voluntary sectors (emphasis added).[137]

In a subsequent Note to the Assembly, the Secretary-General stated that the reconstituted TC could exercise such a collective trusteeship for the integrity of the global environment and common areas (such as the oceans, atmosphere and outer space). Elaborating on the rationale he underscored that:

> While a number of intergovernmental bodies and legal instruments have been put in place, especially following the United Nations Conference on Environment and Development, to address sustainable development and various aspects of the global environment and common areas, *there is no high-level deliberative forum that could take a comprehensive, strategic and long-term view of global trends and provide policy guidance* in those areas to the world community. A new high-level council with a well-defined mandate, that does not create overlaps or conflicts with existing intergovernmental bodies, could serve this purpose (emphasis added).[138]

The Secretary-General's suggestion was construed to be part of the mandate assigned to the 1998 UN Task Force. It was expected that the Task Force would examine the concept of *trusteeship* in greater detail and come out with proposals relating to the role, if any, which the TC could assume in the future. Ironically, the Task Force skirted[139] the issue, resorting to another *Note*[140] of the Secretary-General which proposed convening the Millennium Assembly to

137 Report of the Secretary-General, *Renewing the United Nations: A Programme for Reform*, 51st Session of the General Assembly, UN Doc.A/51/950, 14 July 1997, para 85, p. 27.

138 See Note by the Secretary-General, "A new concept of trusteeship", UN Doc.A/52/849, 31 March 1998.

139 The Task Force instead of coming out with its own view in the matter recommended that the UNEP's Executive Director (i.e. Chair of the Task Force) would undertake consultations with government representatives, non-governmental organizations etc. The burden was shifted to the two day Environment Forum, to be held in conjunction with 20th session of the UNEP Governing Council, for "forward-looking proposals for the protection of the global environment, including the possible future role of the Trusteeship Council"; see UN Doc. A/53/463, *Annex* (Task Force Report), para64 and Recommendation 24, pp. 24–25.

140 Note by the Secretary-General on "A Millennium Assembly, the United Nations system (Special Commission) and a Millennium Forum"; see UN Doc. A/52/850, 31 March 1998, pp. 1–3.

consider institutional arrangements within the United Nations system for dealing with environmental challenges of the next century.

The idea of trusteeship, which was at the basis of the original mandate for TC under the United Nations, comprised of entrusting administration of some territories till the time they attain self-government or independence. The concept now being mooted, however, has a different connotation placing the global commons in *trust* and assigning the task of high-level deliberations to the TC. The areas which might qualify, for the purpose are: oceans (beyond the limits of national jurisdiction), atmosphere, and outer space. These areas could be placed under the tutelage of a supervisory organ of the UN. That, in turn, will have to be in consonance with the different international regulatory frameworks already in place for the purpose. Another potential candidate could be Antarctica, which is subject to the Antarctica Treaty (1959),[141] under which all claims of sovereignty by claimant states have been frozen. Each of this area of global commons has its special characteristics and problems which could be looked after by a high-level supervisory body, such as TC, within the UN system. Any such arrangement shall have to be with the agreement of states parties to respective regulatory frameworks for each of the global commons which might be placed under supervision of the TC.

In case consensus emerges among states to resurrect the TC with a new mandate, it will necessitate an amendment of the UN Charter. Any possibility of amendment of the Charter has been generally thought to be a difficult task. This is especially so in view of the requirement of adoption by two-thirds of the members of the General Assembly and concurrence of all the five permanent members of the Security Council for any amendment.[142] The issue of

---

141 Antarctica Treaty (Washington), 1 December 1959; came into force 23 June 1961; see *UNTS*, vol. 402, 1959, p. 71.

142 Article 108 of the Charter is applicable for normal amendment procedure. Though, in a very rare consensus among veto powers, both memberships of the Security Council (non-permanent) as well as of the Economic and Social Council (from 18 to 27 to 54) have come to be expanded. The voting procedure (Article 27) in the Security Council has also been amended to provide for an affirmative vote of any nine members on procedural matters and on all other matters (non-procedural or substantive) an affirmative vote of nine members including the concurrent votes of five permanent members. Only on three occasions respective Amendments to the Charter were adopted by the General Assembly and were ratified, as required by Article 108: This covered expansion of the Security Council and the Economic and Social Council and the review of the Charter. These amendments took place as: Articles 23, 27 and 61 on 17 December 1963 (came into force 31 August 1965), Article 61 on 20 December 1971 (came into force 24 September 1973) and Article 109(1) on 20 December 1965 (came into force 12 June 1968).

amendment of the Charter has been mired in controversy since the establishment of the UN. In spite of several efforts in the past, no General Conference of the UN members has materialized for the purpose of *review* (Article 109) of the Charter. A review conference can, at least theoretically, be convened by a two-thirds vote of the Assembly and a vote of *any nine* members of the Council. However, any alteration of the Charter proposed at a review conference cannot take effect without consent of all the five permanent members of the Council.

In the light of the experience of half a century of UN's existence, any proposal for amendment of the Charter will be generally treated cautiously. There have been numerous efforts to push for expansion in the membership of the Security Council or even review of the veto power itself. They have still not materialized, as it is feared especially by the veto powers that it would open up the Pandora 's Box. Many states have felt that the UN Charter does not reflect the reality of the present day and would favor making it more democratic. However, the odds are heavily in favor of a *status quo*. If there is a consensus on the utility of the TC in the new context, an appropriate mandate could be worked out which may provide it a meaningful role.

A package for a new mandate for the TC would need to amend chapter XIII of the Charter, especially the composition (Article 86) and functions and powers (Article 87 and 88). In terms of composition, the TC could be a small body whose membership may be limited (ranging from 15 at the minimum to 54 at the maximum). The General Assembly would elect members for a period of three years, with one third of members retiring every three years. The allocation of seats would be on the basis of equitable geographical distribution. Unlike the earlier incarnation of the TC, there will not be any trust areas assigned to it. As such, no distinction would be drawn between members administering trust territories and those not administering trust territories. No member of the TC would be assigned any special role or conferred any privileged voting rights. The functioning of TC would be on the one state one vote basis.

If retained in the present form, the UNEP or the UNEPO will have to work out a special relationship. Figure 6 suggests an organic linkage between the two. In that event the UNEP or the UNEPO would report directly to the TC and, through it, to the General Assembly. The TC would of course be able to avail of the assistance of the ECOSOC and the specialized agencies in regard to matters with which they are respectively concerned (Article 91).

The new mandate for the TC could be formulated as follows:

Article 87: The General Assembly and, under its authority, the Trusteeship Council, in carrying out their functions, may:

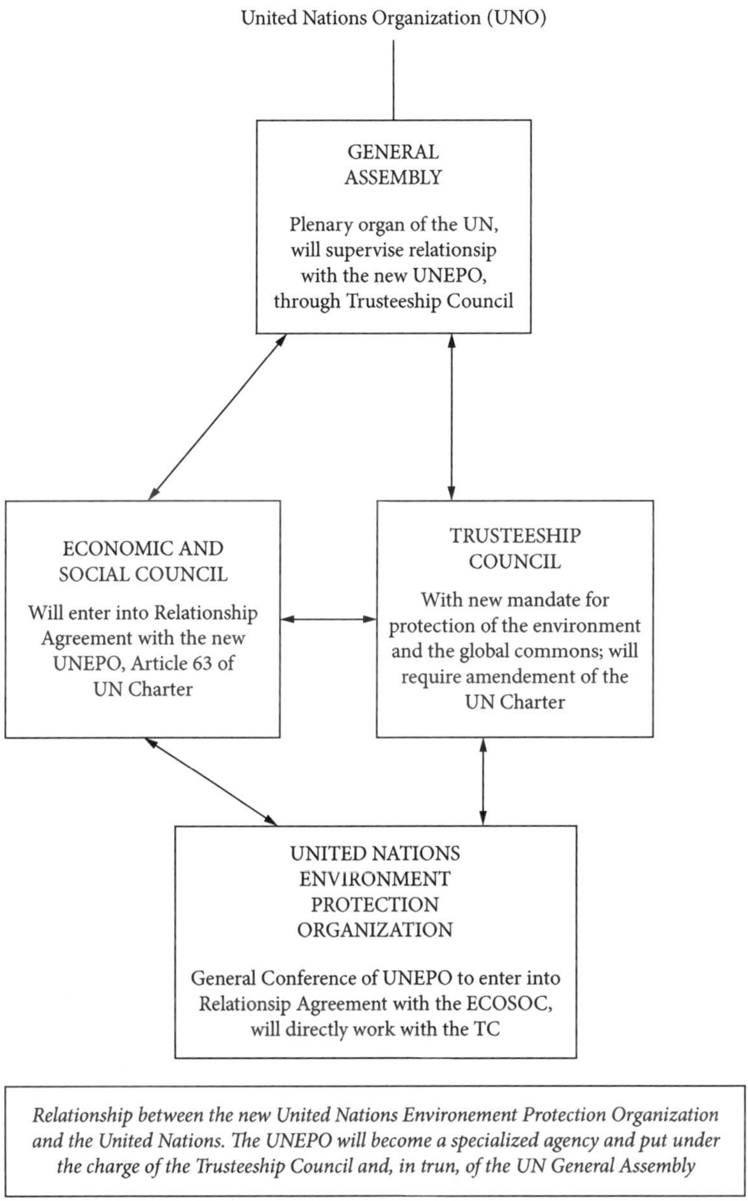

FIGURE 6 *Relationship between the revived UN Trusteeship Council and UNEPO*

a. consider reports submitted by the United Nations Environment Protection Organization (UNEPO);
b. examine progress in reversing global environmental deterioration in consultation with the UNEPO;

c. review the status of each of the designated global commons keeping in view the overall interest of all the inhabitants of the planet earth, in consultation with decision-making organs of the respective regulatory regimes;
d. adopt appropriate decisions and other action, as deemed proper, from time to time, consistent with the respective international agreements and mechanisms.

Article 88: The Trusteeship Council shall prepare the form and modalities for submission of periodic reports by each regulatory regime of the global commons areas. The decision-making organs of the respective regimes shall make an annual report to the Trusteeship Council and, thought it to, the General Assembly.

Conclusion

An evaluation of the excising international environmental institutions, especially UNEP, indicates the need for bold and innovative institutional overhauling. The global environmental challenges warrant institutional responses that are timely, pragmatic and adequate to ensure protection of the global ecological heritage and the survival of the international community. The states members of the UN will need to rise above narrow partisan considerations and muster enough political courage to carve out appropriate international environmental machinery. The tested and recognized contribution of UNEP needs to be factored in this process. The failures of UNEP as an IEIs need to be also attributed to the political neglect of its member states, who in their wisdom thought it fit not to equip it with teeth and requisite authority to enable it function as an effective international environmental institution. UNEP's merger with and becoming the core of a new 'specialized' environmental entity will have to ensure to an enhanced stature and authority. The possibility of endowing a new mandate for the Trusteeship Council must constitute a necessary part of the ongoing exercise of UN restructuring. It would provide an appropriate task for the principal organ of the UN to address a contemporary challenge, and confer new authority to the UN itself.

It needs to be underscored that any endeavor for institutional change within the UN system, will require political support of the states. The states have generally been unwilling to establish powerful institutions, and have sought to stifle institutions that fail to meet the self-designated policy goals. As primary subjects of international law, states continue to be the final arbiters of the strength and authority of international environmental institutions. By the same logic, states have a primary responsibility not to fail the institutions they have established by their political neglect.

PART 3

Sectoral Law Making

CHAPTER 8

Multilateral Environmental Agreements

Introduction

We live in an age of regulation wherein state sovereignty has come to be circumscribed by law.[1] Thus the process of legal regulation of state behaviour is now manifesting in various spheres of international life. As a result the process of 'centralized legalization' concerning sectoral environmental problems has gradually come to be institutionalized. This trend has assumed regularity, intensity and variety in the past four decades so as to cover environmental issues that were hitherto sought to be regulated at national and/or regional level.

The multilateral law making process has worked in a piecemeal,[2] *ad hoc* and sporadic manner. It has, in turn, contributed to the growing web of treaties as most important source of international environmental law. Moreover, it has emerged as a predominant method of regulating state behaviour on a global *problematique*. It appears that law making on environmental issues is greatly facilitated through treaties due to scientific uncertainties and a sense of urgency involved in the matter. As a result multilateral environmental agreements (MEAs) have emerged as a unique technique that encompasses flexibility, pragmatism, in-built law making mechanism as well as step-by-step consensual approach to norm-setting. In fact it has become truism to state that:

> MEAs have emerged as one of the best ways of institutionalizing international (environmental) cooperation and triggering national action in the environmental sector...increasing number of treaties and secretariats responsible for their administration, coherence and coordination of efforts has emerged as a central issue for effective international environmental governance.[3]

1 For a detailed legal thesis on this issue, see Arthur Larson and Clarence Wilfred Jenks, *Sovereignty within the Law* (New York: Oceana Publications, 1965).

2 There is a debate on the issue of 'fragmentation' due to such a piecemeal approach. On this, for example, see UNEP, "Fragmentation of Environmental Pillar and its Impact on Efficiency and Effectiveness", *Issues Brief No.2* (Nairobi: UNEP/DELC); available at http://www.unep.org/environmentalgovernance/Portals/8/InstitutionalFrameworkforSustainabledevPAPER2.pdf.

3 Ibid, p. 3.

 | DOI 10.1163/9789004214552_009

The states, ostensibly, claim to act in 'common' interest while joining multilateral environmental negotiations. The recent history of multilateral negotiations does underscore the dilemma to treaty or no to treaty on a specific environmental problem. In fact precise nature of the instrument that could be desirable as well as its scope – global or regional, falls within the domain of scholarly scrutiny.

In this context, efforts of UNEP to take stock of implementation[4] of MEAs have taken cognizance of only a part of the complex picture of marathon regulatory process at work. As a corollary to it, launch of the *High-Level Colombo Process on Envisioning Next Steps Concerning Compliance with and Enforcement of MEAs* had two sessions in 2006 (Colombo, 21–22 January and Geneva, 31 May-2 June). This brainstorming process (the author was part of it) could short list several shortcomings in this area including lack of adequate resources, inherent deficiencies in the respective legal instruments, inadequate capacities to engage in negotiations and implementation at domestic level, lack of proper coordination and synergies among MEA Secretariats as well as between UNEP and MEA Secretariats, missing linkages between implementation process and socio-economic developmental issues.[5] The exercise led to identifying 'deficits' at several levels including legal instruments, institutional structures, inter linkages and 'trust' of the contracting parties. It was proposed to 'institutionalize' the process for attaining better implementation, compliance with and enforcement of MEAs. UNEP could do this in consultation with MEAs as well as through appropriate mandate from the Governing Council (redesignated as 'UN Environment Assembly' by the UNGA reso.67/251 of 13 March 2013). In fact it is contended that four broad variables[6] such as factors involving the participating States, characteristics of the activity involved, characteristics of the agreements and the international environment could affect the compliance of MEAs.

Often concerns are expressed with regard to problems of coherence and efficiency linked to the increasing number of MEAs. Although the development of this architecture has made positive advances yet international environmental governance (IEG) is perceived to be characterized by fragmentation.

4 For this see http://www.unep.org/delc/MEAImplementationSupport/tabid/54401/Default.aspx.

5 *See* Developing Responses to Factors Inhibiting Implementation and Enforcement of Multilateral Environment Agreements, *UNEP High-Level Meeting Envisioning the Next Steps for Compliance with and Enforcement of Multilateral Environmental Agreements, Colombo, 21–22 January 2006 (on file with the author).*

6 See E.B. Weiss & H. Jacobson, eds. *Engaging Countries: Strengthening Compliance with International Environmental Accords* (MIT Press: 1998).

It often suffers from inconsistency, inefficiency, additional cost and imperfect allocation of human and financial resources. It weakens the capacity of IEG to contribute to sustainable development. In view of such perceived fragmentation of the environmental regulation, there is a need to grapple with the challenge and closely examine key issues such as: (i) workability of the 'centralized law-making' approach; (ii) role of hard scientific evidence in shaping the regulatory tool; (iii) nature of the instruments churned out in multilateral environmental conferences (framework conventions); (iv) scope and applicability of the regulatory tool (global or regional); (v) 'interest' of the contracting states in a specific regime; (vi) contextualizing the regime with developmental goals; (vii) compliance and enforcement (viii) competence of the secretariats (location, personnel, funding, legal capacity); (ix) emergence of 'compliance mechanisms'; do they serve as dispute avoidance and/or dispute settlement mechanisms? (x) relationship between 'host' institutions and convention secretariats.[7]

The current patterns of institutionalized environmental cooperation require closer scrutiny in the backdrop of rapidly deteriorating global environment, expectations of the sovereign states and questions regarding effectiveness/adequacy of the instrumentality adopted to address the *problematique*. Even as the Rio+20 Summit (June 2012)[8] proved to be a dismal global conferencing event, a closer examination could provide a 'sense' of the issues flagged above so as to effectively grapple with the growing corpus and hence challenge of governing the MEAs. It could, in turn, provide a way out for the simmering governance challenge for unprecedented growth of MEAs in the past more than four decades.

Genesis of MEAs

Unique Treaty Making

The initial decades after the UN came into being; there was a flurry of movement for codifying a host of established customary principles of international

7 Bharat H. Desai, *Understanding the Complex Web of Multilateral Environmental Agreements: A Note on Long Term View for the Indian Ministry of Environment & Forests* (Bonn; 8 June 2006), pp. 1–3. Also see, Bharat H. Desai, *Multilateral Environmental Agreements: Legal Status of the Secretariats* (CUP: New York 2010).

8 The United Nations Conference on Sustainable Development (UNCSD) had been organized in pursuance of General Assembly Resolution 64/236 (A/RES/64/236), and took place in Brazil on 20–22 June 2012 to mark the 20th anniversary of the 1992 United Nations Conference on Environment and Development (UNCED), in Rio de Janeiro, and the 10th anniversary of the 2002 World Summit on Sustainable Development (WSSD) in Johannesburg; available at, http://www.uncsd2012.org/about.html.

law. It did unleash an era of codification and 'progressive' development of international law.[9] In essence, it heralded an era of treaty-making in every conceivable area of international law. It seems the UN system itself (for instance 'specialized agencies' like ILO and IMO) regularly churn out conventions that meet the needs of their member states to regulate specific areas (like occupational health and safety as well as maritime safety and pollution). They have in fact unleashed a "gigantic treaty network"[10] that covers many crucial areas of human activities. Thus the mosaic of international law seems to be gradually thickening largely due to proliferation of treaties for regulating state activities in various spheres of international life.

The Vienna Convention on the Law of Treaties (1969) defines a 'treaty' as "an international agreement concluded between States in written form and governed by international law, whether embodied in a single instrument or in two or more related instruments and whatever its particular designation".[11] Thus according to the definition of the Vienna Convention, an international agreement that seeks to address specific sectoral environmental issue is a 'treaty' governed by it. The nomenclature 'multilateral' has to be seen as having two or more sovereign states as parties to it. Thus multilateral environmental agreements do fall within the ambit of traditional 'multilateral' treaties that sovereign states design to address a specific *problematique*. As such, the Vienna Convention governs such treaties as regards their formation, coming into force and subsequent operation through the tools and techniques used, institutional forms put into place and normative rules churned out regularly.[12] They could in fact vary from case to case. Many of the multilateral agreements in the environmental field could be regarded as *sui generis*. This is especially so since barring some common aspects that could be regarded as part of a 'pattern' (in terms of nomenclature, form, enabling provisions for in-built law making and institutions such as plenary and subsidiary organs), these treaty-processes

9 Article 102 of the United Nations Charter (1945).

10 Roy Lee, "Multilateral Treaty-Making and Negotiation Technique: An Appraisal" in Bin Chang and Edward Brown (Eds.), *Contemporary Problems of International Law: Essays in Honour of Georg Schwartzenberger on His Eightieth Birthday* (1998); quoted in Jose E. Alvarez, "The New Treaty Makers", *Boston College International and Comparative Law Review*, vol. XXV, no. 2, 2002, pp. 213–234 at 218.

11 Article 2 (1) (a) of the Vienna Convention; see http://untreaty.un.org/ilc/texts/instruments/english/conventions/1_1_1969.pdf. Also see http://fletcher.tufts.edu/multi/texts/BH538.txt. Also see generally, Oliver Dorr, Kristen Schmalenbach (ed.), *Vienna Convention on the Law of Treaties: A Commentary* (Springer: 2012).

12 See generally, M. E. Villiger, *Commentary on the 1969 Vienna Convention on the Law of Treaties,* (Leiden: Martinus Nijhoff Publishers, 2009].

carry unique features that become necessary to redress a specific problem area. That explains the rationale for development of treaty-making as a testimony of fine craft and innovation, as well as designing of new tools and techniques specific to the sectoral issue at stake.

MEAs are *prima facie* like other treaties governed by international law. Their special characteristics include the very process of initiating such agreements, issues sought to be addressed, relative short time span within which they take shape, scientific uncertainty that surrounds the core issue at stake, participation by a large number (in some cases, like UNCCD, almost universal) of states and in many cases the 'soft' content of such agreements (defying the common understanding of such treaties as 'hard' instruments).[13] Furthermore, as they are not 'one-time affair', they stand apart from conventional treaties as they invariably comprise built-in law making features. As a result, most of the MEAs could be regarded as 'processes' that are generally initiated by international institutions (such as UNEP) and taken over from them by the sovereign states. In many a cases these treaties are initiated due to a 'trigger event'[14] on necessitating urgent negotiations by the states to reach an agreement on regulation of the sectoral issue in question. Once the states are seized of the matter through negotiations, relevant catalyst institution (such as UNEP) takes a back seat.

It is noteworthy that the states have engaged in law making processes that have novelty in terms of issue-specific regulatory process.[15] However, in

13 For details see, Bharat H. Desai, *Multilateral Environmental Agreements: Legal Status of the Secretariats* (CUP: New York 2010).

14 "Trigger events' could include the evidence released by the British Antarctic expedition on stratospheric ozone layer depletion or increasing cases of unregulated dumping of hazardous wastes posing threat to humans and the environment or scientific reports on the accumulation of greenhouse gases in the atmosphere contributing to global climatic changes etc. In each of such case, the trigger provided by these reports/incidents led UNEP on its own or in collaboration with agencies such as WMO to initiate negotiating processes that culminated in respective global treaties: 1985 Vienna Convention on Depletion of the Ozone Layer; 1989 Basel Convention on Transboundary Movements of Hazardous Wastes and their Disposal and 1992 UN Framework Convention on Climate Change.

15 The Minamata Convention on Mercury was signed on 11 October 2013; [for text see, http://www.mercuryconvention.org/Portals/11/documents/publications/Minamata ConventiontextEn.pdf]. The agreement is a response to the realization that mercury pollution is a global problem that no one country can solve alone. However, it was way back in 1956 that Minamata city of Japan had its first case of mercury poisoning and it became so widespread that it was called as Minamata disease. It was due to heavy industrial dumping of methylmercury waste by Chisso Corporation in the Minamata Bay, see,

essence, it reflects a constructive process akin to 'codification' that rests on state practice. The basic legal underpinnings of the process are derived from fundamental principles of state responsibility under international law. The 'process' involves efforts to work out multilateral treaties on even routine issues of international cooperation, apart from dealing with common problems (described more recently as 'common concerns'). It has ushered in an intricate mosaic of treaties at bilateral, regional and global levels.[16] Thus treaties seem to have now become cornerstone of multilateral regulatory enterprise. As a result, this *sui generis* law-making process has started making inroads in to the cherished domain of sovereign jurisdiction of the states. Increasing need for international cooperation has propelled states to come together on common platforms, including institutional ones. As a corollary to it, the notion of 'sharing sovereignties in common' by the states to address some of the global problems (described as common concerns of humankind) is gradually gaining ground.

Interestingly, the law-making process is not the exclusive preserve of the states alone, as it is being effectively influenced and shaped by a host of non-state actors including intergovernmental organizations, non-governmental organizations as well as think tanks, academic institutions, business groups and individual experts.[17] The advent of the 'observer' system[18] within the UN system as well as at other intergovernmental processes (such as multilateral environmental negotiations) has lifted the veil of secrecy and exclusiveness from what is essentially a state-centric law-making process.

'Lessons from Minamata Disease and Mercury Management in Japan', Ministry of the Environment, Japan; available at, http://www.env.go.jp/chemi/tmms/pr-m/mat01/en_full.pdf. Decades after industrial dumping ceased, thousands of survivors of these incidents are still suffering from a host of neurological symptoms, including tremors, dizziness, headaches, memory loss, and vision and hearing problems; the most severe cases also involve developmental disabilities, cognitive and motor dysfunction, and physical abnormalities; see, Rebecca Kessler, The Minimata Convention on Mercury: A First Step toward protecting Future Generations, Environmental Health Perspectives", Vol. 121(10), October 2013; available at: http://ehp.niehs.nih.gov/121–a304/.

16 For more information on global and regional treaties see, United Nations Information Portal on Multilateral Environmental Agreements [InforMEA], http://www.informea.org/treaties/.

17 See generally, Anna Spain, 'Who's going to Copenhagen? The Rise of Civil Society in International Treaty-Making', ASIL Insights, Vol. 13, No. 25, December 11, 2009; available at, http://www.asil.org/insights/volume/13/issue/25/who%E2%80%99s-going-copenhagen-rise-civil-society-international-treaty-making.

18 For more information on observers in UN system, see, http://www.un.org/en/members/aboutpermobservers.shtml.

Global Conferencing Technique

The environment related global conferencing represents an epic form of multilateralism at work. It is a classic example of need-based responses of the states to address specific problems.[19] The range as well as complexity of these MEAs resulting from marathon multilateral negotiations, often instituted by global conferences, is unprecedented. In view of the very nature of present day environmental challenges, the legal responses have started affecting the day-to-day lives of people across the globe, as it is no longer confined only to matters of high state affairs. It can be attributed to the development of MEAs (the so-called *hard law*) on specific sectoral issues as well as a host of other rules and standards (now widely known as *soft law*) for regulating the state behaviour. Thus the critical process of multilateral environmental regulation is getting complex by the day in terms of its range as well as content, notwithstanding its partial and uneven growth. The final form that a treaty (hard law) attains does still require explicit consent of the sovereign states (expressed through signature, followed by ratification or accession of the legal instrument in question).

It was only in the 1970s that issue of protection of the environment came on to the global stage in a big way. The growth and changing character of international environmental law could be mainly assigned to circumstances and responsible factors that prevailed during the pre-1972 period,[20] contribution of the 1972 Stockholm Conference[21] and the 1992 Rio Earth

---

19 See, Peter M Hass (2002), "UN Conferences and Constructivist Governance of the Environment", *Global Governance,* Vol. 8, pp. 73–91 at 78.

20 In the pre-Stockholm period, the treaty-making efforts were primarily guided by short term utility.

21 The 1972 Stockholm Conference that came to be convened by the UN General Assembly launched a formal process of institutionalization of international environmental cooperation. It became major landmark in providing a sound trajectory as far as international environmental policy and law were concerned. The Stockholm Declaration comprised 26 principles that, in addition to the general concern for environment, also took cognizance of developmental concerns of the developing countries. The most notable component of it was principle 21, which sought to put forward a two-part statement that: *"States have, in accordance with the Charter of the United Nations and the principles of international law, the sovereign right to exploit their own resources pursuant to their own environmental policies, and the responsibility to ensure that activities within their jurisdiction or control do not cause damage to the environment of other States or of areas beyond the limits of national jurisdiction."* Report of the United Nations Conference on the Human Environment, *UN Doc.A/CONF.48/14,* pp. 2–65 and Corr. 1 (1972). Also see *International Legal Materials* (ILM), vol. 11, 1972, p. 1416.

Summit[22] that decisively brought to the fore mega – conferencing technique to address global environmental problems. Moreover, incorporation of some of the emerging principles of international environmental law in these agreements, underscored their gradual acceptance for judging the *threshold* of environmental behavior of sovereign states. It seems the Rio Earth Summit heralded coming of age of multilateral environmental regulatory technique.

As a corollary to it, various institutional structures that have emerged (such as conference of parties or subsidiary bodies), provide platforms for continuous institutionalized international cooperation on a specific environmental issue. These institutions provide not only a servicing base to the contracting states of a MEA but also play an important role in giving effect to the in-built law making process.[23] In this organic and continuous treaty-making exercise, states have sought to create and, in turn, rely upon institutional mechanisms as fulcrum to serve specific purposes. As such advent and proliferation of MEAs is best reflection of functional approach at work. It also underscores craving of states for institutional structures as facilitators, catalysts and almost indispensable cooperative frameworks.

Sui Generis *Art*

MEAs have emerged as "predominant legal method for addressing environmental problems that cross national boundaries".[24] As such environmental treaty-making in recent decades has emerged as a fine tool that comprises a great diversity and innovative approaches at regulation. Most of them underscore multidimensional nature of environmental problems that need special sensitivity and *sui generis* approach to address them. The subject matter of

22 An assessment of the contribution made by UNCED may be perceived variously, depending upon what one expected of it. From the perspective of its contribution to the development of international environmental law, however, it may be seen in terms of immediate results obtained as well as UNCED's impact on the norm-setting process *per se*. UNCED itself may be regarded as one of the most remarkable events in the history of multilateral environmental negotiations. It may even be regarded as unparalleled for the coming together of such a large number of states to address global problems, which came to be regarded as 'common concerns of humankind'. When the two multilateral agreements i.e. UN Framework Convention on Climate Change (UNFCCC) as well as Convention on Biological Diversity (CBD) opened for signature at UNCED, more than 150 states put their signatures to them.

23 See, Annecoos Wiersema (2009), "Conference of Parties to Multilateral Environmental Agreements: The New International Law-Makers?", *American Society of International Law Proceedings,* Vol. 103, March 25–28, 2009, pp. 74–76, at 75.

24 "Developments in the Law: International Environmental Law", *Harvard Law Review*, vol. 104, no. 3, 1991, p. 1521.

MEAs range from issues such as protection of a specie (whale) or flora and fauna in general (CITES) or migratory species of wild animals (CMS), cultural and heritage sites (WHC), regulation of trade of hazardous chemicals and wastes (Rotterdam, Basel, Minamata), air pollution (LRTAP) and persistent organic pollutants (Stockholm) to more remote issues like ozone depletion, climate change and biological diversity. The core MEA have come to be categorized into mainly five groups: the biodiversity-related conventions, the atmospheric conventions, the land conventions, the chemicals and hazardous wastes conventions, and the regional seas and related agreements. It seems, as a part of the organic law-making process, MEAs on a host of these issues have in fact "changed over time, just as political, economic, social, and technological conditions have changed over time".[25]

In the pre-Stockholm period, the treaty-making efforts were primarily guided by very limited concerns such as the regulation of marine pollution or nuclear energy issues or conservation of particular specie such as the whale.[26] In this early era, the principles of "unfettered national sovereignty over natural resources and absolute freedom of the seas beyond the three-mile territorial limit"[27] provided the guiding force to emerging international environmental law. The inherent perceptions of the architects of earliest international regulatory efforts were mainly directed towards the use of the living and non-living resources and not environment protection *per se*. Most of them strongly reflected *utilitarian* character. For example, the Convention for the Protection of Birds Useful to Agriculture (1902), sought to address those birds, which were regarded as "useful" to agriculture at the time, as compared to certain "non-useful birds" such as eagles, and falcons, which have now come to be protected. Thus, the negotiators as well as draftsmen of the time essentially took into account "short term utility, the immediate usefulness of protected species",[28]

25 Edith Brown Weiss, "The Five International Treaties: A Living History" in Edith Brown Weiss and Harold K. Jacobson (Eds.), *Engaging Countries: Strengthening Compliance with International Environmental Accords* (Cambridge: MIT Press, 1998), p. 89.

26 Some of the early international conventions in this direction were, for instance, International Convention for the Regulation of Whaling (1946), International Convention for the Prevention of Pollution of the Sea by Oil (1954) Convention on Third Party Liability in the Field of Nuclear Energy (1960) and Supp. Convention (1963), Convention Relating to Intervention on the High Seas in Cases of Oil Pollution Casualties (1969) etc.

27 Edith Brown Weiss, "Global Environmental Change and International Law: The Introductory Framework" in Edith Brown Weiss (Ed.) *Environmental Change and International Law* (Tokyo: United Nations Uni. Press, 1992), p. 7.

28 Alexandre Kiss and Dinah Shelton, *International Environmental Law*, 2nd ed. (New York: Transnational Publishers, 2000), p. 56.

as dictated by the prevailing societal needs. In view of such a *utilitarian* approach at work, the legal responses for regulation of state behavior in this era remained sporadic and catered to specific needs (mainly economic), especially at the regional level.

The range of issues, however, sought to be addressed within the framework of multilateral agreements in the past four decades (post-Stockholm era) is quite remarkable. It appears that states are gradually inclining towards specialized multilateral agreements as a mode of grappling with global environmental problems as they perceive them at a given time. As a corollary, the range and content as well as complexity of these agreements surpasses law-making endeavors in any other sphere of international law. The considerable 'proliferation'[29] of such MEAs underscores the fact that state practice in this respect seem have come to stay. Interestingly, however, their existence is determined by the political will of the contracting states and tailored to the need to address a specific global *problematique*. It also reflects strong sense of multilateralism at work to address some of the common concerns that sovereign states consider necessary to regulate through these instruments. There are, however, some issue-specific common elements and differences in the treaty-making resorted to in some of the sectors (see **Table 4** for a comparative picture of select MEAs).[30]

Quest for Institutionalized Cooperation

As seen earlier, MEAs have emerged as one of the best examples of institutionalized intergovernmental cooperation to address specific environmental issues. This form of governance is *sui generis* as it has all the trappings of an international 'organization' without formally being one. As a matter of fact, these forms of governance cater to the requirement for *ad hoc* bodies flowing from multilateral treaties akin to functional international organizations. The

---

29 It is understood that out of an estimated 500 international conventions related to the environment, almost 300 have been negotiated since the 1972 UN Conference on Human Environment. Multilateral Environment Agreements can be generally put in three categories: (a) core environmental conventions and related agreements of global significance, which have been closely associated with UNEP (in terms of initiative for negotiation, development and/or activities); (b) global conventions relevant to the environment, including regional conventions of global significance, which have been negotiated independently of UNEP and (c) other MEAs, which are restricted by scope and geographical range. For further details on MEAs, see UNEP, "International Environmental Governance: Multilateral Environmental Agreements", *First Meeting of the Open-ended Intergovernmental Group of Ministers or their Representatives on International Environmental Governance*, New York, 18 Aril 2001, Doc. UNEP/IGM/1/INF/3 of 6 April 2001.

30 It is updated as on 20 December 2013 from the websites of respective MEAs.

legal instrument in question provides backbone to the institutionalized cooperative mechanism. Their existence is determined by consensual political will of the contracting states and tailored to address a specific environmental problem. Through treaty-based institutionalized forms (such as plenary political bodies, subsidiary scientific and technical bodies, funding mechanisms and compliance committees), MEAs have sought to establish *processes* of cooperation to address new and complex challenges as they arise.

As treaty-based bodies, MEAs primarily seek to put into place *ad hoc* and autonomous arrangements that are designed to address a sectoral environmental issue. In view of the very nature of this problem-specific institutional arrangement, a MEA is technically expected to be 'wound up' as and when its desired objectives are realized. Furthermore, its autonomous nature is determined by the instrument in question as well as political will of the contracting states as reflected through the decisions (arrived at through lowest common denominator) of the Conference (or Meeting) of the Parties of MEA. Many questions arise as regards the origin, initiation, process and workability of these treaty based regimes. This includes issues such as role of a 'trigger event'[31] that forces states to consider possible legalization on an environmental problem, an institutional catalyst that initiates preparatory process for crystallization of regulatory framework, negotiating process to arrive at consensual text of the instrument, subsequent law-making process to 'flesh out' the gaps or inherent ambiguities, their regulatory contribution, inherent complexities, in-built flexibility, large participation of states, role of non-state actors and issues of implementation and compliance.

Some Key Legal Challenges

Making Sense

Even as we grapple with the challenge of governing MEAs, in some quarters it still remains a matter of debate as regards "sense"[32] of negotiating these instruments for regulating an environmental problem. It could be due to the intricate nature of negotiations, scientific uncertainty plaguing the negotiations as well as negotiated final text of the instrument. Moreover, these treaties have a long gestation period (including entry into force) as they come of age

31 See n. 14.

32 On the issue of reasons going into negotiations on MEAs, see an essay "To Treaty or Not to Treaty? A Survey of Practical Experience", in Peter H. Sand, *Transnational Environmental Law: Lessons in Global Change* (The Hague: Kluwer Law International, 1999), pp. 55–60.

gradually over a long period of time. This has led to some critics describing MEAs as "sleeping treaty"[33] regimes due to relatively long time span they require to become operational. This perception seems to arise due to possible deleterious effect on environment[34] in view of prolonged regulatory inactivity. As such enforcement of and compliance with such treaties intrinsically does pose a challenge.

Most of these agreements do not end up as a one-time process as they do not adopt an all-comprehensive approach in negotiating a MEA that was witnessed especially during the marathon negotiations on the Law of the Sea Convention (1973–1982) resulting in the "Constitution for the Oceans".[35] It provided lessons as regards placing all the issues in a single basket for threadbare negotiations and arriving at a consensual text. MEAs that emerge as an end product from marathon negotiations, spread over relatively short time-span, generally take effect in a whittled down form – sometimes almost as bare skeletons – to facilitate consensual acceptance of the negotiated final text for the states.

Scope of the Treaty: Global v. Regional

Many of the traditional multilateral agreements among states, especially concerning sharing of common international resources such as waters, did enshrine provisions prohibiting fouling or pollution of waters as well as state responsibility for the purpose. Issues of mainly regional concern such as acid rain and air pollution as well as protection of flora and fauna later followed it. Moreover, a large number of regional MEAs have emerged from the 'Regional Seas Programme'[36] that is regarded as 'jewel in the crown'

33 See, generally, S Lyster, *International Wildlife Law: An Analysis of International Treaties Concerned with the Conservation of Wildlife* (New York: Cambridge University Press, 1985).

34 For instance, the first Meeting of Parties (MOP) of the EUROBATS Agreement focused on procedural affairs, leaving little time to discuss anything substantive relating to species conservation. In actual fact, the Parties were only in a position to best determine the requisite measures to be introduced and elaborated upon to address threats to the survival of bats at the third MOP.

35 Remarks by Tommy T. B. Koh, President of the Third U.N. Conference on the Law of the Sea, Montego Bay (Jamaica), 10 December 1982; see United Nations, *U.N. Convention on the Law of the Sea* (New York: UN, 1983), p. xxxiii.

36 The Regional Seas Programme (RSP) has been regarded as one of the biggest achievements of UNEP – 'a jewel in its crown'. The RSP was launched in 1974. The first of the RSP was developed in the Mediterranean with an Action Plan (1975), followed by a Convention (1976). Following success of the RSP for the Mediterranean region, RSP for other regions

of UNEP. It shows systematic "regional approach to protecting the environment and managing natural resources".[37] It seems that geographical contiguity as well as common environmental problems of the coastal states of specific regional seas provides a basic framework to embark upon a regional seas instrument.

The network of RSPs have grown around the world in the past 40 years (since it was launched in 1974) to cover 18 regions and 150 coastal states. It is one of the most globally comprehensive initiatives for the protection of marine and coastal environments. It shows the workability of the concept of regionalization. The underlying logic behind them is that "specific environmental problems of geographically-limited areas usually are better regulated by the affected states".[38] Most of the RSPs are similar in structure but different in specifics. In a way they may be considered to be part of "comprehensive action plans oriented toward overall regional development, including coastal zone planning, monitoring and research, and technical assistance and training".[39] It is no mean achievement that the mosaic of 18 RSPs covers a staggering number of 50 instruments comprising 14 regional conventions, 2 special regional mechanisms and 13 action plans[40] as well

were developed. The Governing Council of UNEP has, in fact, consistently endorsed a regional approach for the control of marine pollution, management of marine and coastal resources and development of regional Action Plans for the purpose. From the first Action Plan adopted in the Mediterranean (1975) as well as the one for the Caspian Sea (2003), the RSPs have multiplied to cover the marine environment of more than 150 of the world's coastal countries.

37 See http://www.unep.org/regionalseas/ (as on 20 January 2014).

38 See Kiss and Shelton, n. 28, p. 33.

39 Peter H. Sand has described five components of the RSPs as: "(a) environmental assessment (the MEDPOL monitoring network); (b) environmental management (the 'Blue Plan' for co-ordinated development of the coastal region; and the 'Priority Actions Programme' for co-operation in coastal settlements, aquaculture, water resources, soils, renewable energy, and tourism); (c) institutional arrangements (permanent secretariat services and periodic conferences); (d) financial arrangements (trust fund shared by coastal states); and (e) regional legal instruments, following a highly uniform pattern and at least partly formulated in near identical language", see Peter H. Sand, *Transnational Environmental Law: Lessons in Global Change* (The Hague: Kluwer Law International, 1999), pp. 175–187 at 181.

40 The eighteen regional seas programmes are: 1. *Antarctic*: Convention on the Conservation of Antarctic Marine Living Resources (1980); entered into force: 7 April 1982 2. *Arctic*: Protection of the Arctic Marine Environment (PAME) established by the Arctic Council Ministers in Nuuk, Greenland, September 1993 3. *Baltic Sea*: The Convention on the Protection of the Marine Environment of the Baltic Sea Area, 1992, entered into force on

17 January 2000 4. *Black Sea*: The Convention on the Protection of the Black Sea Against Pollution was signed in Bucharest in April 1992, and ratified by all six legislative assemblies of the Black Sea countries in the beginning of 1994 5. *Caspian Sea*: Framework Convention for the Protection of the Marine Environment of the Caspian Sea (Tehran, 4 November 2003) 6. *East Africa:* The Nairobi Convention for the Protection, Management and Development of the Marine and Coastal Environment of the Eastern African Region was signed in 1985 and came into force in 1996. The Convention was amended and adopted in April, 2010.7. *East Asian Seas:* Action Plan for the Protection and Development of the Marine Environment and Coastal Areas of the East Asian Seas Region (1981) 8. *Mediterranean:* The Barcelona Convention for the Protection of the Mediterranean Sea against Pollution (1976, as amended in 1995; entered into force 9 July 2004 9. *North-East Atlantic:* Convention for the Protection of the Marine Environment of the North-East Atlantic (OSPAR Convention, 1992); entered into force: 25 March 1998 10. *North-East Pacific:* Convention for Cooperation in the Protection and Sustainable Development of the Marine and Coastal Environment of the Northeast Pacific (Antigua Convention, 2002) 11. *North-West Pacific:* Action Plan for the Protection, Management and Development of the Marine and Coastal Environment of the North-West Pacific Region (1994) 12. *South Pacific:* Noumea Convention for the Protection of Natural Resources and Environment of the South Pacific Region (1986). SPREP is the secretariat for the Apia Convention 1976, the SPREP (or Noumea) Convention 1986 and the Waigani Convention 1995 13. *Red Sea and Gulf of Aden:* Regional Convention for the Conservation of the Red Sea and Gulf of Aden (1982); entry into force: 20 August 1985 14. *ROPME Sea Area:* Action Plan for the Protection and Development of the Marine Environment and the Coastal Areas, the Kuwait Regional Convention for Co-operation on the Protection of the Marine Environment from Pollution, and the Protocol concerning Regional Co-operation in Combating Pollution by Oil and Other Harmful Substances in Cases of Emergency adopted in 1978 15. *South Asian Seas:* SASP is a co-operative partnership, formally adopted in 1995 for the protection and management of the shared marine waters and associated coastal ecosystems of five maritime SACEP countries (Bangladesh, India, Maldives, Pakistan and Sri Lanka) 16. *South-East Pacific:* The Convention for the Protection of the Marine Environment and Coastal Zones of the South-East Pacific (1981): entry into force 19 May 1986;Permanent Commission for the South Pacific (CPPS) is the appropriate Regional Maritime Organization responsible for the coordination of the maritime policies of its Member States: Colombia, Chile, Ecuador and Peru. The Organization was established on 18 August 1952, as a result of "Declaration on the Maritime Zone" subscribed at Santiago by the Governments of Chile, Ecuador and Peru. Colombia joined the CPPS on 9 August, 1979 17. *West & Central Africa:* Abidjan Convention for Co-operation in the protection and Development of the Marine and Coastal Environment of the West and Central African Region (Abidjan Convention, 1981); entered into force 5 August 1984 Action Plan for the protection and Development of the Marine Environment and Coastal Areas of the West and Central African Region (1981); entered into force: 5 August 1984 18. *Wider Caribbean Region*: Cartagena Convention for the Protection and Development of the Marine Environment of the Wider Caribbean Region (1983); see, http://www.unep.org/regionalseas/programmes/default.asp.

as 33 protocols.[41] Out of these, UNEP provides secretariat services for six[42] regional seas programs and five regional organizations[43] have also come into being to implement and administer their respective RSP.

---

41 The protocols include the following: *Mediterranean:* (1) Protocol for the Prevention of Pollution in the Mediterranean Sea by Dumping from Ships and Aircraft (Dumping Protocol); adopted 16 February 1976, in force 12 February 1978 (2) Protocol for the Prevention and Elimination of Pollution in the Mediterranean Sea by Dumping from Ships and Aircraft or Incineration at Sea; adopted on 10 June 1995, not yet in force. (3) Protocol on the Protection of the Mediterranean Sea against Pollution from Land-Based Sources (LBS Protocol); adopted 17 May 1980, in force 17 June 1983 (4) Protocol for the Protection of the Mediterranean Sea against Pollution from Land-Based Sources and Activities; adopted 7 March 1996, not yet in force (5) Protocol Concerning Specially Protected Areas and Biological Diversity in the Mediterranean (SPA and Biodiversity Protocol); adopted 10 June 1995, in force 12 December 1999 (6) Protocol Concerning Cooperation in Preventing Pollution from Ships and, in Cases of Emergency, Combating Pollution of the Mediterranean Sea (Prevention and Emergency Protocol); adopted 25 January 2002, in force 17 March 2004 (7) Protocol for the Protection of the Mediterranean Sea against Pollution Resulting from Exploration and Exploitation of the Continental Shelf and the Seabed and its Subsoil (Offshore Protocol); adopted 14 October 1994, not yet in force (8) Protocol on the Prevention of Pollution of the Mediterranean Sea by Transboundary Movements of Hazardous Wastes and their Disposal (Hazardous Wastes Protocol); adopted 1 October 1996, not yet in force *ROPME Sea Area*: (9) Protocol concerning Regional Co-operation in Combating Pollution by Oil and other Harmful Substances in Cases of Emergency; adopted 24 April 1978, in force 1 July 1979 (10) Protocol concerning Marine Pollution resulting from Exploration and Exploitation of the Continental Shelf; adopted 1989, in force 17 February 1990. (11) Protocol for the Protection of the Marine Environment against Pollution from Land-Based Sources; adopted 1990, in force 2 January 1993 (12) Protocol on the Control of Marine Transboundary Movements and Disposal of Hazardous Wastes and other Wastes; adopted 17 March 1998, not yet in force. *West and Central Africa:* (13) Protocol Concerning Co-operation in Combating Pollution in Cases of Emergency; adopted: 1981, into force 5 August1984. *South-East Pacific:* (14) Agreement on Regional Cooperation in Combating Pollution in the South East Pacific by Hydrocarbons and other Harmful Substances in cases of Emergency; signed: 12 November 1981, participating countries : Chile, Colombia, Ecuador, Peru and Panama (15) Complementary Protocol on the Agreement for Regional Cooperation in Combating Pollution in the South East Pacific by Hydrocarbons and other Harmful Substances in Cases of Emergency; adopted 22 July 1983, in force 1987 (16) Protocol for the Protection of the South East Pacific Against Pollution from Land – Based Sources; adopted 1983, in force 1986 (17) Protocol for the Conservation and Management of Protected Marine and Coastal Areas of the South East Pacific; adopted: 1989, in force 1984 (18) Protocol for the Protection of the South East Pacific from Radioactive Pollution; adopted 21 September 1989, in force 1995 (19) Protocol on the regional program for the study of the El Nino phenomenon in the South East Pacific (ERFEN); adopted 6 November 1992, participating countries: Chile,

Colombia, Ecuador and Peru. *Red Sea and Gulf of Aden:* (20) Protocol Concerning Regional Co-Operation in Combating Pollution by Oil and Other Harmful Substances in Cases of Emergency; adopted 14 February 1982, into force 1985 (21) Protocol Concerning the Conservation of Biological Diversity and the Establishment of Network of Protected Areas in the Red Sea and Gulf of Aden; adopted 2005; Not yet in force (22) Protocol Concerning the Protection of the Marine Environment from Land-Based Activities in the Red Sea and Gulf of Aden; adopted 2005; Not yet in force (23) The Protocol Concerning Technical Cooperation to Facilitate Exchange and Transfer Experts, Technicians, Equipment and Materials in Cases of Emergency; adopted 1 July 2009; Not yet in force. *Wider Caribbean:* (24) The Protocol Concerning Co-operation in Combating Oil Spills; adopted 1983, in force 11 October 1986 (25) The Protocol Concerning Specially Protected Area and Wildlife (SPAW); adopted 1990, in force 18 June 2000 (26) The Protocol Concerning Pollution from Land-Based Sources and Activities (LBS); adopted 6 October 1999, not yet in force. *Eastern Africa:* (27) Protocol Concerning Protected Areas and Wild Fauna and Flora in the Eastern African Region; adopted 21 June 1985, in force 30 May 1996 (28) Protocol Concerning Co-operation in Combating Marine Pollution in Cases of Emergency in the Eastern African Region; adopted 1985, in force 30 May 1996 (29) Protocol for the Protection of the Marine and Coastal Environment of the Western Indian Ocean from Land-Based Sources and Activities; adopted 31 March 2010, not yet in force. *South Pacific:* (30) Protocol for the Prevention of Pollution of the South Pacific Region by Dumping; adopted 1986, in force 1990 (31) Protocol concerning Co-operation in Combating Pollution Emergencies in the South Pacific Region; adopted 1986, in force 1990. *Antarctic*: (32) Protocol on Environmental Protection to the Antarctic Treaty; adopted 1991, in force 14 January 1998. *Black Sea:* (33) Protocol on Protection of the Black Sea Marine Environment Against Pollution from Land Based Sources; adopted 1992, in force 15 January 1994 (34) Protocol on Cooperation in combating pollution of the Black Sea Marine Environment by Oil and Other Harmful Substances in Emergency Situations; adopted 1992, in force 15 January 1994 (35) Protocol on The Protection of The Black Sea Marine Environment Against Pollution by Dumping; adopted 1992, in force 15 January 1994 (36) Black Sea Biodiversity and Landscape Conservation Protocol; adopted 2003, not yet in force (37) Revised Protocol on the Protection of the Marine Environment of the Black Sea from Land-Based Sources and Activities; adopted 2009, not yet in force; see, http://www.unep.org/regionalseas/programmes/default.asp.

42 The six RSPs for which UNEP currently provides permanent/interim secretariat services are: Caribbean Region, East Asian Seas, Eastern Africa Region, Mediterranean Region, North-West Pacific Region and West and Central Africa Region; see http://www.unep.org/regionalseas/programmes/default.asp).

43 These regional organizations for RSP are: 1.Regional Organization for the Protection of the Marine Environment (ROMPE). It comprises Bahrain, Iran, Iraq, Kuwait, Oman, Qatar, Saudi Arabia and United Arab Emirates. 2. Programme of Environment for the Red Sea and the Gulf of Eden (PERSGA). It comprises Egypt, Jordan, Palestine, Saudi Arabia, Somalia, Sudan and Yemen. 3. Permanent Commission of the South Pacific (CPPS). It comprises Chile, Colombia, Ecuador, Panama and Peru. 4. South Pacific Regional Environment Programme (SPREP). Its members are Australia, Cook Islands, Federated

The states, it appears, are gradually inching more towards specialized multilateral agreements as a mode of grappling with environmental problems having a global character. The premise that some of the global environmental problems need global solutions has brought about change in the perception on these issues as *common concerns of mankind*. The efforts by Malta[44] in this connection, however, to have the General Assembly declare conservation of climate as *common heritage of mankind*[45] did not succeed. The Assembly instead recognized the issue of climate change as a *common concern of mankind*. The echo of this salutary declaratory statement came to be reflected in two global conventions on climate change[46] and biological diversity[47] (adopted at the 1992 Rio Earth Summit). In a sense the notion of *common concerns* caters to the requirement of international community interest in a common resource as opposed to limited national interest. It lays down *prima facie* basis for common action for a regulatory framework on those issues, which cannot be addressed, in a bilateral context or by a limited number of states. MEAs arrived at in recent years have a great diversity and most of them underscore the global

States of Micronesia, Fiji, France, Kiribati, Marshall Islands, Nauru, New Zealand, Niue, Palau, Papua New Guinea, Solomon Islands, Tonga, Tuvalu, United Kingdom, United States of America, Vanuatu and Western Samoa. 5. South Asian Cooperative Environment Programme (SACEP). It comprises Bangladesh, India, Maldives, Pakistan and Sri Lanka; see, http://www.unep.org/regionalseas/partners/regional/default.asp.

44 The General Assembly considered the agenda item proposed by the Government of Malta, on "Conservation of climate as part of the common heritage of mankind" and adopted the resolution *Protection of Global Climate for Present and Future Generations of Mankind* on 6 December 1988. The GA resolution 43/53 (1988) was adopted without vote.

45 Article 136 of the United Nations Convention on Law of the Sea provided that: "The Area and its resources are the common heritage of mankind". Article 1(1) of the UNCLOS defines *Area* "means the sea-bed and the ocean floor and subsoil thereof, beyond the limits of national jurisdiction". As per Article 140 the activities in the Area were to be carried out for the benefit of mankind as a whole, irrespective of the geographical location of States. The International Sea-Bed Authority was to provide for the equitable sharing of financial and other economic benefits derived from activities in the Area through appropriate mechanism. The idea of common heritage of mankind was mooted in a Maltese proposal by Arvid Pardo. The UNCLOS came force after a period of 12 years, on 16 November 1994 following

46 The very first para of the *Preamble* to the Framework Convention on Climate Change states: "*Acknowledging* that change in the Earth's climate and its adverse effects are a common concern of humankind"; see *ILM*, vol. 31, 1992, p. 849.

47 The *Preamble* to the Convention on Biological Diversity states: "*Affirming* that the conservation of biological diversity is a common concern of humankind"; see *ILM*, vol. 31, 1992, p. 822.

character as well as multidimensional nature of environmental problems.[48] Interestingly, there is an increasing tendency among the states, especially industrialised ones, to push for a global framework for more and more environmental issues. There is, however, also a lot of scepticism and even some opposition to this approach.

Ad Hoc Law-making

It is generally contended that the advent of MEAs have ushered in an era of *ad hoc* law making and institutional structures. On the contrary, it is advanced that the law making on environmental issues is greatly facilitated by treaties due to a sense of urgency involved in the matter as well as scientific uncertainties intrinsically embedded into them. The sovereign states seem to go for treaties as 'frameworks' that provide them large room for political latitude and convenience. The framework treaties, in turn, could be shaped to grow with availability of scientific evidence, emergence of consensus and convergence of interests of the contracting parties. The process is duly coloured by the atmospherics and posturing of main actors as dictated by circumstances of specific treaty-making exercise. Thus by their very nature, such skeleton (framework) treaties require in-built law-making mechanisms in order to facilitate gradual tightening up of the specific treaty.[49] As a corollary, the whole treaty operates as a 'process', necessitating engagement of the contracting parties at regular intervals and efforts on arriving at convergence/balancing of interests to build up the regime. As a result of such continuous and marathon enterprise, MEAs have emerged as a unique technique containing flexibility, pragmatism, in-built law making mechanism as well as step-by-step consensual approach to norm-setting.

If one examines the growing corpus and mosaic of international environmental law, one cannot but feel the absence of a central law making institution. Such a focal point would have given a coherent shape and direction to the development of law. However, the law making process hitherto has been distinctly characterized by *ad hoc* and need-based responses. The remarkable growth of sectoral environmental regulatory framework testifies to this. As a result, sector-specific rules and principles have proliferated in areas ranging from atmosphere (e.g. air pollution, ozone, climate change etc.), to transboundary movements of substances (e.g. hazardous wastes, chemicals etc.), to conservation of living resources (endangered species, migratory species,

---

48 For more information on global treaties, see, http://www.informea.org/treaties/region/Global/.

49 See generally, Nele Matz-Luck (2009), "Framework Conventions as Regulatory Tools", *Goettingen Journal of International Law*, Vol. 1(3), pp. 439–458.

wetlands, biological diversity etc.). Many of the earlier MEAs were largely a result of the perceived need to take conservation or protection measures. Moreover, except for certain exceptional cases, the main thrust of these sectoral regulatory measures has been, primarily, anthropocentric i.e. to protect long term human *utilitarian* interest in a species or a natural resource.

'Interest' of States

It seems evident that treaty-making on environmental issues has developed into a sustained practice and fine art largely due to inclination of the states to resort to multilateralism[50] to address some of the *common concerns of humankind.* The states, ostensibly, claim to act in the 'common interest' while joining multilateral environmental negotiations. There is a general hypothesis that it is the *common interest* of states that propels them to negotiate a MEA. In general, however, the states are guided by their self-interest rather than any notion of common interest. In many of the cases, move for an international legal instrument is pushed by a *trigger event*, e.g. in case of the ozone layer depletion or the climate change issue. The initiatives in both these cases came in the wake of dire scientific findings, which forced global regulatory action resulting in respective treaty regimes.

It is no mean achievement that most of the global MEAs have been joined by a staggering number of sovereign states as most of the global treaties, among others, on wetlands, cultural and natural heritage, endangered species, ozone layer deletion, transboundary movements of hazardous wastes, climate change, biological diversity, desertification, hazardous chemicals & pesticides in international trade, persistent organic pollutants have more than 100 states parties to them. The gradual formation of frameworks of MEAs has engaged an overwhelming number of states through multilateral negotiations. One of the important factors influencing these negotiations is the balance between "national sovereignty and international interdependence".[51] The unfolding scenario reveals that more and more states are gradually opting for legal as well as institutional cooperation within multilateral frameworks for a wide variety of environmental issues. Such interest and participation of sovereign states could be possible especially due to much needed in-built latitude and accommodation of political convenience to address issues that have underpinnings

50 It has been argued that opportunities for multilateralism "appear to abound", as they have in the "aftermath of both twentieth-century 'non-cold wars'"; see Michael G. Schechter, "International Institutions: Obstacles, Agents, or Conduits of Global Structural Change?" in Michael G. Schechter, *Innovation in Multilateralism* (Tokyo: UNU Press, 1999), p. 3.

51 Richard Elliot Benedick, "Perspectives of a Negotiation Practitioner" in Gunnar Sjöstedt (Ed.), *International Environmental Negotiation* (Newbury Park: Sage Publications, 1993), p. 229 (emphasis in original).

in the crucial socio-economic and developmental priorities of the sovereign states.

Overlapping of Issues

It seems there is a growing penchant on the part of the sovereign states for resolving environmental problem through the means of regulatory tool of a treaty. With the advent of a large number of environmental agreements, some of the concerns such as overlapping and conflicting obligations in different treaties, duplication of resources and efforts have come to the fore.[52] Interestingly, there is a trend at work wherein language from one treaty has been copied and pasted in another environmental agreement of the same era or having similar characteristics.[53] The issue was recognized during the 1992 Rio Earth Summit wherein simultaneous negotiation processes were set in motion for instruments to address issues of climate change, biological diversity, desertification and forestry. Since they all could individually affect management of forests, the potential danger of overlapping and inconsistent provisions were taken into account.[54]

Some other issues of concern are intersection between provisions of different agreements such as the Basel Convention,[55] Rotterdam Convention[56] and Stockholm Convention.[57] These three instruments in general deal with

52 For more information on overlapping and conflation of multilateral environmental agreements mandates see, Karen N Scott (2011), "International Environmental Governance: Managing Fragmentation through Institutional Connection", *Melbourne Journal of International Law*, Vol. 12, pp. 177–216. Also see, Karen Scott (2013), Managing Fragmentation through Governance: International Environmental Law in a Globalised World in A. Byrnes, M. Hayashi and C. Michaelson (Ed.), *New Challenges for International Law in a Globalised World* (Leiden: Martinus Nijhoff Publishers) pp. 207–238.

53 For instance, a standard clause of dispute settlement is found in nearly all the MEAs.

54 For instance, the Convention on Biological diversity addresses the issue of consistency with other agreements explicitly by including a separate article 22 entitled as 'relationship with other international conventions'. This article provides that the Convention does not affect the rights and obligations of state parties to other international agreements, "except where the exercise of those rights and obligations would cause a serious damage or threat to biological diversity".

55 Basel Convention on the Control of Transboundary Movement of Hazardous Waste and Their Disposal, UNEP Doc.IG/80/L.12, adopted and opened for signature Mar. 22 1989, *ILM* vol. 28, 1989, p. 649.

56 Rotterdam Convention on the Prior Informed Consent Procedure in Certain Hazardous Chemicals and Pesticides in International Trade, Rotterdam, 10 September 1998, United Nations, *Treaty Series* , vol. 2244, p. 337.

57 Stockholm Convention on Persistent Organic Pollutants, Stockholm, 22 May 2001, United Nations, *Treaty Series*, vol. 2256, p. 119.

transportation of hazardous wastes and materials. Similarly, important legal implications could arise from the intersection of the Antarctic Treaty[58] and the Law of Sea Convention.[59] Another set of problems came to light from usage of trade sanctions to enforce MEAs and the most favored nation principle of the General Agreement on Tariffs and Trade (GATT).[60] The most significant examples of substantive treaty conflict could occur when countries are members of both a MEA and the GATT.

Another example of conflict due to overlapping of issues could be seen in the case of big leaf mahogany. The debate over limiting trade in big leaf mahogany again came to a head at the Tenth Conference of the Parties of CITES, held in Harare (Zimbabwe) in June 1997.[61] Brazil, Bolivia, and Mexico that are some of the largest exporters of mahogany, pledged to join Costa Rica in listing big leaf mahogany on Appendix III of CITES. Currently, Brazil and Bolivia are members of both the International Tropical Timber Agreement (ITTA) and the CITES. Under the ITTA, Brazil and Bolivia have pledged to manage their forests sustainably by the year 2000. In short, a conflict in obligation could manifest between the two treaties. Thus, on one hand, any listing of mahogany with the CITES as an endangered species would dictate potentially severe restrictions on the trade of mahogany in countries which produce this species of flora. On the other hand, ITTA advocates the sustainable use and trade of this species and frowns upon any ban on mahogany trade.

Outcome

Still, in view of the very nature of these negotiations and participation of a large majority[62] of the states, final outcome is achieved through the notion of

---

58 The Antarctic Treaty 1959, signed at Washington D.C. on December 1, 1959, entered into force on 23 June 1961 , United Nations, *Treaty Series*, vol. 402, p. 71.

59 United Nations Convention on the Law of Sea, signed on 10 December 1982 at Montego Bay, Jamaica, entered into force 16 November 1994, *ILM*, vol. 21, 1982, p. 1261.

60 See generally, Robert A. Brand (1997), Sustaining the Development of International Trade and Environmental Law, *Vermont Law Review*, Vol. 21 at p. 823. Also see, Christine Crawford (1995), Conflict Between the Convention on International Trade in Endangered Species and the GATT in Light of Actions to Halt the Rhinoceros and Tiger Trade, *Georgetown International Environmental Law Review*, Vol. 7 at p. 555 (discussing a conflict between the GATT and the CITES).

61 B L Hicks (1999), Treaty Congestion in International Environmental Law: The Need for Greater International Coordination, *University of Richmond Law Review*, Vol. 32, at p. 1653.

62 Interestingly, almost all of the MEAs negotiated in recent years have seen participation of an unprecedented number of states. For example, the 1992 Framework Convention on Climate Change has been ratified by 198 states (and the European Economic Community, as an organization); The Kyoto Protocol has been ratified by 192 parties; www.unfccc.int.

slowest boat in the race (lowest common denominator). This often makes multilateral environmental negotiations on such issues complicated, contentious and full of calculated ambiguity. In essence, it reflects hard-headed political and economic interests of the states, which often results in a stalemate.[63] As compared to the earlier traditional treaty making experiences, most of the environmental issues are mired in significant amount of scientific uncertainty as well as high political and economic stakes for states, especially the powerful ones. Cumulatively, these factors push states to go for a legal instrument that can gradually evolve and unfold, while it accommodates competing interests. Therefore, in case of most of the recent MEAs, the so-called *hard* law turns out to be not so hard in actual practice.

At the inauguration of a treaty instrument (entry in to force), it resembles like an empty shell that awaits long drawn fleshing out process since the end products resulting from marathon negotiations can be described as having hard shell with a soft belly. The resultant skeleton does necessitate a step-by-step process to harden the commitments, flesh out the gaps and work on the calculated ambiguities that could be part of the finally adopted text of the instrument. It could include definition of the core elements, removing calculated ambiguities and/or spelling out details of the mechanisms in the convention or even launch a separate process to work on issues requiring detailed treatment. If such loose ends or built-in uncertainty are not allowed, the instrument in question will not take off and suffer either premature death or lead to serious 'hold-out' problems. It could force key parties to remain out of the treaty by either refusal to sign or ratify it.

Similarly, the 1994 United Nations Convention to Combat Desertification (UNCCD) has been ratified by 195 parties; see www.unccd.int. The 1992 Convention on Biological Diversity has been ratified by 193 parties, the 2000 Cartagena Protocol on Biosafety has been ratified by 166 parties and the 2010 Nagoya Protocol on Access to Genetic Resources and the Fair and Equitable Sharing of Benefits Arising from their Utilization has received 92 signatures, see www.cbd.int [all as on 20 December 2013].

63 For instance, the refusal of the Unites States to ratify the Kyoto Climate Change Protocol (1997) to the 1992 UN Framework Convention on Climate Change (with 198 parties as on 20 December 2013) is a classic illustration of the vital national interests dictating the state behavior even on an issue regarded as a 'common concern of humankind'. Interestingly, the US not only refused to ratify the Kyoto Protocol but also took an unprecedented step to 'design' the Protocol. The US, being the largest emitter of greenhouse gases has effectively engaged in 'hold-out'. Notwithstanding this, the Protocol did come into force on 16 February 2005. As of 20 December 2013, 192 parties (191 states and 1 regional economic integration organization) have deposited instruments of ratifications, accessions, approvals or acceptances. This took the total percentage of Annex I Parties' emissions to 63.7%.

Hard law –Soft law Dilemma

The 'content' of and final 'form' taken by the treaties is proportional to the sense of urgency involved, paucity of time as well as reluctance of the key actors to permit specificity into the regime so as to apportion concrete obligations to attain basic objectives. As a manifestation of such paradoxical situation – need for a hard instrument having 'soft' or permissive obligations to accommodate political convenience of the states – some of the treaties in fact boldly carry the phrase 'framework convention' in their nomenclature itself. In such cases it is expected that the parties will gradually seek to fill up the gaps carefully left out at the stage of adoption of the instrument. These framework conventions could best be described as having a *hard shell with a soft belly*. This is due to the softness of the language (content) used in the instrument as well as intention of the states parties that these frameworks *per se* will not create 'hard' obligations (such as concrete timetables, quotas, ceilings or other measures). It is such political latitude and 'softness' that facilitates participation of a large number of states in such 'flexible' instruments.

This practice of calculated usage of soft formulations in the very text itself does not *per se* undermine the legal character of the instrument. The parties are at complete liberty to follow any form, any methodology and any time span to realize objectives of the treaty that they have set out for themselves. In such cases, it is the pure convenience of the parties at work to facilitate gradual arrival at consensus on calculated ambiguity or permissive language such as lack of definition of 'hazardous wastes' or usage of formulation such as 'taking into account socio-economic conditions of the parties' or 'as far as possible and as practicable'. These innovative formulations facilitate realization of the states' quest for negotiating a so-called hard treaty and yet keep the language used as soft, open-ended or non-binding[64] for the time being.

Fear of Proliferation

There has been a flurry of interest among sovereign states in the development of MEAs.[65] The law making process hitherto has been distinctly characterized by *ad hoc*, piecemeal and need-based responses. The remarkable growth of sectoral environmental regulatory framework testifies to this. As a result, there

64 For a detailed examination of 'twilight' fate of such agreements, see Oscar Schachter, "Twilight Existence of Non-Binding International Agreements", *American Journal of International Law*, vol. 71, 1977, pp. 296–304.

65 It is estimated that since 1868, there are around 502 international treaties and agreements concerning environment, out of which almost 300 have been entered into since 1972; see UN doc. UNEP/IGM/1/INF/1 of 30 March 2001, pp. 3–4.

has been considerable proliferation in sector-specific rules and principles in areas ranging from atmosphere (e.g. air pollution, ozone, climate change etc.) to transboundary movements of substances (e.g. hazardous wastes, chemicals etc.), to conservation of living resources (endangered species, migratory species, wetlands, biological diversity etc.). However, negotiation of a large number of new environmental agreements has led to a phenomenon called 'treaty congestion'.[66] Treaty congestion could be regarded as a significant challenge in international law because it contributes to inefficiency and non-compliance among parties to the MEAs.

Similarly, there seems to be noticeable dearth of general norms for application to all the environmental issues. Such proliferation of intergovernmental instruments, laying down obligations for the contracting states, has created unique situation and pressure for the participating states. The complex regimes thrown up by different MEAs have generated debate about the need for and efficacy of such form of "global governance"[67] in a sectoral area.

Legal Competence of Secretariats

MEA comprise not only regulatory elements specific to sectoral environmental issue but also a set of institutions that are thought to be necessary to ensure that contracting state parties realize objectives of the 'process' with built-in law making set in motion. There is a critical umbilical linkage between law and institutions[68] since the institutional actors have been regarded as "critical

66 "Treaty congestion" is a term of art used to describe the problems of actual substantive treaty conflict, treaty obligation and objective conflicts, and procedural conflicts which arise as a result of the proliferation of international treaties in the past three decades. See, B L Hicks, *Treaty Congestion in International Environmental Law: The Need for Greater International Coordination,* University of Richmond Law Review, Vol. 32, 1999, p. 1646.

67 For writings on this issue see, generally, Peter H. Sand, *Lessons Learned in Global Environmental Governance* (Washington D.C.: World Resources Institute, 1990, pp. 1–60; Peter M. Haas, "Global Environmental Governance" in Commission on Global Governance, *Issues in Global Governance* (London: Kluwer International), 1995, pp. 333–369; Peter M. Haas and Ernst B. Haas, "Learning to Learn: Some Thoughts on Improving International Governance of the Global *Problematique*", ibid, pp. 295–331. Also see Hilary French, "Strengthening Global Environmental Governance" in *Vanishing Borders: Protecting the Planet in the Age of Globalization* (New York: W.W.Norton & Company, 2000), pp. 144–162; Bharat H. Desai, "Revitalizing International Environmental Institutions: The UN Task Force Report and Beyond", *Indian Journal of International Law*, vol. 40, no. 3, 2000, pp. 455–504; Bharat H. Desai, "Mapping the Future of International Environmental Governance", *Yearbook of International Environmental Law* (OUP), vol. 13, 2002, pp. 43–61.

68 See Bharat H. Desai, *Institutionalizing International Environmental Law* (Ardsley, New York: Transnational Publishers, 2003), chapter 1.

forces in shaping 'real world' environmental governance systems".[69] Moreover, when a multilateral regulatory framework is put into place, it throws up its own set of institutional structures. It covers political bodies such as conference and meeting of the parties, scientific and technical bodies, funding mechanisms and the secretariat. As compared to other institutional structures within a specific legal regime, the secretariat almost becomes indispensable. The practice and procedures revolving around the secretariats are largely governed by international law of international institutions.[70] Still, in the specific context of environmental field, the secretariats have emerged as *sui generis* entities and they do possess some legal status[71] of their own. They, in fact, appear to be most visible symbols of sectoral multilateral regulatory process. Such secretariats could take an independent form or could be provided by an existing institution that serves as a 'host' institution for the purpose.

The secretariat of the convention performs a vital role in the process of 'servicing' the COP and other subsidiary bodies of the convention. This comprises the task of providing vital administrative, technical and scientific support to the COP as well as the subsidiary bodies. The secretariat can also be expected to provide an advice in implementation of the convention when the contracting parties so request. The executive secretary of the convention, as chief executive officer, takes the lead in not only translating the political will of the parties, as reflected in the decisions of the COP, but also in ensuring efficient performance of the institutional mechanism to realize basic objectives of the convention.

The phenomenal growth in the number and types of these MEAs poses a huge governance challenge as regards their legal capacity to carry out activities

---

69 Oran R. Young et. al, *Institutions and Environmental Change* (Cambridge, Mass.: MIT Press, 2008), p. xiii. This work, culmination of a decade long project on the *Institutional Dimensions Programme on Global Environmental Change* (IDGEC), adopted the research definition that institutions are a "system of rights, rules, and decision-making procedures". Moreover, it indicated that "institutions play a role in both causing and addressing problems that arise from human-environment interactions but that the nature of this role is complex"; ibid.

70 For authoritative and detailed works on this see, generally, H.G.Schemers and N.M.Blokker, *International Institutional Law: Unity Within Diversity*, 4th Ed. (Leiden; Brill/Martinus Nijhoff, 2003); Jan Klabbers, *An Introduction to International Institutional Law* (Cambridge: CUP, 2002); P.Sands & P.Klein, *Bowett's Law of International Institutions*, 5th ed. (London: Sweet & Maxwell, 2001); C.F.Amarasinghe, *Principles of Institutional Law of International Organizations* (Cambridge: CUP, 1996).

71 See Bharat H. Desai, *Multilateral Environmental Agreements: Legal Status of the Secretariats* (New York: Cambridge Uni. Press, 2010), chapter 5.

both within the domestic jurisdiction of the state where the seat is located (host country) as well as by virtue of their international legal personality. In view of the differences in the history of each of the MEAs, the content of the treaties, and the secretariat services being provided by an international institutions (such as the UN Educational, Scientific and Cultural Organization (UNESCO), the International Union for Conservation of Nature and Natural Resources (IUCN), and the UN Environment Programme (UNEP), the competence of convention secretariats remains a key legal question. Since MEA is a product of intergovernmental negotiations as and an overwhelming number of sovereign states are parties to it, the legal capacity of the secretariat is vital to give effect to goals of the relevant treaty. As a plenary body, the COP and/or standing committee could only express its view on the legal capacity of the MEA. It is manifested through actions of the secretariat. Interestingly, many of the texts of MEAs remain silent as far as legal capacity is concerned. As a result, most of the MEAs– as represented by their secretariats – try to decipher their legal capacity not only from their constituent instrument but also from their headquarters agreement (with the host state) and any specific relationship agreement (with the host institution).

The work of various institutional mechanisms under MEAs reveals that they evolve along with evolution and development of the treaty regime itself. In a way they provide fine testimony to the working, in actual practice, of the institutionalized international environmental cooperation. It is a remarkable legal process that works slowly and steadily. In fact it is literally a 'creeping' process of institutionalization to cater to requirements of the sovereign states for institutionalized environment cooperation through a specific treaty regime.

Relationship of 'Host' Institution and MEA Secretariat

A treaty, as soon as it finds a base in a host country, it also generally gets located in a 'host' institution. Such a host institution could be the one that initially floated the idea of regulating the subject matter of a treaty or an institution that could provide the best support to give effect to the treaty objectives. It is the text of the treaty that provides the relevant mandate as regards the nature and character of 'host arrangements' necessary for the purpose. Almost all the MEAs that took shape in the post-Stockholm period have contained provisions for such host institution arrangements. There is, however, a common trend that is seen at the final stage of negotiation stage itself. This includes formally making a request to an 'existing' international institution to perform and/or provide such secretariat services. As per the practice, generally, it is the institution that has played role in initiating negotiation process and/or has been working closely on the issue in question becomes a natural choice for this purpose.[72]

The crucial formulation – as regards making a 'request' in the text of the treaty itself – holds the key in unraveling the complex web of relationship between the existing institution and the requesting decision making body of the treaty. It is, however, not necessary that the secretariat will be located at the 'headquarters' of the international institution that has been requested to provide such a service. In fact the question of location (seat) of the secretariat is dictated by the offers made by the state parties that wish to 'host' the secretariat. The best offer acceptable to the Conference of the Parties (COP) paves the way for establishment of the secretariat.[73] Thus, in principle, they could be away from the headquarters of an international institution that has agreed to 'house' the secretariat. In such cases, the secretariat in question acts as an *out-posted* office that could not only be in a different country but also in a different continent. For instance the CBD Secretariat (Montreal) as well as CMS (Bonn), CITES (Geneva) and Basel (Geneva) located in Americas and Europe respectively are being administered by UNEP located in Nairobi (Africa).

It is the COP that has the final say in deciding about 'instituting' a secretariat, its nomenclature, host institution and, finally, the location. There is no standard formulation used for bringing such a secretariat to fruition. As such it is the language used that can provide basic 'clue' to be deciphered in this respect. The language formulation used to ignite relationship with a host institution is often bland and explicit as it states the secretariat functions *shall* be "performed" (POPs, PIC, Ramsar)[74] or "provided" (CITES, CMS)[75] or "appointed"

---

72 For instance, when UNEP has initiated such negotiations on the basis of a mandate from the Governing Council and its ten-year action plan under the *Montevideo Programme*.

73 It is the 'plenary' body of the treaty (generally called the Conference or Meeting of the Parties) that has the legal capacity to put such a request and invite an entity to perform 'secretariat' functions. The plenary body in question controls the levers of 'supervising' the relationship. The requested entity is described as a 'host institution'. It is the text of the instrument in question that has to be primarily relied upon to examine the nature of request made to an existing institution to provide secretariat support.

74 Article 8, Convention on Wetlands of International Importance (1971), 11 *ILM* 963 (1972); Article 20, Stockholm Convention on Persistent Organic Pollutants (Stockholm, 22 May 2001) at www.pops.int; Article 19, Rotterdam Convention on the Prior Informed Consent Procedure for Certain Hazardous Chemicals and Pesticides in International Trade (Rotterdam, 10 September 1998) at www.pic.int.

75 Article XII, Convention on International Trade in Endangered Species (1972), 12 *ILM* 1055 (1973); Article IX, Convention on the Conservation of Migratory Species of Wild Animals (1979), 19 *ILM* 15 (1980).

(WHC)[76] or "carry out" (LRTAP)[77] by an existing international institution (UNEP, FAO, IMO, UNESCO, ECE, IUCN as the case may be). In some other cases, the text of the convention leaves decision to the plenary body of the convention (i.e. COP) at its first session for a formal designation of secretariat responsibility to an existing institution as well as ensuring arrangements for its functioning (Basel, CBD, UNFCCC, UNCCD etc.). This practice seems to have been well institutionalized.

Interestingly, in all the cases, where there is an explicit reference as regards performing or providing secretariat services by an institution, it is refers to the respective head of the institution (POPs, PIC, CMS, CITES, WHC etc.). The reference to 'host institution' (IUCN)[78] can be found in general only in case of the Ramsar Convention, and not to the IUCN Director-General. In fact commonality in formulations could be seen especially in case of 'request' made to the executive director of UNEP that has often played role of a 'catalyst' in initiating negotiations concerning many of the sectoral environmental issues. The net effect of any such language formulation is that the 'secretariat' has come into effect and the task is assigned to UNEP as an 'institution'. It is the head of UNEP (executive director) who is, in turn, expected to take a series of successive steps that fully realize the role UNEP is expected to make. It is probably to perform such continuing role that UNEP has constituted a full – fledged Division of Environmental Law and Conventions (DELC).[79] It is DELC that gives full effect to the role of UNEP headquarters to perform 'secretariat' role for a series of conventions 'administered' by it. Interestingly, this relationship need not necessarily be given effect to at the main 'seat' (headquarters in Nairobi) of UNEP. Except location of the ozone secretariat at the headquarters, all other convention secretariats being 'administered' by UNEP are located away from the main seat.[80] This, in turn, unleashes a chain of legal

76 Article 14, Convention for the Protection of the World Cultural and Natural Heritage (1972), 12 *ILM* 1385 (1972).

77 Article 11, Convention on Long Range Transboundary Air Pollution (1979), 18 *ILM* 1442 (1979).

78 The World Conservation Union was founded in October 1948 as the International Union for the Protection of Nature (IUPN) at an international conference in Fontainebleau, France. The organization changed its name to the International Union for Conservation of Nature and Natural Resources in 1956. It is the world's largest and most important conservation network that has under its umbrella membership comprising 91 States, 127 government agencies, more than 1000 non-governmental organizations (NGOs), and some 11,000 scientists and experts from 181 countries; see http://www.iucn.org/about/union/members/who_members/members_database/.

79 For details see, http://www.unep.org/delc/.

80 For instance, out of the seven MEAs to whom UNEP provides secretariat support – Ozone, CBD, CITES, Basel, CMS, PIC and POPs (with FAO) – they are located in Africa,

implications. As such it will require usage of multiple legal steps engaging the standing committee of the COP, host institution and the host country where the 'seat' of the secretariat is to be physically located.

In cases where an existing international institution is 'requested' to provide secretariat services for the convention, the purpose is to take advantage of the already established structure. The new arrangement sought to be created involves carving out a part of the existing institution that works exclusively and performs role of a 'secretariat' for the convention. It does trigger delicate relationship between the existing institutions that will play role of a 'host' for the functions earmarked under an international legal instrument. The common usage of the language, for instance, that "Secretariat functions shall be performed (provided) by the Executive Director of UNEP"[81] does not mean that the concerned person shall 'personally' carry out the task. The phrase appears to have been used as a metaphor and could be construed to mean that UNEP Executive Director shall put into place suitable institutional arrangement that will perform the role of a 'secretariat' for the concerned convention.[82] That role triggers a series of institutional and legal implications to ensure that an entity caters to the specific mandate laid down in the text of the instrument. In fact making sense of this complicated maze remains a scholarly challenge.[83]

Future Direction

Clustering

It has been widely recognized that this multilateral law making *modus operandi* has worked in a piecemeal, *ad hoc* and sporadic manner. This underscores need to streamline the system of international environmental

---

North America and Europe. Similarly, in cases of several regional seas programmes (RSPs) where UNEP directly provides secretariat support, the task is carried out by the respective 'regional coordination units' that are located away.

81 See POPs (Article 20), PIC (Article 19; along with FAO D-G), CMS (Article IX) and CITES (Article XII).

82 In accepting the 'request' made by the Conference of Parties to the convention, head of UNEP accepts to carry out the relevant tasks and obligations. Thus he is answerable to the COP as far as his role and that of the secretariat carved out from UNEP is concerned. The convention text is generally devoid of clear guidelines as regards discharge of UNEP Executive Director's responsibilities.

83 For one such rare scholarly effort see, Bharat H. Desai, *Multilateral Environmental Agreements: Legal Status of the Secretariats* (New York: Cambridge University Press, 2010), Chapter 4.

governance that is characterized by the existence of a multitude of inter-governmental agreements. The concept of 'clustering' of MEAs was introduced into the debate within the working group of UNEP.[84] The debates that ensued over coherence and integration were largely based on the political debates that had taken place on coordination both at Stockholm (1972) and Rio (1992). However, in the present case they were to be more sophisticated because they sought to build upon the existing system of environmental treaties and environmental institutions. Unlike past attempts to have an integrated governance system for the environment, this time the debates "did not call for a new organization to replace all existing ones; rather they advocated a simple notion of better cooperation between existing MEAs and international organizations and institutions", calling for these bodies to resolve their conflicts, end their turf wars[85] and create synergies in their work.

In 2005 (14–16 September), the World Summit,[86] with largest ever gathering of 170 heads of state/governments reaffirmed the need to explore the possibility of a more coherent institutional framework to address this need, including a more integrated structure, building on existing institutions, and internationally agreed instruments, as well as the treaty bodies and the specialized agencies.[87] One aspect of this coherence related to the environmental regime and included the promotion of synergies among MEAs and the mainstreaming of their goals within broader poverty-reduction strategies and plans.

The 'coherence' approach received strong impetus recently in the form of proposal from the Executive Secretaries of the Basel, Rotterdam and Stockholm Conventions for the organization of the secretariats of the three conventions,[88]

84 UNEP, Governing Council, Decision 21/21, on the issue of international environmental governance.

85 On turf wars and cooperation problems among MEAs see Kristin Rosendal and Steinar Andresen (2004), *UNEP's Role in Enhancing Problem-Solving Capacity in Multilateral Environmental Agreements: Co-ordination and Assistance in the Biodiversity Conservation Cluster*, FNI Report Oct. 2003. Lysaker, Norway: Fridtjof Nansen Institute, p. 29.

86 For details see the World Summit Outcome document, A/RES/60/1 of 24 October 2005; available at: http://www.un.org/ga/59/hl60_plenarymeeting.html.

87 See, http://responsibilitytoprotect.org/world%20summit%20outcome%20doc%202005%281%29.pdf.

88 The decisions on enhanced cooperation and coordination among the three conventions, also called "synergies decisions" were considered and adopted by the Conferences of the Parties to the Basel Convention (decision BC-IX/10, June 2008), Rotterdam Convention (decision RC-4/11,October 2008) and Stockholm Convention (decision SC-4/34, May 2009) without any substantive amendments. The "synergies decisions" concern synergies at the national, regional and global levels in the following areas: 1.Organizational issues in the field; 2.Technical issues; 3.Information management and public awareness issues;

as requested by the three Conferences of the Parties (COPs; held in 2011) through their decisions on joint managerial functions.[89] The three MEAs had set the ball rolling, through simultaneous extraordinary meetings of the COPs to the Basel, Rotterdam and Stockholm conventions, in Bali, Indonesia (22 to 24 February 2010).[90] The meetings examined and decided upon futuristic issues that include joint activities; joint managerial functions; joint services; synchronization of budget cycles; joint audits and review arrangements.[91]

The COPs to the Basel, Rotterdam and Stockholm conventions respectively requested the Executive Secretary, in consultation with the parties to the conventions, to prepare a proposal for the organization of the secretariats of the three conventions, including staffing levels, numbers and structure, to be implemented by 31 December 2012.[92] The proposed plan included a shift from the current structure, generally referred to as a programmatic structure, to a future matrix structure. The current structure principally consists of three separate secretariats dedicated to each of the three conventions plus a joint

---

4.Administrative issues; 5.Decision-making; available at, http://synergies.pops.int/Implementation/AboutSynergies/History/tabid/2615/language/en-US/Default.aspx .

89 By decision SC-2/15 of the Conference of the Parties to the Stockholm Convention, decision RC-3/8 adopted by the Conference of the Parties to the Rotterdam Convention and decision VIII/8 of the Conference of the Parties to the Basel Convention it was agreed to establish an ad hoc joint working group (the "AHJWG") to prepare joint recommendations on enhanced cooperation and coordination among the three conventions for submission to the Conference of the Parties of all three conventions.See, paragraph 4 of section II on Joint Managerial Functions of decisions BC-10/29, RC-5/12 and SC-5/27 of the respective Conferences of the Parties. The recommendations of the ad hoc joint working group available at http://ahjwg.chem.unep.ch/documents/3rdmeeting/ahjwg03_03_REP.pdf#page=9.

90 The simultaneous extraordinary Conferences of the Parties (ExCOPs) to the Basel, Rotterdam and Stockholm Conventions took place during 22–24 February 2010 in Nusa Dua, Bali (Indonesia). They were followed by the eleventh special session of the United Nations Environment Programme (UNEP) Governing Council/Global Ministerial Environment Forum (GCSS-11/GMEF) that was held from 24–26 February 2010; see *Earth Negotiations Bulletin*, Vol. 16 No. 84, 1 March 2010; available at http://www.iisd.ca/download/pdf/enb1684e.pdf.

91 See, Report of the simultaneous extraordinary meetings of the conferences of the Parties to the Basel, Rotterdam and Stockholm conventions, UNEP/FAO/CHW/RC/POPS/EXCOPS.1/8, 22–24 February 2010; available at, http://synergies.pops.int/Implementation/AboutSynergies/History/tabid/2615/language/en-US/Default.aspx.

92 See http://synergies.pops.int/SynergiesProcess/JointManagerialFunctions/OrganizationoftheSecretariats/tabid/2619/language/en-US/Default.aspx.

convention services group dedicated to providing common support services to each secretariat. The structure proposed was to establish a single integrated secretariat dedicating to serving all three conventions equally, and would consist of four branches covering administrative services, convention operations, technical assistance and scientific support.[93] It was expected that the future structure would also considerably simplify the organization of the secretariat, and ultimately reduce the number of senior managers.[94] The proposed structure was put into effect on 18 February 2012 and endorsed by the 2013 COP meetings.

The second simultaneous extraordinary meetings of the COPs to the three conventions (ExCOPs2) convened from (28 April–10 May 2013) in Geneva, Switzerland. Among others, the COPs endorsed the matrix-based management approach and organization of the Secretariat and adopted recommendations on follow-up to the review of the synergy arrangements.[95] An omnibus decision was adopted on enhancing cooperation and coordination among the conventions that include synergies; joint activities; measures to further

93 See, Joint Managerial Functions: Proposals from the Executive Secretary of the Basel, Rotterdam and Stockholm Conventions for the organization of the secretariats of the three conventions, 21 December 2011; see, http://synergies.pops.int/SynergiesProcess/JointManagerialFunctions/OrganizationoftheSecretariats/tabid/2619/language/en-US/Default.aspx.

94 United Nations Conference on Sustainable Development, held in June 2012 at Rio de Janerio [referred to as Rio+20 Summit]. Rio+20 outcome document entitled 'The Future We Want' (Doc. A/66/L.56) outlines the international community's common vision of an economically, socially, and environmentally sustainable future for present and future generations. It took note of significant contributions to the sustainable development made by the multilateral environmental agreements. It acknowledged the synergies developed in the chemical waste cluster. It also noted, '[w]e encourage parties to multilateral environmental agreements to consider further measures, in these and other clusters, as appropriate, to promote policy coherence at all relevant levels, improve efficiency, reduce unnecessary overlap and duplication, and enhance coordination and cooperation among the multilateral environmental agreements, including the three Rio conventions, as well as with the United Nations system in the field'; available at http://www.uncsd2012.org/thefuturewewant.html. The General Assembly endorsed the Rio+20 Outcome document without vote through Res./66/288; see http://www.un.org/News/Press/docs//2012/ga11264.doc.htm (27 July 2012).

95 See, Report of the second simultaneous extraordinary meetings of the conferences of the parties to the Basel, Rotterdam and Stockholm conventions, UNEP/FAO/CHW/RC/POPS/EXCOPS.2/4, 28 April – 10 May 2013; see, http://synergies.pops.int/2013COPsExCOPs/Overview/tabid/2914/mctl/ViewDetails/EventModID/9163/EventID/297/xmid/9411/language/en-US/Default.aspx.

increase cooperation and coordination; the modality of the next meetings of the COPs; the Programme of Work and the budget for joint activities; and the Programmes of Work and budgets for the three conventions.[96]

The above mentioned case exemplifies that it could be possible to weed out problems affecting the MEAs in terms of duplicity of work, issues, efforts, resources and outcomes. Therefore, some form of clustering approach is already at work (apart from MEAs in the chemicals group), in the biodiversity group (CBD, CITES, Ramsar, ITPGRFA, CMS and WHC) through the 'liaison group'.[97] The recent decision from the UNEP Governing Council has also called for an enhanced synergies among the biodiversity-related MEAs.[98] It provided that:

---

96 See, Report of the second simultaneous extraordinary meetings of the conferences of the parties to the Basel, Rotterdam and Stockholm conventions, UNEP/FAO/CHW/RC/POPS/EXCOPS.2/CRP.5/Rev.1, Add.1/Rev.1, Add.2 and Add.3., 28 April – 10 May2013; see, http://synergies.pops.int/2013COPsExCOPs/Overview/tabid/2914/mctl/ViewDetails/EventModID/9163/EventID/297/xmid/9411/language/en-US/Default.aspx. For more details see, Earth Negotiations Bulletin, Vol. 15 (No. 210), 13 May 2013; available at, http://www.iisd.ca/vol15/enb15210e.html.

97 See, e.g., Secretariats of the *Convention on Biological Diversity*, the *United Nations Convention to Combat Desertification* and the *United Nations Framework Convention on Climate Change, Note by the Secretariat – Options for Enhanced Cooperation among the Three Rio Conventions*, UN Doc FCCC/SBSTA/2004/INF.19 (2 November 2004). This paper sets out options to improve cooperation between the members of the Joint Liaison Group, which comprises the 1992 *Convention on Biodiversity*, the 1992 *UNFCCC* and the *United Nations Convention to Combat Desertification in Those Countries Experiencing Serious Drought and/or Desertification, Particularly in Africa*, opened for signature 14 October 1994, 1954 UNTS 3 (entered into force 26 December 1996) ('*UNCCD*'); Executive Secretary, Convention on Biological Diversity, *Options for Enhanced Cooperation among the Biodiversity Related Conventions: Note by the Executive Secretary*, UN Doc UNEP/CBD/WG-RI/1/7/Add.2 (14 July 2005); Conference of the Parties, United Nations Environment Programme, *Note by the Secretariat – Study on Improving Cooperation and Synergies between the Secretariats of the Basel, Rotterdam and Stockholm Conventions*, UN Doc UNEP/POPS/COP.2/INF/12 (20 March 2006). Also see, Report of the Meeting of the Liaison Group of Biodiversity-related Conventions, 2–3 September 2013; available at: https://www.cbd.int/cooperation/doc/blg-2013-09-09-en.pdf.

98 See, Twelfth Special Session GC/GMEF, Decision SS.XII/3, February 2012; available at, http://www.unep.org/gc/gcss-xii/docs/in_L-docs.asp. Also see, Earth Negotiations Bulletin, Summary of the Twelfth Special Session of the UNEP Governing Council/ Global Ministerial Environment Forum, 20–22 February 2012, Vol. 16 (no. 98), 25 February 2012; available at, http://www.iisd.ca/download/pdf/enb1698e.pdf.

> (T)he importance of enhancing synergies, including at the national and regional levels, among the biodiversity-related conventions, without prejudice to their specific objectives and recognizing their respective mandates, and encourages the conferences of the parties to those conventions to strengthen efforts further in that regard, taking into account relevant experiences... (and, furthermore, requested) the Executive Director to explore the opportunities for further synergies in the administrative functions of the multilateral environmental agreement secretariats administered by the United Nations Environment Programme and to provide advice on such opportunities to the governing bodies of those multilateral environmental agreements.[99]

The governing bodies of all six global biodiversity-related agreements have adopted decisions or resolutions calling for enhanced synergies with other conventions.[100] The Rio Conventions Pavilion is another platform for raising awareness and sharing information about the latest practices and scientific findings on the co-benefits that can be realized through implementation of the three Rio Conventions.[101] The Pavilion is a collaborative effort between the Secretariats of the three Rio Conventions and the Global Environment Facility, in addition to a growing list of other global and local partners.

A similar scope remains to be duly worked out as regards the atmosphere related conventions (LRTAP, Ozone and UNFCCC).

Co-location

The location of secretariat in a host country triggers a chain of legal implications. It is a two stage exercise. As soon as the respective convention comes into force, the first step is to establish an 'interim secretariat' to organize convening of the first meeting of the COP. It is this first meeting of the COP that takes decision on the establishment of permanent secretariat of the

99 Ibid. Also see, Promoting Synergies within the cluster of biodiversity-related multilateral environmental agreements, UNEP World Conservation Monitoring Centre, April 2012; available at, http://www.unep-wcmc.org/medialibrary/2012/04/27/8b832e8c/Final_MEA_synergies_27April2012_cover.pdf.

100 The most recent decisions or resolutions including CBD decision X/20, CITES decision 14.38 (Rev. CoP15) and resolution Conf. 10.4 (Rev. CoP14), CMS resolutions 10.21 and 10.25, ITPGRF resolution 8/2011, Ramsar Convention resolution X.11 and WHC resolution 34 COM 5D; see, https://www.cbd.int/cooperation/doc/blg-modus-operandi-en.pdf.

101 The Rio Conventions Pavilion was launched during the International Year of Biodiversity in 2010, convened at the margins of the CBD Conference of the Parties (CBD COP10) in Nagoya, Japan; see, http://www.riopavilion.org/.

convention, location of the secretariat within an existing institution as well as various ground rules for the functioning of the servicing arm. In most of the cases, an existing international institution is requested to 'house' and provide the secretariat to the convention. It also necessitates a crucial decision as regards location of the 'seat' of the convention in a 'host' country.

A possible solution to the growing incoherence and overlapping of MEAs is to house the secretariats of related environmental treaties together in the same building such as International Environment House (Geneva), Platz der Vereinten Nationen (Bonn) and the UN Gigiri Complex (Nairobi). Agenda 21, adopted at the Rio Earth Summit, also suggested co-location of the secretariats. It is contended that common housing will lessen the communication gap between the secretariats of MEAs. It will also help in quick exchange of information between the secretariats with regard to issues dealt by each of them. Further, common housing would reduce overhead costs and economize on various functions of the secretariat. Hence this could bring about smooth coordination among the different but interrelated MEAs. On the contrary, there are doubts that such a common location in the same place may not accrue much benefit especially since it will not melt the (institutional) egos of secretariats working in their separate spheres. For instance, UNEP did shift some of the convention secretariats into one building.[102] Ostensibly, it was felt that this change did not bring about any perceptible attitudinal change in the working of secretariats inspite of common sharing of communication and information facilities.

Conclusion

It appears that the process of multilateral environmental regulation is quite diffused, highly fragmented, and more "poorly coordinated".[103] This does not, however, reflect true picture since MEAs are a *sui generis* method of grappling with sector-specific environmental problems. They, in general, depart from the traditional treaty-making enterprise known to have been followed by the sovereign states in the field of international law. MEAs seem to be 'new' treaty-based response mechanisms in the sense that they put up their own dynamics through a built-in law-making mechanism. The treaty making enterprise

102 E B Weiss, "International Environmental Law: Contemporary Issues and the Emergence of New World Order", *The Georgetown Law Journal*, Vol. 81, 1993, 675.

103 Paul C. Szasz, "International Norm-making" in Edith Brown Weiss (Ed.), *Environmental Change and International Law: New Challenges and Dimensions* (Tokyo: UNU Press, 1992), p. 47.

functions as almost a 'work-in-progress'. Still they are designed in such a way that they remain *ad hoc* in nature even as they address sector-specific environmental goals. Thus, instead of following the traditional treaty-making approach, MEAs become virtual "processes".[104] The process itself comes to the fore duly couched in different legal formulations. It is, however, essentially based on the bedrock of evolving scientific evidence, cost-effective measures, institutional structures as well as political convenience of the state parties to the Convention.

It seems states are now comfortable with this particular mode of treaty-making. The pattern has come to stay and duly institutionalized. Still, the process remains amorphous in some respects notwithstanding participation of a large number of sovereign states that testifies to its utility as an institutionalized form of international cooperation. This makes the scholarly task hazardous as regards making full 'sense' of the sectoral international environmental law-making enterprise. In the midst of euphoria, posturing and atmospherics of treaty-making, it is important to determine whether the targeted environmental problem or issue could be effectively solved with the help of MEA. There appears dearth of relevant data reflecting on the status of the environmental problem after states have measured the status of implementation and compliance with obligations under an agreement. For instance, the Montreal Protocol was a product of pressing problem of thinning of ozone layer. Now after nearly 26 years of its working, we still need to decipher status of the ozone layer on the basis of conclusive data that the perceived change in the state behavior brought about by the Protocol helped in redeeming the ozone layer. This question will need to be probed in case of each of the MEA since they are *ad-hoc* in nature. We need to galvanize scholarly efforts in this direction so as not only to grapple with the challenge of governing MEAs but also to make sense of the perennial dilemma to treaty or not to treaty as well as regulatory *modus vivendi* on sectoral global environmental problems.

The challenge needs to be squarely addressed as a part of the larger architecture of IEG. Thus the mushrooming growth of MEAs needs to be made 'sense' in earnest to ensure that the multilateral regulatory technique does not get over-stretched as well as does not repel states with fatigue effect. The questions of mounting scientific evidence, growing concerns for environment protection and natural resource conservation, issues of funding and transfer of technology as well as drawing synergies and location remain to be seriously

104 For that reason, the entire canvas of international law could also be described as a process because it evolves over time. For relevant work on this, see, generally, Rosalyn Higgins, *Problems and Process: International Law and How We Use It* (Oxford: Clarendon Press, 1994).

looked into so as to provide best cost-effective regulation of state behavior concerning a *problematique*. Since these MEAs are *sui generis* instruments they can be subordinated neither to the UN nor any of the UN specialized agencies or subsidiary organs or even international non-governmental organization. UNEP's Division of Environmental Law and Conventions is too feeble an entity to provide any redress in the matter. Therefore, the coming challenge would be how best to coordinate the work, draw the best synergy as well as to provide additional mandates to the existing MEAs rather than encourage growth of more MEAs unless they are inevitable. Sorting out the mosaic of clogged terrain of MEAs will be the biggest IEG challenge in the coming decades.

TABLE 4 *Comparative status of select Multilateral Environmental Agreements [as on 20 December 2013]*

MEAS	Year	Entry into force	Parties ratification	Host institution	Seat	Decision-making organ	Issues covered
Convention on wetlands of international importance	1971	21.12.1975	168	IUCN	Gland	COP	Conservation and wise use of wetlands, primarily as habitat for the waterbird
Convention for the protection of world cultural and natural heritage	1972	17.12.1975	190	UNESCO	Paris	General assembly of states parties	Protection and conservation of cultural and natural heritage
Convention for the prevention of marine pollution by dumping of wastes	1972	30.08.1975	87	IMO	London	Consultative meeting of the parties	All sources of pollution of the marine environment especially dumping of waste
Protocol to the convention on the prevention of marine pollution by dumping of wastes	1996	24. 03. 2006	43	IMO	London	Meetings of the parties	All sources of pollution of the marine environment especially dumping of waste

TABLE 4 *Comparative status of select Multilateral Environmental Agreements* (cont.)

MEAS	Year	Entry into force	Parties ratification	Host institution	Seat	Decision-making organ	Issues covered
Convention on international trade in endangered species [CITES]	1973	1.07.1975	179	UNEP	Geneva	COP	International trade in endangered species of wild fauna and Flora
Convention on migratory species of wild animals (CMS)	1979	1.11.1983	119	UNEP	Bonn	COP	Conservation & management [wise use of migratory species of wild animals and their habitats
Agreement for the conservation of bats in europe [EUROBATS]	1991	16.01.1994	35	UNEP collocated with CMS	Bonn	MOP	Conservation of bats, especially threats from habitat degradation, disturbance of roosting sites and certain pesticides
Agreement for the conservation of small cetaceans of the baltic and north sea [ASCOBANS]	1992	29.03.1994	10	UNEP collocated with CMS	Bonn	MOP	To achieve and maintain a favorable conservation status for small cetaceans
Agreement on the conservation of african-eurasian migratory water birds [AEWA]	1995	1.11.1999	72	UNEP collocated with CMS	Bonn	MOP	To maintain favorable conservation status for migratory waterbirds, especially endangered species

MEAS	Year	Entry into force	Parties ratification	Host institution	Seat	Decision-making organ	Issues covered
Convention on substances that deplete the ozone layer [Vienna]	1985	22.09.1988	197	UNEP	Nairobi	COP	Atmospheric ozone layer above the planetary boundary layer
protocol on substances that deplete the ozone layer layer [Montreal]	1987	1.01.1989	London (197) Copen'gen (197) Montreal (195) Beijing (193)	UNEP	Nairobi	COP	Atmospheric ozone layer above the planetary boundary layer
Convention on transboundary mmovements of hazardous wastes and their Disposal [Basel]	1989	5.05.1992	180	UNEP	Geneva	COP	Transboundary movements of hazardous wastes and their disposal
Protocol on liability and compensation for damage resulting from transboundary movements of hazardous wastes and their disposal [Basel]	1999	NOT IN FORCE	13 (signatures) 11(ratifica-tions)	UNEP	Geneva	MOP	comprehensive regime for liability and for adequate and prompt compensation for damage
United nations framework convention on climate change [UNFCCC]	1992	21.03.1994	198	UN	Bonn	COP	changes in the earth's climate system due to anthropogenic interference

TABLE 4 *Comparative status of select Multilateral Environmental Agreements* (cont.)

MEAS	Year	Entry into force	Parties ratification	Host institution	Seat	Decision-making organ	Issues covered
Protocol to the UNFCCC [Kyoto]	1997	16.02.2005	192	UN	Bonn	MOP	Quantified emission limitation and reduction commitments for Annex I parties
Convention on biological diversity [CBD]	1992	29.12.1993	193	UNEP	Montreal	COP	Biological diversity and biological resources
Protocol on biosafety to the CBD [Cartagena]	2000	11.09.2003	166	UNEP	Montreal	MOP	Transboundary movement, transit, handling and use of living modified organisms
Nagoya protocol on access to genetic resources and the fair and equitable sharing of benefits arising from their utilization to the convention on biodiversity	2010	NOT IN FORCE	92 (signatures) 26 (ratifications)	UNEP	Nagoya	MOP	Access, fair and equitable sharing of benefits arising from the utilization of genetic resources, traditional knowledge
United Nations convention to combat desertification	1994	26.12.1996	195	UN	Bonn	COP	combating desertification and mitigate the effects of drought, particularly in africa

MEAS	Year	Entry into force	Parties ratification	Host institution	Seat	Decision-making organ	Issues covered
Rotterdam convention on the prior informed consent procedure for certain hazardous chemicals and pesticides in international trade	1998	24.02.2004	154	UNEP FAO	Geneva & Rome	COP	Promote shared responsibility and cooperative Effort among the Parties in the international trade of certain hazardous chemicals, in order to protect human health and the environment from potential harm and to contribute to their environmentally sound use
Stockholm convention on persistent organic pollutants	2001	17.05.2004	179	UNEP	Geneva	COP	Protect human health and the environment from persistent organic pollutants
Minimata covention on mercury	2013	NOT IN FORCE	94 (signatures) 1 (ratification)	UNEP	nil	COP	Protect human health and the environment from the adverse effects of mercury

PART 4

The Future

CHAPTER 9

Conclusions

In the era of organizational proliferation, the effort to carve out appropriate and robust mechanism for governance of the environment appears to be need of the hour in the face of simmering global environmental challenges. The perceived crisis has, over the past four decades, found telling expressions in various Reports (such as *Only One Earth, Our Common Future* and *The Future We Want as well as scholarly works* (such as Limits to Growth and This Endangered Planet). The crisis is considered to be of '*planetary*' proportions notwithstanding the scientific prowess and technological strides attained by the humankind. Still, this glittering so-called human progress has been marred by predicament, as the Club of Rome report noted, that:

> It is the predicament of mankind that man can perceive the *problematique*, yet, despite his considerable knowledge and skills, he does not understand the origins, significance, and interrelationships of its many components and thus is unable to devise effective responses. This failure occurs in large part because we continue to examine single items in the *problematique* without understanding that the whole is more than the sum of its parts, that change in one element means change in the others.[1]

The quest for addressing the global environmental *problematique*, comprises a system of legal and institutional framework that can be characterized under the rubric of international environmental governance (IEG). This marathon

1 *The Club of Rome* (at the outset, in April 1968, it comprised some 30 persons from 10 different nationalities) sought to examine the complex of problems troubling all nations: poverty in the midst of plenty; degradation of the environment; loss of faith in institutions; uncontrolled urban spread; insecurity of employment; alienation of youth; rejection of traditional values; and inflation and other monetary and economic disruptions. The Club of Rome called this "world problematique" having three characteristics in common: they occur to some degree in all societies; they contain technical, social, economic, and political elements; and, most important of all, they interact. See Donella H. Meadows (et. Al), *The Limits to Growth: A Report for the Club of Rome's Project on the Predicament of Mankind* (New York: Universal Books, 1972), pp.10–11; available at: http://www.donellameadows.org/wp-content/userfiles/Limits-to-Growth-digital-scan-version.pdf.

 | DOI 10.1163/9789004214552_010

process takes place in the midst of general apprehension that "the major problems facing mankind are of such complexity and are so interrelated that traditional institutions and policies are no longer able to cope with them, nor even to come to grips with their full content".[2]

Thus IEG mosaic provides a logical corollary to multiple apparatus placed within the UN system as well as *ad hoc* responses in addressing environmental problems having global character. In view of the global environmental challenges, which are expected to remain for the foreseeable future, the IEG reforms shall have to be timely, pragmatic and effective enough to ensure protection of the global ecological heritage as well as long term survival of life on this planet. The UN member states now need to rise above narrow partisan considerations as well as streamline priorities and define expectations from the human institutions put into place to address the challenge that largely arises from our mindless quest for material wealth. Institutional structures do provide a basis for the states to have an orderly form of cooperation for debating and arriving at consensus on the future of IEG. Therefore, any such future exercise to reform current IEG regime would need to clearly define the structure, mandates, powers, funding, location and composition of the relevant institutions designed for the purpose.

On the international institutional landscape, the arrival of environmental institutions has witnessed significant patterns, processes and developments. These institutional structures reflect the need for interdependence in the arena of global protection of the environment. There are many innovations in the process of institution building which are designed to cater to the nature and location of the environmental problems as well as expectation of the sovereign states. Most of the institutions also appear to be mirror images of the experiences of the states within their domestic sphere. As such they are expected to adjust to the changing circumstances and priorities of the states. In the wake of this, the pace as well as the content of multilateral environmental law-making as well as institution-building processes has intensified in the past four decades. It is generally taken for granted that environmental regulatory frameworks also throw up institutional mechanisms. In fact, there is a remarkable synergy in the growth of both multilateral environmental law-making and international environmental institution-building.

Ironically, the law-making as well as institution building processes are designed in an *ad hoc* and piecemeal manner. No single entity provides an overall birth, direction and sustenance to the *sui generis* process. As a result, the role played by various specialized IEIs as well 'greening' of other international

2 *Ibid*, pp. 9–10.

institutions has, in a sense, created unexpected multiplicity, overlapping and clogging of the institutional landscape. The role of multiplicity of institutional actors appears to hamper intergovernmental efforts in designing a coherent and well coordinated approach to address the environmental challenges. Moreover, the growing fragmentation of the environmental agenda has made the task complicated. It has also aggravated the problem of coordination. Hence, the need of the hour is to firmly put into place a well-knit and coherent governance framework as well as to augment coordination in order to address global environmental challenges, while avoiding duplication and wastage of resources.

The states have, generally, been unwilling to establish powerful institutions, and sought to stifle institutions that fail to meet the self-designated 'national interest' driven policy goals. The failures of UNEP as an international environmental institution need to be also attributed to the political neglect of its member states, who in their wisdom thought it fit not to equip it with adequate funding as well as requisite institutional status to function effectively. The arrival of various international institutions on the environmental scene has led to considerable 'encroachment' upon UNEP's domain and, in turn, dilution of its authority as an entity that could set the global environmental agenda through democratic and transparent process.

As a part of overhauling of the institutional structure, various innovations have been witnessed over the years within UNEP itself. This includes closure of environment coordination board, formation of a committee of permanent representatives (CPR), advent (2000) of global ministerial environment forum (GMEF) and its closure (2013) as well as coordination mechanism of Environment Management Group (EMG). Similarly, commission on sustainable development (CSD) was set as a follow up measure to the Rio Earth Summit (1992). The CSD outlived its utility in 2013 with the advent of high level political forum (HLPF) on sustainable development. This replacement of CSD by HLPF on the radar screen of sustainable development agenda is largely seen as a welcome and timely step.

Thus the birth and death of institutions appear to be logical corollary to genuine expectations of the sovereign states. The quest for internalization of culture of sustainable development, especially within the UN system, also signifies 'inner' institutional engineering at work. The mandate of the new entity is quite broader than its predecessor CSD as well as UNEP. The HLPF has been created to provide political leadership to the overarching agenda of sustainable development that includes environmental, economic and social pillars. It does in some way put to rest the earlier concerns that new entity would weaken UNEP's authority. Yet in view of complex challenges that are expected to remain for the foreseeable future, HLPF shall have to tread the difficult path with caution, pragmatism and effectiveness to ensure implementation of global sustainable development agenda as well as the post-2015 development agenda. It remains to be seen as to how HLPF measures up to the simmering global challenge of sustainable development.

However, there seems to be growing realization that IEG reform cannot stand alone – UNEP's transformation must occur in parallel with installation of a sustainable development structure. In fact the case for upgrading UNEP into a UN 'specialized agency' could have been addressed head-on alongside the replacement of CSD with HLPF at the Rio+ 20 Summit (UNCSD, 2012) itself. In order to ensure better balance among the three pillars of sustainable development, both the institutional processes concerning sustainable development and the goal of effective system of IEG need to be mutually supportive and remain interconnected.

Given the prognosis of the problems in hand, a void is being felt as regards the need for a centralized environmental institution which can lead from the front and form a strong environmental pillar to give a push to the quest for 'sustainable' development in the larger interest. Hence, there is an urgent need to strengthen the UN's primary environmental governance framework. UNEP – being UN's environmental conscience – has the best credentials to spearhead this vital process. Given the political will and consensus among the key sovereign actors, there appears to be strong justification – and the growing support of sovereign states (GC/GMEF 12th Special Session, Feb. 2012) – for UNEP's logical up-gradation into a UN 'specialized' agency as a logical culmination of institutional evolution within the UN system. This incremental process could follow the pattern of the UN Industrial Development Organization (UNIDO)[3] set up by a General Assembly resolution 2152 (XXI) of 17 November 1966. The General Assembly set in motion a process for its up gradation into a

3 On 17 November, 1966, the United Nations General Assembly passes resolution 2152 (XXI) establishing the United Nations Industrial Organization (UNIDO) as an autonomous body within the United Nations.

In 1975, the General Assembly, in resolution 3362 (S-VII), endorsed the recommendation of the Conference that UNIDO be converted into a specialized agency. As a sequel, the UN conference on the "Establishment of UNIDO as a specialized agency," at its second session (1979) in Vienna (Austria) adopted the new Constitution. As such the new Constitution of UNIDO, the Constitution enters into force on 21 June 1985. The first session of the General Conference of UNIDO as a specialized agency met in August 1985 and elected Domingo L. Siazon Jr. (Philippines) as its Director General. For details on this see, http://www.unido.org/fileadmin/user_media/UNIDO_Header_Site/About/UNIDO_Constitution.pdf Also see http://www.unido.org/fileadmin/user_media_upgrade/Who_we_are/In_Brief/IntrodUNIDO_July2009_SC.pdf

UN specialized agency by resolution 3362 (S-VII) of 16 September 1975 (that finally took shape with adoption of UNIDO Constitution on 8 April 1979 at the second session of the UN Conference on the Establishment of UNIDO as a Specialized Agency in Vienna). Thus, as and when the UN General Assembly crystallizes requisite political will of the member states, it could trigger a similar process for the functional area of 'environment'.

Thus, the time tested and recognized contribution of UNEP, howsoever it may fall short of expectations of the sovereign states, could be factored in this vital process. While building on past experience, the proposed new structure (with nomenclature such as UNEPO) will need to be *sui generis* in view of the nature and uniqueness of this functional area. The contours of the new entity could emerge on the basis of expectations of the sovereign states. UNEP's merger with and becoming the core of a new international environmental entity could ensure an enhanced stature and authority as regards the institutional structure dedicated for the environment. Under these circumstances, the merits and demerits of having a UN specialized agency for the 'functional' area of environment protection will need to be considered in terms of possibility of improvement over the existing situation. The core issue in the matter revolves around the desirability of enhancing UNEP's status or carving out a new organization altogether. The institution-building history shows that it is difficult to negotiate a *de novo* international organization. Therefore, enhancing UNEP's status through an international agreement duly negotiated through a mandate given by the plenary organ of the UN, the General Assembly, could be a logically preferred option. The process of institutional restructuring will depend upon the political will of the states, which may reflect in the merger of some UN departments and programmes in the new organization with UNEP at its core. However, this could be determined by interests and priorities of the UN member states as well as the strength of the environmental, economic and social pillars in the UN system.

The possibility of endowing a new mandate for the UN *Trusteeship Council* could also constitute a crucial part of the ongoing exercise for restructuring of the UN. It would provide an appropriate task for one of the principal organs of the UN to address a contemporary challenge and, in turn, confer new authority to the UN itself. Such a revival of the Trusteeship Council could serve the need for a supervisory organ within the UN itself especially since both the General Assembly and the Economic and Social Council (ECOSOC) are overburdened with their respective political as well as socio-economic agendas. Thus a new mandate for the revived Trusteeship Council could be given effect through amendment of the UN Charter (Articles 87 and 88) for a 'new trust' to cater to the growing environmental challenges as well as for the global commons.

The 'up-graded' UNEP into a 'specialized agency' (called UNEPO) will be part of the larger restructuring of the UN. This agency could report to the Trusteeship Council (and the ECOSOC) and through them to the General Assembly (see chapter 7 for detailed blueprint).

In the course of the deliberations at the twelfth Special Session of the GC/GMEF (2012), though strengthening of the IEG has been on the agenda of UNEP for over a decade, the chasm of infusing "broader" versus "incremental" reforms has polarized the intergovernmental deliberations. The European Union, led by France and Germany, with support from African countries, argued that only a new specialized agency can overcome the perceived weaknesses of UNEP. However, the US, China, India, Russia, Egypt and a few others remained, for their own reasons, skeptical about changing UNEP's status at this juncture. They argued that a centralized body would be unwieldy and inflexible, and would de-emphasize countries' obligations under specific treaties. In fact, the discussion on future of UNEP also shows signs of vacillation from time to time since "specialized agency" supporters (including several members of the African Union) insisted they have opted for an "international specialized institution" rather than a UN specialized agency. Switzerland has been referring to "a strengthened IEG anchor institution". However, if States sincerely wish to realize the ambitious objectives expressed in the 1997 Nairobi Declaration, the 2000 Malmö Ministerial Declaration as well as the 2012 UNCSD outcome (*The Future We Want*), they shall have to articulate a forward-looking consensus on reform objectives and seek a realistic and yet futuristic road-map for strengthening the architecture of IEG.

The 'outcome' document of the UNCSD did provide an impetus to strengthen UNEP underscoring universal membership of the Governing Council (GC); stable, adequate and predictable financial resources; enhancement of UNEP's coordination role in the UN system; a strong science-policy interface; and active participation of all relevant stakeholders. The first Universal Session of UNEP Governing Council (2013) squarely underscored the application of incremental approach – revitalizing the mandate of the UNEP's Governing Council by renaming it as the UN Environment Assembly as a deliberative global environmental forum with a universal membership – and UNEP to be provided with adequate, stable and predictable funding. Hence, it will now attain far greater institutional legitimacy and authority. The decision to re-designate the Governing Council as 'United Nations Environment Assembly of UNEP' reflects the latent intent of sovereign states to enhance UNEP's status. Similarly, the decision to discontinue the GMEF which has often been dubbed as 'ministerial talk-shop' and, instead, convene a high-level segment at the end of each Environment Assembly meeting, reflects a desire to confer higher status upon future UNEP EA decisions. The new hesitant makeover of the UNEP would help in garnering more political clout then its previous incarnation. Still, it remains a step short of the final call on becoming a full-fledged 'functional' international organization – a specialized agency as per Articles 57 and 63 of the UN Charter – in the field of environment.

In the present scenario, however, while UNEP's mandate remains the same, funding has not still become adequate and predictable to meet growing environmental challenges and some incremental changes made in its structure. Still, expectations from the body have steadily grown. The process signifies a remarkable incremental institutional innovation at work. In the face of perceived skepticism among many of the countries, it appears, UNEP's 'creeping' institutional elevation into a specialized agency could come through the 'back door'. Thus, as and when, the final call is made to turn UNEP into a functional IO, it could be designated as the United Nations Environment Protection Organization (UNEPO) so as to provide it logical 'up-gradation' from a UN programme into a specialized agency – as it was done in the case of UNIDO (established in 1966 through a General Assembly resolution and became a specialized agency through adoption of a constitution in 1979 at a UN conference in Vienna).

It is now widely accepted that such up-gradation for the UN's environment pillar, could directly help in addressing the crisis of perception as well as legitimacy that UNEP currently faces from the UN member States, specialized agencies, the secretariats of MEAs, international governmental and non-governmental organizations. Thus the gradual meaning of effective 'revitalization' of UNEP (as mandated by the 1997 Nairobi Declaration) could be construed as the key goal in the immediate future to upgrade UNEP and environment protection within the UN system (on the pattern of UNIDO up gradation) as well as strengthen its location in Nairobi. The process could be evolutionary as already seen in the through intergovernmental processes during the period of 1997 to 2013. Even then, the challenges that lie ahead of UNEP are daunting given the emerging landscape of sustainable development governance that UNEP must navigate as well as 'hesitant' changes brought about in its own institutional arrangements.

Similarly, MEAs are a *sui generis* method of grappling with sector-specific environmental problems and seem to be 'new' treaty-based response mechanisms in the sense that they put up their own dynamics through a built-in law-making mechanism. The treaty making enterprise functions literally as 'work-in-progress'. Still they are designed in such a way that they remain *ad hoc* in nature even as they address sector-specific environmental goals. Thus, instead of following the traditional treaty-making approach, MEAs become virtual 'processes'. The process itself comes to the fore duly couched in different legal formulations. It is, however, essentially based on the bedrock of evolving scientific evidence, cost-effective measures, institutional structures as well as political convenience of the state parties to the specific regulatory instrument (MEA in question).

It seems states are now comfortable with this particular mode of treaty-making as well as the pattern has now come to stay and duly institutionalized. Still, the process remains amorphous in some respects notwithstanding participation of a large number of sovereign states that testifies to its utility as an institutionalized form of intergovernmental environmental cooperation. Considering the manner in which MEAs have progressed as sectoral legal restraints upon the behavior of States, it would be difficult either to dismantle them or to bring them under the control of a single entity or even expect that UNEP would be in a position to effectively coordinate work of all the different MEAs. Depending upon how it is designed, given effect to and how much consensus could be attained among the parties to various MEAs, co-location or clustering could be one of the effective modes to address this lingering challenge of governance. The chemicals and hazardous wastes clusters provide testimony that such initiatives are doable and could be replicated in other clusters too (such as atmosphere and biodiversity). However, any such move will need to essentially respect the autonomous legal status of each MEA.

The challenge needs to be squarely addressed as a part of the larger architecture of IEG. The mushrooming growth of MEAs needs to be made 'sense' of in earnest to ensure that the multilateral regulatory technique does not get over-stretched as well as does not repel states with fatigue effect. The questions of mounting scientific evidence, growing concerns for environment protection and natural resource conservation, issues of funding and transfer of technology as well as drawing synergies and location remain to be seriously looked into so as to provide best cost-effective regulation of state behavior concerning a *problematique*. Since these MEAs are *sui generis* instruments, they can be subordinated neither to the UN nor any of the UN specialized agency or subsidiary organs or even international non-governmental organization. UNEP's Division of Environmental Law and Conventions is a feeble entity to provide any redress in the matter. Therefore, the coming challenge would be how best to coordinate the work, draw the best synergy as well as to provide additional mandates to the existing of the MEAs rather than encourage growth of more MEAs unless they become inevitable. Sorting out the mosaic of clogged terrain of MEAs will be the biggest IEG challenge in the coming decades.

In the wake of challenge of designing an appropriate architecture of IEG, it seems, the reluctance of many of the sovereign states is borne out of perceived fears and fuelled by envy from other institutional actors in the field. Thus, even as different pieces of the jigsaw are still in the process of gradually falling into place, UNEP's emergence as a 'specialized agency' seems to be written on the wall – just like the nomenclature 'to be born a nation' characterized plight of Namibia for decades. It seems to be no longer a question as to 'why' but 'when' and 'how'. The question of a 'new trust' for the UN Trusteeship Council – as a supervisory organ for the global environment and the commons – that still forms part of the UN Charter and lies dormant, can also be addressed as a part of the larger issue of UN reform as and when conducive climate and sagacity come to the fore. It will vindicate the time tested truism that both law and the institutions must change with the change of circumstances as well as needs of the society at a given time.

As the plenary organ of the UN, the General Assembly will need to step in to address the complexity of the institutional dimensions of international environmental governance. As such, the future direction of IEG will be dictated more by the political will of States – how far they wish to go in the process, how best they want to translate their international environmental commitments into action, and how much they are willing to allow transparency in the functioning of different institutional structures –in order to address the challenge of the global environment and the commons. Notwithstanding this, the UN General Assembly has a role cut out for itself in the coming decade if there is a genuine desire to ensure that the IEG jigsaw falls into its place that serves the long term interests of the 'peoples' of the United Nations. One hopes that 'doing' rather than 'talking' becomes the crucial *mantra* as regards governance of the environment during this century that will prove crucial for long-term survival of life itself on this small endangered planet.

PART 5

Appendices

I The General Assembly Resolution 67/290

The General Assembly

Recalling its resolution 66/288 of 27 July 2012, by which it endorsed the outcome document of the United Nations Conference on Sustainable Development, entitled "The future we want",

Emphasizing the need for an improved and more effective institutional framework for sustainable development, which should be guided by the specific functions required and mandates involved; address the shortcomings of the current system; take into account all relevant implications; promote synergies and coherence; seek to avoid duplication and eliminate unnecessary overlaps within the United Nations system and reduce administrative burdens and build on existing arrangements,

Recalling the decision contained in paragraph 84 of the outcome document of the Conference[1] to establish a universal, intergovernmental, high-level political forum, building on the strengths, experiences, resources and inclusive participation modalities of the Commission on Sustainable Development, which would subsequently replace the Commission, as well as the decision that the high-level political forum should follow on the implementation of sustainable development and should avoid overlap with existing structures, bodies and entities in a cost-effective manner,

Reaffirming the role and authority of the General Assembly on global matters of concern to the international community, as set out in the Charter of the United Nations, and its central position as the chief deliberative, policymaking and representative organ of the United Nations, and recognizing the need for it to further integrate sustainable development as a key element of the overarching framework for United Nations activities,

Reaffirming also the commitment to strengthen the Economic and Social Council, within its mandate under the Charter, as a principal organ in the integrated and coordinated follow-up of the outcomes of all major United Nations conferences and summits in the economic, social, environmental and related fields, and recognizing the key role of the Council in achieving a balanced integration of the three dimensions of sustainable development,

---

* The General Assembly adopted resolution on Format and organizational aspects of the high-level political forum on sustainable development, adopted on 9 July, 2013, UN Doc. A/RES/67/290, 23 August 2013; available at, http://www.un.org/ga/search/view_doc.asp?symbol=A/67/L.72&Lang=E.

1 Resolution 66/288, annex.

 | DOI 10.1163/9789004214552_011

Recalling the Rio Declaration on Environment and Development,[2] Agenda 21,[3] the Programme for the Further Implementation of Agenda 21,[4] the Plan of Implementation of the World Summit on Sustainable Development (Johannesburg Plan of Implementation)[5] and the Johannesburg Declaration on Sustainable Development,[6]

Recalling also the Programme of Action for the Sustainable Development of Small Island Developing States (Barbados Programme of Action)[7] and the Mauritius Strategy for the Further Implementation of the Programme of Action for the Sustainable Development of Small Island Developing States,[8]

Recalling further the Programme of Action for the Least Developed Countries for the Decade 2011–2020 (Istanbul Programme of Action),[9] the Almaty Programme of Action: Addressing the Special Needs of Landlocked Developing Countries within a New Global Framework for Transit Transport Cooperation for Landlocked and Transit Developing Countries,[10] the political declaration on Africa's development needs[11] and the New Partnership for Africa's Development,[12]

Recalling the commitments in the outcomes of all the major United Nations conferences and summits in the economic, social and environmental fields, including the

---

2 *Report of the United Nations Conference on Environment and Development, Rio de Janeiro, 3–14 June 1992*, vol. I, *Resolutions adopted by the Conference* (United Nations publication, Sales No. E.93.I.8 and corrigendum), resolution 1, annex I.

3 Ibid., annex II.

4 Resolution S-19/2, annex.

5 *Report of the World Summit on Sustainable Development, Johannesburg, South Africa, 26 August–4 September 2002* (United Nations publication, Sales No. E.03.II.A.1 and corrigendum), chap. I, resolution 2, annex.

6 Ibid., resolution 1, annex.

7 *Report of the Global Conference on the Sustainable Development of Small Island Developing States, Bridgetown, Barbados, 25 April–6 May 1994* (United Nations publication, Sales No. E.94.I.18 and corrigenda), chap. I, resolution 1, annex II.

8 *Report of the International Meeting to Review the Implementation of the Programme of Action for the Sustainable Development of Small Island Developing States, Port Louis, Mauritius, 10–14 January 2005*

(United Nations publication, Sales No. E.05.II.A.4 and corrigendum), chap. I, resolution 1, annex II.

9 *Report of the Fourth United Nations Conference on the Least Developed Countries, Istanbul, Turkey, 9–13 May 2011* (A/CONF.219/7), chap. II.

10 *Report of the International Ministerial Conference of Landlocked and Transit Developing Countries and Donor Countries and International Financial and Development Institutions on Transit Cooperation, Almaty, Kazakhstan, 28 and 29 August 2003* (A/CONF.202/3), annex I.

11 Resolution 63/1.

12 A/57/304, annex.

United Nations Millennium Declaration,[13] the 2005 World Summit Outcome,[14] the Monterrey Consensus of the International Conference on Financing for Development,[15] the Doha Declaration on Financing for Development: outcome document of the Follow-up International Conference on Financing for Development to Review the Implementation of the Monterrey Consensus,[16] the outcome document of the High-Level Plenary Meeting of the General Assembly on the Millennium Development Goals,[17] the Programme of Action of the International Conference on Population and Development,[18] the key actions for the further implementation of the Programme of Action of the International Conference on Population and Development[19] and the Beijing Declaration and Platform for Action,[20]

Recalling also its resolution 67/203 of 21 December 2012,

1. *Takes note* of the report of the Secretary-General on the lessons learned from the Commission on Sustainable Development[21];
2. *Decides* that the high-level political forum, consistent with its universal intergovernmental character, shall provide political leadership, guidance and recommendations for sustainable development, follow up and review progress in the implementation of sustainable development commitments, enhance the integration of the three dimensions of sustainable development in a holistic and cross-sectoral manner at all levels and have a focused, dynamic and action-oriented agenda, ensuring the appropriate consideration of new and emerging sustainable development challenges;
3. *Also decides* that the meetings of the forum shall be convened under the auspices of the General Assembly and of the Economic and Social Council;
4. *Further decides* that all meetings of the forum shall provide for the full and effective participation of all States Members of the United Nations and States members of specialized agencies;

---

13 Resolution 55/2.

14 Resolution 60/1.

15 *Report of the International Conference on Financing for Development, Monterrey, Mexico, 18–22 March 2002* (United Nations publication, Sales No. E.02.II.A.7), chap. I, resolution 1, annex.

16 Resolution 63/239, annex.

17 Resolution 65/1.

18 *Report of the International Conference on Population and Development, Cairo, 5–13 September 1994*
(United Nations publication, Sales No. E.95.XIII.18), chap. I, resolution 1, annex.

19 Resolution S-21/2, annex.

20 *Report of the Fourth World Conference on Women, Beijing, 4–15 September 1995* (United Nations publication, Sales No. E.96.IV.13), chap. I, resolution 1, annexes I and II.

21 A/67/757.

5. *Decides* that, in all meetings of the forum, every effort shall be made to reach consensus;
6. *Also decides* that the meetings of the forum under the auspices of the General Assembly:
   (a) Shall be convened at the level of Heads of State and Government;
   (b) Shall be convened every four years by the President of the Assembly for a period of two days, at the beginning of the session of the Assembly, as well as on other occasions, on an exceptional basis, upon a decision by the Assembly;
   (c) Shall be chaired by the President of the Assembly;
   (d) Shall result in a concise negotiated political declaration to be submitted for the consideration of the Assembly;
7. *Further decides* that the meetings of the forum under the auspices of the Economic and Social Council:
   (a) Shall be convened annually by the President of the Council for a period of eight days, including a three-day ministerial segment to be held in the framework of the substantive session of the Council, building on and subsequently replacing the annual ministerial review as from 2016;
   (b) Shall be chaired by the President of the Council;
   (c) Shall have a thematic focus reflecting the integration of the three dimensions of sustainable development, in line with the thematic focus of the activities of the Council and consistent with the post-2015 development agenda;
   (d) Shall follow up and review progress in the implementation of all the outcomes of the major United Nations conferences and summits in the economic, social and environmental fields, as well as their respective means of implementation, improve cooperation and coordination within the United Nations system on sustainable development programmes and policies, promote the sharing of best practices and experiences relating to the implementation of sustainable development and, on a voluntary basis, facilitate sharing of experiences, including successes, challenges and lessons learned, and promote system-wide coherence and coordination of sustainable development policies;
   (e) Shall take into account the work of the Development Cooperation Forum, as well as other activities of the Council relating to the integration and implementation of sustainable development;
   (f) Shall benefit from regional preparatory processes;
   (g) Shall result in a negotiated ministerial declaration for inclusion in the report of the Council to the General Assembly;

8. *Decides* that the forum, under the auspices of the Economic and Social Council, shall conduct regular reviews, starting in 2016, on the follow-up and implementation of sustainable development commitments and objectives, including those related to the means of implementation, within the context of the post-2015 development agenda, and further decides that those reviews:
   (a) Shall be voluntary, while encouraging reporting, and shall include developed and developing countries, as well as relevant United Nations entities;
   (b) Shall be State-led, involving ministerial and other relevant high-level participants;
   (c) Shall provide a platform for partnerships, including through the participation of major groups and other relevant stakeholders;
   (d) Shall replace the national voluntary presentations held in the context of the annual ministerial-level substantive reviews of the Council, building upon the relevant provisions of General Assembly resolution 61/16 of 20 November 2006, as well as experiences and lessons learned in this context;
9. *Also decides* that all meetings convened under the auspices of the General Assembly shall operate under the rules of procedure of the main committees of the Assembly, as applicable, unless otherwise provided in the present resolution, and that all meetings convened under the auspices of the Economic and Social Council shall operate under the rules of procedure of the functional commissions of the Council, as applicable, except as otherwise provided in the present resolution;
10. *Underlines* that the arrangement established by the Economic and Social Council for the Commission on Sustainable Development in Council decision 1995/201 of 8 February 1995 shall apply to the meetings of the forum held under the auspices of the Council, and that the arrangements established by the General Assembly in the annex to its resolution 65/276 of 3 May 2011 shall apply to the meetings of the forum held under the auspices of the Assembly;
11. *Decides* that the meetings of the forum shall devote adequate time to the discussion of the sustainable development challenges facing developing countries, including the most vulnerable countries, in particular the least developed countries, small island developing States, landlocked developing countries and African countries, with the aim of enhancing engagement and implementing commitments and that they will recognize the particular challenges facing the middle-income countries in achieving sustainable development, and reiterates that the efforts of middle-income countries should be adequately supported by the international community, in various forms, taking into account the needs of those countries and their capacity to mobilize domestic resources;

12. *Encourages* States to ensure that their participation in the meetings of the forum reflect the balanced integration of the social, economic and environmental dimensions of sustainable development from their national perspectives;
13. *Acknowledges* the importance of the regional dimension of sustainable development, and invites the United Nations regional commissions to contribute to the work of the forum, including through annual regional meetings, with the involvement of other relevant regional entities, major groups and other relevant stakeholders, as appropriate;
14. *Stresses* the need for the forum to promote transparency and implementation by further enhancing the consultative role and participation of the major groups and other relevant stakeholders at the international level in order to make better use of their expertise, while retaining the intergovernmental nature of discussions, and in this regard decides that the forum shall be open to the major groups, other relevant stakeholders and entities having received a standing invitation to participate as observers in the General Assembly, building on arrangements and practices observed by the Commission on Sustainable Development, including Economic and Social Council decision 1993/215 of 12 February 1993 and Council resolution 1996/31 of 25 July 1996, which shall be applicable to the forum;
15. *Decides*, in this regard, that, while retaining the intergovernmental character of the forum, the representatives of the major groups and other relevant stakeholders shall be allowed:
    (a) To attend all official meetings of the forum;
    (b) To have access to all official information and documents;
    (c) To intervene in official meetings;
    (d) To submit documents and present written and oral contributions;
    (e) To make recommendations;
    (f) To organize side events and round tables, in cooperation with Member States and the Secretariat;
16. *Encourages* the major groups identified in Agenda 213 and other stakeholders, such as private philanthropic organizations, educational and academic entities, persons with disabilities, volunteer groups and other stakeholders active in areas related to sustainable development, to autonomously establish and maintain effective coordination mechanisms for participation in the high-level political forum and for actions derived from that participation at the global, regional and national levels, in a way that ensures effective, broad and balanced participation by region and by type of organization;
17. *Invites* the organizations of the United Nations system, including the Bretton Woods institutions and other relevant intergovernmental organizations, including the

World Trade Organization, to contribute within their respective mandates to the discussions of the forum;

18. *Emphasizes* that the forum shall provide a dynamic platform for regular dialogue and for stocktaking and agenda-setting to advance sustainable development and that the agenda of all meetings of the high-level political forum shall be focused, while allowing flexibility to address new and emerging issues;
19. *Reaffirms* that the forum shall contribute to the enhanced integration of the three dimensions of sustainable development in a holistic and cross-sectoral manner at all levels, and in this regard invites the forum to take into account the contributions and work of relevant United Nations intergovernmental bodies in the social, economic and environmental fields;
20. *Decides* that the forum shall strengthen the science-policy interface by examining documentation, bringing together dispersed information and assessments, including in the form of a global sustainable development report, building on existing assessments, enhancing evidence-based decision-making at all levels and contributing to the strengthening of ongoing capacity-building for data collection and analysis in developing countries, and requests the forum to consider, in 2014, the scope and methodology of a global sustainable development report, based on a proposal of the Secretary-General reflecting the views and recommendations of Member States, and relevant United Nations entities, including the Committee for Development Policy;
21. *Also decides* that the forum may provide recommendations to the board of the 10-year framework of programmes for sustainable consumption and production, as well as to the United Nations Environment Programme, as the secretariat of the 10-year framework, taking into account their reports;
22. *Requests* the President of the General Assembly and the President of the Economic and Social Council to coordinate with the Bureau of the Council and with the bureaux of the relevant committees of the Assembly to organize the activities of the forum so as to benefit from the inputs and advice of the United Nations system, the major groups and other relevant stakeholders, as appropriate;
23. *Decides* that the forum shall be supported by the Department of Economic and Social Affairs of the Secretariat in close cooperation with all relevant entities of the United Nations system, including funds and programmes, multilateral financial and trade institutions, the secretariats of the three Rio conventions and other relevant treaty bodies and international organizations within their respective mandates;
24. *Requests* the Secretary-General to carry over all the remaining funds from the Trust Fund for Support of the Work of the Commission on Sustainable

Development to a voluntary trust fund of the forum in order to facilitate the participation of developing countries, the least developed countries, representatives of major groups and other relevant stakeholders, as appropriate, in the work of the forum and to support the preparations of the forum, and in this regard invites Member States, financial institutions and other organizations to contribute to the voluntary trust fund of the forum;

25. *Decides* that travel expenses for one representative of each of the least developed countries shall be paid from the regular budget of the United Nations for participation in all formal meetings of the forum;
26. *Recommends* that the Economic and Social Council abolish the Commission on Sustainable Development effective upon the conclusion of its twentieth session, to be held prior to the first meeting of the forum, pursuant to General Assembly resolution 67/203 of 21 December 2012;
27. *Decides* that the first meeting of the forum under the auspices of the General Assembly shall have an inaugural character, requests the President of the Assembly to convene the meeting at the beginning of the sixty-eighth session for the duration of one day, and decides that, on an extraordinary basis and only for the purpose of that meeting, the outcome of the meeting shall consist of the summary of the President;
28. *Also decides* to consider at its sixty-ninth session the need to convene a meeting of the forum under the auspices of the General Assembly in 2015 in relation to the launch of the post-2015 development agenda;
29. *Further decides* to review at its seventy-third session the format and the organizational aspects of the forum, unless otherwise decided;
30. *Emphasizes* that the review of the implementation of General Assembly resolution 61/16 should take into account the present resolution in order to avoid duplication.

II UN GA Resolution of 67/251, 13 March 2013

The Governing Council

Welcoming the outcome document, "The future we want", of the United Nations Conference on Sustainable Development held from 20 to 22 June 2012 in Rio de Janeiro, Brazil, which invited the General Assembly to adopt at its sixty-seventh session a resolution strengthening and upgrading the United Nations Environment Programme, as outlined in paragraph 88, subparagraphs (a)–(h), of the outcome document, and recalling General Assembly resolution 66/288 of 27 July 2012,

Reaffirming the need to strengthen international environmental governance within the context of the institutional framework for sustainable development in order to promote a balanced integration of the economic, social and environmental dimensions of sustainable development, as well as coordination within the United Nations system,

Recognizing General Assembly resolution 67/213 of 21 December 2012 on, *inter alia*, the implementation of section IV.C, entitled "Environmental pillar in the context of sustainable development", of the outcome document of the United Nations Conference on Sustainable Development and under which the first universal session of the Governing Council of the United Nations Environment Programme is held,

1. *Recommends* to the General Assembly that the Governing Council of the United Nations Environment Programme, an intergovernmental body established pursuant to article 22 of the United Nations Charter, be renamed as the United Nations Environment Assembly of the United Nations Environment Programme;
2. *Reaffirms* the commitment to strengthen the role of the United Nations Environment Programme as the leading global environmental authority that sets the global environmental agenda, promotes the coherent implementation of the environmental dimension of sustainable development within the United Nations system and serves as an authoritative advocate for the global environment;
3. *Decides* that the governing body of the United Nations Environment Programme[1] will convene its sessions in Nairobi on a biennial basis, starting in 2014, and will

* Adopted by the General Assembly on 13 March 2013; Doc.A/RES/67/251, 25 July 2013.

1 The Governing Council of the United Nations Environment Programme, whose designation is subject to change pursuant to paragraph 1 of the present decision and a resolution of the General Assembly to that effect.

 | DOI 10.1163/9789004214552_012

carry out its mandate as set out in General Assembly resolution 2997 (XXVII) of 15 December 1972 and all other relevant resolutions that reinforce its mandate as well as the 1997 Nairobi Declaration on the Role and Mandate of the United Nations Environment Programme, the 2000 Malmö Ministerial Declaration, the 2010 Nusa Dua Declaration and paragraph 88 of the outcome document of the United Nations Conference on Sustainable Development as endorsed by the General Assembly in resolution 66/288;

4. *Decides* to discontinue the Global Ministerial Environment Forum;

5. *Decides* that each session of the governing body of the United Nations Environment Programme will conclude with a two-day high level segment as an integral part of the governing body of the United Nations Environment Programme, which will take strategic decisions and provide political guidance and will perform *inter alia* the following functions:
   (a) Setting the global environmental agenda;
   (b) Providing overarching policy guidance and defining policy responses to address emerging environmental challenges;
   (c) Undertaking policy review, dialogue and exchange of experiences;
   (d) Setting the strategic guidance on the future direction of the United Nations Environment Programme;
   (e) Organizing a multi-stakeholder dialogue;
   (f) Fostering partnerships for achieving environmental goals and resource mobilization;

6. *Decides* that the Bureau of the governing body of the United Nations Environment Programme shall be composed of 10 members to reflect the universality of the governing body, in accordance with equitable geographical distribution, and will assist the governing body and perform the functions as set out in the rules of procedure of the governing body;

7. *Decides* that the governing body will ensure the active participation of all relevant stakeholders, particularly those from developing countries, drawing on best practices and models from relevant multilateral institutions and will explore new mechanisms to promote transparency and the effective engagement of civil society in its work and that of its subsidiary bodies, *inter alia* by:
   (a) Developing by 2014 a process for stakeholder accreditation and participation that builds on the existing rules of procedure and takes into account inclusive modalities of the Commission on Sustainable Development and other relevant United Nations bodies;
   (b) Establishing by 2014 mechanisms and rules for stakeholders' expert input and advice;
   (c) Enhancing by 2014 working methods and processes for informed discussions and contributions by all relevant stakeholders towards the intergovernmental decision-making process;

8. *Decides* that the governing body of the United Nations Environment Programme will promote a strong science-policy interface by reviewing the state of the environment, by building on existing international instruments, assessments, panels and information networks, including through an enhanced summary for policy makers of the Global Environment Outlook and, in this regard, requests the Executive Director to identify critical gaps and present a report, with recommendations, to the governing body;
9. *Decides* that an open-ended Committee of Permanent Representatives will be the intersessional subsidiary body of the governing body of the United Nations Environment Programme and, in addition to its mandate2 and in open and transparent manner, will perform the following functions:
   (a) Contributing to the preparation of the agenda of its governing body;
   (b) Providing advice to its governing body on policy matters;
   (c) Preparing decisions for adoption by its governing body and overseeing their implementation;
   (d) Convening thematic and/or programmatic debates
   (e) Promoting effective ways and means to facilitate participation of the non-resident members of the Committee, particularly from developing countries
   (f) Performing any other functions delegated to it by its governing body;
10. *Decides* to convene an open-ended meeting of the Committee of Permanent Representatives, while ensuring support to developing country representatives, to enable the participation of capital-based representatives as well as stakeholders for a period of five days in an even year to contribute to preparation of the agenda of its governing body, and to provide advice to its governing body on policy matters;
11. *Decides* to establish a subcommittee of the Committee of Permanent Representatives that will meet annually for a period of five days to review, with the support of the secretariat, the medium-term strategy and programme of work and budget, in a manner coherent with the budgetary cycle of the United Nations, to be endorsed by the Committee of Permanent Representatives and for the governing body's approval, and to oversee their implementation and accountability by the Secretariat;
12. *Decides* that the Committee of Permanent Representatives will consider the frequency, schedule and programmatic focus of its meetings to enhance its efficiency and effectiveness and will improve upon its working methods;
13. *Commits* to progressively consolidate headquarters functions of the United Nations Environment Programme in Nairobi and in this context requests the Executive Director to present a report to the governing body at its next session and to include recommendations in the programme of work for the period 2016–2017 to be acted upon and implemented in a timely manner;

14. *Decides* to strengthen the United Nations Environment Programme's regional presence in order to assist countries in the implementation of their national environmental programmes, policies and plans and in this regard requests the Executive Director to increase the Programme's participation in United Nations country teams;
15. *Stresses* the importance of the regional ministerial environment forums for which the United Nations Environment Programme serves as secretariat, and invites these forums to contribute, as appropriate, to the work of the governing body of the United Nations Environment Programme;
16. *Decides* to consider additional measures to strengthen the United Nations Environment Programme's voice and ability to fulfil its coordination mandate on environmental matters and, in this regard, invites the Secretary-General to take necessary steps to enhance the United Nations Environment Programme's role in key United Nations coordination bodies;
17. *Decides* to enhance transparency and openness in its work and in this regard requests the Executive Director to establish a written access-to-information policy;
18. *Invites* the Executive Director to continue improving the timeliness and responsiveness to the needs and requests by Member States and recalls the relevant provisions of paragraph 13 of its decision 19/32;
19. *Stresses* the need by no later than 2016 to implement the provisions of paragraph 88 (b) of the outcome document of the United Nations Conference on Sustainable Development and requests the Executive Director to report thereon;
20. *Decides* to implement paragraph 88 (f) of the outcome document of the United Nations Conference on Sustainable Development and, in this context, requests the Executive Director to enhance the operationalization of the Bali Strategic Plan for Technology Support and Capacity-building;
21. *Invites* the General Assembly to adopt a resolution to change the designation of the Governing Council along the lines of the text contained in the annex to the present decision.

III UNEP GC as First Universal Session 27/2, 22 February 2013

The General Assembly

Recalling its resolution 2997(XXVII) of 15 December 1972, concerning institutional and financial arrangements for international environmental cooperation, by which the Governing Council of the United Nations Environment Programme was established,

Also recalling its resolution 67/213 of 21 December 2012, on the report on the Governing Council of United Nations Environmental Programme on its twelfth special session and on the implementation of section IV C, "Environmental pillar in the context of sustainable development", of the outcome document of the United Nations Conference on Sustainable Development,

1. *Takes note* of Governing Council decision 27/2 of 22 February 2013, by which the Governing Council recommends to the General Assembly to change its designation to the United Nations Environment Assembly of the United Nations Environment Programme, it being understood that this change of designation in no way changes, nor will change, the present mandate, aims and purposes of the United Nations Environment Programme or the role and functions of its governing body;
2. *Decides* to change the designation of the Governing Council of the United Nations Environment Programme to the United Nations Environment Assembly of the United Nations Environment Programme.

---

* Adopted at Twenty seventh Session of the Governing Council/ GMEF, Nairobi, 18–22 February 2013; Doc.UNEP/ GC.27/17, 12 March 2013, pp. 25–28.

 | DOI 10.1163/9789004214552_013

IV The General Assembly Resolution 67/213, 21 December 2012

The General Assembly

Reaffirming the mandate contained in its resolution 2997 (XXVII) of 15 December 1972, which established the United Nations Environment Programme, and other relevant resolutions that reinforce its mandate, as well as the 1997 Nairobi Declaration on the Role and Mandate of the United Nations Environment Programme of 7 February 1997[1] and the 2000 Malmö Ministerial Declaration of 31 May 2000,[2]

Recalling its resolutions 53/242 of 28 July 1999, 55/200 of 20 December 2000, 57/251 of 20 December 2002, 64/204 of 21 December 2009, 65/162 of 20 December 2010, 66/203 of 22 December 2011 and other previous resolutions relating to the Governing Council/Global Ministerial Environment Forum of the United Nations Environment Programme,

Reaffirming its commitment to strengthening the role of the United Nations Environment Programme as the leading global environmental authority that sets the global environmental agenda, promotes the coherent implementation of the environmental dimension of sustainable development within the United Nations system and serves as an authoritative advocate for the global environment,

Taking into account Agenda 21[3] and the Plan of Implementation of the World Summit on Sustainable Development (Johannesburg Plan of Implementation),[4]

Reaffirming the Rio Declaration on Environment and Development[5] and its principles,

---

* Adopted by the General Assembly on 21 December 2012; Doc.A/RES/67/213, 15 March 2013; available at http://www.unep.org/gc/gc27/Docs/GA-RES-67-213-UNEP.pdf.

1 *Official Records of the General Assembly, Fifty-second Session, Supplement No. 25* (A/52/25), annex, decision 19/1, annex.

2 Ibid., *Fifty-fifth Session, Supplement No. 25* (A/55/25), annex I, decision SS.VI/1, annex.

3 *Report of the United Nations Conference on Environment and Development, Rio de Janeiro, 3-14 June 1992*, vol. I, *Resolutions Adopted by the Conference* (United Nations publication, Sales No. E.93.I.8 and corrigendum), resolution 1, annex II.

4 *Report of the World Summit on Sustainable Development, Johannesburg, South Africa, 26 August-4 September 2002* (United Nations publication, Sales No. E.03.II.A.1 and corrigendum), chap. I, resolution 2, annex.

5 *Report of the United Nations Conference on Environment and Development, Rio de Janeiro, 3-14 June 1992*, vol. I, *Resolutions Adopted by the Conference* (United Nations publication, Sales No. E.93.I.8 and corrigendum), resolution 1, annex I.

 | DOI 10.1163/9789004214552_014

Recalling the 2005 World Summit Outcome,[6]

Recalling also the Bali Strategic Plan for Technology Support and Capacity-building,[7]

Committed to strengthening international environmental governance within the context of the institutional framework for sustainable development in order to promote a balanced integration of the economic, social and environmental dimensions of sustainable development as well as coordination within the United Nations system,

Recalling the outcome document, entitled "The future we want",[8] of the United Nations Conference on Sustainable Development, held from 20 to 22 June 2012 in Rio de Janeiro, Brazil, which invited the General Assembly to adopt, at its sixty-seventh session, a resolution strengthening and upgrading the United Nations Environment Programme, in the manner outlined in paragraph 88, subparagraphs (a) to (h) of the outcome document,

Recalling also paragraph 89 of the outcome document of the United Nations Conference on Sustainable Development, encouraging parties to multilateral environmental agreements to consider further measures, in the chemicals and waste cluster and other clusters, as appropriate, to promote policy coherence at all relevant levels, improve efficiency, reduce unnecessary overlap and duplication and enhance coordination and cooperation among the multilateral environmental agreements, including the three Rio conventions, as well as with the United Nations system in the field,

Reiterating the need for secure, stable, adequate and predictable financial resources for the United Nations Environment Programme, and, in accordance with its resolution 2997 (XXVII), underlining the need to consider the adequate reflection of all the administrative and management costs of the Programme in the context of the United Nations regular budget,

Reiterating also that capacity-building and technology support to developing countries in environment-related fields are important components of the work of the United Nations Environment Programme,

1. *Takes note* of the report of the Governing Council of the United Nations Environment Programme on its twelfth special session and the decisions contained therein[9];
2. *Reiterates* the continuing need for the United Nations Environment Programme to conduct up-to-date, comprehensive, scientifically credible and policy-relevant

6 Resolution 60/1.

7 UNEP/GC.23/6/Add.1 and Corr.1, annex.

8 Resolution 66/288, annex.

9 *Official Records of the General Assembly, Sixty-seventh Session, Supplement No. 25* (A/67/25).

global environment assessments, in close consultation with Member States, in order to support decision-making processes at all levels, and in this regard takes note of the fifth report in the Global Environment Outlook series and its related summary for policymakers, and stresses the need to enhance the policy relevance of the Outlook by, *inter alia*, identifying policy options to speed up the achievement of the internationally agreed goals and to inform global and regional processes and meetings where progress towards the agreed goals will be discussed;

3. *Also reiterates* the importance of the Nairobi headquarters location of the United Nations Environment Programme, and requests the Secretary-General to keep the resource needs of the Programme and the United Nations Office at Nairobi under review so as to permit the delivery, in an effective manner, of necessary services to the Programme and to the other United Nations organizations and entities in Nairobi;

4. *Decides* to:

   (a) Strengthen and upgrade the United Nations Environment Programme in the manner set out in subparagraphs (a) to (h) of paragraph 88 of the outcome document, entitled "The future we want",8 of the United Nations Conference on Sustainable Development, as endorsed by the General Assembly in its resolution 66/288 of 27 July 2012;

   (b) Establish universal membership in the Governing Council of the United Nations Environment Programme, and mandates it, as from its first universal session to be held in Nairobi in February 2013, using its applicable rules of procedure and applicable rules and practices of the General Assembly, pending the adoption of its new rules of procedure, to expeditiously initiate the implementation of the provisions contained in paragraph 88 of the outcome document in its entirety; make a recommendation on its designation to reflect its universal character; and decide on future arrangements for the Global Ministerial Environment Forum;

   (c) Request the Executive Director of the United Nations Environment Programme to continue to provide support for the full and effective participation of representatives of developing countries in the Governing Council meeting and invite the Governing Council to consider further arrangements in this regard;

5. *Recalls* the decision to have secure, stable, adequate and increased financial resources from the regular budget of the United Nations and voluntary contributions to fulfil the mandate of the United Nations Environment Programme, and:

   (a) Requests the Secretary-General, in line with paragraph 88 (b) of the outcome document of the United Nations Conference on Sustainable

Development, to reflect in the 2014-2015 biennium budget proposal resources that take into account the proposed revised programme of work of the United Nations Environment Programme and the implementation of paragraph 88, subparagraphs (a) to (h), of the outcome document of the United Nations Conference on Sustainable Development, as well as opportunities for increasing the efficient use of resources;

(b) Urges donors to increase voluntary funding to the United Nations Environment Programme, including to the Environment Fund;

(c) Requests the Secretary-General to maintain the resource needs from the regular budget of the United Nations for the United Nations Environment Programme under review, in the light of the implementation of paragraph 88 of the outcome document, in accordance with United Nations budgetary practices;

6. *Decides* to include in the provisional agenda of its sixty-eighth session, under the item entitled "Sustainable development", a sub-item entitled "Report of the Governing Council of the United Nations Environment Programme on its first universal session".

V UNEP Governing Council Twelfth Special Session Decision SS.XII/3, 20–22 February 2012

The Governing Council

Recalling its decision 26/1 of 24 February 2011 on international environmental governance,

Taking note of the implementation by the Executive Director of the incremental reforms that were identified in the set of options presented to the Governing Council at its eleventh special session, in February 2010, by the Consultative Group of Ministers or High-level Representatives on International Environmental Governance established under Governing Council decision 25/4 of 20 February 2009,[1]

Taking note also of the continuing consultations, in the context of the United Nations

Conference on Sustainable Development, on the institutional framework for sustainable development, and considering that international environmental governance is one particularly important component of those consultations,

Recalling the commitment set out in the 2010 Nusa Dua Declaration[2] to strengthening the role of the United Nations Environment Programme as the leading global environmental authority that sets the global environmental agenda, promotes the coherent implementation of the environmental dimension of sustainable development within the United Nations system and serves as an authoritative advocate for the global environment, as set out in the 1997 Nairobi Declaration on the Role and Mandate of the United Nations Environment Programme,[3]

1. *Recognizes* the importance of enhancing synergies, including at the national and regional levels, among the biodiversity-related conventions, without prejudice to their specific objectives and recognizing their respective mandates, and encourages the conferences of the parties to those conventions to strengthen efforts further in that regard, taking into account relevant experiences;
2. *Invites* the Executive Director to undertake, as appropriate, further activities to improve the effectiveness of and cooperation among multilateral environmental

* Adopted as Decision SS XII/3 at the Twelfth Special Session of the UNEP Governing Council; Doc. UNEP/GCSS.XII/14 of 2 March 2012; available at, http://www.unep.org/gc/gcss-xii/.

1 UNEP/GCSS.XI/11, annex II.

2 Ibid., annex I, decision SS.XI/9.

3 UNEP/GC.19/34, annex I, decision 19/1, annex.

 | DOI 10.1163/9789004214552_015

agreements, taking into account the autonomous decision-making authority of the conferences of the parties, and to enhance cooperation with the International Strategy for Disaster Reduction;

3. *Requests* the Executive Director to explore the opportunities for further synergies in the administrative functions of the multilateral environmental agreement secretariats administered by the United Nations Environment Programme and to provide advice on such opportunities to the governing bodies of those multilateral environmental agreements;
4. *Also requests* the Executive Director to explore the possibility of signing or updating memorandums of understanding with other United Nations bodies, in particular with the specialized agencies and regional commissions, in order to coordinate endeavours by United Nations secretariats, avoid overlapping, enhance cooperation and build on synergies in the implementation of the programmes and policies of those bodies in support of sustainable development;
5. *Recalls* the invitation by the General Assembly to the relevant United Nations funds, and programmes and the specialized agencies and multilateral environmental agreements to consider mainstreaming the Bali Strategic Plan for Technology Support and Capacity-building into their overall activities, and calls upon Governments and other stakeholders in a position to do so to provide the funding and technical assistance and capacity-building necessary to advance further and implement fully the Bali Strategic Plan, and invites the General Assembly to examine the possibility of developing a system-wide capacity-building framework for its implementation;
6. *Invites* the General Assembly to examine the possibility of developing a system-wide strategy for the environment;
7. *Requests* the Executive Director to instruct and give guidance to the regional offices of the United Nations Environment Programme to strengthen the cooperation between the Programme and other United Nations bodies, including regional commissions and other regional bodies, and to promote collaboration between the Programme and the secretariats of regional integration organizations in an effort to promote actions pertinent to the environmental dimension of sustainable development;
8. *Encourages* member States to provide, on a voluntary basis, extrabudgetary funding to strengthen the regional offices of the United Nations Environment Programme.

VI The Nairobi-Helsinki Outcome, 23 November 2010

Origins and Mandate of the Consultative Group

1. The Consultative Group of Ministers or High-level Representatives on International Environmental Governance (the Consultative Group) was established by the Governing Council of the United Nations Environment Programme in its decision SS.XI/1 of 26 February 2010.
2. Decision SS.XI/1 builds upon the work of an earlier consultative group of ministers and high-level representatives established by the Governing Council in its decision 25/4 of 20 February 2009. The work of that group, which has come to be known as the "Belgrade Process" in reference to the site of its first meeting, resulted in the identification of some objectives and functions of an international environmental governance system and the elaboration of a "set of options for improving international environmental governance", which were presented to the Governing Council at its eleventh special session.
3. Decision SS.XI/1 requested the Consultative Group "to consider the broader reform of the international environmental governance system, building on the set of options developed during the Belgrade Process, but remaining open to new ideas". It also requested the Group to conclude its work in a timely fashion and to present a final report to the Governing Council at its twenty-sixth session, in anticipation of the Council's contribution to the second meeting of the open-ended preparatory committee of the United Nations Conference on Sustainable Development and the sixty-fifth session of the United Nations General Assembly.
4. The decision requested the Executive Director of the United Nations Environment Programme (UNEP), in his capacity as Chair of the Environment Management Group, "to invite the United Nations system to provide input to the group", and requested the consultative group, through the UNEP secretariat, "to seek relevant inputs from civil society groups from each region."

* Adopted at the Second Meeting of the Consultative Group of Ministers or High-level Representatives on International Environmental Governance, Espoo, Finland, 21–23 November 2010.

 | DOI 10.1163/9789004214552_016

Work and Outcome of the Consultative Group

5. The Consultative Group met in Nairobi from 7 to 9 July 2010 and in Espoo, Finland, from 21 to 23 November 2010. Representatives of 58 countries attended the Nairobi meeting and those of 44 countries attended the Espoo meeting. Inputs from civil society were provided to the process through the UNEP secretariat and inputs from the United Nations system through the Environment Management Group.
6. The President of the Republic of Finland, Tarja Halonen, who is also a co-Chair of the High-Level Panel on Global Sustainability, opened the meeting. She welcomed the work of the Consultative Group, saying that the Panel would be listening to the signals that it sent.

Strengthening the International Environmental Governance System: Functions and System-Wide Responses

7. Having considered the objectives and functions of an international environmental governance system identified during the Belgrade Process, and after reviewing gaps and options discussed in the co-chairs' document on elaboration of ideas on broader international environmental governance reform (UNEP/CGIEG.2/2/2), the Consultative Group identified a number of potential system-wide responses to the challenges in the current system of international environmental governance, including:
   (a) To strengthen the science-policy interface with the full and meaningful participation of developing countries; to meet the science-policy capacity needs of developing countries and countries with economies in transition, including improvement of scientific research and development at the national level; and to build on existing international environmental assessments, scientific panels and information networks. The overall purpose would be to facilitate cooperation in the collection, management, analysis, use and exchange of environmental information, the further development of internationally agreed indicators, including through financial support and capacity-building in developing countries and countries with economies in transition, early warning, alert services, assessments, the preparation of science-based advice and the development of policy options. In this context, the Global Environment Outlook process must be strengthened and work in cooperation and coordination with existing platforms;

(b) To develop a system-wide strategy for environment in the United Nations system to increase the effectiveness, efficiency and coherence of the United Nations system and in that way contribute to strengthening the environmental pillar of sustainable development. The strategy should increase interagency cooperation and clarify the division of labour within the United Nations system. It should be developed through an inclusive process involving Governments and seeking input from civil society;

(c) To encourage synergies between compatible multilateral environmental agreements and to identify guiding elements for realizing such synergies while respecting the autonomy of the conferences of the parties. Such synergies should promote the joint delivery of common multilateral environmental agreement services with the aim of making them more efficient and cost-effective. They should be based on lessons learned and remain flexible and adaptive to the specific needs of multilateral environmental agreements. They should aim at reducing the administrative costs of secretariats to free up resources for the implementation of multilateral environmental agreements at the national level, including through capacity-building;

(d) To create a stronger link between global environmental policy making and financing aimed at widening and deepening the funding base for environment with the goal of securing sufficient, predictable and coherent funding and increasing accessibility, cooperation and coherence among financing mechanisms and funds for the environment, with the aim of helping to meet the need for new and additional funding to bridge the policy-implementation gap through new revenue streams for implementation. Enhanced linkage between policy and financing is needed along with stronger and more predictable contributions and partnerships with major donors and the pooling of public and supplementary private revenue streams. To consider the development of financial tracking systems, including their costs and benefits, based on existing systems to track financial flows and volumes comprehensively at the international and regional levels, as well as a strategy for greater involvement of private sector financing;

(e) To develop a system-wide capacity-building framework for the environment to ensure a responsive and cohesive approach to meeting country needs, taking into account the Bali Strategic Plan for Technology Support and Capacity-Building. The framework should be targeted at strengthening national capacities required to implement multilateral environment agreements and agreed international environmental objectives;

(f) To continue to strengthen strategic engagement at the regional level by further increasing the capacity of UNEP regional offices to be more responsive to country environmental needs. The aim of such strengthening should be to increase country responsiveness and implementation. Environmental expertise within United Nations country teams should be strengthened, including through UNEP.

8. The Consultative Group suggests that the Governing Council at its twenty-sixth session give consideration to the contribution of UNEP to identifying the implementation of, and actors responsible for, follow-up on the functions and system-wide responses.

Form Related Aspects of Broader Institutional Reform

9. Having identified the potential system-wide responses above, the Consultative Group considered institutional forms that would best serve to implement those responses and achieve the objectives and functions identified during the Belgrade Process.

10. It was generally accepted that form should follow function and that UNEP should be strengthened and enhanced. Differing views were expressed in respect of institutional reform.

11. Strengthening the global authoritative voice, as well as other voices, for the environment is a key outcome of the international environmental governance reform process, providing credible, coherent and effective leadership for environmental sustainability under the overall framework of sustainable development. During the Belgrade Process and in the Co-Chairs' document on elaboration of ideas for broader reform of international environmental governance (UNEP/CGIEG.2/2/2), various options for broader institutional reforms were put forward, including the following five options:
    (a) Enhancing UNEP;
    (b) Establishing a new umbrella organization for sustainable development;
    (c) Establishing a specialized agency such as a world environment organization;
    (d) Reforming the United Nations Economic and Social Council and the United Nations Commission on Sustainable Development;
    (e) Enhancing institutional reforms and streamlining existing structures.

12. The Consultative Group recognized the need to develop all the options further and suggested that options (b) and (d) would best be addressed in the wider sustainable development context.

13. Based on the principle that form follows function, and recognizing that it had not achieved consensus on institutional form, the Group suggested that existing institutions be strengthened and enhanced and that options (a) (enhancing UNEP), (c) (establishing a specialized agency such as a world environment organization) and (e) (enhancing institutional reforms and streamlining

existing structures) were potential options for strengthening the form of the environment pillar in the context of sustainable development and achieving effective international environmental governance.

Next Steps

14. The Consultative Group hereby presents its final report to the Governing Council in accordance with paragraph 10 of decision SSXI/1.
15. The Consultative Group is of the view that the Governing Council should further consider how to secure political momentum and efficient follow-up of the international environmental governance process.
16. The Consultative Group expresses its sincere thanks to the Governments of Kenya and Finland and notes that it was honoured by the presence of Tarja Halonen, President of the Republic of Finland at the opening of the its second meeting.

VII Informal Consultations of the General Assembly on the Institutional Framework for the United Nations' Environment Work, 10 February 2009

The Mandate

The General Assembly –in paragraph 169 of its World Summit Outcome Document (A/RES/60/1) –recognized the need for more efficient environmental activities in the United Nations System, with enhanced coordination, improved policy advice and guidance, strengthened scientific knowledge, assessment and cooperation, better treaty compliance, while respecting the legal autonomy of the treaties, and better integration of environmental activities in the broader sustainable development framework at the operational level, including through capacity-building. It agreed to explore the possibility of a more coherent institutional framework to address this need, including a more integrated structure, building on existing institutions and internationally agreed instruments, as well as the treaty bodies and the specialized agencies.

Based on this decision, on 26 January 2006, the President of the 60th session of the General Assembly appointed Ambassador Enrique Berruga (Mexico) and Ambassador Peter Maurer (Switzerland) as Co-Chairs of the informal consultations of the General Assembly on the institutional framework for the UN's environment work. He also circulated a background note entitled "The institutional framework for the United Nations system's environmental activities", prepared by the Secretariat at his request.

The Consultation Process

First Stage

In order to have a structured debate, the Co-Chairs decided to engage delegations in an analytical discussion on the basis of a questionnaire relating to the issues mentioned in paragraph 169 of the Outcome Document.

Initial consultations were held in New York in March and April 2006, followed by discussions in Nairobi, from 2 to 5 May 2006, and Geneva on 16 and 17 May 2006, with Delegations, UNEP officials, representatives of Multilateral Environmental Agreements (MEA), civil society and representatives of specialized Agencies.

* Report of the Co-Chairs (Ambassadors Peter Maurer and Claude Heller) dated 10 February 2009; see http://www.un.org/ga/president/63/issues/environmentalgovernanee.shtml.

 | DOI 10.1163/9789004214552_017

On 27 June 2006, the Co-Chairs presented a written summary, in which they highlighted the discrepancy between environmental degradation and insufficient efforts to cope with such challenges, as weil as a significant gap in finance and a lack of capacity to deliver results. In spite of a lively debate on environmental governance and consensus on some policy issues, little concrete action had resulted in the past years.

Proposals from delegations during these early discussions could be put in two broad categories:

a) incremental improvements, based on existing institutions; and b) transformational proposals, looking into a more fundamental overhaul of lEG. Many delegations highlighted the importance

Second Stage

In a letter dated 5 October 2006, the PGA of the 61 st session of the General Assembly informed Member States that she had asked the Co-Chairs to resume their consultations following the issuance of the report of the High-level Panel on System-wide Coherence.

On 18 and 23 January 2007, the Co-Chairs held a second round of consultations based on a more detailed set of questions that they had sent to delegations in advance, in order to facilitate a structured discussion.

On 2 and 3 February 2007, the Co-Chairs participated in the Paris Conference for Global Ecological Governance, convened by France. From 5 –9 February 2007, they took also part in the 24th Session of the Governing Councill Global Ministerial Environment Forum of the United Nations Environment Programme in Nairobi, to brief participants on the process and receive inputs from environmental Ministries.

In a letter dated 24 May 2007, the PGA of the 6lst session of the General Assembly announced that she had asked Ambassador Claude Heller, the new Permanent Representative of Mexico to the United Nations, to continue the work of his predecessor.

At this stage of the consultations some common views and persistent messages emerged, while important divergences of opinions endured.

Delegations supported the ideas that environmental degradation needed a stronger institutional UN set-up, improved international environmental governance (lEG), while avoiding duplications, and reinforced activities for capacity-building, partnerships, and scientific research.

However, in addressing these issues, delegations presented different, even divergent views: disagreements were about whether the system suffered from fragmentation or whether it had the advantage of a multiplicity of specialised bodies addressing specific environmental issues; there were also lively debates on the level of financial resources, and the scope of necessary changes.

Taking into account both the common and diverging messages, as weil as suggestions for improvement, the Co-Chairs prepared a document entitled “Options Paper”, with the aim to present in a schematic way the findings of the consultations, to translate suggestions into concrete proposals for strengthening the current international environmental governance, and to systematize options for decision-making.

On 14 June 2007, the Options Paper was presented to the Membership. It consisted of two parts: one dealt with the strengthening of current institutions, the other with the broader transformation of the system. This two-tier approach was intended to allow the Membership to move forward step-by-step while remaining attentive to longer-term perspectives.

The Co-Chairs remain of the firm opinion that reconciling the short-term and long-term, captured in the notion of “ambitious incrementalism”, is the only way to find agreement on a way forward:

The Options Paper also offered an analysis of the weaknesses of the system, made proposals structured around seven building blocks with a view of improving the present international environmental governance and addressed the issue of a more fundamental transformation in the future. The seven building blocks take up key issues addressed in previous reform attempts and make proposals for better implementation.

The proposals in the Options Paper were based on a series of principles, premises and conditions highlighted by delegations. They recognized the importance of sustainable development as an overarching concept for the discussion, mainstreaming and financing environmental activities, balancing capacity-building and compliance, and implementing previous decisions.

The Proposals Contained in the Seven Building Blocks Included:

1 *Scientific assessment, monitoring and early warning capacity:*

Make UNEP a leading authority within the UN system for scientific assessment and monitoring on the state of the global environment, and create the position of a chief scientist at UNEP.

Strengthen the Programme's capacity by building a network of scientific activity both within and beyond.

Strengthen the Programme's capacity to provide Member States with authoritative advice on key aspects of global environmental challenges and early warning.

2 *Coordination and cooperation at the level of agencies*

Aim to improve coordination on the operational and the policy levels.

Strengthen the policy coordination capacities of UNEP and thus its ability to cooperate with other UN entities and the World Bank.

Enhance the capacities within the UN system to integrate environmental objectives into related areas such as development cooperation, trade, and health.

3 *Multilateral Environmental Agreements*

Cluster the MEAs by topics, programmatic and administrative tasks.
Enhance cooperation and coordination amongst MEAs.
Rationalise secretariat activities.

4 *Regional presence and activities at the regional level*

Use regional offices of UNEP as entry points for scientific activities.
Strengthen offices with regional organizations outside the UNO.

5 *Bali Strategic plan, technology support and capacity building*

Deepen and broaden capacity-building and technology support throughout the international environmental governance system.
Foster implementation of the Bali Strategic Plan.
Promote the Bali Strategic Plan as reference framework for operational activities.

6 *Information Technologies, partnerships and advocacy*

Use Information Technologies for electronic meetings.
Create a unified clearinghouse of best practices and lessons learned.
Encourage partnerships with scientific entities, NGOs and business.

7 *Funding*

Improve financing for environmental governance and for environmental activities through timely and adequate funding.

With regard to long-term perspectives, the Options Paper proposed to decide not later than by the end of the 62nd session of the General Assembly on the terms of reference for formal negotiations on a broader transformation of the IEG system, negotiations which should start no later than the beginning of the 63rd session of the General Assembly.

Before holding consultations on the Options Paper, the Co-Chairs participated in the "Meeting of Ministers of Foreign Affairs and Environment on Governance for Sustainable Development" in Rio de Janeiro, Brazil, on 3 and 4 September 2007. During the meeting, Ambassador Heller explained the Options Paper and its rationale.

On 10 September and 26 October 2007, the Co-Chairs held a round of consultations in order to receive feedback from Delegations on the Options Paper.

In a letter dated 4 October 2007, the President of the 62nd session of the General Assembly informed Member States that he had asked the Co-Chairs to continue consultations on the strengthening of environmental governance.

Consultations confirmed concurrent analysis and proposals on strengthening UNEP, the linkages between UNEP and UNDP, and better coordination between UNEP and the MEAs.

Other issues such as the clustering of MEAs, financing and the transformation of UNEP into a UNEO were discussed controversially. Nevertheless, there was support from Delegations to continue the process.

Third Stage

From 20–22 February 2008, the Co-Chairs participated in the 10th Special Session of the Governing Council I Global Ministerial Environment Forum of the United Nations Environment Programme in Monaco, to brief participants on the process and get inputs. On 25 and 26 February, the Co-Chairs also held aseries of briefings in the UN Offices in Geneva for Delegations, representatives of UN bodies and of civil society.

On 11 March 2008, the Co-Chairs had a series of exchanges with representatives of the World Bank and the Global Environmental Facility in Washington, DC.

During the consultations, financial issues emerged as of particular importance. In this regard, the Co-Chairs convened a panel on financing environmental activities on 17 March 2008, with the participation of the GEF, UNDP and the Inter-American Development Bank, in order to discuss these issues informally.

Another recurrent issue was capacity-building and a similar panel discussion on capacity building for environmental governance was held on 24 April 2008, in New York.

Based on the feedback of the previous two years, the Co-Chairs drafted a proposal for a

General Assembly resolution that was aimed at translating the Options Paper and the input received in subsequent discussions into legislative language. The draft resolution was presented to the Membership on 2 May 2008. It was modeled after the seven building blocks of the Options Paper, with proposals for:

- Strengthening the authority of UNEP, and giving the Secretary General enhanced leadership on the Environmental Management Group
- Scientific assessment, monitoring and early warning capacity
- Coordination at the level of agencies
- Multilateral Environmental Agreements
- Regional processes
- The Bali Strategic Plan, technology support and capacity-building
- Information Technology and partnerships
- Funding
- Next steps on broader transformation and institutional set-up

A few days after the presentation of the text, the Co-Chairs participated in the "Ministerial Meeting on International Environmental Governance", sponsored by Costa Rica and held in New York on 13 May 2008.

On 21 and 28 May and on 4 June 2008, consultations with Member States on the draft resolution were held. Delegations welcomed the draft resolution as a solid basis for discussion and engaged constructively. Although some of the comments were of general character, there were some recurring comments and suggestions for improving the text in order:

- to better reflect the issue of sustainable development throughout the resolution, in particular
- on regional presence and activities, the Bali Strategic Plan and financing;
- to better reflect the mandate of UNEP;
- to clarify wording on the relationship between the General Assembly and the Multilateral

Environmental Agreements, as well as on the scope and limits of cooperation among them, taking into account the legal autonomy of the MEAs;

- to better explain the role of the Environment Management Group (EMG) and the Chief Executives Board (CEB) in international environmental governance;
- to further define financial proposals.

On the basis of the comments received, the Co-Chairs prepared a revised draft resolution, which was presented to the Membership on 23 July 2008. On 12 September 2008, a first feedback session was held.

The Co-Chairs were re-appointed by the President of the 63rd session of the General Assembly, as stated in his letter dated 7 October 2008.

On 30 October and 25 November 2008, a full and detailed reading of the revised draft resolution was held. At these readings, Delegations proposed specific amendments, additions and deletions to the text.

The detailed inputs presented were rich and substantive. Although some proposals might have offered opportunities for consensus, others faced more fundamental opposition, thus creating an serious divide.

There was general support for strengthening international environmental governance, but the extent and ambition of that strengthening presented difficult dilemmas:

A group of States advocated giving more weight to sustainable development in general and in particular to the importance of eradicating poverty. Other countries preferred an approach that focused on the environmental pillar of sustainable development and UNEP's role and interaction with other key actors in the UN system. A proposal of one group to better integrate environmental activities in development programmes could not found general support.

The scope and limits of the mandate of UNEP were discussed controversially, and while some States were of the opinion that part of the draft provisions sought to enlarge UNEP's mandate, other States were comfortable with the way the draft resolution reflected the mandate of UNEP.

One group of States explicitly supported the proposals on the EMG, including the idea to integrate the EMG in the framework of the CES in order to ensure a coordinated approach of the UN system to sustainable development. However, a significant number of countries remained unconvinced of the usefulness of these proposals.

Even though many countries had complained in an earlier stage of the process about the workload that reporting and meeting obligations of an increasing number of MEAs placed on Member States, many delegations met proposals which tried to specify the cooperation expected from MEAs and the nature of their interaction with UNEP with reluctance and often referred to the legal autonomy of the MEAs. In this context, the distinction between recommendations to management and governance responsibility was once again an issue of concern.

Discussions took place on the Bali Strategic Plan for Technology Support and Capacity-building: should it serve as an overall guidance for operational activities of all environmental actors of the UN system or should it guide the work of UNEP only? Member States had diverging views.

Key proposals of the draft resolution, such as UNEP presenting to Member States a biannual consolidated overview of research activities, an annual consolidated appeal with needs, planned activities and estimated funding levels for all environmental capacity-building activities in the UN system as well as a call for a web-based, global environmental financial tracking mechanism were still not well understood and met with reluctance.

Not surprisingly, the issue of funding proved to be difficult. States had different views on whether new and additional resources are needed, but also on how to provide additional funding.

Whereas the proposal to continue discussions in the future to follow up on the implementation of the resolution and decide on additional steps to further strengthen environmental governance was not opposed as such, any attempt to specify the scope and direction of such discussion was met with resistance, and there was no unanimity on the best moment to request are port of the Secretary-General as a basis for continuing the discussions on environmental governance.

The Co-Chairs found themselves in a situation, in which the attempt to move to a decision increased the difficulties in finding consensus. While agreement on a consensual resolution might be possible, a consensus document would likely fail to add value to existing decisions or could even risk to fall behind improvements decided in other intergovernmental fora, in particular in the context of UNEP's Governing Council/ GMEF.

Given the opposing views on some fundamental issues, the Co-Chairs consider the chance of reaching a substantive decision during the 63rd session of the General Assembly to be very small. The Co-Chairs recommend to all interested parties to make the best use of upcoming intergovernmental meetings to remain seized of the matter.

Among such meetings, the upcoming 25th session of the Governing Council of UNEP would present an important opportunity to take stock and debate the course of action. International environmental governance is an important component of the decision SSVII/1 from the Governing Council of UNEP, the so-called "Cartagena Package". The Co-Chairs hope that the discussions in Nairobi will allow Ministers of Environment to find a political compromise and entrust their delegations in New York with pragmatic, creative and constructive proposals, which allow improving the current system.

The Co-Chairs do not intend to call consultations, but they will remain available to Delegations for further informal interaction, in order to make a proposal on how best to continue this process during the 64th session of the General Assembly.

The Co-Chairs encourage Member States and interested organizations to offer other informal opportunities for interaction on this important issue.

VIII The High-level Panel on United Nations System-wide Coherence in the areas of development, humanitarian assistance and the environment [Excerpts], 9 November 2006

Environment

There is an increasingly compelling case for taking urgent action on the environment. Environmental priorities have too often been compartmentalized in isolation from economic development priorities. However, global environmental degradation – including climate change – will have far-reaching economic and social implications that affect the world's ability to meet the Millennium Development Goals. Because the impacts are global and felt disproportionately by the poor, coordinated multilateral action to promote environmental sustainability is urgently required.

We recommend that international environmental governance be strengthened and made more coherent in order to improve the effectiveness and targeted action of environmental activities in the United Nations system.

We recommend that, as a basis for reforms to improve system-wide coherence, the Secretary-General commission an independent assessment of international environmental governance within the United Nations system and related reform.

We recommend that the United Nations Environment Programme be upgraded and given real authority as the environmental policy pillar of the United Nations system.

We further recommend that United Nations entities cooperate more effectively on a thematic basis and through partnerships, with a dedicated agency at the centre.

As the major financial mechanism for the global environment, the Global Environment Facility should be strengthened to help developing countries build their capacity. It should have a significant increase in resources to address the challenge posed by climate change and other environmental issues. We have also made a number

* United Nations General Assembly, Sixty-first Session (Agenda Item 113, Follow up to the Outcome of the Millennium Summit, UN Doc.A/61/583, 20 November 2006. *Delivering as One: Report of Secretary-General's High-level Panel on UN System-wide Coherence in the Areas of Development, Humanitarian Assistance, and the Environment* (Co-Chaired by the Prime Ministers of Pakistan, Mozambique and Norway), New York, 9 November 2006, pp.1-67 at pp.14-15 and 28-32 [excerpts edited by the author].

 | DOI 10.1163/9789004214552_018

of recommendations to make sure that the United Nations helps countries mainstream environment in their strategies and actions, to elevate the status of sustainable development in the United Nations institutional architecture and in country activities, and to achieve the needed balance among the three pillars (economic, social and environmental) of sustainable development.

[page 14-15]

Environment: Building a Global Consensus and Capacity for Action

Deteriorating environmental trends have far-reaching economic, social and health implications and affect the world's ability to meet the Millennium Development Goals. Substantial gains in efficiency and effective responses can be made through enhanced coordination and improved normative and operational capacity, in particular through the integration of environment into national development strategies and United Nations system country operations. To improve effectiveness and targeted action of environmental activities, the system of international environmental governance should be strengthened and more coherent, featuring an upgraded UNEP with real authority as the United Nations environment policy pillar. Synergy needs to be pursued between the United Nations organizations that address environment, and multilateral environmental agreements should continue to pursue efficiencies and coordination among themselves. An independent assessment of the current United Nations system of international environmental governance is required to support ongoing efforts at reform.

30. There can be no long-term development without environmental care. In a global and interdependent world economic objectives and environmental objectives increasingly reinforce each other. Environmental priorities – including climate change – have too often been compartmentalized and separated from economic development priorities. However, because the impacts are global and felt disproportionately by the poor, environmental sustainability is not an option – it is an imperative. The Panel is united in its conviction that addressing worsening trends of environmental degradation is one of the greatest collective challenges for economic development and human welfare.
31. We possess fairly comprehensive knowledge and understanding of what we individually and collectively need to do to reverse these trends – all spelled out in reports, declarations, treaties and summits since the early 1970s. While we have made significant advances within the United Nations framework, what is needed now is a substantially strengthened and streamlined international environmental governance structure, to support the incentives for change required at all levels.

32. The Panel recognizes that relatively little headway has been made in integrating the environment in development strategies at the country level, or in implementing internationally agreed goals. Environmental issues and goals must now be better integrated within United Nations system country operations, as critical components of national poverty reduction strategies and sustainable development plans. Bearing in mind that environmental sustainability is the foundation for achieving all the other Millennium Development Goals, there must be a strengthening of human, technical and financial capacities in developing countries to mainstream environmental issues in national decision-making, particularly through the resident coordinator.

33. The increase in the incidence and severity of natural disasters with environmental causes demonstrates the need to strengthen the links between environmental and humanitarian activities and between environmental and development activities. The United Nations system needs to incorporate more knowledge in its work on preparedness and risk reduction for natural disasters and for post-disaster recovery and reconstruction.

34. The United Nations institutions for the environment must be optimally organized and tooled, drawing on expertise in different parts of the United Nations system. Unless the United Nations adopts more comprehensive approaches, it will continue to fall short of its goals. The Panel is cognizant of the ongoing General Assembly informal consultative process on international environmental governance and has interacted with the process. Our recommendations should give it greater impetus.

35. Fragmented institutional structures do not offer an operational framework to address global issues, including water and energy. Water is an essential element in the lives of people and societies, and the lack of access to water for basic needs inflicts hardship on more than 1 billion people. Similarly, energy is a main driver of development, but current systems of energy supply and use are not sustainable (more than 2 billion people in developing countries do not have access to modern energy services). More than 20 United Nations organizations are engaged at some level in water and energy work, but there is little evidence of overall impact.

36. The inadequacy of the current system is the result of having outgrown its original design. Developing countries are unable to cope with the extensive reporting and participation requirements of the current multilateral environmental structure, which has depleted expertise and resources for implementation. A survey by the Panel revealed that the three Rio Conventions (biodiversity, climate and desertification) have up to 230 meeting days annually. Add the figures for seven other major global environmental agreements (not including regional agreements) and that number rises to almost 400 days.

37. As environmental issues have become more clearly defined and interlinked, they have come to influence the work of practically every United Nations organization, all competing for the same limited resources. The institutional complexity is further complicated by the substantial environment portfolios of the World Bank and regional development banks, which are not well coordinated with the rest of the United Nations system. In addition, UNEP, the principal environment organization of the United Nations – with its normative, scientific, analytical and coordinating mandate – is considered weak, under-funded and ineffective in its core functions.

38. Climate change, desertification, ecosystem decline, and dispersion of hazardous chemical substances have the potential to affect every part of the globe and require clear and forceful responses by the United Nations system. Cooperation should be close among UNEP, UNDP, WMO, the Global Environment Facility (GEF) and the World Bank for building scientific and technical capacity, managing investment and infrastructure components, supporting adaptation measures and facilitating an effective integration of global environmental concerns into the development policy frameworks at the country level. GEF, the specialized funding instrument to help developing countries undertake projects and programmes that protect the global environment, has been replenished in 2006 – but will require a significant increase in resources to address future challenges. Its policy requirements and operational procedures need to be made much more simple and compatible with the development framework at the country level.

39. It is the judgement of the Panel that the international community must transcend differences and move forward. Economic growth, social justice and environmental care, advance best when they advance together. It is in our shared interest to have institutions that enable us to respond collectively to the threats of environmental degradation that challenge us all. To deliver on the internationally agreed goals and commitments, the United Nations will require stronger leadership and greater capacity for environmental activities. In this regard, cooperation and partnerships with civil society organizations, including the private sector, are essential.

Recommendation: International environmental governance should be strengthened and more coherent in order to improve effectiveness and targeted action of environmental activities in the United Nations system. It should be strengthened by upgrading UNEP with a renewed mandate and improved funding.

Recommendation: An upgraded UNEP should have real authority as the environment policy pillar of the United Nations system, backed by normative and analytical capacity and with broad responsibility to review progress towards improving the

global environment. UNEP should provide substantive leadership and guidance on environmental issues.

- The technical and scientific capacity of UNEP should be strengthened as the environmental early-warning mechanism of the international community and for monitoring, assessing and reporting on the state of the global environment. This can be achieved through a system of networking and drawing on the work of existing bodies, including academic institutions and centres of excellence and the scientific competence of relevant specialized agencies and scientific subsidiary bodies of multilateral environmental agreements.
- Capacity should be built to promote the implementation of international commitments. The Bali Strategic Plan for Technology Support and Capacity building should be strategically implemented to provide cutting-edge expertise and knowledge resources for the sustained expansion of capacity at the country level. Where necessary, UNEP should participate in United Nations country teams through the resident coordinator system, as part of One United Nations at the country level.
- UNEP should take the lead in assisting countries in the two-step process of quantifying environmental costs and benefits and incorporating them into mainstream policymaking, in cooperation with UNDP and the Department of Economic and Social Affairs of the Secretariat.

Recommendation: United Nations agencies, programmes and funds with responsibilities in the area of the environment should cooperate more effectively on a thematic basis and through partnerships with a dedicated agency at the centre (such as air and water pollution, forests, water scarcity, access to energy and renewable energy). This would be based on a combined effort towards agreed common activities and policy objectives to eliminate duplication and focus on results.

- Greater coordination at Headquarters should promote coherence at the country level, and greater coordination efforts at the country level should promote coherence at the international level. There is a need to strengthen UNEP coordination of system-wide environmental policies in order to improve cohesion and consistency. In this regard, the Environmental Management Group should be given a clearer mandate and be better utilized. It should be linked with the broader framework of sustainable development coordination.

Recommendation: Efficiencies and substantive coordination should be pursued by diverse treaty bodies to support effective implementation of major multilateral environmental agreements. Such coordination is being pursued by the Basel,

Rotterdam and Stockholm convention secretariats (pending decisions of their respective conferences of the parties).

- Stronger efforts should be made to reduce costs and reporting burdens and to streamline implementation. National reporting requirements for related multilateral environmental agreements should be consolidated into one comprehensive annual report, to ease the burden on countries and improve coherence.
- Countries should consider integrating implementation needs of multilateral environmental agreements into their national sustainable development strategies, as part of the One Country Programme.
- Governing bodies of multilateral environmental agreements should promote administrative efficiencies, reducing the frequency and duration of meetings, moving to joint administrative functions, convening back-to-back or joint meetings of bureaux of related conventions, rationalizing knowledge management and developing a consistent methodological approach to enable measurement of enforcement and compliance.

Recommendation: GEF should be strengthened as the major financial mechanism for the global environment. Its contribution in assisting developing countries in implementing the conventions and in building their capacities should be clarified, in conjunction with its implementing and executing agencies. A significant increase in resources will be required to address future challenges effectively.

Recommendation: The Secretary-General should commission an independent and authoritative assessment of the current United Nations system of international environmental governance. To be completed as soon as possible and taking previous work into account, the assessment would review global needs as well as the specific roles and mandates of UNEP and other United Nations agencies and multilateral environmental agreements. It would provide the basis for further reforms towards improving system-wide coherence, effectiveness and targeted action. It should be complementary to the General Assembly informal consultative process on the institutional framework for the United Nations environmental activities, which should continue its work and provide guidance on the subject. The assessment should include an analysis of proposals to upgrade UNEP from among a range of organizational models.

IX The Cartagena Report on International Environmental Governance, 15 February 2002

The Governing Council

Recalling the Malmö Ministerial Declaration[1] of 31 May 2000, in which it was stated that the 2002 conference should review the requirements for a greatly strengthened institutional structure for international environmental governance, based on an assessment of future needs for an institutional architecture that has the capacity to effectively address wide-ranging environmental threats in a globalizing world and that in this regard, the role of the United Nations Environment Programme should be strengthened and its financial base broadened and made more predictable,

Recalling General Assembly resolution 53/242 of 28 July 1999, on the report of the Secretary-General on environment and human settlements in which the General Assembly established the Global Ministerial Environment Forum, and supported proposals, *inter alia*, for the establishment for an environmental management group for the purpose of enhancing inter-agency coordination, and for enhancing linkages and coordination within and among environmental and environment related conventions,

Further recalling its decision 21/21 of 9 February 2001 on international environmental governance in which it established an open-ended intergovernmental group of ministers or their representatives, with the Executive Director as an ex-officio member, to undertake a comprehensive policy-oriented assessment of existing institutional weaknesses as well as future needs for strengthened international environmental governance, including the financing of the United Nations Environment Programme, with a view to presenting a report containing analysis and options to the next session of the Governing Council/Global Ministerial Environment Forum and to undertake an in depth discussion of the report with a view to providing its input on future requirement of international environmental governance,

Expressing its appreciation to the Executive Director for the excellent support provided to the Intergovernmental Group of Ministers in its deliberation of international environmental governance, which enabled it to conduct its work in an open, transparent and inclusive manner,

---

* Decision SS.VII/1 of the UNEP Governing Council adopted at its seventh special session in Cartagena, Colombia, on 15 February 2002; see http://www.unep.org/IEG/Meetings_docs/index.asp

1 Governing Council decision SS.VI/1, annex.

 | DOI 10.1163/9789004214552_019

1. *Adopts* the report of the Open-ended Intergovernmental Group of Ministers or Their Representatives on International Environmental Governance[2] in the appendix to the present decision;
2. *Invites* the President of the Governing Council to transmit the present decision and the report of the Open-ended Intergovernmental Group of Ministers or Their Representatives on International Environmental Governance to the Commission on Sustainable Development acting as the preparatory committee for the World Summit on Sustainable Development[3] at its third session;
3. *Requests* the Executive Director to present this decision and the report of the Open-ended Intergovernmental Group of Ministers or Their Representatives on International Environmental Governance to the Preparatory Committee for the World Summit on Sustainable Development at its third session;
4. *Decides* to review the implementation of the recommendations contained in the report of the Open-ended Intergovernmental Group of Ministers or Their Representatives on International Environmental Governance at its twenty-second session, subject to the outcome of the World Summit on Sustainable Development;
5. *Also decides* to consider further measures for the strengthening of the United Nations Environment Programme in light of the outcome of the World Summit on Sustainable Development at its twenty-second session.

Report of the Open-Ended Intergovernmental Group of Ministers or their Representatives on International Environmental Governance

I. *Background*

1. The current debate on the requirements for a more coherent and more effective international environmental governance regime is a continuation of international efforts over the past decade to develop institutional responses to underpin international action to confront the increase of environmental threats faced by all countries. The growing body of scientific evidence as to the seriousness of environmental degradation has led to a proliferation of legal and institutional arrangements for international cooperation aimed at addressing specific environmental problems. As a result, the international community has become increasingly concerned with not only establishing a strengthened framework for coordinated international action but also ensuring that the limited resources available are deployed in the best possible manner for optimal effect.

2 UNEP/GCSS.VII/L.4/Add.1.

3 General Assembly resolution 55/199 of 20 December 2000.

2. The context within which international environmental policy formulation takes place has also evolved. Increasingly, environmental objectives are being pursued in the broader context of sustainable development as is evident in the work programmes of the recent mechanisms that have been established. Agenda 21 reaffirmed the role of the United Nations Environment Programme (UNEP) as the principal body within the United Nations system in the field of the environment but also added that it should take into account the development aspects of environmental questions.
3. A further step in the evolution of the current system was the establishment by the Secretary-General of the United Nations of a Task Force on Environment and Human Settlements as part of the overall reform of the United Nations. In establishing the Task Force, the Secretary-General noted the formidable challenge facing the international community in attaining "a sustainable equilibrium between economic growth, poverty reduction, social equity and the protection of the Earth's resources, common and life support systems", thus reaffirming the sustainable development context. The Secretary-General also concluded that experience had demonstrated the need for a more systemic approach to policies and programmes through mainstreaming the United Nations commitment to sustainable development.
4. The General Assembly adopted resolution 53/242 of 28 July 1999 on the Secretary-General's Task Force recommendations and took action on a number of important institutional measures including the creation of the Environmental Management Group, the creation of the Global Ministerial Environment Forum and on support for and enhancing linkages among environmental and environment-related conventions.
5. At its first meeting in Malmö in May 2000, the Global Ministerial Environment Forum adopted the Malmö Declaration, which stated that the "2002 conference should review the requirements for a greatly strengthened institutional structure for international environmental governance based on an assessment of future needs for an institutional architecture that has the capacity to effectively address wide-ranging environmental threats in a globalizing world. The role of the United Nations Environment Programme in this regard should be strengthened and its financial base broadened and made more predictable".

II. *The UNEP Governing Council International Environmental Governance Initiative*

6. Against the backdrop of the preparations for the World Summit on Sustainable Development, the UNEP Governing Council at its twenty-first session adopted

decision 21/21 on international environmental governance, which established the Open-ended Intergovernmental Group of Ministers or Their Representatives to undertake a comprehensive policy-oriented assessment of existing institutional weaknesses as well as future needs and options for strengthened international environmental governance, including the financing of UNEP, with a view to presenting a report containing analysis and options to the next session of the Governing Council/Global Ministerial Environment Forum, which is being held in February 2002. In that same decision, the Council also decided that the next Governing Council/Global Ministerial Environment Forum should undertake an in-depth discussion of that report with a view to providing input on future requirements of international environmental governance in the broader context of multilateral efforts for sustainable development to the preparatory body for the World Summit on Sustainable Development as a contribution to the Summit.

7. The work of the Intergovernmental Group of Ministers is intended to build on recent advances, including the report of the United Nations Task Force on Environment and Human Settlements and General Assembly resolution 53/242 which supported the establishment of the Global Ministerial Environment Forum and the Environmental Management Group and made other important recommendations on strengthening the current environmental governance regime.

8. Six meetings of the Intergovernmental Group of Ministers have taken place: in New York, on 18 April 2001, in Bonn, on 17 July 2001, in Algiers, on 9 and 10 September 2001, in Montreal, on 30 November to 1 December 2001, in New York, on 25 January 2002 and in Cartagena, on 12 February 2002. All meetings were well attended and witnessed a rich and extensive exchange of views between delegations. The second meeting benefited from having at its disposal the outcome of intersessional consultations between non-governmental and civil society organizations, agencies and experts. The third meeting was presented with suggestions of the President of the Governing Council in the form of "building blocks", which were discussed in two working groups. Working Group I addressed the role and the structure of the Global Ministerial Environment Forum and strengthening the role, authority and financial situation of UNEP. Working Group II addressed improved coordination and coherence among multilateral environmental agreements and enhanced coordination across the United Nations system – the role of the Environment Management Group. The meetings also benefited from the valuable inputs of the UNEP Committee of Permanent Representatives and generated a number of ideas that provide a sense of what the expectations are in this process. These ideas were summarized by the chair as follows:

(a) The international environmental governance process encompasses all international environmental efforts and arrangements within the United Nations system, including at the regional level, and is not restricted to UNEP;

(b) The process of strengthening international environmental governance should be evolutionary in nature and be based on implementing General Assembly resolution 53/242. A prudent approach to institutional change is required, with preference given to making better use of existing structures;

(c) The meetings on international environmental governance should lead to comprehensive inputs into the preparations for the World Summit on Sustainable Development, which should be presented for consideration by it. Decision 10/1 of the Commission on Sustainable Development, which invited the Governing Council to submit its progress report and results to the Preparatory Committee at its second session and the final results to the third session so that they can be fully considered in the preparatory process, clearly establishes this link;

(d) Some issues being considered go beyond the mandate of environment ministries alone, and other branches of Government should be involved in order to enhance national level coordination and to bring environmental considerations into the mainstream of economic and social decision-making at all levels. In this regard, international environmental governance should be viewed within the broader context of sustainable development;

(e) The increasing complexity and impact of trends in environmental degradation require an enhanced capacity for scientific assessment and monitoring and for provision of early warnings to Governments;

(f) The design and implementation of environmental policy at all levels requires a clear link to the sustainable development context as well as greater involvement and engagement of non-governmental organizations, and civil society and the private sector, allowing them a meaningful role in intergovernmental policy-making, and also requires strengthened national frameworks of governance;

(g) The international environmental governance process should take into account the needs and constraints of developing countries on the basis of common but differentiated responsibility;

(h) An essential complement to international cooperative arrangements is the requirement to strengthen the capacity of developing countries to participate actively in policy formulation and implementation. In this regard there is a need to emphasize and support capacity-building and technology transfer, and the role of UNEP in this regard was emphasized;

(i) As the principal United Nations body in the field of the environment, UNEP should be strengthened. This requires a clear solution to the issue of adequate, stable and predictable financing;
(j) A variety of proposals were considered, including the proposal to establish UNEP as a United Nations specialized agency, which met with differing views;
(k) The Global Ministerial Environment Forum should be placed as the cornerstone of the international institutional structure of international environmental governance;
(l) In addition, UNEP headquarters in Nairobi must be maintained and strengthened as a centre for international meetings on the environment;
(m) The proliferation of institutional arrangements, meetings and agendas, while having the benefit of specialization, may weaken policy coherence and synergy and put further strain on limited resources;
(n) The clustering approach to multilateral environmental agreements holds some promise, and issues relating to the location of secretariats, meeting agendas and also programmatic cooperation between such bodies and with UNEP should be addressed.

9. The conclusions and recommendations emanating from the international environmental governance process and agreed by consensus are contained in the following chapter.

III *Recommendations of the Intergovernmental Group of Ministers to the Governing Council/Global Ministerial Environment Forum*

A Improved Coherence in International Environmental Policy-making – the Role and Structure of the Governing Council/Global Ministerial Environment Forum

10. The Global Ministerial Environment Forum is constituted by the UNEP Governing Council as envisaged in General Assembly resolution 53/242, which states, in paragraph 6, that the Governing Council would constitute "the forum in the years that it meets in regular session and, in alternate years, with the forum taking the form of a special session of the Governing Council".

11. The international environmental governance process has highlighted the need for a high-level environment policy forum as one of the cornerstones of an effective system of international environmental governance. To this end, the Governing Council/Global Ministerial Environment Forum should be utilized more effectively both in promoting international cooperation in the field of the environment, in providing broad policy advice and guidance, identifying global environmental priorities, and making recommendations, in accordance with

paragraphs 2(a) and 2(b) of General Assembly resolution 2997 (XXVII) of 15 December 1972. Such an approach should be pursued with full respect for the independent legal status and governance structures of other entities, and would be consistent with the mandate provided to the UNEP Governing Council in General Assembly resolution 2997 (XXVII), which states, in paragraphs 2 (b) and 2 (c), that it should provide general policy guidance for the direction and coordination of environmental programmes within the United Nations system, keep their implementation under review and assess their effectiveness. This approach could be achieved through a series of measures such as those proposed below:

(a) Universal participation of Members States of the United Nations and members of its specialized agencies in the work of the Governing Council/ Global Ministerial Environment Forum should be ensured. The question of establishing universal membership for Governing Council/Global Ministerial Environment Forum is an important but complex issue that should be considered in the broader context of the preparatory process of the World Summit on Sustainable Development and be reviewed at the twenty-second session of the Governing Council/Global Ministerial Environment Forum based on the outcome of the Summit;

(b) The Nairobi Declaration on the Role and Mandate of the United Nations Environment Programme reaffirmed the continuing relevance of the mandate of UNEP deriving from General Assembly resolution 2997 (XXVII) and as further elaborated by Agenda 21. The core elements of the focused mandate of UNEP contained in the Nairobi Declaration highlighted, *inter alia*, the role of UNEP in the analysis of the state of the global environment, provision of policy advice and catalysing and promoting international cooperation; in further developing its international environmental law aimed at sustainable development, including the development of coherent interlinkages among existing international environmental conventions; in advancing the implementation of agreed international norms and policies and strengthening its role in the coordination of environmental activities in the United Nations system in the field of the environment;

(c) To play its role as the high-level environmental policy forum in the United Nations system, and in accordance with General Assembly resolution 2997 (XXVII), the Governing Council/Global Ministerial Environment Forum will:

    (i) Keep under review the world environment situation and develop policy responses in order to ensure that emerging environmental problems of wide international significance receive appropriate and adequate consideration based on sound science;

(ii) Provide general policy guidance for the direction and coordination of environmental programmes and make cross-cutting recommendations, in accordance with paragraphs 2 (a) and 2 (b) of General Assembly resolution 2997 (XXVII), to other bodies while respecting the independent legal status and autonomous governance structures of such entities;

(iii) Promote international cooperation in the field of the environment and recommend, as appropriate, policies to this end;

(iv) Strengthen further the coordination and institutional requirements for international environmental policy in view of the outcome of the World Summit on Sustainable Development and in light of the Malmö Declaration;

(b) The Governing Council/Global Ministerial Environment Forum should identify ways and means of improving and strengthening its interrelationship with autonomous decision-making bodies, such as conferences of the parties to multilateral environmental agreements;

(c) The Governing Council/Global Ministerial Environment Forum should promote the meaningful participation of representatives of major groups and non-governmental organizations including the private sector, giving them clear channels for providing Governments with their views, to inform intergovernmental decision-making bodies, within the established rules and modalities of the United Nations system. A particular effort to enable civil society organizations from developing countries to participate should be a priority. In line with Governing Council decision 21/19 of 9 February 2001, the relationship between UNEP and its governance structures, as well as among civil society, the private sector and other major groups, should be developed;

(d) Consideration should be given to having the Governing Council/Global Ministerial Environment Forum meet every other year at UNEP headquarters in Nairobi with meetings in alternate years, if possible, at another United Nations region. This would enhance its interaction with other policy forums in the economic and social fields and assist in the objectives of sustainable development mainstreaming. In addition, the possibility of having back-to-back meetings between the Governing Council/Global Ministerial Environment Forum and multilateral environmental agreements could be explored, with due regard to their legal status and governance structures;

(e) The Governing Council/Global Ministerial Environment Forum should institute a regular dialogue, to address the apparent disparity between policy and funding, with multilateral financial institutions, including the

Global Environment Facility (GEF). In this regard the Governing Council/Global Ministerial Environment Forum should play a stronger environmental policy advisory role and strengthen UNEP's efforts to enhance its relationship with GEF through the Action Plan on Complementarity between GEF activities and its programme of work, in line with Governing Council decisions 20/7 of 5 February 1999 and 21/25 of 9 February 2001. Better coordination of decision-making on international environmental policy with decision-making on financing should benefit the funding of environmental aspects of sustainable development;

(f) The Governing Council/Global Ministerial Environment Forum should enable ministers to concentrate on policy issues and have the opportunity to promote international cooperation, including making cross-cutting recommendations in the field of the environment, in accordance with paragraphs 2 (a) and 2 (b) of General Assembly resolution 2997 (XXVII), take policy decisions, identify priorities on matters within its area of competence, and provide broad direction and advice, as well as oversight of the programme of work and budget of UNEP. The Governing Council/Global Ministerial Environment Forum should also regularly review reports on the follow-up of its previous decisions. The agenda could be grouped in segments as follows:

   (i) The Governing Council/Global Ministerial Environment Forum should take into account emerging environmental trends and should consider issues related to environmental assessment and monitoring, monitoring of its previous decisions, early warning and emerging issues, based on a strengthened scientific capacity of UNEP. Further consideration should be given to strengthening UNEP's scientific base by improving its ability to monitor and assess global environmental change including, *inter alia*, through the establishment of an intergovernmental panel on global environmental change. The effective participation of developing countries in the work of the panel should be ensured, and the mandate, modalities and composition of any mechanism are to be decided by the Governing Council/Global Ministerial Environment Forum;

   (ii) The Governing Council/Global Ministerial Environment Forum could address environmental aspects of one or two selected sectoral issues on an annual basis (such as chemicals, water, oceans), as well as the environmental contribution to major development challenges. In this context relevant sectoral national ministries could be invited to interact with environment ministers to assist in a decision-making process that would aim at bringing environmental considerations into the mainstream of policy discussions and promote sustainable development. Progress in the follow-up of such work should be monitored and reported to the Governing Council/ Global Ministerial Environment Forum;

(iii) Taking advantage of its high-level and cross-cutting environmental perspective and its coordination role on environmental matters in the United Nations system, the Governing Council/Global Ministerial Environment Forum could engage in periodic stocktaking and, *inter alia*, review synergies and linkages undertaken between multilateral environmental agreements, as well as review reports of the Environment Management Group and progress in inter-agency collaboration. The Governing Council/Global Ministerial Environment Forum would give policy guidance and advice in the field of the environment by making recommendations, in accordance with paragraphs 2 (a) and 2 (b) of General Assembly resolution 2997 (XXVII). In this context, UNEP should carry out further scientific analysis in cooperation with secretariats of conventions and their subsidiary bodies and other relevant international scientific bodies, in order to identify possible activities with potential multiple benefits and to bring them to the attention of conferences of the parties, in conformity with General Assembly resolution 54/217 of 22 December 1999. Officials of United Nations agencies and heads of multilateral environmental agreement secretariats should be invited to participate and interact with ministers at meetings of the Governing Council/Global Ministerial Environment Forum;

(iv) The Governing Council/Global Ministerial Environment Forum agenda would also include a separate segment providing for the negotiation and adoption of the biennial programme of work and budget of UNEP and review of its implementation. The UNEP Committee of Permanent Representatives, as a subsidiary body, would continue to play its mandated role in monitoring the implementation of Governing Council/Global Ministerial Environment Forum decisions as well as preparation of its sessions, which would take place in an open and transparent manner, so as to facilitate the participation in substantive preparations of Governments not represented in Nairobi.

B Strengthening the Role and Financial Situation of UNEP

12. The Nairobi Declaration of 1997, which was endorsed by the United Nations General Assembly, established UNEP as the leading global environmental

authority that sets the global environmental agenda, promotes the coherent implementation of the environmental dimension of sustainable development and serves as an authoritative advocate for the global environment. While UNEP is the centrepiece of the international community's efforts to safeguard the environment, its role continues to fall short of the expectations expressed in the Nairobi Declaration primarily because UNEP remains hampered by insufficient and unpredictable resources.

13. Given the major environmental challenges of the twenty-first century, one way to address discrepancies between commitments and action is to improve the financial situation of UNEP.

14. While commendable efforts have been made by the United Nations to fund some of the administrative costs of UNEP through its regular budget, this funding has been declining in terms of percentage of the total UNEP resources over the past years. Hence it is recommended that, in accordance with General Assembly resolution 2997 (XXVII), consideration be given by the United Nations General Assembly to making available from its regular budget the amount which is necessary to cover all administrative and management costs of UNEP. There is also an urgent need to improve the financial situation of UNEP's Environment Fund.

15. Several steps should be taken to address the overall financial situation of UNEP. These include:
    (a) More predictable funding from all Member States of the United Nations and members of its specialized agencies;
    (b) More efficient and effective use of available resources, including the possibility of utilizing external management review mechanisms, taking into account the recommendations of prior management reviews of UNEP;
    (c) Strong focus on agreed priorities of UNEP and ongoing review of previous priorities;
    (d) Greater mobilization of resources from the private sector and other major groups in accordance with applicable United Nations rules and procedures.

16. All Member States of the United Nations and members of its specialized agencies, taking into account their economic and social circumstances should contribute financially to UNEP. The financial contributions should be made to the Environment Fund to finance the activities of UNEP to enable it, *inter alia*, to implement the provisions and achieve the objectives of the Fund set forth in General Assembly resolution 2997 (XXVII). Resources mobilized from major groups should also finance activities for the implementation of the programme of work of the Environment Fund.

17. To broaden the base of contributions to, and to enhance predictability in the voluntary financing of the Environment Fund, there should be a voluntary

indicative scale of contributions, to be developed specifically for UNEP's Environment Fund, taking into account, *inter alia*, the United Nations scale of assessment as well as the following:

(a) A minimum indicative rate of 0.001 per cent;
(b) A maximum indicative rate of 22 per cent;
(c) A maximum indicative rate for the least developed countries of 0.01 per cent;
(d) Economic and social circumstances of the Member States, in particular those of developing countries and countries with economies in transition;
(e) Provisions to allow for any Member State, in a position to do so, to increase its level of contributions over and above its current level.

18. All contributions to the Fund remain voluntary and each State reserves the right to determine whether or not it wishes to contribute voluntarily to the Fund. However, all Member States, taking into account their economic and social circumstances, will be encouraged to contribute to the Environment Fund either on the basis of the indicative scale of contributions, or on the basis of any of the following:

(a) Biennial pledges;
(b) United Nations scale of assessment;
(c) Historical level of contributions;
(d) Any other basis identified by a Member State.

19 The Executive Director of UNEP will notify all Member States, in a timely manner, of the indicative scale of contributions he intends to propose for the biennial budget. All Member States are urged to inform the Executive Director, in a timely manner, whether or not they will use the proposed indicative scale of contributions. The biennial budget will be submitted for consideration of the Governing Council/Global Ministerial Environment Forum, prior to the commencement of the financial period that it covers. It will also be circulated to all Member States at least six weeks before the meeting of the Governing Council/ Global Ministerial Environment Forum at which it will be considered.

20. The Executive Director will notify all Member States that choose the indicative scale of contributions by 15 October of the preceding calendar year, of the amount, in United States currency, of its indicative scale of contributions based on contributions for each year of the biennium. Any Member State which decides not to use the indicative scale of contributions will notify the Executive Director by this date of the basis it intends to use for its contributions, taking into account paragraph 18 above. In either case, each Member State will, prior to 1 January of each year, inform the Executive Director of UNEP of the contribution it intends to make that year and of the projected timing of that contribution. Contributions should

be made by 1 January of each calendar year, or as soon as possible thereafter, recognizing that there are differences in the budget cycles of Member States. All contributions should be paid in convertible currencies into a bank account identified in the notification of the Executive Director.

21. In addition to the contributions identified in paragraph 20 above, the resources available to UNEP for implementation of its programme of work will also consist of additional voluntary contributions which may be made by Member States or by major groups; other voluntary contributions, including contributions to support the participation of the representatives of developing countries, in particular the least developed and the small island developing States amongst them, as well as representatives from countries with economies in transition, in the Governing Council/Global Ministerial Environment Forum; the uncommitted balance of appropriations from previous financial periods; and miscellaneous income.

22. All Member States are encouraged to make prompt payment of their contributions to the Environment Fund, and a balance should be sought between earmarked and non-earmarked contributions.

23. The Executive Director of UNEP will submit to the Governing Council/Global Ministerial Environment Forum at its special session in the year 2004, a report on the implementation of paragraphs 15 to 22 above. The Governing Council/Global Ministerial Environment Forum will review the effectiveness of the system and take a decision, as appropriate.

24. Progress in implementing the international environmental agenda and creating a stronger link between environmental trends and policy dialogue at the Governing Council/Global Ministerial Environment Forum will be increasingly dependent on the availability of information required for decision-making, and in particular on providing developing countries with the means of implementation. In this regard, higher priority should be given to developing independent and authoritative scientific assessment and monitoring capacity for emerging issues. UNEP is well situated to build on its current strengths in these areas, and could also build a greater capacity to assist developing countries with their needs and requirements in such areas. An enhanced capacity would also require an enhanced financial base. UNEP should continue efforts to attract additional resources and support from partnerships with civil society and the private sector.

25. The UNEP/GEF Action Plan on Complementarity adopted by the UNEP Governing Council at its twentieth session and the GEF Council at its thirteenth meeting identified the establishment of a UNEP/GEF strategic partnership as an important modality for achieving complementarity. Recently, an initial phase of the UNEP/GEF strategic partnership, in the areas of environmental assessment, global environmental knowledge management and global environmental

outreach including the mobilization of the scientific community, has been successfully completed. Strategic partnerships with the World Bank and the United Nations Development Programme (UNDP) are also being undertaken. GEF could fund mutually agreed activities of UNEP which are of relevance to the global environment and the GEF. The existing partnership could focus on the following areas: assessment; scientific information, best practice, and policy analysis; capacity-building and training for the environment; and, country-level coordination for sustainable development. The partnership between UNEP and GEF could be further pursued and should also facilitate the mobilization of additional multilateral and bilateral financial resources for targeted activities consistent with the GEF mandate and global environmental priorities identified by the Governing Council/Global Ministerial Environment Forum.

C Improved Coordination among and Effectiveness of Multilateral Environmental Agreements

26. The negative impact of the increasing burdens on Governments' ability to participate meaningfully in the proliferating meetings and agendas of multilateral environmental agreements has been underscored as a major constraint to effective international policy-making. While the benefits of being able to concentrate on issue-specific areas are recognized, the perception of a growing potential for overlap in the international environmental agenda makes it difficult to benefit from potential synergies and linkages between the various agreements. In this regard the authority and the autonomy of the governing bodies of the conference of the parties and the accountability of their secretariat to their respective governing bodies should be respected.
27. One approach that has emerged from the debate is that of enhancing the synergies and linkages between multilateral environmental agreements with comparable areas of focus or of a regional character with due regard to their respective mandates. In particular, there is support for enhancing collaboration among multilateral environmental agreement secretariats in specific areas where common issues arise, such as current work among the chemicals and waste multilateral environmental agreement secretariats and including the interim secretariats, as well as biological diversity-related conventions, where efforts are underway to improve national reporting mechanisms of and among these conventions. The initiation of pilot projects should be further pursued. In this regard the study on chemicals- and wastes-related conventions, as well as the joint liaison group that has been convened by the secretariats of the Rio conventions, including the United Nations Convention to Combat Desertification in those Countries Experiencing Serious Drought and/or Desertification, particularly in Africa as

approved by their governing bodies, are steps in the right direction. More consideration should be given to the proposed measures suggested by the study. Such synergies and linkages must be promoted in close consultation and with the full agreement of the Conference of the Parties. UNEP should continue, in close cooperation with the secretariats of the multilateral environmental agreements, to enhance such synergies and linkages including on issues related to scientific assessments on matters of common concern.

28. A periodic review of the effectiveness of multilateral environmental agreements is critical to their success. As an important factor in their effectiveness compliance factors and mechanisms should be supported in conformity with the different regime under each multilateral environmental agreement and including designing multilateral environmental agreements with realistic and achievable goals which could be implemented. States should have regard for the advisory and non-binding UNEP guidelines on compliance with and enforcement of multilateral environmental agreements, once approved by the Governing Council/Global Ministerial Environment Forum. Capacity-building and, for some multilateral environmental agreements, technology transfer and the provision of financial resources to developing countries to facilitate compliance, are of great importance for supporting the effectiveness of multilateral environmental agreements.

29. While taking fully into account the autonomous decision-making authority of the conference of the parties, considerable benefits could accrue from a more coordinated approach to areas such as scheduling and periodicity of meetings of the conferences of the parties; reporting; scientific assessment on matters of common concern, capacity-building, transfer of technology; and enhancing the capacities of developing countries before and after the entry into force of legal agreements to implement and review progress on a regular basis by all parties concerned. Biennial meetings as well as shorter duration of conference of the parties should be promoted as well as the need to consider, as far as possible and practical, back-to-back or parallel conference of the parties meetings. The merit of convening meetings at the United Nations headquarters or in other locations will be considered on a case-by-case basis by the conference of the parties involved. In the future, careful consideration should be given to the effectiveness and resource efficiency of establishing additional subsidiary institutions of the conference of the parties, and the co-location of future multilateral environmental agreement secretariats should be encouraged, and where possible in developing countries, with a view of enhancing collaboration and effectiveness. Enhanced coordination at the convention level will also require improved coordination of positions at the national level concerning multilateral environmental agreements. Priority should be given to synergies at the country level, including the provision of means of implementation.

30. Coordination could be fostered by having the Governing Council/Global Ministerial Environment Forum review the progress made by the conference of the parties of multilateral environmental agreements, with due regard to their respective mandates, in developing synergies in areas where common issues arise.

D Capacity-Building, Technology Transfer and Country-level Coordination for the Environment Pillar of Sustainable Development

31. Environmental governance should be considered from a multi-level approach – international, regional, subregional and national. The ability of developing countries, as well as countries with economies in transition, to participate fully in the development of international environmental policy and to support those countries in their efforts towards achieving the environmental objectives of sustainable development, and to undertake the requisite implementation of international agreements at the national level, must be strengthened. The need to strengthen the capacity and capability of developing countries, as well as those with economies in transition, remains a major requirement for sustainable development and in particular on issues related to poverty eradication. Such efforts must include all relevant partners and emphasize in particular capacity-building and training, as well as national-level coordination, under leadership of national governments and according to national priorities, of the environmental component of sustainable development. To this end, effective and time-bound measures will be required at international, regional and national levels. In this regard the strengthening of national institutions, including the ministries of environment, in developing countries is an important aspect. Arrangements for the access to, and transfer of, environmentally sound technologies to developing countries should be established and facilitated as they are very important for achieving sustainable development. For progress in this field, steps should be taken expeditiously for the transfer of publicly owned technology.
32. International environmental governance should also cover and support regional and subregional efforts. UNEP, in cooperation with relevant regional and subregional organizations could provide support to the strengthening of regional environmental governance to improve coordination, implementation, capacity-building and technology transfer in support of regional initiatives. The New Partnership for Africa's Development (NEPAD) initiative should be supported as the framework for sustainable development in Africa.
33. In its resolution 53/242, the General Assembly stressed the need to ensure that capacity-building and technical assistance, in particular with respect to institutional strengthening in developing countries, remained an important

component of the work of UNEP. This should build on the ongoing capacity-building needs assessment being carried out by GEF through its implementing agencies, including UNEP. A strengthened programme of capacity-building should be clearly defined in the work of UNEP, building on its demonstrated comparative advantage and in the context of pursuing the ongoing strategic partnership with GEF, respecting its governance structure and in close cooperation with the United Nations organizations and other international organizations active in the area of the environment.

34. In this regard, an intergovernmental strategic plan for technology support and capacity-building to developing countries should be developed to improve the effectiveness of capacity-building, and to address the gaps identified by assessments of existing activities and needs, including the ongoing GEF inventory, subject to the availability of funds other than the Environment Fund, taking into account that additional resources need to be made available for this purpose. Such a strategic plan could be implemented through enhanced coordination between UNEP and other relevant bodies, including GEF and UNDP. It could include an increased role for UNEP in country-level capacity delivery in particular through greater collaboration with UNDP. This could be built on the following two components:

(a) Capacity-building and training: The strengthening of the national institutions responsible for environment and the implementation of multilateral environmental agreements which will promote the achievement of the objectives of the environmental component of sustainable development. Efforts by UNEP, in response to requests by Governments, to develop local and national capacity in environmental issues and for dissemination of best practices and experiences will build on its role as one of the three implementing agencies of GEF as well as on the expected benefits from the multi-year UNEP/GEF strategic partnership as envisaged in the UNEP/GEF Action Plan on Complementarity;

(b) National-level coordination of the environmental component of sustainable development: In addition to the mobilization of domestic resources, developing countries require access to financial, technological and technical resources from the international community, as well as better internal coordination to implement sustainable development strategies. Efforts for environmental improvement at all levels and the implementation of multilateral environmental agreements must converge for countries to achieve their national priorities and objectives. Countries are encouraged to promote the coordination of the multiple national frameworks that currently exist in the field of environment at the ministerial level.

35. The strategic partnership between UNEP and GEF should be based on the decisions of their respective governing bodies and involve strengthening the capacity of UNEP to fulfil its role as provided for in the UNEP/GEF Action Plan on Complementarity. UNEP's strength as one of the three GEF implementing agencies should be fostered. It should also take into account the special relationship with UNDP, building on its unique national field capacity, which can contribute to these efforts and also facilitate the mobilization of additional resources with positive results for the environment at both national and global levels.

E Enhanced Coordination Across the United Nations System – the Role of the Environmental Management Group

36. Considerable emphasis has been placed on enhancing coordination within the United Nations system and the role of the Environmental Management Group in this regard. The Environmental Management Group was established following the adoption of General Assembly resolution 53/242, and includes amongst its members the specialized agencies, funds and programmes of the United Nations system and the secretariats of multilateral environmental agreements. It follows an issue-management approach whereby issue-management groups are established within the organizations concerned in order to address specific issues identified by the Environmental Management Group within an established time frame. Issue-management groups may include institutions from outside the United Nations in their work. Issues selected so far have included the harmonization of biodiversity-related reporting, the development of a system-wide approach to environmental education and training, waste management and chemicals. The Environmental Management Group has only met a few times and it is therefore too early to make an assessment of its functioning. It is clear, however, that there is a need to ensure that the functionality of the Environmental Management Group as envisaged by resolution 53/242 should be realized as soon as possible. It is also clear that:
   (a) For the Governing Council/Global Ministerial Environment Forum to effectively play its policy role, it requires an instrument at the inter-agency level to enhance policy coordination across the environmental activities of the United Nations system. The Environmental Management Group is such an instrument and should be charged with reporting annually to the Forum, taking into account the provisions of General Assembly resolution 54/217, as well as on specific issues arising from the work of the United Nations system in the environmental area on which the Forum could make recommendations on the work of the Environment Management Group;

(b) The Environmental Management Group also provides potential for bringing the environment into the mainstream of relevant activities of the United Nations system. UNEP should join the United Nations Development Group, which brings together the operational agencies of the United Nations in the economic and social fields;

(c) The technical capacities of the specialized agencies and organizations participating in the Environmental Management Group could also be used to support the implementation of a strategic partnership between UNEP and other relevant bodies, including UNDP and GEF, *inter alia*, for capacity-building.

37. The efficient functioning of the Environmental Management Group requires a clear relation with intergovernmental processes which includes a clearly defined reporting relationship with the Governing Council/Global Ministerial Environment Forum, the Commission on Sustainable Development, and other forums in the United Nations system. It will also require senior-level participation by member institutions, transparency in operations, adequate resources to support its functioning and the possibility of financial support for specific activities, including a coordinated approach to capacity-building.

F Future Perspective

38. The present report takes as its foundation the debate within the international environmental governance process and the recommendations deal with specific weaknesses and opportunities within the current system. Some of the proposals and recommendations in the report could help build incrementally not only towards meeting the needs identified, but also towards the renewed efforts required to be undertaken by all countries pursuant to the internationally agreed development goals, including those contained in the Millennium Declaration. Our efforts are not only underpinned by a sense of protection of the global environment, but by the clear framework set in Malmö in May 2000. The Malmö Ministerial Declaration states that the World Summit on Sustainable Development "should review the requirements for a greatly strengthened institutional structure for international environment governance based on an assessment of future needs for an institutional architecture that has the capacity to effectively address wide-ranging environmental threats in a globalizing world".

39. We must therefore not only ensure a solid foundation on which to build, but also begin to shape a vision for the future of a robust, versatile regime that will allow us to respond quickly and effectively to emerging environmental challenges. In this context it has been recognized that the implementation of Agenda 21, requires improved international governance in all dimensions of sustainable

development as a prerequisite for achieving successful protection of the environment, economic growth and social equity. The 2002 Johannesburg Summit will have to address this crucial issue, and our input will be of significant value in the forthcoming debate. The mandate of UNEP, re-enforced at the 1992 Earth Summit in Rio, has placed it in a unique position to provide not only policy guidance and coordination in the field of the environment, but also to promote international cooperation in this field, while taking into account development perspectives. By improving and strengthening international environmental governance the decisions taken at the seventh special session of the Governing Council/Global Ministerial Environment Forum on 15 February 2002 should be considered as the commencement of a longer-term enterprise to develop international understanding, commitment and resolve towards ensuring the sustainability of the global environment in accordance with the Rio principles, including the principle of common but differentiated responsibilities.

X The Intergovernmental Group of Ministers on IEG, First Meeting, 18 April 2001

Summary of Selected Papers
State of International Environmental Governance

United Nations, "Report of the United Nations Task Force on Environment and Human Settlements" (A/53/463, annex) – 15 June 1998

The first major intergovernmental conference on the environment was the United Nations Conference on the Human Environment, held in Stockholm in June 1972. The Conference adopted a far-sighted Declaration and Programme of Action and led to the creation of the United Nations Environment Programme (UNEP) by the General Assembly with a mandate to catalyse and coordinate environmental actions within the United Nations system. The General Assembly decided that UNEP's headquarters should be located in Nairobi, Kenya. The UNEP Governing Council became the world's primary environmental forum. The two decades following the Stockholm saw many international actions to protect the environment, including the negotiation of many global and regional conventions.

Twenty years after Stockholm, the United Nations Conference on Environment and Development (the Earth Summit) was held in Rio de Janeiro in June 1992. The Conference approved the Rio Declaration, Agenda 21 and a set of non-legally binding principles on forest management. It also witnessed the signature of major conventions on climate change and biological diversity.

From the time of the Stockholm Conference, it was recognized that environmental issues could not be treated as afterthoughts or dealt with solely by "end-of-pipe" approaches, but that environmental considerations must be integrated into the activities of sectoral and development-oriented institutions. The international agenda for environment and development has been transformed, and the context in which the United Nations must operate has changed radically. The changes within the United Nations system have been conceptual and organizational; meanwhile the context has been altered by the emergence or continuation of sweeping global trends.

* UNEP, Report of the Executive Director on "International Environmental Governance", Open-ended Intergovernmental Group of Ministers of their Representatives on International Environmental Governance, First Meeting, New york, 18 April 2001; Doc.UNEP/IEM/1/2, 4 April 2001.

 | DOI 10.1163/9789004214552_020

The concept of sustainable development links economic, social and environmental concerns, and has been adopted by the world community. Agenda 21 assigns a broad range of responsibilities for action to United Nations organizations and bodies, national Governments and many other international and national groups. Environmental issues have appeared increasingly on the agendas of development-oriented institutions including the United Nations Development Programme (UNDP), the World Bank, the regional multilateral development banks, and such specialized agencies as the World Health Organization (WHO), the World Meteorological Organization (WMO), the Food and Agriculture Organization of the United Nations (FAO), the United Nations Educational, Scientific and Cultural Organization (UNESCO) and the United Nations Industrial Development Organization (UNIDO), as well as the United Nations regional commissions. The "greening" of these bodies has been a necessary and welcome step, but the integration of environmental considerations in their programmes clearly needs to go further. There has also been a welcome recognition of the need to move in these directions among some sections of business and industry.

The United Nations structure was altered after the Rio Conference by the creation of the United Nations Commission on Sustainable Development, which provides a high-level forum for discussion of environmental, developmental, social and economic issues. The Inter-Agency Committee on Sustainable Development (IACSD), a standing committee of the United Nations Administrative Committee on Coordination, has brought together the United Nations bodies concerned with these issues and has helped to coordinate their work. IACSD's system of designating agencies to be "task managers" for specific issues has decentralized responsibility for developing coordinated policy positions in key areas of sustainable development, especially as inputs to the Commission on Sustainable Development. The Global Environment Facility (GEF) has been established as a mechanism for financing activities to deal with some global environmental problems.

The establishment of the Commission on Sustainable Development, IACSD and GEF has created additional institutional arrangements alongside UNEP in the field of environment and sustainable development, and has highlighted the need to review the role of UNEP and its Governing Council in this context. The number of international legal instruments concerned with the environment has continued to grow. Demands on ministers and Governments have increased because of the multiplication of high-level meetings, including those of the Conferences of the Parties to international conventions. At the same time, the financial resources available to support international and national actions for sustainable development have fallen far short of what is required, and UNEP's own Environment Fund has declined substantially.

Human demands on the global life support system continue to mount as poverty and affluence spread in parallel all over the globe. Despite all the efforts made since the

Stockholm Conference, the environment continues to deteriorate in many parts of the world. Some social, economic and technological trends are exacerbating these problems. In addition, rapid urbanization is outstripping the provision of the services needed for health and welfare. New and unexpected problems will certainly continue to arise.

The main roles of the United Nations in the field of environment and human settlements are to:

- Facilitate intergovernmental consensus and international cooperation on environmental components of policies and actions for sustainable development, including legally binding commitments
- Promote support, especially from developed to developing countries, so as to facilitate the implementation of agreed environmental and human settlements action plans, especially Agenda 21 and the Habitat Agenda
- Involve, encourage and support relevant "stakeholders" so that they make their appropriate contributions at the global, regional, national and local levels
- Monitor and assess existing and emerging environmental problems, alert policy makers and the world public to them, and advocate and coordinate measures and action to tackle these problems and their causes, thereby reducing future risks
- Provide support and resources to enable the effective implementation of global and national commitments relating to the environment and human settlements, and to build capacity for environmental action in developing countries.

United Nations, "Renewing the United Nations: a programme for reform" (A/51/950) – 14 July 1997

A particularly important product of the Earth Summit has been the proliferation of new actors in the field of environment and sustainable development and their expanding participation in United Nations deliberations, negotiations and actions. This has led to changes in the scope of the international and environmental agenda to focus on the environment as a critical component of sustainable development.

UNEP is the environmental voice of the United Nations and the principal source of the environmental input into the work of the Commission on Sustainable Development. High priority must be given to according to it the status, strength and access to resources it requires to function effectively as the environmental agency of the world community. This has been confirmed by the Nairobi Declaration. UNEP's role as the focal point for harmonization and coordination of environment-related activities must be strengthened.

Strengths and Weaknesses in The existing Arrangements

Canada, International Environmental Institutions: Where from Here? – *Discussion paper for the Bergen Informal Ministerial Meeting (Bergen, Norway, 15-17 September 2000)*

The number and range of international institutions and instruments dealing with environmental issues have grown steadily over the past quarter century. A strong base of international environmental law exists. The focus now is on challenges to implementation. Compliance and enforcement mechanisms remain underdeveloped and unexplored, undermining the effectiveness of agreements.

Current approaches to global environmental management and sustainability are inadequate. To date, international action has focused primarily on transboundary movements of pollution and sectoral issues. We need to move toward a coherent and integrated management framework which addresses individual challenges in the context of the global ecosystem. The institutional structures which govern international environmental agreements are fragmented. Agreements are often managed independently, with little coherence or coordination.

There is no doubt that the environmental agenda of the 1960s and 1970s has expanded and grown in complexity. Today, it can be argued that the most crucial challenge to achieving environmental results is integration – integration of the environmental science and policy agenda itself as well as integration of environmental perspectives into the larger agendas of sustainable development and economic globalization.

It is through international institutions that information is shared, negotiations are conducted, norms and standards are elaborated and common action can be pursued. However, despite its many achievements, the existing machinery remains fragmented, often with vague mandates, inadequate resources and marginal political support. Competing for scarce funds and political commitment, existing institutions are frequently torn between competing priorities which are driven by overlapping and unfocused demands. Weak support and scattered direction have left institutions less effective than they could be, while demands on their resources continue to grow.

Canada, Global Environmental Governance: Moving Ahead, *January 2001*

The current structure of international environmental institutions belongs to a different age. As we enter a new century, our approach to managing the global environment must reflect what we have learned over the past decades, and where we are going. New scientific knowledge is illustrating the close interconnectedness of environmental issues, calling the traditional "issue-by-issue" problem-solving approach into question. Compelling evidence of the truly global nature of many environmental problems, such as climate change and persistent organic pollutants, highlights the critical nature of international cooperation. However, a growing number of environmental institutions, issues and agreements are placing stress on current systems, and our ability to manage them. Increasing globalization, both economic and social, is also complicating matters. Greater connectedness offers many opportunities for sharing knowledge and information for the better; it also presents real challenges. For example, increased social integration is resulting in the spread of unsustainable, consumption-dominated lifestyles. In addition, increased industrial activity in some regions of the world is exacerbating existing environmental pressures. Globalization is also transforming international relations and institutions, and represents a new phase in the ordering of global affairs.

Norway, Chairman's Summary of the Bergen Informal Ministerial Meeting (*Bergen, Norway, 15-17 September 2000*) *by H.E. Siri Bjerke, Minister of the Environment of Norway*

Key issues highlighted by participants:

- Need for 4 Cs: coherence, coordination, compliance and capacity-building
- Lack of coordination between different environmental organizations/structures and multilateral environmental agreements
- Weak international dispute mechanism for environmental agreements
- Lack of financial resources for international environmental cooperation
- No environmental counterweight to the World Trade Organization (WTO)
- Need for implementation and compliance of multilateral environmental agreements
- Need to increase environmental security.

Financing for the Global environment

European Union, Global Environmental Governance – Conclusions, *2321st Council meeting* (*Brussels, 18 and 19 December 2000*)

Stable, predictable and adequate funding is a prerequisite for improving governance. As regards UNEP, the 1997 Nairobi Declaration should be respected. Various methods could be contemplated with a view to stabilizing and strengthening UNEP's financial foundations, such as a system of negotiated multiannual agreements or assessed contributions covering all or part of the programme requirements. The possibility of extending the domains of action of GEF, and of adapting its resources accordingly, should be examined on the occasion of the replenishment of its resources and the meeting of its Assembly in autumn 2002.

G8, Communiqué: G8 Environment Ministers' Meeting *in Trieste, Italy (2-4 March 2001)*

Stable, predictable and adequate funding is a prerequisite for improving governance of international institutions. As regards UNEP, various methods could be contemplated to achieve this. All countries should be ready to play their part in the common effort.

Norway, Chairman's Summary of the Bergen Informal Ministerial Meeting *(Bergen, Norway, 15-17 September 2000) by H.E. Siri Bjerke, Minister of the Environment of Norway*

Lack of financial resources for developing countries to prepare, participate and follow up in a meaningful way (North-South imbalance).

United Nations, "Renewing the United Nations: a programme for reform" (A/51/950) – 14 July 1997

Overall the response to the needs of developing countries for new and additional financial resources has been disappointing, and official development assistance has declined since the Rio Conference. GEF, established to finance the incremental costs of certain sustainable development projects, has functioned well and now needs to be replenished at higher levels and its scope expanded.

Needs and Options

Canada, International Environmental Institutions: Where from Here? *– Discussion paper for the Bergen Informal Ministerial Meeting (Bergen, Norway, 15-17 September 2000)*

Given the expanding environmental agenda and the fragmented approach to international action, the international community needs to consider whether the existing international institutional machinery can confront the challenges of the twenty-first century. Building on the United Nations and UNEP reform efforts since 1997, should we also consider a more fundamental restructuring of existing governance mechanisms and institutions, including the creation of a centralized environmental authority? The basic premise for charting a new course for institutional strengthening is that existing institutions do not (or will not) adequately address current and future needs.

In essence, the debate concerns the relative merits of further centralized governance and decision-making through the creation of a new organization – which some have identified as a World Environment Organization – versus a decentralized but strengthened system similar to that which currently exists. While much has been written about strengthening the existing United Nations system, particularly in the context of United Nations and UNEP reform, there has been no detailed analysis and assessment of alternative options like a World Environment Organization. Ideally, debates on form (i.e. institutional and financial matters) should follow discussions on function (i.e. mandate and authority). Questions about mandate and authority should precede any debate about institutional structure.

European Union, Global Environmental Governance – Conclusions, *2321st Council meeting (Brussels, 18-19 December 2000)*

The continuous increase in the number of international bodies with environmental competence carries the risk of reduced participation of States owing to an increased workload, and makes it necessary to create or strengthen the synergies between all these bodies. We should consider in this context the role of UNEP and its status, with a view to giving it the resources it needs to promote better coordination. The Global Ministerial Environment Forum should further promote the enhancement of UNEP's authority by providing political impulse and direction.

There is a need to explore other directions to improve the synergies between institutions, including:

- Setting up a coordination mechanism bringing together, under the aegis of UNEP, all institutions with a largely environmental remit, in order to harmonize, in particular on a thematic basis, schedules, assessments, actions and strategies;
- Strengthening coherence and improving existing structures of cooperation between conventions and between their secretariats, notably within thematic clusters;
- Reinforcing the links between environmental and non-environmental institutions.

The development of a large number of multilateral agreements on the environment has resulted in a very diversified body of rules. It is therefore important to ensure consistency in the development of standards. With regard to implementation of environmental agreements, consideration should be given to ways of making the agreements more effective, by studying which compliance mechanisms, non-judicial and possibly judicial, would be most appropriate, and ways of streamlining the reporting mechanisms.

To increase the effectiveness of environmental standards, it is central to examine the link between multilateral environmental agreements and WTO.

The success of environmental policies will ultimately depend, both internally and internationally, on the integration of environmental concerns in sectoral policies. At the global level, the Environmental Management Group should make it possible to strengthen links between the various institutions in order to pass on the environmental message and promote environmental mainstreaming, where UNEP should play a key role.

Discussions on improving international environmental governance should be an integral part of international efforts to promote sustainable development.

The strengthening of international environmental governance should be based on existing structures, in particular UNEP, should aim gradually to adapt them to the new requirements and could ultimately lead to a World Environment Organization, respecting existing headquarters; it should try to respond to current challenges, particularly as regards the implementation of environmental agreements.

For international environmental architecture to be credible, all players must be encouraged to participate effectively. Firstly, care must be taken to promote the participation of all regions of the world. Harmonization of the timetables of international meetings would allow rationalizing the work of national delegations; training and information on the issues of international negotiations should be discussed.

As regards the participation of non-governmental players, it is desirable, on the one hand, to encourage increased participation by civil society in existing international bodies (UNEP, the Commission on Sustainable Development, etc.) and in major international negotiations, and on the other hand, to encourage common norms throughout the various States on access to information and public participation.

G8, Communiqué: G8 Environment Ministers' Meeting *in Trieste, Italy* (*2-4 March 2001*)

The strengthening of international environmental governance is important to meet the challenges of the twenty-first century and to implement multilateral environmental agreements. Effective, accountable governance not only helps to strengthen democracy and human rights, promote economic prosperity and social cohesion and reduce poverty, but is critical to enhance environmental protection and the sustainable use of natural resources, and deepen confidence in government and public administration.

The strengthening of international environmental governance should be based on the existing structures, in particular UNEP, with its headquarters in Nairobi, with a view to adapting them to new requirements.

We underline the need to improve UNEP's coordinating role in international environmental management and the need to foster voluntary exchanges of information between all international environmental institutions and bodies with a largely environmental remit, to provide coherence, in particular on a thematic basis, among schedules, assessments, reporting strategies and actions, mindful of the autonomous nature of the separate treaties involved; improve existing structures of cooperation between conventions and between their secretariats, notably within thematic clusters; and reinforce the links between environmental and non-environmental institutions, increasing the participation of civil society.

Norway, Chairman's Summary of the Bergen Informal Ministerial Meeting (Bergen, Norway, 15-17 September 2000) by H.E. Siri Bjerke, Minister of the Environment of Norway

Key issues highlighted by participants:

- Support for action to strengthen global environmental institutions, building on existing institutions, and to take incremental steps towards a World Environment Organization
- Developed and developing countries to agree on how environmental governance within the United Nations institutions should be improved. The Environmental Management Group should be fully used
- UNEP must be given broad and strong political and financial support to fulfil its mandate on the basis of common but differentiated responsibilities (reference was made to the United Nations scale of contributions)
- Need to set strategic objectives and targets for coherent governance
- Better integration of environment with other sectors and socio-economic policies
- Better coordination and integration of multilateral environmental agreements
- Functions of convention secretariats should be streamlined and Conferences of the Parties and meetings better coordinated
- More participation and input at high political level would improve cooperation
- System of reporting should be streamlined in order for countries to produce fewer reports. It was suggested that only one national report integrating all the conventions should be submitted annually
- Use information technology, such as videoconferencing, to facilitate participation
- Global environmental and sustainable development governance/institutional reform should be on the agenda for the 2002 World Summit on Sustainable Development.

European Commission, Communication from the Commission to the Council and European Parliament: Ten Years after Rio: Preparing for the World Summit on Sustainable Development in 2002 (*COM (2001) 53 final*), *Brussels, 6 February 2001*

There is growing momentum for the Summit to address global governance on sustainable development. The current institutional setting was designed a long time ago and it might not be able to respond to the new challenges of a globalizing world. It is therefore necessary to consider what the prospects are for strengthened governance on sustainable development. The Commission on Sustainable Development's role and the adequacy of current United Nations structures to deal with sustainable development should therefore be addressed, taking into account the overall development structures of the United Nations. Lack of regional structures in most parts of the world is another item worth exploring.

World Commission on Environment and Development, Our Common Future (*A/42/427*) – *1987*

The integrated and interdependent nature of the new challenges and issues contrasts sharply with the nature of the institutions that exist today. These institutions tend to be independent, fragmented and working to relatively narrow mandates with closed decision processes. Those responsible for managing natural resources and protecting the environment are institutionally separated from those responsible for managing the economy. The real world of interlocked economic and ecological systems will not change; the policies and institutions concerned must.

The ability to choose paths that are sustainable requires that the ecological dimensions of policy be considered at the same time as the economic, trade, energy, agricultural, industrial and other dimensions – on the same agendas and in the same national and international institutions. That is the chief institutional challenge of the 1990s. The Commission's proposals for institutional change at the national, regional and international levels are embodied in six priority areas:

- Getting at the sources;
- Dealing with the effects;
- Assessing global risks;
- Making informed choices;
- Providing the legal means;
- Investing in our future.

Together, these priorities represent the main directions for institutional and legal change needed to make the transition to sustainable development.

German Advisory Council on Global Change (WBGU), World in Transition: New Structures for Global Environmental Policy: Summary for Policy Makers, September 2000

The Council's vision of an Earth Alliance to reform the framework of international environmental institutions and organizations builds on existing structures and develops them further as needed. The Earth Alliance consists of an Earth Assessment, an Earth Organization and an Earth Funding, which are to be linked one another through mutual commitments for information and communication exchange, joint activities and common financing models.

- *Earth Assessment*: we propose the establishment of an independent entity (Earth Commission) to serve as a special authority for the evaluation of environmental problems. 10-15 members of the Earth Commission would be appointed by the General Assembly. The duty of this authority would be to issue timely warnings of environmental risks. This authority, of deliberately limited size, would have certain rights to make proposals vis-à-vis scientific panels, some of which are yet to be established, and would be entitled to address the public as needed. The scientific panels might include the Intergovernmental Panel on Climate Change, an

Intergovernmental Panel on Biological Diversity, an Intergovernmental Panel on Soils and a Risk Assessment Panel. In the structure of Earth Assessment, the Commission on Sustainable Development would assume an important role in fostering linkages and dialogue among the various countries involved, the United Nations organizations, the Earth Commission, the scientific community and non-governmental organizations.

- *Earth Organization*: we propose the restructuring of the existing system in a series of steps. The first step is geared to improve cooperation among the various organizations and programmes, working together on an equal basis. The several functions currently exercised by the Commission on Sustainable Development, GEF, various conferences of the parties, the convention secretariats and the environmental divisions and programmes of the specialized agencies are not to be altered. UNEP could, at this point, be assigned a different institutional structure within the United Nations system , as a specialized agency (like WHO) or an internal United Nations entity (like the United Nations Conference on Trade and Development (UNCTAD)). If the first step does not eliminate shortcomings in the system, the second step would be taken to create a certain amount of hierarchy within the organizational structure, for which WTO might serve as a model. Various conferences of the parties to international environmental agreements might be integrated within a framework agreement establishing an international environmental organization. They could continue to exist as separate and largely independent committees to the ministers' conferences, as in the case of WTO. The third step would be to centralize and establish a hierarchical order for international policy-making. The decision-making process should be speeded up by moving beyond the consensus principle and/or by introducing smaller decision-making bodies – an "environmental security council", for example.
- Besides the above proposal, the following proposals for good regime design are made: using protocols to advance the purposes of framework agreements; making voting procedures more flexible; strengthening the right of access to environmental information and linking it to reporting procedures; possibilities of flexible reaction to complications encountered during implementation; integrating non-governmental organizations as partners in environmental protection; and ensuring that environmental certification or labelling systems are fair.
- *Earth Funding*: we propose three measures for financing global environmental policy which – in addition to a desirable increase in available funds – would lead to more efficient use of these funds: reorganizing both internal and external control structures in multilateral institutions; levying utilization fees for resources belonging to the global community (global commons); and stepping up integration of private and public financing mechanisms.

Duncan Brack and Joy Hyvarinen, Global Environmental Institutions: Analysis and Options for Change – *report prepared for the Department of Environment, Transport and the Regions of the United Kingdom, Royal Institute of International Affairs, September 2000*

An effective global environmental governance structure needs to enable, support and encourage policy-making and decision-making leading to an effective response to environmental management needs which require (or benefit from) a response at the global level.

The management goals of an effective structure include: avoiding further harm, in particular irreversible harm, to the natural environment; halting and reversing negative trends; repairing damage; and generating positive trends. Global dialogue, leading to action that takes into account the needs of both developing and developed countries, is an essential prerequisite for effective global environmental governance. An effective global environmental governance structure must be conducive to such a dialogue. In order to enable an assessment of the existing global environmental governance set-up, we identify 12 key features which an effective structure should possess: 1. Transformational leadership (leadership that is capable of bringing about fundamental change through action that is perceived as legitimate); 2. Clear and early identification of problems; 3. Identification and assessment of response options and management objectives; 4. Effective implementation at the international level; 5. Coordination of activities; 6. Effectiveness of activities; 7. Policy integration; 8 Mobilization of private-sector resources; 9 Transformation of the traditional industrialized-country development model; 10. International equity; 11. Legitimacy; 12. Institutional adaptability: innovation and learning.

Bharat H. Desai, Revitalizing International Environmental Institutions: The UN Task Force Report and Beyond, Indian Journal of International Law, *vol.40, No.3, July–September 2000*

Various suggestions have been put forward on the nomenclature of the new organization, ranging from an international (world) environmental organization to a world environment and development organization. It appears that the primary purpose of such a specialized agency could be to enhance UNEP's status and authority. Thus, any sculpting of a new institution would comprise UNEP at its core. The question of a merger of other existing organs and programmes would depend upon the extent to which States prefer to make the exercise ambitious. At the minimum level, a new institutional structure should result in an enhancement of UNEP's status from a United Nations programme to that of a specialized agency. It would be ideal if the General Assembly seriously reviewed the requirements for a "greatly strengthened institutional structure for international environmental governance", as called for by the first meeting of the Global Ministerial Environment Forum. It would be appropriate if the Assembly decided this issue and provided a mandate for the purpose. It could give shape to a United Nations Environment Protection Organization wherein the existing UNEP could merge.

Akiko Domoto (President, GLOBE International, former Vice-President, IUCN), International Environmental Governance: Its Impact on Social and Human Development, *April 2000*

While many of the global environmental challenges we face can best be addressed at the international level, solutions arrived at by those who govern at this level will be sustainable only on two conditions. First, they must be found and implemented in partnership with the broad range of people they are designed to benefit. Whereas governance was seen largely as the job of governments throughout much of the twentieth century, there is an increasing realization that good governance necessitates the participation of all sectors of society. Second, solutions need to be based on the understanding that human society and the environment are interconnected and that, without a sound environment, society cannot function. This means both that environmental agreements need to take into greater consideration the development needs of the poor, and that more economically oriented governance mechanisms need to operate with a fuller understanding of the linkages between the economy and the environment. It is only an interlinked, holistic approach to governance which puts the environment and people's needs first that will suffice for the coming century. International environmental governance can be effective only if it is integrated into local, national and regional governance structures which encompass governments as well as civil society and the business sector.

Konrad von Moltke, The Organization of the Impossible – *Working Paper, International Institute for Sustainable Development, 2001*

The ultimate purpose of an environmental regime is to safeguard environmental quality – however defined – but no regime can actually control the environment. All it can do is work to modify human behaviour in ways that, it is hoped, will result in more satisfactory environmental conditions. The outcome is a long chain of uncertain causalities. An environmental regime can be thought effective if it changes perceptions; it if causes laws to be changed; if these laws cause changes in behaviour; if these changes in behaviour result in changes in the standards that are used as surrogates for the environment; and/or if some ecosystem or other environmental good is left obviously intact. Finally, a regime can be effective by doing any of these things more efficiently than alternative regimes.

Most international environmental regimes exhibit some degree of effectiveness according to one or more of these criteria, but none fulfils them all. Recent analysis suggests that the sources of effectiveness in international environmental regimes lie in areas that are largely outside the scope of traditional international research. This new approach argues that international environmental regimes are based on science, in that they have an objective core that is not politically determined. Arguably the climate regime would not exist without the Intergovernmental Panel on Climate Change. International environmental regimes have deep roots in the domestic society of States, that is, they can bypass the national authorities which are nominally in control in international society. International environmental regimes have contributed to the emergence of an international civil society, and benefit from this new phenomenon. International environmental regimes have been institutionally innovative. Whatever proposals are made for a World Environment Organization, it is essential to preserve these critical characteristics of the existing international environmental management structure. At the very least a World Environment Organization will need to be an international organization unlike any other that exists.

Good environmental governance at all levels has been characterized by reliance on science; the use of the precautionary approach; the ability to accommodate actions at different levels of governance (subsidiarity); the use of economic incentives and the avoidance of physical coercion as an implementation strategy; and high degrees of transparency and participation. The result is a series of policy complexes that exhibit highly specific characteristics and are not amenable to hierarchical organization. A World Environment Organization that actually improves environmental governance will need to exhibit all of these characteristics, and will consequently be as difficult as the current structure to comprehend from the limited perspective of economic liberalization.

XI The Malmö Ministerial Declaration, 31 May 2000

We, Ministers of Environment and heads of delegation meeting in Ma l mö, Sweden from 29 to 31 May 2000, on the occasion of the First Global Ministerial Environment Forum, held in pursuance of United Nations General Assembly resolution 53/242 of 28 July 1999 to enable the world's environment ministers to gather to review important and emerging environmental issues and to chart the course for the future,

Recalling the Stockholm Declaration of the United Nations Conference on the Human Environment and the Rio Declaration of the United Nations Conference on Environment and Development, the Barbados Declaration on the Sustainable Development of Small Island Developing States as well as the Nairobi Declaration on the Role and Mandate of the United Nations Environment Programme,

Deeply concerned that, despite the many successful and continuing efforts of the international community since the Stockholm Conference, and some progress having been achieved, the environment and the natural resource base that supports life on Earth continue to deteriorate at an alarming rate,

Reaffirming the importance of the speedy implementation of the political and legal commitments entered into by the international community, in particular at the Rio Conference,

Convinced that urgent and renewed efforts are required to be undertaken by all countries in a spirit of international solidarity, and recognizing, *inter alia*, the principle of common but differentiated responsibility as contained in the Rio Principles to manage the environment so as to promote sustainable development for the benefit of present and future generations,

Conscious that the root causes of global environmental degradation are embedded in social and economic problems such as pervasive poverty, unsustainable production and consumption patterns, inequity in distribution of wealth, and the debt burden,

Also conscious that success in combating environmental degradation is dependent on the full participation of all actors in society, an aware and educated population, respect for ethical and spiritual values and cultural diversity, and protection of indigenous knowledge

Aware that the 10-year review and appraisal of the implementation of Agenda 21 to be conducted in 2002 will provide a further opportunity for the international community to take action to implement its commitments and to strengthen international

* The Malmö Ministerial Declaration, adopted vide Decision GCSS.VI/1 of 31 May 2000 by the Governing Council of UNEP at its Sixth Special Session/ Global Ministerial Environment Forum; see http://www.unep.org/malmo/malmo_ministerial.htm

 | DOI 10.1163/9789004214552_021

cooperation urgently required to address the challenges of sustainable development in the twenty-first century,

Convinced that the Millennium Summit of the fifty-fifth session of the United Nations General Assembly provides a unique opportunity to address at the highest level the role of the United Nations in the field of sustainable development, and noting in this regard the proposals of the Secretary-General of the United Nations as contained in his report "We the peoples: the role of the United Nations in the twenty-first century", which will serve as the basis of discussion at the Summit,

Determine to contribute to this historic endeavour from an environmental perspective, and having requested the President of the Governing Council to bring the following matters to the attention of the fifty-fifth session of the General Assembly, the Millennium Assembly,

Declare that:

Major Environmental Challenges of the Twenty-First Century

1. The year 2000 marks a defining moment in the efforts of the international community to ensure that the growing trends of environmental degradation that threaten the sustainability of the planet are arrested and reversed. Hence there is an urgent need for reinvigorated international cooperation based on common concerns and a spirit of international partnership and solidarity.
2. There is an alarming discrepancy between commitments and action. Goals and targets agreed by the international community in relation to sustainable development, such as the adoption of national sustainable development strategies and increased support to developing countries, must be implemented in a timely fashion. The mobilization of domestic and international resources, including development assistance, far beyond current levels is vital to the success of this endeavour.
3. The evolving framework of international environmental law and the development of national law provide a sound basis for addressing the major environmental threats of theday. It must be underpinned by a more coherent and coordinated approach among international environmental instruments. We must also recognize the central importance of environmental compliance, enforcement and liability, and promote the observation of the precautionary approach as contained in the Rio Principles, and other important policy tools, as well as capacity-building.
4. The Global Environment Outlook 2000 of the United Nations Environment Programme provides a compelling assessment of the serious nature of the environmental threats faced by the international community. Special attention should be paid to unsustainable consumption patterns among the richer

segments in all countries, particularly developed countries. Environmental stewardship is lagging behind economic and social development, and a rapidly growing population is placing increased pressures on the environment.

5. Environmental threats resulting from the accelerating trends of urbanization and the development of megacities, the tremendous risk of climate change, the freshwater crisis and its consequences for food security and the environment, the unsustainable exploitation and depletion of biological resources, drought and desertification, and uncontrolled deforestation, increasing environmental emergencies, the risk to human health and the environment from hazardous chemicals, and land-based sources of pollution, are all issues that need to be addressed.
6. Opportunities however exist that can redress this situation. Technological innovation and the emergence of new resource-efficient technologies, in which the private sector plays major role, provide a source of great hope and increased opportunities to avoid the environmentally destructive practices of the past including through clean technologies.
7. To confront the underlying causes of environmental degradation and poverty, we must integrate environmental considerations in the mainstream of decision-making. We must also intensify our efforts in developing preventive action and a concerted response, including national environmental governance and the international rule of law, awareness-raising and education, and harness the power of information technology to this end. All actors involved must work together in the interest of a sustainable future.
8. It is necessary that the environmental perspective is taken into account in both the design and the assessment of macro-economic policy-making, as well as practices of government and multilateral lending and credit institutions such as export credit agencies.
9. The trends of globalization in the world economy, with the attendant environmental risks and opportunities, require international institutions to adopt new approaches and to engage the major actors involved in globalization in new ways. We should encourage a balanced and integrated approach to trade and environment policies in pursuit of sustainable development, in accordance with the decision of the Commission on Sustainable Development at its eighth session.
10. The role and responsibility of nations based on the Rio Principles, as well as the role and responsibility of the main actors including Governments, the private sector and civil society, must be emphasized in addressing the environmental challenges of the twenty-first century. Governments are the primary agents in this process, whose actions revitalizing implementing United Nations environment-related instruments since Stockholm, institutional capacity-building and strengthened international cooperation.

The Private Sector and the Environment

11. The private sector has emerged as a global actor that has a significant impact on environmental trends through its investment and technology decisions. In this regard, Governments have a crucial role in creating an enabling environment. The institutional and regulatory capacities of Governments to interact with the private sector should be enhanced. A greater commitment by the private sector should be pursued to engender a new culture of environmental accountability through the application of the polluter-pays principle, environmental performance indicators and reporting, and the establishment of a precautionary approach in investment and technology decisions. This approach must be linked to the development of cleaner and more resource efficient technologies for a life-cycle economy and efforts to facilitate the transfer of environmentally sound technologies.
12. The potential of the new economy to contribute to sustainable development should be further pursued, particularly in the areas of information technology, biology and biotechnology. The ethical and social implications must be carefully considered. There must be recognition of the public interest in knowledge related to biodiversity, including the interest of indigenous and local communities. A corporate ethic guided by public interest should be promoted.
13. The Global Compact established by the Secretary-General of the United Nations with the private sector provides an excellent vehicle for the development of a constructive engagement with the private sector. UNEP should continue to enhance its engagement and collaboration with the private sector and consider the relation between foreign direct investment and the environment, with a view to minimizing negative environmental implications.

Civil Society and the Environment

14. Civil society plays a critically important role in addressing environmental issues. The role, capabilities and involvement of civil society organizations has seen a substantial increase over recent years, which highlights the need for national Governments and for UNEP and international organizations to enhance the engagement of these organizations in their work on environmental matters.
15. Civil society has found new and effective modes of expression of popular sentiments and concerns. It provides a powerful agent for promoting shared environmental purpose and values. Civil society plays an important role in bringing emerging environmental issues to the attention of policy makers, raising public

awareness, promoting innovative ideas and approaches, and promoting transparency as well as non-corrupt activities in environmental decision-making.

16. The role of civil society at all levels should be strengthened through freedom of access to environmental information to all, broad participation in environmental decision-making, as well as access to justice on environmental issues. Governments should promote conditions to facilitate the ability of all parts of society to have a voice and to play an active role in creating a sustainable future.
17. Science provides the basis for environmental decision-making. There is a need for intensified research, fuller engagement of the scientific community and increased scientific cooperation on emerging environmental issues, as well as improved avenues for communication between the scientific community, decision makers and other stakeholders.
18. We must pay special attention to threats to cultural diversity and traditional knowledge, in particular of indigenous and local communities, which may be posed by globalization. In this context we welcome the proclamation by the United Nations General Assembly of the year 2001 as the International Year of Dialogue among Civilizations.
19. Greater emphasis must be given to the gender perspective in decision-making concerning the management of the environment and natural resources.
20. There is a need for independent and objective media at all levels in enhancing awareness and developing shared environmental values in global society. The media can serve the cause of sustainable development by identifying emerging issues, awareness-raising and promoting appropriate action.

The 2002 Review of UNCED

21. The 2002 review of the implementation of the outcome of the United Nations Conference on Environment and Development (UNCED) should be undertaken by an international conference at the summit level. The objective should not be to renegotiate Agenda 21, which remains valid, but to inject a new spirit of cooperation and urgency based on agreed actions in the common quest for sustainable development. In this regard, the ratification of all environmental conventions and protocols, in particular those related to climate, desertification, biosafety and chemicals, should be urgently pursued by Governments.
22. Governments and UNEP have to play a major role in the preparation for the 2002 review of UNCED at the regional and global levels and ensure that the environmental dimension of sustainable development is fully considered on the basis of a broad assessment of the state of the global environment. The preparations for the conference should be accelerated. The 2002 conference should aim at

addressing the major challenges to sustainable development, and in particular the pervasive effects of the burden of poverty on a large proportion of the Earth's inhabitants, counter posed against excessive and wasteful consumption and inefficient resource use that perpetuate the vicious circle of environmental degradation and increasing poverty.

23. The 2002 conference should review the requirements for a greatly strengthened institutional structure for international environmental governance based on an assessment of future needs for an institutional architecture that has the capacity to effectively address wide-ranging environmental threats in a globalizing world. UNEP's role in this regard should be strengthened and its financial base broadened and made more predictable.

Conclusion

24. At the dawn of this new century, we have at our disposal the human and material resources to achieve sustainable development, not as an abstract concept but as a concrete reality. The unprecedented developments in production and information technologies, the emergence of a younger generation with a clear sense of optimism, solidarity and values, women increasingly aware and with an enhanced and active role in society – all point to the emergence of a new consciousness. We can decrease poverty by half by 2015 without degrading the environment, we can ensure environmental security through early warning, we can better integrate environmental consideration in economic policy, we can better coordinate legal instruments and we can realize a vision of a world without slums. We commit ourselves to realizing this common vision.

XII The General Assembly Resolution 53/242, 10 August 1999

The General Assembly

Recalling its resolution 52/12 A of 12 November 1997, entitled "Renewing the United Nations: a programme for reform",

Reaffirming its determination to strengthen the role, capacity, effectiveness and efficiency of the United Nations, including in the field of environment and human settlements, and thus improve its performance in order to realize the full potential of the Organization,

Taking note of the report of the Secretary-General on environment and human settlements[1] and the report of the United Nations Task Force on Environment and Human Settlements annexed thereto, which contain recommendations on reforming and strengthening the activities of the United Nations in the field of environment and human settlements,

Expressing its appreciation to the Chairman and members of the Task Force for their commendable work,

Conscious of the continued deterioration of the global environment and the state of human settlements, despite some positive achievements, as well as of the need to strengthen the institutions of the United Nations charged with responsibility for environment and human settlements, to improve their performance and to promote coordination in the implementation of the environmental and human settlements dimension of sustainable development within the United Nations system,

Emphasizing the importance of strengthening the capacity of the United Nations Environment Programme and the United Nations Centre for Human Settlements (Habitat) in their Nairobi location and of ensuring the provision of requisite support and stable, adequate and predictable financial resources necessary to both organizations for the fulfilment of their mandates, as contained in General Assembly resolutions 2997 (XXVII) of 15 December 1972 and 32/162 of 19 December 1977, as well as in the Nairobi Declaration on the Role and Mandate of the United Nations Environment Programme, adopted by the Governing Council of the United Nations Environment Programme in its decision 19/1 of 7 February 1997,[2] and the Istanbul

---

* **Report of the Secretary-General on environment and human settlements,** adopted on 28 July 1999. See UN doc. A/RES/53/242, 10 August 1999.

1 A/53/463.

2 *Official Records of the General Assembly, Fifty-second Session, Supplement No. 25* (A/52/25), annex.

 | DOI 10.1163/9789004214552_022

Declaration on Human Settlements,[3] adopted by the United Nations Conference on Human Settlements (Habitat II) on 14 June 1996, including by seeking additional financial resources through broadening the range of sources of funding for both organizations, in accordance with the Financial Regulations and Rules of the United Nations,

Taking into account the views of Member States on the report of the Secretary-General on environment and human settlements,

Taking into account also the views contained in decision 20/17, adopted on 5 February 1999 by the Governing Council of the United Nations Environment Programme,[4] and Commission on Human Settlements resolution 17/6 of 14 May 1999,[5] concerning the report of the Secretary-General on environment and human settlements,

1. *Welcomes* the efforts undertaken to strengthen the United Nations in the field of environment and human settlements, and in that context takes note of the general thrust of the recommendations contained in the report of the Secretary-General on environment and human settlements,[1] proposing actions to be taken by the Secretary-General, the Executive Director of the United Nations Environment Programme and the Executive Director of the United Nations Centre for Human Settlements (Habitat), and takes note also of the recommendations outlined in section IV of the report;
2. *Requests* the Secretary-General to strengthen the United Nations Office at Nairobi, in its capacity as the only United Nations headquarters located in a developing country, through the provision of requisite support and stable, adequate and predictable financial resources, including by proposing additional regular budget resources, as envisaged by the General Assembly in its resolution 52/220 of 22 December 1997, for the consideration of the Assembly, with due regard for proper United Nations budgetary procedures;
3. *Encourages* the Director-General of the United Nations Office at Nairobi to take steps to increase the level of utilization of the Office, and in this regard encourages other agencies, funds and programmes to consider increasing their utilization of its facilities for their activities;
4. *Calls upon* the United Nations Environment Programme and the United Nations Centre for Human Settlements (Habitat) to increase cooperation in and

3 *Report of the United Nations Conference on Human Settlements (Habitat II), Istanbul, 3–14 June 1996* (United Nations publication, Sales No. E.97.IV.6), chap. I, resolution 1, annex I.

4 See A/54/25, annex I. For the final text, see *Official Records of the General Assembly, Fifty-fourth Session, Supplement No. 25.*

5 See A/54/8, annex I. For the final text, see *Official Records of the General Assembly, Fifty-fourth Session, Supplement No. 8.*

strengthen coordination of their activities, within the framework of their respective mandates and separate programmatic and organizational identities, as well as their separate Executive Directors;

5. *Supports* the proposal of the Secretary-General regarding the establishment of an environmental management group for the purpose of enhancing inter-agency coordination in the field of environment and human settlements, and requests the Secretary-General to develop, in consultation with the Member States and members of the Administrative Committee on Coordination, the mandate, terms of reference, appropriate criteria for membership and flexible, cost-effective working methods of the proposed environmental management group and to submit them to the General Assembly for consideration at its fifty-fourth session;
6. *Welcomes* the proposal to institute an annual, ministerial-level, global environmental forum, with the Governing Council of the United Nations Environment Programme constituting the forum in the years that it meets in regular session and, in alternate years, with the forum taking the form of a special session of the Governing Council, in which participants can gather to review important and emerging policy issues in the field of the environment, with due consideration for the need to ensure the effective and efficient functioning of the governance mechanisms of the United Nations Environment Programme, as well as possible financial implications, and the need to maintain the role of the Commission on Sustainable Development as the main forum for high-level policy debate on sustainable development;
7. *Supports* the proposals for the facilitation of and support for enhancing linkages and coordination within and among environmental and environment-related conventions, including by the United Nations Environment Programme, with full respect for the status of the respective convention secretariats and the autonomous decision-making prerogatives of the conferences of the parties to the conventions concerned, and emphasizes in this regard the need to provide the United Nations Environment Programme with adequate resources to perform this task;
8. *Welcomes* the proposals for the involvement, participation and constructive engagement of major groups active in the field of environment and human settlements, with due consideration for the relevant rules, regulations and procedures of the United Nations;
9. *Reiterates* the importance of strengthening the capacity and capability of the United Nations Environment Programme and the United Nations Centre for Human Settlements (Habitat), within the framework of their existing mandates, in the areas of information, the monitoring and assessment of global and regional environmental and human settlements trends and early warning

information on environmental threats, so as to catalyse and promote international cooperation and action, and in this context emphasizes the importance of strengthening the system-wide Earthwatch as an effective, accessible and strictly non-political science-based system;

10. *Reaffirms* that, in accordance with its mandate, the United Nations Environment Programme should not become involved in conflict identification, prevention or resolution;

11. *Stresses* the need to ensure that capacity-building and technical assistance, in particular with respect to institutional strengthening in developing countries, as well as research and scientific studies in the field of environment and human settlements, must remain important components of the work programmes of both the United Nations Environment Programme and the United Nations Centre for Human Settlements (Habitat), within their existing mandates, and also stresses, in this regard, the need for adequate financial resources as well as the need to avoid duplication of efforts;

12. *Also stresses* the need to enhance further the role of the United Nations Environment Programme as an implementing agency of the Global Environment Facility, consistent with its role as defined in the Instrument for the Establishment of the Restructured Global Environment Facility;[6]

13. *Reaffirms* the role of the Commission on Human Settlements in the implementation of the Habitat Agenda,[7] emphasizes the need for it to take steps to prepare for the review of its implementation in 2001, and welcomes the proposals that the United Nations Centre for Human Settlements (Habitat) should strengthen its core activities and develop into a centre for excellence with regard to human settlements;

14. *Welcomes* the proposal to continue ongoing work in the development of indicators in the field of environment and human settlements, and in this regard stresses the importance of the need to avoid duplication of efforts;

15. *Requests* the Secretary-General to submit to the General Assembly at its fifty-fourth session a report on the implementation of the present resolution.

---

6 UNEP/GCSS.IV/2.

7 *Report of the United Nations Conference on Human Settlements (Habitat II), Istanbul, 3–14 June 1996* (United Nations publication, Sales No. E.97.IV.6), chap. I, resolution 1, annex II.

XIII The Report of the Secretary-General on Environment and Human Settlements, 6 October 1998

I Introduction

1. The report of the Secretary-General entitled "Renewing the United Nations: a programme for reform" (A/51/950) was the result of a thorough review of the activities of the United Nations with the objective of identifying ways in which the United Nations could more effectively and efficiently meet the challenges that lie ahead as we enter the new century and a new millennium. The report noted, however, that reform is not an event but a process, and that although the proposals made are important for the ways in which they would produce a stronger, more resilient and more flexible United Nations in the short term, they are also important for the general direction they would impart for the future evolution of the Organization.
2. An important aspect of the work of the Organization that was addressed by the report was the area of "Environment, habitat and sustainable development". The report reviewed the experience and achievements of the United Nations in this area, and noted that of all the challenges facing the world community in the next century, none will be more formidable or pervasive as the attainment of a sustainable equilibrium between economic growth, poverty reduction, social equity and the protection of the Earth's resources, common and life-support systems. The report also noted that the General Assembly, at its nineteenth special session, had emphasized the difficulties and divisions that continue to impede progress towards agreement on the cooperative measures required to deal with these issues and to ensure enforcement of existing agreements.
3. The report further reviewed developments since the United Nations Conference on Environment and Development (UNCED), including the proliferation of new actors in the field and their expanding participation in United Nations forums; the emergence of the Commission on Sustainable Development as an important policy forum; augmented environmental capacities in United Nations organizations; the transition to a predominantly urban world; and the disappointing response to the needs of developing countries for new and additional resources. The report concluded that this experience demonstrated the need for a

* UN, United Nations reform: measures and proposals – Report of the Secretary-General on Environment and human settlements, Fifty-third session, Agenda item 30, 6 October, 1998.

 | DOI 10.1163/9789004214552_023

more integrated systemic approach to policies and programmes throughout the range of United Nations activities in the economic and social field through mainstreaming the Organization's commitment to sustainable development. This would require closer cooperation and interaction between the United Nations Environment Programme (UNEP) and the United Nations Centre for Human Settlements (Habitat), and between both entities and other departments, funds and programmes in the economic, social and development areas.

4. The report reaffirmed the role of UNEP as the environmental voice of the United Nations, and that high priority must be given to according it the status, strength and access to resources it required to function as the environmental agency of the world community, as confirmed by the Nairobi Declaration adopted by the nineteenth session of the UNEP Governing Council. The report emphasized the need to strengthen UNEP's role as the focal point for harmonization and coordination of environment-related activities, and noted that the Secretary-General intended to lend his full support to that process. It was considered timely to take immediate steps to strengthen UNEP and Habitat, while considering the fundamental changes that might be required to clarify and focus their structures and functions within a reformed United Nations and to revitalize political and financial support for them.

5. In order to initiate this process, action 12 of the Report provided that the Secretary-General, in consultation with Governments, the Executive Director of UNEP and the Executive Director of Habitat, would develop new measures for strengthening and restructuring the two organizations, based on General Assembly resolution 2997 (XXVII) and 32/162, and taking into account the decisions and recommendations of the Governing Council of UNEP and the Commission on Human Settlements, and would make recommendations to the General Assembly at its fifty-third session.

II United Nations Task Force on Environment and Human Settlements

6. In order to initiate the process of preparing recommendations for the fifty-third session of the General Assembly, the Secretary-General established the Task Force on Environment and Human Settlements under the chairmanship of the Executive Director of UNEP. The Task Force was composed of 21 eminent persons, including ministers, senior government officials, senior United Nations officials and non-governmental organizations representatives. Its terms of reference included a review of current structures and arrangements through which environmental activities are carried out within the United Nations to evaluate

the efficacy of those arrangements and make recommendations for such changes and improvements required to optimize the work and effectiveness of the United Nations environmental work, as well as the work of UNEP as the leading environmental organization. The proposals were to be prepared for the consideration of the Secretary-General and subsequent submission to the General Assembly.

7. The Task Force met four times, and delivered its report to the Secretary-General on 15 June 1998; the report of the Task Force, including its composition and terms of reference, is contained in the annex.

8. The recommendations of the Task Force report represent the completion of another important step in the overall reform of the United Nations, as well as the beginning of a process designed to equip the United Nations to concretely address the pressing environmental and sustainable development problems currently facing the international community. In making its recommendations, the Task Force proceeded on a commonly shared conviction that the institutional fragmentation and loss of policy coherence as a result of the number of separate environment-related intergovernmental processes had resulted in a loss of effectiveness in the work of the United Nations in the area of environment and human settlements. The Task Force examined the existing organizational arrangements within the United Nations to determine how they might be changed to better meet international environmental and human settlements challenges, and how existing United Nations structures and arrangements could be optimally redesigned to deal with the problems that will concern the international community in the coming decades. The Task Force derived its overall guidance from the conviction of the Secretary-General, as expressed in his 1997 reform report, that the United Nations must take the lead in building a new international system through greater unity of purpose, greater coherence of efforts, and greater agility in responding to an increasingly dynamic and complex world.

9. The main findings of the Task Force are reflected in 24 recommendations contained in seven sections on:
   (a) Inter-agency linkages;
   (b) Linkages among and support to environmental and environment-related conventions;
   (c) UNEP, Habitat and the United Nations Office at Nairobi;
   (d) Information, monitoring, assessment and early warning;
   (e) Intergovernmental forums;
   (f) Involvement of major groups;
   (g) Future initiatives.

10. The recommendations are designed to enhance coordinated action by the United Nations and begin the process of improving overall policy coherence,

and represent the sum of measures that, in the view of the Task Force, must be taken to revitalize the work of the United Nations in the environment and human settlements in the short term. Similar to the approach of the initial proposals of the Secretary-General on reform, the recommendations require decisions and measures to be taken at different levels, i.e., both at the Secretariat level and at the intergovernmental level. The recommendations are spelled out in detail, together with their underlying rationale, in the report of the Task Force (see annex). However, they are summarized briefly below, clustered according to the level at which the decisions have to be taken.

III Recommendations for Action at the Secretariat Level

A *Inter-Agency Coordination*

11. Recommendation 1 of the Task Force relates to improved inter-agency coordination. In response to the perceived need for effective coordination, the Task Force recommended that the Secretary-General establish an environmental management group under the chairmanship of the Executive Director of UNEP. The group would adopt a problem-solving, results oriented approach that would enable United Nations bodies and their partners to share information, consult on proposed new initiatives and contribute to a planning framework and develop agreed priorities and their respective roles in the implementation of those priorities in order to achieve a more rational and cost-effective use of their resources. It would also provide a forum and a mechanism to enhance complementarity between the analytical and normative activities of UNEP with the operational role of the United Nations Development Programme (UNDP). As such, the group would follow the "issue management" approach outlined by the Secretary-General in his reform report. The group would be supported by Secretariat arrangements that would draw on the existing substantive capacity of UNEP and Habitat. The reports of the group could be made available to relevant intergovernmental bodies to enhance intergovernmental policy coherence. The Task Force recommended that following the conclusion of the current General Assembly session, the Secretary-General consult with members of ACC and decide on the establishment of the group.

B *Linkages Among and Support to Environmental and Environment-Related Conventions*

12. A series of actions are recommended under recommendation 2 of the Task Force that have implications both at the secretariat and intergovernmental levels for

UNEP, and are consistent with the mandate of UNEP as contained in relevant General Assembly resolutions and UNEP Governing Council decisions.

13. In pursuance of these recommendations, the Executive Director of UNEP would take action to:
   (a) Base UNEP support to global and regional conventions on its capacities for information, monitoring and assessment, which should also be strengthened (recommendation 2 (a));
   (b) Continue to sponsor joint meetings of heads of convention secretariats to ensure that the work programmes established by conferences of parties to conventions and the substantive support provided by UNEP are complementary, fill gaps and take advantage of synergy (recommendation 2 (b)).

14. The Task Force also recommended that the Secretary-General, through the Executive Director of UNEP, invite Governments and conferences of parties to consider the implications of operational inefficiencies and costs arising from the geographical dispersion of convention secretariats and ways of overcoming this. Further consultations among the relevant United Nations entities will be required to develop the modalities for the implementation of this recommendation, and should result in specific proposals being made to the relevant intergovernmental bodies for their consideration (recommendation 2 (d)).

C *United Nations Environment Programme, United Nations Centre for Human Settlements and United Nations Office at Nairobi*

15. The Task Force recognized and emphasized the central importance of stabilizing and strengthening the Nairobi location of the United Nations. In its recommendations 3, 4, 5, 6, 7 and 8, which are intended for action by the Secretary-General and the Executive Director of UNEP and of Habitat, the Task Force has addressed, *inter alia*, security, the strengthening of the United Nations Office at Nairobi, the exploitation of the synergy deriving from the co-location of UNEP and Habitat, and the development of a financial strategy.

16. Although several of these measures can be implemented immediately, others will require further consultation with Governments or the presentation of further proposals to intergovernmental bodies. Action that can be taken immediately involves the implementation of recommendations 3, 4, 5 and 6. In this regard, the Secretary-General of the United Nations Office at Nairobi will commence a consultative process with the Government of Kenya with a view to improving physical security, as well as recommending to heads of United Nations organizations with representation at Nairobi that they relocate their offices to the United Nations compound.

17. With respect to recommendation 5, steps have already been taken for the strengthening of the United Nations Office at Nairobi to provide common administrative services to both UNEP and Habitat. The provision of additional regular budget resources, as well as the possibility of relieving UNEP and Habitat of paying rent, is currently under positive consideration by the Secretary-General, in particular in the context of the 2000 2001 biennial budget.
18. The Secretary-General has already designated the current Executive Director of UNEP as Director-General of the United Nations Office at Nairobi, as well as acting Executive Director of Habitat, thus partially implementing recommendation 6. Further consideration will be given to the full implementation of this recommendation by the Secretary-General.
19. In recommendation 7, the Task Force proposes that UNEP and Habitat derive greater benefit from their common location in terms of administrative efficiency and programmatic synergy. It recommends that UNON be utilized to unify the administrative services of the two organizations; that common support services for information, press and library facilities be established, that the planning and implementation of the two programmes be more tightly linked given their complementarity; and that the possibility of co-locating regional offices be assessed. These recommendations constitute practical measures that can be undertaken in the short term by the Executive Director of UNEP and Habitat to make significant economies and enhance synergy. Action taken will be notified to the UNEP Governing Council and the Commission on Human Settlements, while also indicating the means through which the respective oversight and policy guidance roles of the two governing bodies will be maintained.
20. In view of the urgent need to ensure a sound financial basis for both organizations, proposals for a financial strategy will also be presented to the governing bodies of the two organizations consistent with recommendation 8.

D *Information, Monitoring, Assessment and Early Warning*

21. Both organizations carry important responsibilities related to the monitoring and assessment of critical developments in their respective fields of expertise, as well as the responsibility to provide relevant and useful information for decision makers in developing countries. In addition, both must be equipped to notify Governments at an early stage of negative or harmful developments in their respective fields that require either preventive or remedial action to be taken by the international community.
22. The Task Force recognized the central importance of strengthening and focusing the capabilities of the two organizations to play an important role in servicing the information requirements of member countries. In recommendations 9 and

10, a series of measures are proposed to be carried out by the secretariats of the two organizations. The recommendations are consistent with decisions and recommendations made in the respective governing bodies of UNEP and Habitat, as well as by the General Assembly and the United Nations Conference on Human Settlements (Habitat II), and comprise the following complementary measures:

(a) High priority should be given to developing capacity in the field of information, monitoring and assessment and serving as an "environment guardian" in providing the necessary information to enable the sound stewardship of the global environment by the international community;
(b) The Earthwatch system should be reviewed and a determination made of the steps required to transform it into an effective, accessible, well advertised, science-based system capable of meeting the needs of decision makers;
(c) Intensive networking and cooperation should be undertaken with national and international partner institutions to this end;
(d) Problems, action- and result-oriented environment and human settlements indicators for sustainable development should be elaborated;
(e) Capacity should be strengthened and developed to serve as a clearing house for data and information, including information from non-governmental organizations and other grass-roots sources;
(f) A system of information, monitoring and assessment should be designed and maintained so as to maximize its ability to provide early warning of emergencies;
(g) UNEP should consider establishing a capability to identify potential environmental and related conflicts, and to provide information and analysis for the development of preventive measures.

23. All the above recommendations are complementary to existing intergovernmental guidance emanating from the UNEP Governing Council, the Commission on Human Settlements and Habitat II. In the case of UNEP in particular, the Executive Director will be preparing a report for the consideration of the Governing Council of UNEP at its forthcoming session that will elaborate his proposals further in the context of the biennial work programme of UNEP for 2000 2001.

E *Intergovernmental Forums*

24. The recommendations made by the Task Force in relation to intergovernmental forums have been formulated in direct response to the perception of

institutional fragmentation and loss of policy coherence with the growth in the number of separate environment-related intergovernmental processes, and they thus constitute a comprehensive set of measures intended to begin the process of regaining policy coherence in the field of the environment and human settlements.

25. The proposed measures are contained in recommendations 11 to 17 and are primarily directed to intergovernmental bodies. Measures calling for action at the secretariat level are complementary, and would underpin intergovernmental action.

26. In recognition of the importance of integrating regional perspectives into the global agenda, recommendation 12 proposes that UNEP regional offices assist Governments in the regions in defining regional priorities reflecting regional needs and promoting their integration in the global agenda. It also proposes that in the implementation of regional priorities, UNEP involve specialized agencies and other institutions, including financial institutions. These proposed measures are consistent with the evolving role of regional offices of UNEP and the Executive Director will further elaborate on the implementation of this recommendation at the next session of the UNEP Governing Council.

27. With respect to Habitat, recommendation 15 (a) proposes that the Executive Director consider ways to build the capacity of the Habitat Centre to implement the Habitat Agenda, in particular by strengthening the normative core activities of Habitat and developing it into a well financed centre of excellence. The implementation of this resolution is central to the currently ongoing development of proposals for the reform and restructuring of Habitat being undertaken by the Executive Director. Concrete proposals and report on progress in this respect will be provided to the next session of the Commission on Human Settlements.

28. The Task Force also noted the importance of the effective use of Global Environment Facility (GEF) resources, and proposed in recommendation 17 that collaboration between the three GEF implementing agencies be intensified. This recommendation will be conveyed to the concerned agencies, and will inform the further development of the UNEP/GEF strategy.

F *Involvement of Major Groups*

29. The Task Force recognized the global trends that imply a growing role for elements outside Governments in actions and decisions affecting environment and human settlements, including the activities of the United Nations system. Agenda 21 was of particular importance in this regard. The Task Force reviewed the experience of international processes, and made a series of proposals in rec-

ommendations 18 to 23 at both the intergovernmental and secretariat levels with the intention of facilitating a coherent approach to the need to constructively engage non-governmental organizations and civil society in the work of the United Nations.

30. Recommendations 19, 21, 22 and 23 contain the following proposals for action by the secretariat:
    (a) UNEP and Habitat should examine ways of constructively engaging business and industry in their work. This is already an ongoing process in both organizations, and will be strengthened within guidelines established by the respective governing bodies;
    (b) UNEP and Habitat, with UNDP, should identify and make provision to meet the needs of southern non-governmental organizations for capacity-building, keeping in mind the importance of networking. Inter-agency consultations are proposed on this issue, among others, to develop a cooperative approach;
    (c) UNEP and Habitat should establish a specialized unit to provide non-governmental organizations with necessary information, in collaboration with UNDP, and to ensure that the capacities and contributions of non-governmental organizations are utilized. The Executive Director is currently considering modalities for the implementation of this recommendation in the context of the reorganization of Habitat and UNEP;
    (d) Non-governmental organizations should improve collaboration amongst themselves to contribute effectively to the work of UNEP and Habitat, and establish focal points for this purpose;
    (e) United Nations agencies involved in environment and human settlements should take steps to enable major groups to participate in their activities and meetings. The Secretary-General, through the Executive Director, will bring this recommendation to the attention of the relevant agencies;
    (f) UNEP and Habitat should strengthen their systems of receiving and responding to information from non-governmental organizations, especially on emerging problems, and encourage non-governmental organizations to provide information on new problems.

G *Future Initiatives*

31. The Task Force, in concluding its work, also considered a number of forward-looking proposals designed to project the process initiated by its report more into the future. On recommendation 24, the Task Force made a number of proposals, including:

(a) The Executive Director of UNEP would undertake wide-ranging consultations in preparation for the next session of the UNEP Governing Council;
(b) These consultations would culminate in a two-day "environment forum" immediately before the next session of the Council, and would include wide representation from Governments and the non-governmental sector;
(c) The Commission on Human Settlements would provide forward-looking perspectives as part of this process, which would also contribute to the preparations for the five-year review of the Habitat Agenda in the year 2001.

32. The Executive Director is currently reviewing modalities for how this process of preparation both for the Governing Council and the Commission on Human Settlements may best be organized, and will be consulting Governments through the Committees of Permanent Representatives of UNEP and Habitat on this issue.

IV Recommendations for Action by Intergovernmental Bodies

33. In addition to the recommendations for action at the level of the respective secretariats of the United Nations, the Task Force recommended a number of actions to be taken by various intergovernmental bodies. Taken together, it was the view of the Task Force that the totality of its report provided a comprehensive approach to commencing the required reform in the area of environment and human settlements. The actions proposed at the intergovernmental level are an essential component of the overall reform package, and are directly related to the major concern of the Task Force in terms of enhancing the policy coherence and coordinated action by the United Nations system in the field of environment and human settlements.

34. The recommendations requiring intergovernmental action are reviewed briefly below, together with an indication of the appropriate intergovernmental body to which the recommendation is addressed. The Secretary-General supports the recommendations of the Task Force, and considers that their implementation will go a long way in enhancing policy coherence and coordination within the United Nations system.

35. Recommendations for action by intergovernmental bodies are made primarily with regard to environmental and environment-related conventions, intergovernmental forums and involvement of major groups, and are outlined below.

A *Linkages Among and Support to Environmental and Environment-Related Conventions*

36. In addition to the various recommendations on which action will be taken by the Secretary-General and the Executive Director and that will lead to proposals to be reviewed at the intergovernmental level, the Task Force (recommendation 2 (c)) proposed that the President of the UNEP Governing Council be invited to consult the presidents of the conferences of parties of selected conventions on arrangements for periodic meetings to address cross-cutting issues arising from the various conventions. The Executive Director of UNEP and the heads of the respective convention secretariats would organize and participate in these meetings, the results of which would be brought to the attention of the UNEP Governing Council and respective conferences of parties.
37. The implementation of this recommendation would be consistent with the mandate of UNEP arising from the nineteenth special session of the General Assembly, and would also facilitate the review of progress achieved by the conventions, as indicated in Assembly decision 52/445 of 18 December 1997.

B *Intergovernmental Forums*

38. Most of the recommendations of the Task Force in this area are intended for action by intergovernmental bodies, and constitute a comprehensive series of measures designed to enhance coherent and coordinated action at the intergovernmental level on environment and human settlements issues throughout the United Nations system.
39. The proposals include general recommendations to Governments, as well as specific measures to be taken by the General Assembly, the UNEP Governing Council, the Commission on Human Settlements and the Committee of Permanent Representatives to UNEP as a formal subsidiary body of the UNEP Governing Council.
40. Recommendation 11 is rooted in the conviction of the Task Force that Governments must provide consistent guidance to the different intergovernmental organizations in the United Nations system, and recommends that Governments make additional efforts to achieve consistency of national positions in different intergovernmental forums. In this regard, an effective environmental management group mechanism would be invaluable in providing coordinated overviews of activities, plans and policy approaches in various issue areas by concerned United Nations agencies. Modalities for making relevant

information from the environmental management group available to intergovernmental bodies will be defined as the group is established.

41. Recommendation 13 proposes significant and important institutional adjustments designed to begin to overcome the fragmented approach to intergovernmental policy-making and provide a forum in which high-level debate on global issues is informed by a comprehensive approach to the international environmental agenda.

42. The Task Force (recommendation 13 (a)) proposes that an annual, ministerial-level, global environmental forum be instituted with a number of important functions. It also proposes that regular biennial sessions of the UNEP Governing Council constitute that forum in the years that it meets, and that in alternate years the forum should take the form of a special session of the Governing Council meeting in different regions of the world and including regional issues on its agenda. The Governing Council of UNEP is a subsidiary body of the General Assembly, and the Secretary-General recommends that action on this proposal be taken by the Assembly at its current session.

43. Recommendation 13 (b) makes a number of very useful recommendations on future agendas of the Governing Council and the structuring and timing of its meetings to enhance coordination with the Commission on Sustainable Development and the conferences of parties of environmental and environment-related conventions. The Executive Director will provide concrete modalities for the consideration of the UNEP Governing Council at its next session for the implementation of these proposals.

44. Recommendation 13 (c) contains an important proposal with significant institutional implications that require the action of the General Assembly at its current session. The Task Force proposes that the membership of the UNEP Governing Council be made universal. The recommendation is made in the context of the increasing importance of global environmental issues that touch on all countries with significant implications for them, and the need for a coordinated policy to those problems and wide participation in those discussions by member countries. This would be consistent with the mandate of UNEP as contained in General Assembly resolution 2997 (XXVII), and would further enhance the coordinating authority of the Council as envisaged by the General Assembly with regard to the development of international environmental policy, which is currently made in a fragmented manner.

45. In recommendation 14, in order to further streamline the functioning of intergovernmental oversight, the Task Force proposes that matters relating to the programme, budget and operations of UNEP and Habitat be reviewed by their respective Committees of Permanent Representatives. In this regard and in the light of the recommendation to establish an annual ministerial forum, the future

role of the UNEP High-Level Committee of Ministers and Officials should be considered. The Executive Director will provide a number of options to the Governing Council at its next session in the light of the decisions of the Assembly at its fifty-third session.

46. In support of its recommendation to the Executive Director to build the capacity of Habitat to implement the Habitat Agenda (recommendation 15 (a)) the Task Force proposes in recommendation 15 (b) that the Commission on Human Settlements pay particular attention to its role in monitoring the implementation of the Agenda and take steps to prepare for the review of the Agenda in 2001. The Executive Director will present proposals on these issues to the Commission at its next session, taking into account the outcome of the fifty-third session of the General Assembly. In line with the importance that the Task Force attached to the effective use of GEF resources, it is proposed in recommendation 16 that UNEP's role in providing environmental advocacy, analysis and advice in shaping GEF priorities and programmes be strengthened consistent with UNEP's envisaged role in the GEF instrument and as the lead agency in the United Nations system for environment. Specific proposals in this regard will be presented to the next session of the Governing Council by the Executive Director, and the Council will also be invited to make its recommendations to the GEF Assembly on the strengthened role of UNEP.

C *Involvement of Major Groups*

47. Several recommendations were made by the Task Force on the involvement of major groups that require action at the intergovernmental level, which would be augmented by secretariat actions described above.

48. In recognition of the positive experience of Habitat II at Istanbul, the Task Force proposes that the Commission on Human Settlements consider the establishment of a special status for local authorities. Proposals in this regard will be put before the Commission at its next session by the Executive Director.

49. In recommendation 18 (b), it was also proposed that structured meetings of major groups be organized in conjunction with meetings of the Commission on Human Settlements and the UNEP Governing Council, and that representatives of major groups be accorded the opportunity to formally present their views to these bodies.

50. Recommendation 18 (c) recognizes the valuable experience gained with respect to major groups in the Commission on Sustainable Development process, and proposes that all United Nations agencies encourage participation by major groups, and that the Secretary-General issue general guidelines on these matters. This matter will be considered further in the context of the deliberations of

ACC on relations with civil society, including the question of preparation of guidelines.

51. Finally, in recommendation 20 it is recommended that the accreditation process of the Economic and Social Council and other agencies dealing with environment and human settlements be speeded up. This recommendation will be conveyed to the relevant bodies by the Secretary-General.

V Conclusion

52. It is the view of the Secretary-General that the report of the United Nations Task Force on Environment and Human Settlements constitutes an important step, both in the overall process of United Nations reform and in undertaking the urgent adjustments required in the international system to tackle the pervasive and serious threats to the global environment and decisively move the process of urbanization in a sustainable direction.

53. This is, however, the beginning of a process. The positive consideration of these recommendations by the General Assembly will allow the commencement of a process that can bring substantial gains to the international community in future and allow it to have institutions at its service that are capable of addressing the immense challenges of the future.

Report of the United Nations Task Force on Environment and Human Settlements

I *Introduction*

1. The Secretary-General, in his report entitled "Renewing the United Nations: a programme for reform" (A/51/950), recognized the need for a more integrated, systemic approach to policies and programmes throughout the whole range of United Nations activities in the economic, social, and development fields. As part of this effort, he informed the General Assembly that he would, in consultation with Governments and the heads of the United Nations Environment Programme (UNEP) and the United Nations Centre on Human Settlements (Habitat), develop new measures for strengthening and restructuring those two organizations, based on General Assembly resolutions 2997 (XXVII) and 32/162 and taking into account decisions and recommendations of the Governing Council of UNEP and the Commission on Human Settlements. He committed himself to making recommendations to the General Assembly at its fifty-third session, in 1998.

2. To assist him in this respect, in 1998 the Secretary-General constituted a Task Force composed of high-level advisers from Governments, civil society and within the United Nations. The membership of the Task Force is listed in appendix I and its terms of reference in appendix II.
3. The Task Force met four times: on 1 April 1998 at New Delhi; on 26 and 27 April 1998 at New York; on 29 and 30 May 1998 at Bonn; and on 13 to 15 June 1998 at Geneva.

II Historical Background

4. The first major intergovernmental conference on the environment was the United Nations Conference on the Human Environment, held at Stockholm in June 1972. That Conference adopted a farsighted Declaration and Programme of Action and led to the creation of UNEP by the General Assembly with a mandate to catalyse and coordinate environmental actions within the United Nations system. The General Assembly decided that UNEP's headquarters should be located at Nairobi. The UNEP Governing Council became the world's primary environmental forum. The two decades following the Stockholm Conference saw many international actions to protect the environment, including the negotiation of many global and regional conventions.
5. The Stockholm Conference recognized that the built environment deserved special attention, and recommended the holding of a further United Nations conference on this subject. The United Nations Conference on Human Settlements was held at Vancouver from 31 May to 11 June 1976. One of the perceptions that emerged at Vancouver and has since been reinforced is that human settlements are an integral element of development, and should be a high priority at the national level.
6. The Vancouver Conference decided on the Vancouver Declaration and Action Plan, which made national Governments and the international community aware of the plight of human settlements worldwide. It also led to the creation of the United Nations Centre for Human Settlements (Habitat), which was established in 1978. In view of the substantial overlap between environmental and human settlements issues, Habitat was located at Nairobi alongside UNEP. Existing United Nations activities and programmes, including the Centre for Housing, Building and Planning established in the mid-1960s and the United Nations Habitat and Human Settlements Foundation established by UNEP, were integrated into Habitat. Habitat was to service a new intergovernmental body, the United Nations Commission on Human Settlements, and carry out an integrated work programme, including research, policy guidance, training, technical

cooperation and information. Mechanisms were put in place to encourage cooperation between UNEP and Habitat.

7. Twenty years after Stockholm, the United Nations Conference on Environment and Development (UNCED) was held at Rio de Janeiro in June 1992. UNCED drew even more popular participation and media coverage than the Stockholm Conference, including greater participation by non-governmental organizations and other major groups of society from developing countries. Unlike the Stockholm Conference, UNCED was attended by scores of heads of Government. UNCED approved the Rio Declaration on Environment and Development, Agenda 21 (a compendium of actions needed to achieve sustainable development) and the Non-legally Binding Authoritative Statement of Principles for a Global Consensus on the Management, Conservation and Sustainable Development of All Types of Forests (Forest Principles). It also witnessed the signature of major conventions on climate change and biological diversity.

8. The United Nations Conference on Human Settlements (Habitat II) was held at Istanbul in June 1996. It adopted the Istanbul Declaration, in which the nations present endorsed the universal goals of ensuring adequate shelter for all and making human settlements safer, healthier and more liveable, equitable, sustainable and productive.

   The Habitat Agenda that was agreed on at Habitat II is the global plan of action to improve human settlements conditions for the next 20 years. Habitat is charged with coordinating its implementation among United Nations agencies and facilitating its application by Governments, as well as among other major groups of society.

9. From the time of the Stockholm Conference, it was recognized that environmental issues could not be treated as afterthoughts or dealt with solely by "end-of-the-pipe" approaches, but that environmental considerations must be integrated into the activities of sectoral and development-oriented institutions. Many changes of this kind occurred during the 1970s and 1980s, and the pace of change has accelerated since UNCED and Habitat II. As a result, the international agenda for environment and development has been transformed, and the context in which the United Nations must operate has changed radically. The changes within the United Nations system have been conceptual and organizational; meanwhile, the context has been altered by the emergence or continuation of sweeping global trends.

10. The concept of sustainable development links economic, social, and environmental concerns, and has been adopted by the world community. Agenda 21 assigns a broad range of responsibilities for action to United Nations organizations and bodies, national Governments, and many other international and national groups. Environmental issues have appeared increasingly on the

agendas of development-oriented institutions, including UNDP, the World Bank, the regional multilateral development banks and such specialized agencies as the World Health Organization (WHO), the World Meteorological Organization (WMO), the Food and Agriculture Organization of the United Nations (FAO), the United Nations Educational, Scientific and Cultural Organization (UNESCO) and the United Nations Industrial Development Organization (UNIDO), and the regional commissions. The "greening" of these bodies has been a necessary and welcome step, but the integration of environmental considerations in their programmes clearly needs to go further. There has also been a welcome recognition of the need to move in these directions among some sections of business and industry.

11. The United Nations structure was altered after UNCED by the creation of the Commission on Sustainable Development, which provides a high-level forum for environmental, developmental, social and economic issues. The Inter-Agency Committee on Sustainable Development (IACSD), a standing committee of the Administrative Committee on Coordination (ACC), has brought together the United Nations bodies concerned with these issues and has helped to coordinate their work. IACSD's system of designating agencies to be task managers for specific issue areas has decentralized the responsibility for developing coordinated policy positions in key areas of sustainable development, especially as inputs to the Commission on Sustainable Development. The Global Environment Facility (GEF) has been established as a mechanism for financing activities to deal with some global environmental problems.

12. The establishment of the Commission on Sustainable Development, IACSD and GEF has created additional institutional arrangements alongside UNEP in the field of environment and sustainable development, and has highlighted the need to review the role of UNEP and the UNEP Governing Council in this context. The number of international legal instruments concerned with the environment has continued to grow. Demands on ministers and Governments have increased because of the multiplication of high-level meetings, including those of the conferences of parties to international conventions. At the same time, the financial resources available to support international and national actions for sustainable development have fallen far short of what is required, and UNEP's own Environment Fund has declined substantially.

13. Whereas there were institutional changes in the United Nations structure in the field of environment following UNCED, there were no such institutional developments in the field of human settlements following Habitat II. Rather, the Commission on Human Settlements was assigned a central role in monitoring, within the United Nations system, the implementation of the Habitat Agenda; acting as a catalyst to promote adequate shelter for all and sustainable

human settlements development; advising the Economic and Social Council on human settlements issues; and assisting the Economic and Social Council in coordinating the implementation of the Habitat Agenda within the United Nations system. Unfortunately, the situation has deteriorated and Habitat has lacked the capacity to carry out these tasks. The absence of any significant institutional change subsequent to the Habitat II Conference has hampered the effective implementation and follow-up of the outcome of that Conference.

14. Human demands on the global life support system continue to mount as poverty and affluence spread in parallel through the globe. Despite all the efforts made since the Stockholm Conference, the environment continues to deteriorate in many parts of the world. Some social, economic and technological trends are exacerbating these problems. In addition, rapid urbanization is outstripping the provision of the services needed for health and welfare. New and unexpected problems will certainly continue to arise. Much more vigorous and effective coordinated action will then be required at all levels. Better monitoring and assessment and enhanced means of providing effective information to Governments will also be crucial.

15. International action will continue to be essential in meeting these challenges. The United Nations system must play a central part in this action, in cooperation with other components of society. Agenda 21 and the global plan of action contained in the Habitat Agenda broke new ground by addressing a broad spectrum of stakeholders who should be involved in the process of developing and implementing policies and actions for environment and human settlements.

III *Needs and Responses*

16. These developments, trends, and challenges will influence and to a great extent define the role of the United Nations in the field of environment and human settlements. The ways of the past will not suffice in this new era. The Task Force has concluded that the United Nations and its governmental and non-governmental partners will need reformed structures and new methods in order to optimize their effectiveness.

17. The main roles of the United Nations in the field of environment and human settlements are to:

    (a) Facilitate intergovernmental consensus and international cooperation on environmental components of policies and actions for sustainable development, including legally binding commitments;

    (b) Promote support, especially from developed to developing countries, so as to facilitate the implementation of agreed environmental and human settlements action plans, especially Agenda 21 and the Habitat Agenda;

(c) Involve, encourage, and support relevant stakeholders so that they make their appropriate contribution at the global, regional, national, and local levels;
(d) Monitor and assess existing and emerging environmental problems, alert policy makers and the world public to them, and advocate and coordinate measures and action to tackle these problems and their causes, thereby reducing future risks;
(e) Provide support and resources to enable the effective implementation of global and national commitments relating to the environment and human settlements, and to build capacity for environmental action in developing countries.

18. The remaining sections of the present report consider:
(a) The linkages at the inter-agency level between the United Nations institutions concerned with environment, sustainable development and human settlements, including environmental and environment-related conventions;
(b) Linkages among and support to environmental and environment-related conventions;
(c) The internal needs of the United Nations system, especially those of UNEP and Habitat at Nairobi;
(d) The United Nations role (the Earthwatch function) in collecting, evaluating, and disseminating environmental data and information, including the United Nations responsibility for early and emergency response in the field of environment and human settlements;
(e) The intergovernmental structure of the United Nations in the field of environment and human settlements;
(f) The involvement of civil society and of profit-making enterprises;
(g) The possible role of a reconstituted United Nations Trusteeship Council.

A Inter-agency Linkages

19. The Task Force considers that the United Nations system needs a strong and respected UNEP as its leading environmental organization. For this purpose, UNEP needs to be given adequate financial, staff and information capacities. In particular, it should be the recognized centre of a network of information, monitoring, assessment and early warning, and should play to the full its role as an implementing agency of GEF.

20. The Task Force's review of existing United Nations structures and arrangements in the field of environment and human settlements, linked to different issues

and including in-depth examination of the energy and water sectors, has revealed that current United Nations activities are characterized by substantial overlaps, unrecognized linkages and gaps. These flaws are basic and pervasive. They prevent the United Nations system from using its scarce resources to best advantage in addressing problems that are crucial to the human future; harm the credibility and weight of the United Nations in the environmental arena; and damage the United Nations working relationship with its partners in and outside of Government.

21. What is needed is a problem-solving, results-oriented approach that enables United Nations bodies and their partners to share information about their respective plans and activities; to inform and consult one another about proposed new initiatives; to contribute to a planning framework that permits the plans and activities of each participant to be reviewed within the framework of the whole range of activities being carried on by all participants; and to consult with each other with a view to developing an agreed set of priorities and on the measures through which each participating organization can best contribute to those priorities and achieve a more rational and cost-effective use of their respective capacities and resources.

22. These needs were recognized by the Secretary-General in his report on reform under the heading "Strategy 8: Institute an issue management system" (see A/51/950, paras.248–250).

Recommendation 1

The Task Force recommends that in order to meet these needs with respect to the environment and human settlements, the Secretary-General should establish an environmental management group. It would replace the existing Inter-Agency Environment Coordination Group, which should be abolished.

23. The environmental management group would be chaired by the Executive Director of UNEP, supported by a secretariat. The Chair would report to the Secretary-General.

The group would include as core members the main United Nations entities concerned with environment and human settlements. Particular meetings would involve additional United Nations entities, financial institutions, and organizations outside the United Nations system that have experience and expertise relevant to the issues on the agenda.

24. The environmental management group would be concerned with environment and human settlement issues in the context of the linkages between environment and development, as defined at UNCED and subsequently elaborated. Habitat should be a prominent participant in the group, which should structure its operations so as to achieve an integrated United Nations work programme

that bridges the gaps that have existed between the two areas.

25. The most important goal of the environmental management group should be to achieve effective coordination and joint action in key areas of environmental and human settlements concern. Another important objective should be to assist intergovernmental bodies in the area of environment and human settlements, in particular the UNEP Governing Council and the commission on Human Settlements, in the preparation of coordinated inputs to intergovernmental forums, notably the Commission on Sustainable Development. The group should report on an informational basis to ACC, and should bring an environmental perspective into the work of IACSD. The group should establish time-bound task forces or working groups covering clusters of issues in which representatives of the main institutions involved in a particular issue can work together quickly to solve important problems (for example, the recently reconstituted Ecosystem Conservation Group).

26. The environmental management group should include convention secretariats among its participants, when needed. In addition to facilitating the kinds of linkages among conventions that are recommended in section III.B below, the group should act to ensure that there are appropriate linkages among activities that occur under conventions and relevant activities elsewhere in the international system.

27. The Task Force considered the question whether the environmental management group should produce a single United Nations environmental programme, similar to the former system-wide, medium-term environment programme. The Task Force concluded that in view of fast-moving global trends, a static programme, no matter how frequently it is updated, is bound to lag behind real needs. Instead, the group should create a dynamic process for review of planned activities and modification of goals and activities in the light of new knowledge. However, subgroups of the environmental management group may agree on sharply focused action plans as a means of coordinating actions at the programme level and allocating resources in the most effective manner.

28. Regional action and regional coordination are essential in the field of environment and human settlements. At the level of field operations, the existing system of United Nations resident coordinators is responsible for effective coordination of activities related to environment and human settlements, and should be strengthened. The environmental management group should from time to time review the effectiveness of this coordination.

B Linkages among and Support to Environmental and Environment-Related Conventions

29. The creation of a large number of legally binding instruments in areas of environmental concern has been a major success of the international community.

However, as a result of decisions by Governments, the secretariats of environmental and environment-related conventions have been located in diverse geographic locations, with little regard to the functional relationships among conventions. That dispersal has resulted in loss of efficiency because of inability to take advantage of synergies among conventions and substantial costs through loss of economies of scale and fragmentation of administrative, conference and infrastructure services. The period after UNCED led to a significant increase in activities related to environmental and environment-related conventions, and the number of international meetings of relevant treaty bodies has increased significantly. This has created additional burdens, especially for ministers.

30. Bearing in mind that the main policy decisions under conventions are taken by their respective conferences of parties, which are autonomous bodies, strengthening of the linkages between conventions with a view to achieving synergies and multiple benefits and promoting coherence of policies and actions should be a long-term strategic goal of the international community. Intergovernmental bodies, including the General Assembly in paragraphs 119 and 123 of the Programme for the Further Implementation of Agenda 21 (see General Assembly resolution S/19–2 of 28 June 1997, annex), have identified the need for more effective linkages and support. Decisions of the General Assembly at its nineteenth special session, in 1997, and prior decisions by the General Assembly and the UNEP Governing Council have provided a clear basis for UNEP to foster such linkages. Pursuant to these mandates, UNEP has sponsored annual meetings of the secretariats of selected environmental conventions, which have addressed common issues, such as implementation at the national level, including development of relevant national legislation and institutions, capacity-building and technical assistance.

31. Further steps are needed to strengthen linkages and provide support that will ensure that the international community derives maximum benefit from the investments it has made in this system of international instruments.

Recommendation 2

The Task Force recommends that, in addition to integrating convention secretariats and convention-related issues in the work of the environmental management group, the following actions should be taken by UNEP in pursuance of the above-mentioned mandate from the General Assembly at its nineteenth special session:

(a) UNEP's substantive support to global and regional conventions should be founded on its capacities for information, monitoring and assessment, which need to be strengthened substantially and urgently for this purpose. UNEP should build its capacity and its networks of support in order to ensure the scientific underpinning of conventions, to respond to their requests for specialized analysis and technological assessments, and to facilitate their implementation;

(b) The Executive Director of UNEP should continue to sponsor joint meetings of heads of secretariats of global and regional conventions, and should use this forum to recommend actions to ensure that the work programmes established by the conferences of parties to the conventions, together with substantive support offered by UNEP, are complementary, fill gaps and take advantage of synergy, and avoid overlap and duplication. These meetings also should explore ways of fulfilling common substantive and administrative needs. Recommendations from these meetings should be presented to the conferences of parties by the respective secretariats;

(c) The Governing Council of UNEP should invite its President to consult the presidents of conferences of parties to selected conventions on arrangements for periodic meetings between representatives of those conventions in order to address cross-cutting issues arising from the work programmes of these bodies and policy approaches being followed by them. The Executive Director of UNEP and the heads of the respective convention secretariats would organize and participate in these meetings. The conclusions of these meetings would be brought to the attention of UNEP's Governing Council and the respective conferences of parties by the respective secretariats;

(d) Concerned about the operational inefficiencies and costs arising from the geographical dispersal of convention secretariats, the Task Force recommends that the Secretary-General, through the Executive Director of UNEP, invite Governments and Conferences of Parties to consider the implications of this trend and ways to overcome the resulting problems. Every effort should be made to co-locate new conventions with other conventions in the same functional cluster (for example, biological resources, chemicals/waste, marine pollution) and with institutions with which they have a particular affinity. With respect to existing conventions, approaches should include promoting cooperation among the secretariats within each cluster with a view to their eventual co-location and possible fusion into a single secretariat, and, in the longer term, should include the negotiation of umbrella conventions covering each cluster.

C UNEP, Habitat and the United Nations at Nairobi

32. It was recognized at the time of the Stockholm Conference that environment and human settlements issues are closely related. In consequence, the Vancouver Conference decided to locate Habitat alongside UNEP at Nairobi. Subsequent

events have strengthened this relationship, and the worldwide trend towards urbanization seems certain to forge even closer links. Yet cooperation between UNEP and Habitat is still limited.

33. The Task Force discussed the Nairobi location of the United Nations, and agreed that there is an urgent need to strengthen it. Nairobi is the only location of a major United Nations office in the developing world (the other major offices, in addition to United Nations Headquarters in New York, are the United Nations Offices at Geneva and Vienna). The United Nations Office at Nairobi should have arrangements in keeping with its status. There are several requirements for achieving this goal in addition to the already mentioned need for closer coordination between UNEP and Habitat. They include better communications capabilities, improved physical security, an enhanced United Nations presence at Nairobi and adequate access to the regular budget of the United Nations with respect to administrative costs. The Task Force:
    (a) Commends the Government of Kenya for the efforts already taken to improve communication between the Nairobi location and the rest of the world, but urges the Executive Director to work together with the Government to enhance and strengthen communications capabilities by allowing unrestricted access to the Mercure satellite at a reasonable cost;
    (b) Is aware of the socio-economic problems of the region and the difficulty of ensuring physical security for United Nations staff and related personnel, yet recognizes that lack of security makes it difficult for UNEP and Habitat to attract and retain the highly qualified staff that they must have to succeed in their missions;

Recommendation 3

The Task Force recommends that the Secretary-General, through the Director General of the United Nations Office at Nairobi, request the Government of Kenya to address further the problem of physical security

Recommendation 4

The Task Force recommends that other United Nations agencies, funds, and programmes be stimulated to establish or expand activities at Nairobi so as to transform the United Nations compound at Nairobi into a fully active United Nations Office.

(c) Notes that UNEP and Habitat are the only United Nations entities with global responsibilities that have their headquarters in a developing country, reflecting the commitment of the international community to strengthen capacity in developing nations to address the issues of environment and human settlements. Currently, these organizations conduct their work under difficult financial conditions;

Recommendation 5

The Task Force recommends that the United Nations Office at Nairobi, which provides common services to UNEP and Habitat, be strengthened and be provided, as an exceptional measure, with sufficient resources from the regular budget to fulfill its tasks, and that the United Nations consider the possibility of relieving UNEP and Habitat from paying rent.

(d) Believes that the Secretary-General acted wisely when he designated one individual to head UNEP, Habitat and the United Nations Office at Nairobi;

Recommendation 6

The Task Force recommends that UNEP, Habitat and the United Nations Office at Nairobi continue in the future to be directed by one person.

(e) Sees the measures suggested above as important ingredients in a process that would enhance confidence in UNEP and Habitat, facilitating the attainment of a broader, more stable and predictable financial basis for the two organizations.

34. There are a number of ways in which UNEP and Habitat can benefit from their co-location. Among them are common administrative functions, common support institutions, common programme activities and the possibility of co-located regional offices.

Recommendation 7

The Task Force recommends that the Executive Director of UNEP and Executive Director of Habitat:

(a) Utilize the United Nations Office at Nairobi to unify the administration of the two organizations to the fullest extent feasible;
(b) Make full use of the synergistic co-location of the two organizations by establishing common institutions for:
    (i) Information and databases and the clearing house function;
    (ii) Press and information services;
    (iii) Library and other forms of support;
(c) Ensure that the planning and implementation of the programmes of the two organizations are tightly linked through monitoring, assessment, and information and joint working parties on such overlapping issues as environmental health and the sustainability of cities. This should in no way compromise the distinctive nature of UNEP and Habitat but should be complementary;
(d) Assess the possibility of co-locating the regional offices of the two organizations.

35. The Task Force is concerned that UNEP and Habitat must have adequate human and financial resources if they are to fulfil the mandates of the Nairobi Declaration and decisions of the Governing Council and the General Assembly. Accordingly, the Task Force agrees with and underlines the decision made at the May 1998 special session of the UNEP Governing Council that there is an urgent need for stable and predictable funding.

Recommendation 8

The Task Force recommends that the Executive Director of UNEP and Executive Director of Habitat develop a financial strategy, in close cooperation with the Committee of Permanent Representatives at Nairobi, and report on it at the next meetings of the UNEP Governing Council and the Commission on Human Settlements. The financial strategy should address such matters as policies concerning secondment, including geographical balance; conditions for accepting in-kind contributions; the role of counterpart contributions in implementing the programmes of UNEP and Habitat; and the possibility of obtaining funds from foundations and other private sources.

D Information, Monitoring, Assessment and Early Warning

36. Pursuant to the action plan that was adopted at the Stockholm Conference, UNEP developed during the 1970s the Earthwatch system for assessing the condition of the global environment. Chapters 38 and 40 of Agenda 21 called on UNEP to strengthen Earthwatch, especially in the areas of urban air, freshwater, land resources (including forests and rangelands), desertification, other habitats, soil degradation, biodiversity, the high seas and the upper atmosphere, and to make the resulting information more available for decision-making.

37. UNEP was named as task manager for Earthwatch by IACSD. The mission of Earthwatch, as agreed in 1994 by the inter-agency Earthwatch Working Party, is to coordinate, harmonize and integrate observing, assessment and reporting activities across the United Nations system in order to provide environmental and appropriate socio-economic information for national and international decision-making on sustainable development, and for early warning of emerging problems requiring international actions. This should include timely information on the pressures on, status of and trends in key global resources, variables and processes in both natural and human systems, and on the response to problems in these areas.

38. The Earthwatch system seeks to fulfill this mandate by integrating data and analyses from a variety of scientifically proven sources. These include, among others, the Global Environmental Monitoring System (GEMS), the Global Resource Information Database (GRID), and three Global Observing Systems (the Global Climate Observing System, the Global Oceans Observing System and the Global

Terrestrial Observing System). Earthwatch uses up-to-date communications technologies to maintain an excellent site on the World Wide Web. However, the Earthwatch system and its capabilities are largely unknown to the large universe of decision makers and environmentally concerned members of the public who could benefit from it. Moreover, there are gaps and deficiencies in the underlying systems of data collection and analysis, and in the methods by which data and analysis are translated into information that is understandable to non-experts. UNEP's depleted staff in the area of monitoring and assessment lacks the ability to identify and correct these flaws.

39. Human settlement conditions are monitored and assessed by Habitat, which also collects, collates and publishes statistics on human settlements conditions and trends. A new monitoring and assessment framework for the implementation of the Habitat Agenda will involve inputs from partners in Government and other elements of society.

Recommendation 9

The Task Force recommends that UNEP and Habitat:

(a) As a matter of high priority, develop their capacity in the field of information-monitoring and assessment in order to serve as an "environmental guardian," mobilizing the necessary resources from Governments, foundations, and international bodies;

(b) Carry out a short-term review to determine the steps needed to transform Earthwatch into an effective, accessible, well-advertised, science-based system that meets the needs of environmental and human settlements decision makers and the informed public, and employs expert analysis and user feedback to correct deficiencies and update itself to meet changing needs;

(c) Take the actions, in intensive networking cooperation with national and international partner institutions, including non-governmental organizations and other major groups, that are needed to transform Earthwatch and sustain it as a fully effective system of information, monitoring and assessment;

(d) Continue to elaborate problem-, action-,and result-oriented indicators for sustainable development in the field of environment and human settlements;

(e) Strengthen and further develop their capacity to serve as a clearing house for collecting and disseminating information and data relevant to the condition of the environment and human settlements, including information from and to non-governmental organizations and other grass-roots sources.

40. The Earthwatch system should be designed, *inter alia*, to alert the world to emerging environmental problems and threats. Information about such problems

should be communicated in understandable terms to relevant decision makers, the media and the informed public. Earthwatch also can contribute importantly to such syntheses as UNEP's GEO series and Habitat's periodic Global Report on Human Settlements.

41. Monitoring and assessment are closely linked to early warning of possible environmental emergencies through the prediction of extreme events or unusual environmental conditions. This kind of warning is extremely valuable for environmental and economic decision makers; for example, advance warning of drought conditions can enable farmers to plant drought-resistant crops. It may be possible to identify, on a long-term basis, potential "hot spots" or areas that are likely to be subject to rates of change that exceed the limits of sustainability and thus pose threats to regional or global security.

Recommendation 10

The Task Force recommends that UNEP and Habitat design and maintain the system of information, monitoring and assessment so as to maximize its ability to provide early warning of possible environmental and human settlements emergencies. It further recommends that UNEP consider establishing a capability to identify potential environmental and environment-related conflicts and provide information and analysis to guide the development of preventive measures, for example by the negotiation of joint actions.

E Intergovernmental Forums

42. The United Nations is an intergovernmental organization. Organs and agencies of the United Nations can perform their functions efficiently only if they receive clear guidance from Member States. This is true in the field of environment and human settlements, as in all others. There is a need for intergovernmental forums to give that guidance.

43. There is a lack of coherent guidance at this level. Specialized agencies, for example, are responsible only to their governing bodies. In the environmental field, some specialized agencies have sectoral missions that correspond to specific elements within national Governments; hence, the agendas of those agencies may reflect very different priorities.

44. The only entities that can give consistent guidance to these different bodies are national Governments. In view of the important role that is played in the field of environment and human settlements by international institutions not under the authority of the Secretary-General, coordination cannot be fully effective unless Governments themselves give coordinated guidance. In short, coordination at the international level should begin at home.

Recommendation 11

The Task Force recommends that Governments make additional efforts to achieve consistency of national positions in different intergovernmental forums. The environmental management group should assist Governments in achieving such coherence by providing coordinated overviews of activities, plans and policy approaches in the United Nations system as a whole.

Recommendation 12

The Task Force recommends that UNEP regional offices assist Governments in each region in their discussion of the global agenda, in defining priorities reflecting the particular needs of each region, and in promoting those regional priorities in the global agenda. In the implementation of regional priorities, UNEP should involve specialized agencies and other institutions concerned with environment and human settlements, as well as those that can provide financing.

45. Current intergovernmental forums are inadequate to give the kind of guidance that is needed in the environmental field. Those forums, consisting primarily of the UNEP Governing Council, the Commission on Sustainable Development, and meetings of the conferences of parties of leading conventions, are scattered as to time and place. They are attended by different constellations of ministers. They differ in their outcomes: some are decision-making bodies, whereas others serve primarily as forums for policy debates, consensus-building, review of United Nations activities and plans, and exchanges with major groups. Ministers have expressed dissatisfaction because attendance at so many meetings is time-consuming for them. Moreover, the scattering of different meetings on different subjects makes it hard for participants to get the "big picture" perspective that is important for setting global priorities.
46. In addition, the traditional United Nations format for intergovernmental meetings does not fully meet the need for high-level consideration of environmental issues. The traditional United Nations format has featured formal discussion leading to agreement on the exact wording of a text. That format is ill-suited to many of the purposes that intergovernmental meetings on environment and human settlements should fulfill. Those purposes require a format that allows for actual debate and fewer statements, more in-depth discussions, more interaction with major groups and structured efforts to produce innovative strategies that can meet tomorrow's challenges.
47. The Task Force affirms that the Commission on Sustainable Development and the Governing Council of UNEP have necessary and distinctive roles. The Commission on Sustainable Development provides a forum for high-level debate, including ministerial debate, that bridges and relates environmental,

developmental, and socio-economic elements. The UNEP Governing Council is and should remain the primary forum within which Ministers and senior officials of Governments can review the environmental performance of the United Nations system as a whole and define priorities for new action.

Recommendation 13

The Task Force recommends:

(a) That there be an established annual, ministerial-level, global environmental forum in which environment ministers can gather to review and revise the environmental agenda of the United Nations in the context of sustainable development; oversee and evaluate the implementation of that agenda; discuss key issues in depth; identify challenges requiring international environmental cooperation and develop plans of action for meeting them; review the role of UNEP in relation to GEF; and engage in a variety of discussions with their peers, with representatives of international institutions and with major groups. In the years when it meets, the UNEP Governing Council should be that intergovernmental forum. In alternate years, the forum should be a special session of the UNEP Governing Council, which would focus on issues of high priority. The venue of these special sessions should move from region to region, and regional issues should feature prominently on their agenda;

(b) That the agenda of each session of the Governing Council be a lively one, designed to foster debates on topical issues and to attract media attention. Each session should cover topics of global importance, and in the case of meetings held in the regions, should cover issues of special significance to the region where the meeting is held. Each session should be structured so as to provide input to that year's Commission on Sustainable Development meetings. A major item on the agenda of each session should be to review, from a cross-cutting perspective, progress made under the various environmental conventions;

(c) That the membership of the UNEP Governing Council be made universal. This recommendation would not apply for the Commission on Human Settlements because it is a subsidiary body of ECOSOC.

48. The regular and special sessions of the Governing Council should receive reports from the Executive Director of UNEP on the work of the environmental management group in promoting linkages among components of the United Nations system. The joint meetings of representatives of the conferences of parties of selected conventions that was recommended previously might be held "back to back" with sessions of the Governing Council.

49. There is a need for stronger links between environmental and human settlements at the intergovernmental as well as the inter-agency levels. It would not be

appropriate to merge the UNEP Governing Council with the Commission on Human Settlements, because those bodies have distinctive characters and partially different substantive agendas, and because they typically involve two distinct sets of ministers, those responsible for the environment and those responsible for housing, and it is unlikely that many Governments would send two ministers to the same meeting. However, the agendas of the two bodies should be cross-linked and designed to complement one another. Environmental matters should be standing items on the agenda of the Commission on Human Settlements, and human settlements-related issues should occupy a similar place on the agenda of the Governing Council. To the extent feasible, the Nairobi meetings of the two bodies should overlap.

Recommendation 14

The Task Force recommends that continuing international liaison on matters relating to the programme, budget and operations of UNEP and Habitat be undertaken at Nairobi by the Committees of Permanent Representatives and High-Level Officials convened by the Executive Director on behalf of their Chairmen. In the light of the changes recommended in the present report, the Governing Council of UNEP should consider the future role of the High-Level Committee of Ministers and Officials.

50. The special identity and distinctive character of Habitat should be retained, bearing in mind its mandate in General Assembly resolution 32/162 of 19 December 1977, as clarified and developed in the Habitat Agenda. A particularly important consideration for the Task Force is that Habitat has been designated as a focal point for the implementation of the Habitat Agenda, and that the Commission on Human Settlements has a central role in monitoring its implementation.

51. Habitat has a large, demand-driven technical cooperation programme with a clear development agenda. The financial support for that programme comes solely from earmarked sources. The financial basis of Habitat has been seriously eroded in recent years, particularly in regard to core funds, which are crucial for its normative activities. If Habitat is to fulfill its role in promoting the implementation of Habitat Agenda, it is imperative that its normative functions be strengthened substantially. This will require a stronger financial base, especially with regard to core funding. In addition, existing overlaps between the technical cooperation programmes and the activities of other parts of Habitat should be eliminated.

Recommendation 15

The Task Force recommends:

(a) That the Executive Director of Habitat consider ways of building capacity to facilitate the implementation of the Habitat Agenda, particularly by strengthening the normative core activities of Habitat and developing it into a centre of excellence for urban development, and ways to obtain the necessary financial resources;

(b) That the Commission on Human Settlements devote particular attention to its role in monitoring the implementation of the Habitat Agenda, and take steps to prepare for the five-year review of the implementation of the Habitat Agenda, which will occur in 2001.

52. The Task Force attaches the greatest significance to the effective use of GEF resources.

Recommendation 16

The Task Force recommends that, consistent with the GEF instrument, UNEP's role in providing environmental advocacy, analysis and advice in shaping GEF priorities and programmes should be strengthened, building on UNEP's current responsibility for ensuring the scientific underpinning of GEF activities. UNEP should act as catalyst and advocate for new directions, and should take the lead among the three GEF implementing agencies in providing environmental advice. This role is consistent with UNEP's status as the lead agency in the United Nations system for identifying large-scale environmental threats and proposing remedial measures.

Recommendation 17

The Task Force recommends that there be increased collaboration among the three GEF implementing agencies, in accordance with relevant GEF decisions [unbold]

F Involvement of Major Groups

53. Global trends imply a growing role for elements outside government in actions and decisions affecting the environment and human settlements, including activities and decisions of the United Nations system. Agenda 21 recognized this reality in its description in chapters 24 to 32 of the roles of "major groups, "including women, youth, indigenous people, non-governmental organizations, local authorities, trade unions, business and industry, the scientific and technological community, and farmers. Governments and international bodies need the wisdom, experience, knowledge and resources of these groups if they are going to make environmental and human settlements decisions, in the context of sustainable development, that are scientifically based, economically sound, suited to local conditions and in accord with the desires of ordinary people.

54. The Stockholm Conference on the Human Environment and the accompanying Non-Governmental Organization Forum marked a breakthrough in the way that major groups related to and sought to influence an intergovernmental decision-making process. UNCED was another watershed event, attended by representatives of some 8,000 non-governmental organizations from more than 160 countries. The Habitat II Conference in 1996 was attended by some 20,000 people and representatives of more than 500 local authorities. It featured the following innovative mechanisms for involving major groups from the beginning of the preparatory process:
    (a) All Governments were invited to create national Habitat II committees involving a wide spectrum of society;
    (b) The drafting group that prepared the Habitat Agenda included representatives of local authorities and non-governmental organizations;
    (c) The Conference itself featured a "partners' committee" (Committee II), in which representatives of civil society were officially invited to assemble in their own forum and present their views to the representatives of Governments;
    (d) United Nations officials joined with representatives of civil society in making possible a set of "Dialogues for the twenty-first century," which explored in details key issues concerning the future of cities, including water and energy;
    (e) Statements produced in the dialogue sessions, together with the Chairperson's summaries of the discussions in Committee II, were included in the official record of Habitat II.
55. The Commission on Sustainable Development also has been a leader in its relations with major groups. Commission on Sustainable Development meetings are attended by representatives of a wide variety of interests. Non-governmental organization participation is facilitated by a broad-based Non-Governmental Organization Steering Committee. New participants are welcomed, and the Commission on Sustainable Development secretariat prepares guidelines on a regular basis to help them participate and contribute. The practice at Commission on Sustainable Development meetings has been that representatives of major groups are allowed to speak virtually on an equal basis with representatives of Governments. The sixth session of the Commission on Sustainable Development, in 1998 featured an innovative industry segment that included participants from various major groups. Additional "economic sector" segments are planned for future Commission on Sustainable Development meetings.
56. The extensive involvement of major groups at Habitat II and in the work of the Commission on Sustainable Development has enlivened and enriched

deliberations that are important to the world's future. Further steps are needed to ensure that this kind of involvement is the rule in the United Nations. They should begin with the Commission on Human Settlements and the UNEP Governing Council.

Recommendation 18

The Task Force recommends:

(a) That the Commission on Human Settlements consider establishing a special status for representatives of local authorities;

(b) That future sessions of the UNEP Governing Council and of the Commission on Human Settlements be preceded by or overlap with substantial, structured meetings of major groups, covering the same substantive agenda topics that are to be covered at the intergovernmental meetings. Representatives of the major groups should be given an opportunity to discuss the findings of these meetings in a round-table meeting with ministers, and should report this to the Governing Council and the Commission, which should record their responses;

(c) The practices of the Governing Council and the Commission on Human Settlements should be reformed, as an initial step, to come up to the standard of the Commission on Sustainable Development with respect to the involvement of major groups, and the Governing Council and Commission secretariats should take steps (for example, the preparation of guidelines) to facilitate their participation. All other United Nations agencies involved with environment and human settlements should re-examine their rules and practices with the aim of encouraging and facilitating participation by major groups to the fullest extent practicable, consistent with the principle that the final decisions must rest with representatives of Governments. The Task Force further recommends that the Secretary-General issue general guidelines on these matters, and urges all United Nations agencies to conform with them.

57. It is apparent, in view of global trends and the need for cleaner methods of production, that environment and human settlements policy must be more integrated with economic decision making. This means that there must be a well balanced and effective continuing dialogue with business, industry, and other economic interests.

Recommendation 19

The Task Force recommends that UNEP and Habitat examine, together with representatives of business, industry and other economic interests, ways of involving that community constructively in their deliberations.

58. Non-governmental organizations commonly must obtain consultative status with the Economic and Social Council in order to gain access to intergovernmental meetings and other United Nations processes. Consultative status is not often denied; however, it currently takes about a year to obtain accreditation.

Recommendation 20

The Task Force recommends that the Economic and Social Council accreditation process, and those of other United Nations entities concerned with environment and human settlements, be speeded up to the fullest extent possible.

59. Non-governmental organizations from developing countries commonly have fewer resources and less capacity than those from industrialized nations. UNEP and Habitat should take actions to help them build their capacity for constructive participation.

Recommendation 21

The Task Force recommends:

(a) That UNEP, Habitat and UNDP systematically identify, in consultation with non-governmental organizations and non-governmental organization leaders, the needs of southern non-governmental organizations for capacity- building, and act to meet those needs, both directly and by mobilizing funds from other donors. In so doing, they should keep in mind the importance of networking among non-governmental organizations, especially via electronic communications, and should help southern non-governmental organizations to build their capacity in that area;
(b) That UNEP and Habitat establish a specialized unit to provide concerned non-governmental organizations with necessary and updated information, and together with UNDP, assist them technically and financially to carry out their work effectively at national, regional and global levels. They should also establish mechanisms to ensure that the expertise and contributions of non-governmental organizations can be utilized by UNEP and Habitat;
(c) That non-governmental organizations be encouraged to strengthen their capacities to contribute effectively to the activities of UNEP and Habitat, including improving collaboration and networking among themselves and establishing focal points to liaise with UNEP and Habitat at global and regional levels [unbold]

60. Major groups from developing countries often find it difficult to attend international negotiations and meetings even when they have a right to do so, because of lack of funds for travel and subsistence.

Recommendation 22

The Task Force recommends that to the fullest extent possible, the United Nations agencies involved in environment and human settlements take steps to enable major groups from these countries to participate meaningfully in their activities, both through capacity- building to make possible meaningful participation in negotiations and meetings, and through establishment of funds to which Governments and others are encouraged to contribute.

Recommendation 23

The Task Force recommends that UNEP and Habitat strengthen their system for receiving and responding to information from non-governmental organizations on environmental and human settlements problems, especially emerging problems. In this regard, UNEP and Habitat should encourage non-governmental organizations to provide information on new problems that might arise, for example, from the introduction of new technologies or new production activities or changes in economic or social policies.

G Possible Role of a Reconstituted United Nations Trusteeship Council

61. In paragraphs 84 and 85 of his report on United Nations reform (A/51/950), the Secretary-General recommended to the international community a new concept of trusteeship, and proposed that the United Nations Trusteeship Council be reconstituted as the forum through which Member States exercise their collective trusteeship for the integrity of the global environment and common areas, such as the oceans, atmosphere and outer space, as well as linking the United Nations and civil society in addressing these areas of global concern. In a subsequent note to the General Assembly (A/52/849), the Secretary-General recalled this proposal and noted that it has become increasingly evident that issues relating to the integrity of the global environment and common areas have a direct bearing on the future of mankind, and that those issues need to be understood and addressed in a strategic and long-term perspective. The Secretary-General also suggested that the Task Force should elaborate further on his proposals.
62. In reviewing the proposals of the Secretary-General, the Task Force was cognizant of the note of the Secretary-General to the General Assembly (A/52/850) concerning a Millennium Assembly and Millennium Forum. That note proposed that the fifty-fifth session of the General Assembly be designated as the "Millennium Assembly" and include a high-level segment to be called the "Millennium Summit". The Summit would be asked to provide guidance to the

United Nations for meeting the challenges of the new century, including such matters as the nature and fundamental goals of the United Nations and the way it should relate to and interact with the growing number of international institutions, an increasingly robust global civil society, and ever more integrated global markets and systems of production. The Secretary-General's note also proposed that non-governmental organizations and other civil society actors organize a Millennium Forum to be held in conjunction with the Assembly.

63. In the same note to the General Assembly, the Secretary-General announced that in order to facilitate focused discussions and concrete decisions, he would prepare a report on the theme of the Millennium Assembly, entitled "The United Nations in the twenty-first century." The report would draw on a series of informal events involving Member States and other actors to be held in regional centres around the world; on events of a more specialized nature in the United Nations; and on the results of consultations currently taking place within ACC.

64. The Task Force also recalled the decision of the UNEP Governing Council at its recent fifth special session on the revitalization, reform and strengthening of UNEP. In that decision, the Governing Council, *inter alia*, decided to review at its next regular session the status of the ongoing reform of UNEP and to provide the Millennium Assembly with its conclusions concerning institutional arrangements within the United Nations system for dealing with the environmental challenges of the next century and the role of UNEP in that context. The Task Force believes that these conclusions will provide an important environmental perspective for the Millennium Assembly and will enhance the preparatory process.

Recommendation 24

The Task Force recommends:

(a) That the Executive Director of UNEP, in preparing for the next regular session of the UNEP Governing Council, undertake wide-ranging consultations concerning institutional arrangements for dealing with the environmental challenges of the next century;

(b) That these consultations include Government representatives, non-governmental organizations, and other representatives of civil society and the private sector, and culminate in a two-day environment forum to be held immediately before and in conjunction with the next session of the Governing Council. The forum should suggest to both the Governing Council and the Millennium Assembly and Forum forward-looking proposals for the protection of the global environment, including the possible future role of the Trusteeship Council;

(c) That the Commission on Human Settlements provide forward-looking perspectives on human settlements issues as part of this process. These perspectives would also contribute to the preparations for the five-year review of the Habitat Agenda to be undertaken in 2001.

Appendix I
Membership of the Task Force

Task Force members:
Klaus Toepfer (Chair), Executive Director,United Nations Environment Programme
Maria Julia Alsogaray, Minister of Natural Resources and Sustainable Development of Argentina
Christina Amoako-Nuama, Minister of Education of Ghana
John Ashe, Ambassador/Deputy Permanent Representative of Antigua and Barbuda to the United Nations
Julia Carabias Lillo, Minister of Natural Resources and Fisheries of Mexico
Nitin Desai, Under-Secretary-General, Department for Economic and Social Affairs of the United Nations Secretariat
Lars-Goran Engfeldt, Permanent Representative of Sweden to UNEP and Habitat
Guro Fjellanger, Minister of Environment of Norway
Jean-Pierre Halbwachs, Assistant Secretary-General/Controller, United Nations Office of Programme Planning, Budget and Accounts
Sir Martin Holdgate, United Kingdom of Great Britain and Northern Ireland
Martin Khor, Director, Third World Network, Malaysia
Ashok Khosla, Development Alternatives, India
Tommy Koh, Ambassador-At-Large, Ministry of Foreign Affairs, Singapore
Julia Marton LeFevre, LEAD International, Inc., New York
James Gustave Speth, Administrator, United Nations Development Programme
Maurice Strong (ex officio), Special Adviser to the Secretary-General
Mostafa K. Tolba, President, International Centre for Environment and Development, Cairo
Joseph Tomusange, High Commissioner of the Republic of Uganda to India
Makarim Wibisono, Permanent Representative of Indonesia to the United Nations
Timothy E. Wirth, President, United Nations Foundation
Michael Zammit Cutajar, Executive Secretary, Secretariat of the United Nations Framework Convention on Climate Change
Advisers to the Task Force
Eileen Claussen,
Peter Thacher

Secretariat to the Task Force
Per Bakken
Donald Kaniaru
Donatus Okpala
Lesly Puyol
Thomas Stoel

Appendix II
Terms of Reference of the Task Force

The terms of reference of the United Nations Task Force on Environment and Human Settlements are:

(a) To review existing structures and arrangements through which environment and environment-related activities are carried out within the United Nations, with particular reference to departments, funds and programmes that report to the Secretary-General but also taking into account the relevant programmes and activities of the specialized agencies;
(b) In this respect, to focus particularly on the distinctive functions of policy, development of norms and standards, programme development and implementation, and financing, as well as relationships among those functions;
(c) To evaluate the efficacy and effectiveness of existing structures and arrangements, and make recommendations for such changes and improvements as will optimize the work and effectiveness of United Nations environmental work at the global level and of UNEP as the leading environmental organization or "authority", as well as the role of UNEP as the principal source of environmental input into the work of the Commission on Sustainable Development;
(d) To prepare proposals for consideration by the Secretary-General and subsequent submission to the General Assembly on reforming and strengthening United Nations activities in the area of environment and human settlements.

XIV The Nairobi Declaration, 7 February 1997

The Nairobi Declaration was agreed by ministers of the environment and heads of delegation attending the nineteenth session of the Governing Council held during January & February, 1997. The declaration defining the future role and mandate of UNEP was endorsed by the special session of the United Nations General Assembly held in New York in June, 1997.

The Heads of Delegation declare:

That the United Nations Environment Programme has been and should continue to be the principal United Nations body in the field of the environment and that we, the ministers of the environment and heads of delegation attending the nineteenth session of the Governing Council, are determined to play a stronger role in the implementation of the goals and objectives of the United Nations Environment Programme;

1. That the role of the United Nations Environment Programme is to be the leading global environmental authority that sets the global environmental agenda, that promotes the coherent implementation of the environmental dimension of sustainable development within the United Nations system and that serves as an authoritative advocate for the global environment;
2. That to this end, we reaffirm the continuing relevance of the mandate of the United Nations Environment Programme deriving from General Assembly resolution 2997 (XXVII) of 15 December 1972 and further elaborated by Agenda 21. The core elements of the focused mandate of the revitalized United Nations Environment Programme should be the following:
    a) To analyse the state of the global environment and assess global and regional environmental trends, provide policy advice, early warning information on environmental threats, and to catalyse and promote international cooperation and action, based on the best scientific and technical capabilities available;
    b) To further the development of its international environmental law aiming at sustainable development, including the development of coherent interlinkages among existing international environmental conventions;

* The Nairobi Declaration on the Role and Mandate of the United Nations Environment Programme (decision 19/1) was adopted at the 7th meeting of the Nineteenth Session of the Governing Council of UNEP on 7, February 1997, on the basis of the draft decision on this subject (UNEP/GC.19/L.44/Rev.1), submitted by the President of the Council; see http://www.unep.org/Documents.Multilingual/Default.asp?DocumentID=287&ArticleID=1728&l=en

 | DOI 10.1163/9789004214552_024

c) To advance the implementation of agreed international norms and policies, to monitor and foster compliance with environmental principles and international agreements and stimulate cooperative action to respond to emerging environmental challenges;

d) To strengthen its role in the coordination of environmental activities in the United Nations system in the field of the environment, as well as its role as an Implementing Agency of the Global Environment Facility, based on its comparative advantage and scientific and technical expertise;

e) To promote greater awareness and facilitate effective cooperation among all sectors of society and actors involved in the implementation of the international environmental agenda, and to serve as an effective link between the scientific community and policy makers at the national and international levels;

To provide policy and advisory services in key areas of institution-building to Governments and other relevant institutions.

Index

Accidents, Major Industrial 212
Action Plan 107
  National Environmental 75
Administrative Committee on Coordination (ACC) 203
African Development Bank 74
Agenda
  environmental 207
  —, global 38, 159
  sustainable development 41, 42, 44
  —, implementation of 268
  setting 41
Agenda 21, 7, 52, 68, 119, 185, 199, 255
  implementation 29, 32, 37, 61, 76, 121, 187, 197
  —, *Program for further* 37
  international institutional arrangements envisaged by 122, 188
Agreement, Environmental 240
Agriculture 54
Antarctica Treaty 215, 241
Arab Bank for Economic Development in Africa 74
John, Ashe 42
Asian Development Bank 74
Assistance in the Case of a Nuclear Accident or Radiological Emergency 55

Basel Convention 8, 85, 114, 162, 163, 179, 240
  at the International Environment House in Geneva 138
Basel Protocol 114
  adoption of 181
Biosafety, Cartagena Protocol on 114
UNEP, birth of 103, 116, 183
Bonn Convention 8
Brundtland Commission 60

Caribbean Development Bank 74
catastrophes, environmental 212
Centre for Human Settlements (Habitat) 192
Certain Hazardous Chemicals and Pesticides in International Trade 112
challenge,
  environmental 90
  —, global 147, 168, 265, 266
  legal 231
Chernobyl nuclear power plant accident 55
CITES 8, 138, 162, 229, 247
Climate Change 8, 239, 240
  development of UN Framework Convention on 180
Clustering 249
CMS 8, 138, 162, 229, 247
Commission on Human Settlements 202
Commission on Sustainable Development (CSD) 21, 25, 28, 39, 48, 51, 61, 84, 99, 127, 139, 152, 164, 171, 186, 194
commissions, intergovernmental 50
Committee of Permanent Representatives (CPR) 267
Committee on Science & Technology 71
Conference of Parties (COPs) 71, 72, 73, 212, 247, 251
Conference on Environment and Development (UNCED) 24
Conferencing
  global 28
  —, technique 18, 227
Conscience
  keeper 8
  environmental 60, 206
Conservation
  of living resources 244
  of natural resource 256
Constitution for the Oceans 232
Consultative Group of Ministers 92
Convention
  atmosphere related 254
  Biological Diversity (CBD) 8, 60, 72, 85, 135, 160, 162, 180, 247
  Climate Change (UNFCCC) 8
  Conservation of Migratory Species of Wild Animals (the Bonn Convention) 59, 72, 85, 112, 115, 135, 160, 182
  and coordination 253

Convention (cont.)
International Trade in Endangered Species of Wild Fauna and Flora (CITES) 72, 85, 134, 160
LRTAP 72
for the Protection of Birds Useful to Agriculture 229
for the Protection of the Ozone Layer (Ozone) 72
for the Protection of the World Cultural and Natural Heritage 134
Wetlands of International Importance Especially as Waterfowl Habitat 159
Cooperation
coexistence 20
institutional 21, 46
institutionalized,
—, quest for 230
—, sustainable development 42
environmental, intergovernmental 172, 272
international 20, 58, 226
—, environmental 7, 14, 46, 57, 105, 106, 174
—, for environmental crisis 15
—, forums for 46
South-South 15
country progress reports 34
CSD 20, 38
establishment of 22
inclusive participation modalities of 40
working of the 29

Deliberations
final, of the IGM in Cartagena 147, 167
intergovernmental 167
at the Johannesburg Summit 142, 166
and recommendations of the IGM process 139, 164
Desertification 163, 181
and forestry 240
Convention 8
global environmental 217
Developing Countries 42
Development
banks, multilateral 74, 171
of international environmental law 131, 156
official, assistance 191
Diversity, Biological 244
Dolzer, Rudolf 187
Dowdeswell, Elizabeth 128, 154
Drought, Serious 181

Earth Summit 76
Economic and Social Council (ECOSOC) 26, 39, 40, 63, 84, 187, 216, 269
Economic Commission Europe (ECE) 72
Emergencies Relief Council 14
emergencies, environmental 95, 295
Environment Assembly 16, 17
Environment Fund 117, 123, 124, 152, 189
contributions to 124, 129, 189
downward trend in 128, 153
pledges to the 154
UNEP's voluntary 123, 153, 183
Environment
closure of, coordination board 267
global 213
—, concerns 12
ministers 43
policy for dam and reservoir projects 75
proposals for a world, organization 147, 167
protection 201, 227, 256
—, efforts for 37
—, specialized agency for 93
related global conferencing 227
Secretariat within the UN 7
and sustainable development institutions 44
Environmental Law Council (ELC) 211
Environmental Management Group (EMG) 9, 86, 118, 131, 155, 196, 203, 267
Environmentally Sound Management of the *Common Zambezi River System* 181
European Community (EC) 137, 162
ExCOPs 2, 252
expert watchdog 60, 118, 184
explosion, organizational 47

firefighters, *green* 212
Food and Agricultural Organization (FAO) 52, 58, 106, 175, 180

Forest 35
critical issues concerning 35
fires 212
intergovernmental panel on 35
management 55
Funding,
mechanism for environmental agreements 67
of UNEP 138
base, secured 142

General Agreement on Tariffs and Trade (GATT) 241
Global Environment Facility (GEF) 21, 28, 51, 65, 66, 70, 71, 127, 152, 171
grants 70
implementing agency of 203
institutional structure of 64
restructured 68, 69
Global Environment Trust Fund (GETF) 65, 66, 69, 70
Global Environmental Authority 97
Global Environmental Forum 87, 166
Global Environmental Organization (GEO) 129
Global Ministerial Environment Forum (GMEF) 9, 14, 86, 128, 131, 142, 156, 204, 267
launching of 9, 86, 157
Global Programme of Action for the Protection of the Marine Environment from Land-Based Activities (GPA) 111, 178
Governance 1
architecture 12
environmental 4, 205, 265, 273
—, international 3, 9, 81, 98, 99, 132, 148, 222, 265
global 47
—, environmental 12, 91, 93, 209
—, environmental, architecture 12, 91
hybrid, systems 41
real world environmental, systems 245
Governing Council 145
of UNEP 9, 103, 120
green fund 70
green protectionism 209
greening 9, 189, 266
of multilateral financial institutions 47
of the other multilateral institutions 170
Group of 77 (G-77) 137

Hague Declaration 208
Harare Agreement 181
Hard Law 227
Soft law Dilemma 243
Heritage Fund 71
High-Level Political Forum (HLPF) 10, 21, 23, 33, 39
advent of the 39, 42
birth of 42
meetings of 41, 43
organizational modalities of 40
replacement of CSD by 267

implementation of sustainable development 39
Informal Consultation Process 91
on the Institutional Framework for the United Nations Environmental Activities 81
Institution Building 42
history of 144
host 248, 249
Institutional Structure
specialized environmental 56
in the environmental field 146
institutionalization 3, 48
institution-building, international environmental 77
institutions,
environmental,
—, ill-defined 207
—, specialized 56
interactions, inter-state 46
Inter-Agency Committee on Sustainable Development (IACSD) 171, 194, 196
Inter-American Development Bank 74
Interdependence 20
among states 46
Intergovernmental Negotiating Committee 113
inter-governmental organizations (IGOs) 5, 52, 226

Intergovernmental Panel on Climate Change (IPCC) 85, 95
International Action on Certain Persistent Organic Pollutants 180
International Atomic Energy Agency (IAEA) 55, 59, 175
International Committee of the Red Cross (ICRC) 212
International Court of Justice (ICJ) 57, 100, 104, 173
International Environment House (Geneva) 255
international environmental commitments 12, 273
international environmental governance (IEG) 12, 13, 91, 148, 210
  consensus on the future of 266
  problems afflicting 165
  at the WSSD and the UN General Assembly 164
International Environmental Institutions (IEIs) 5, 101, 46, 83, 169, 211, 267
  challenges faced by 168
  emergence of 49
  as legal creatures 48
  types of 51
international environmental law 50
international environmental regulatory measures 77
international institutional forms 46
international institutions 225
International Labour Organization (ILO) 52, 53, 135, 175
International Law Commission 99
international law, principles of 97
International Maritime Organization (IMO) 56, 59, 175
international organization (IO) 48
International Tropical Timber Agreement (ITTA) 241
International Union for Conservation of Nature and Natural Resources (IUCN) 246
Involuntary Resettlement 75

Johannesburg
  Plan of Implementation 37, 140, 164
  Summit 164
    —, expectations at the 139
    —, PrepCom for the 37

Law of the Sea Convention 232
Law-making
  ad hoc 238
  centralized 223
  contribution to 107
  on environmental issues 221, 238
  international
    —, environmental 48, 49, 98
    —, process 51
League of Nations 53
least developed countries 42
living document 136
LRTAP 229
Lusaka Agreement 181

Malmö Ministerial Declaration 17, 132, 147, 157, 161, 205, 270
Man and the Biosphere (MAB) programme 54
Management of the Common Zambezi River System 113
Mandate
  and structure of CSD 31
  of ILO 53
Mankind
  common concerns of 237
  common heritage of 237
Maurice Strong 128, 153
meetings, intergovernmental ministerial 81
Membership
  universal 9, 16, 17, 137, 166
    —, of the UNEP 145
    —, of the UNEP GC 16
minimalist strategy of efficiency improvement 208
Ministerial Forums 132
mobilization, resource 153
Montevideo Programme 59, 101, 111
  launching of an ambitious 102
Montreal Protocol for the Protection of the Ozone Layer (1987) 66, 112, 179, 256
multilateral environmental agreements (MEAs) 21, 44, 48, 50, 71, 149, 170, 221, 221, 224, 227, 255, 257, 272
  coordination and synergies among Secretariats 222
  advent and proliferation of 228
  challenge of governing the 223

clustering of 250
growth in 51
incoherency and overlapping of 255
multilateral financial institutions 34
Multilateral Fund 71
Multiplicity
of institutions 23, 127, 128, 152
—, environmental 119

Nairobi Declaration 9, 86, 130, 147, 155, 189, 191, 204, 271
Nairobi-Helsinki Outcome 15
national sustainable development strategies (NSDS) 34
natural disasters 212
Negotiations
international environmental 48, 48, 84
multilateral 227
New York Declaration 171
non-governmental organizations 52, 226
nuclear energy issues 229

Operational Directives on Environmental Assessment 75
Ozone
Layer 4, 162, 229, 239
regime 73

Permanent Representatives of Mexico and Switzerland to the UN 81
Persistent Organic Pollutants (POP) 112
plant genetic resources 54
Platz der Vereinten Nationen (Bonn) 255
Pollution
marine 134
—, regulation of 229
oil
—, disasters 212
—, regulation of 56
transfrontier 212
Premier Environmental Entity 99
Preparatory Committee (PrepCom) 24
problematique, global environmental 265
problems
environmental 3
—, having global dimensions 169
—, global environmental 228, 237

Proliferation 27
fears of 243
institutional 42, 46, 126, 152
of environmental secretariats 121
of institutions 150
of intergovernmental instruments 244
of MEAs 138, 163

Quest for an Environmental Entity 84

Ramsar 7, 72
Regime Specific Institutions 71
Regional Seas Programme (RSP) 8, 59, 85, 107, 176, 232, 235
Report
of the Secretary-General on Environment and Human Settlements 202
on Environment and Human Settlements 202
revitalization 191
of UNEP 271
Quest for 9
Rio Conventions Pavilion 254
Rio Earth Summit 9, 75, 118, 228, 255
Rio mandate 63
Rio+ 20
Summit (UNCSD) (2012) 39, 93, 223, 268
decision of 43
Rotterdam Convention on Prior Informed Consent Procedure (PIC) 35, 180, 240
Ruggiero, Renato 209

Science & Technology Council 211
Scientific and Cultural Organization (UNESCO) 58
Secretariat 71
independent 177
legal competence of 244
organization of the 250
relationship of 'Host' Institution and MEA 246
services 235
Small Island Developing States (SIDS) 36
soft law 227
sovereignty, state 46
Steiner, Achim 165

Stockholm
  Conference 36, 52, 54, 171, 183, 227
    —, influence of the historic 56
  Convention 236, 240
  Declaration 74, 107
    —, and the Action Plan 176
  mandate 7, 58, 84, 106, 175
Subsidiary Body for Science and Technology Advice (SBSTA) 95, 212
Subsidiary Body on Implementation (SBI) 71
Sustainable Development 34
  challenges 42
  dimensions and sectors of 37
  goal of 44
  HLPF on 38
  institutional architecture for 39
  recommendations for 40
  scientific contributions to 38
  three dimensions of 41
Sustainable Development Council (SDC) 39
Sustainable Development Indicators (SDI) 34
Sustainable Development Goals, (SDG) 43

Task Force
  mandate of the 194
  on Environment and Human Settlements 126, 151
  report,
    —, recommendations of the 202
    —, UN 202, 205
The Future We Want, UNCSD outcome document 42
Toepfer Task Force 27, 86, 126, 127, 129, 151
  inauguration of the 155
Töpfer, diplomatic blitzkrieg of 128
Tolba, Mostafa K. 128, 153
Toepfer, Klaus 9, 27, 154, 126, 128, 151, 128
Treaty Making
  environmental 228
  sui generis 4
  unique 223
Tropical Forestry Action Plan 55
Trust Fund 182, 189
  scope of the 70
Trusteeship Council 200, 201, 217, 218, 269
  collective 201, 213
  concept of 200, 201
  idea of 215
  revival of the 269
  UN 13, 19, 136, 213, 273
    —, mandate for the 269

UN
  affiliated functional international organizations 56
  bureaucracy 143
  bureaucracy, criticism of 209
  Centre for Human Settlements (Habitat) 203
  Conference on Environment and Development (Rio Earth Summit) 150
  Conference on Environment and Development (UNCED) 6, 41, 60, 61, 83, 99, 112, 118, 184, 214
  Conference on Sustainable Development (Rio+20) 15, 23, 39, 92
  Convention to Combat Desertification in those Countries Experiencing Serious Drought and/or Desertification 113
  Educational, Scientific and Cultural Organization (UNESCO) 7, 72, 246
  Environment Organization (UNEO) 87
  Environment Programme (UNEP) 246
  Environment Protection Organization (UNEPO) 10, 11, 13, 91, 145, 147, 211, 217, 271
  environmental conscience-keeper of the 9
  environmental programme 206
  Forum on Forests (UNFF) 35
  Framework Convention on Climate Change (UNHCCC) 85, 113
  General Assembly 56
  Gigiri Complex (Nairobi) 255
  Industrial Development Organization (UNIDO) 268, 271
  Informal Consultative Process on Oceans 35
  Office in Nairobi (UNON) 199, 202
  Task Force on Environment and Human Settlements 27
  Task Force Report 192, 206

UNCCD 138
  (Rio+20) 42
  lack of consensus at 35
UNEP 6, 7, 14, 56, 143, 154, 216, 235, 272
  and other entities 197
  birth of the, at the Stockholm Conference 173
  contribution of 269
  conversion of, into a specialized agency 167
  drafters of UNEP's constituent instrument 101
  efforts to revitalize the 86
  establishment, of 158
  failures of 267
  functioning of 49, 213
  GC Global Ministerial Environment Forum Nairobi, meetings in 87
  Governing Council and Commission on Human Settlements (CHS) 196
  Governing Council 129, 132, 198
  mandate 271
  marginalization of 189
  place of, within the UN hierarchy 31
  role and authority of 134, 159, 189
  up-graded 270
  weaknesses of 270
UNFCCC 138
UNGA 12, 40
United Nations Conference on Human Environment (UNCHE) 103, 169
United Nations Educational, Scientific and Cultural Organization (UNESCO) 52, 53, 106, 146, 175
United Nations Environment Program (UNEP) 3, 6, 21, 48, 51, 56, 164
United Nations Environment Programme Governing Council (UNEPGC) 81
United Nations Environment Programme 81, 172
    financing of the 150
    role of the 15, 155
United Nations Office in Nairobi (UNON) 193
United Nations Task Force on Environment and Human Settlements 192
Upgradation
    of UNEP 11, 16
    issue of 10

Vienna Convention (1985) 85, 112, 179, 224
    on the Law of Treaties 224
voluntary exchange of information 34, 64

Wastes
  hazardous 239, 243
    —, and their disposal 112
    —, transboundary movements of
    —, transportation of, and materials 241
wetlands of international importance 4
wild animals 4
World Health Organization (WHO) 59
World Bank 58, 65, 74, 171
World Commission on Environment and Development (Brundtland Commission) 118, 184
World Commission on Environment and Development (WCED) 24
World Conservation Union (IUCN) 52, 72, 135, 171
World Environment Organization (WEO) 11, 88, 144, 162
World Environmental and Sustainable Development Organization (WESDO) 129
World Environmental Organization (WEO) 129
World Health Organization (WHO) 52, 175
World Meteorological Organisation (WMO) 52 59, 85, 175
World Summit 250
  on Sustainable Development (WSSD) 36, 98, 149
  Outcome 81, 146
World Trade Organization (WTO) 209
World Wide Fund for Nature (WWF) 51, 52, 171